# TWENTIETH-CENTURY SOUTH AFRICA

**William Beinart** is Rhodes Professor of Race Relations at the University of Oxford—a post that, despite its name, is concerned very largely with African Studies. He studied at the universities of Cape Town and London, and taught in the Department of Historical Studies, University of Bristol (1983–97). He was joint editor of the *Journal of Southern African Studies* (1982–7) and chair of its editorial board (1992–8). His publications include books, articles, and edited collections especially on the rural areas of southern Africa; he is currently researching in the field of environmental history.

# Twentieth-Century South Africa

## WILLIAM BEINART

**OXFORD**
UNIVERSITY PRESS

# OXFORD
## UNIVERSITY PRESS

Great Clarendon Street, Oxford OX2 6DP

Oxford University Press is a department of the University of Oxford.
It furthers the University's objective of excellence in research, scholarship,
and education by publishing worldwide in

Oxford  New York

Athens Auckland Bangkok Bogotá Buenos Aires Cape Town
Chennai Dar es Salaam Delhi Florence Hong Kong Istanbul Karachi
Kolkata Kuala Lumpur Madrid Melbourne Mexico City Mumbai Nairobi
Paris São Paulo Shanghai Singapore Taipei Tokyo Toronto Warsaw

with associated companies in Berlin Ibadan

Oxford is a registered trade mark of Oxford University Press
in the UK and in certain other countries

Published in the United States
by Oxford University Press Inc., New York

British Library Cataloguing in Publication Data

Data available

Library of Congress Cataloging in Publication Data

Data available

ISBN 0–19–289318–1

1 3 5 7 9 10 8 6 4 2

Typeset in Times
by RefineCatch Limited, Bungay, Suffolk
Printed in Great Britain by
Cox & Wyman Ltd., Reading, Berkshire

# PREFACE AND ACKNOWLEDGEMENTS

For this second edition, no significant changes have been made to the overall structure of the first, published in 1994. The first nine chapters have not been extensively rewritten, although errors brought to my notice have been corrected, and some material has been added, especially in Chapter 7. Reference has been made to a few important new books and articles; it has not been possible to do justice to all of the vast and lively academic output on South Africa since the early 1990s. Chapter 10 has been reworked and extended to explore the negotiations of 1990–4 and the constitutional settlement. Chapters 11–13, focusing largely on the period 1994–2000, are new. I would like to thank Shamil Jeppie, Tony Lemon, and Gavin Williams for their comments on this additional material and on my interpretation of the transition in South Africa.

Writing history requires the identification of major political trends and social changes. It is always difficult to be confident about the very recent past or to understand historical processes when they are still so fresh. Encapsulating the social realities of complex societies within a set of clear and convincing generalizations is an awkward exercise. There is no shortage of material on the current politics of the country, nor any lack of opinion. Southern African studies remains a particularly fertile academic field, ever more eclectic and varied in its intellectual influences. There have been valuable debates in such spheres as democratization, reconciliation, economic policy, ethnicity and identity, cultural studies, as well as the significance of civil society. Gender, health, and environment, amongst other issues, have been intensively explored. In some senses the historian contemplating contemporary society is blessed, but the very multiplication of academic concerns makes them all the more difficult to represent, distil, and contain in a few short chapters.

The transition to democracy in South Africa, after years of authoritarianism, political violence, and tortuous negotiation, must be a central theme for both celebration and analysis in the final part of the book. But, as I have suggested in the introduction, South Africa's transformation and the accession to power of the African National Congress have also stimulated new historiographical concerns. Some of the themes stressed in the first edition were intended to anticipate issues that might become central to a post-apartheid historiography. Certainly, it is increasingly important to understand critically African history, African heritages, and comparative African experiences in writing history about the new South Africa.

William Beinart
*August 2000*

# CONTENTS

vii

# Contents

# Contents

# LIST OF MAPS

# LIST OF TABLES

# LIST OF FIGURES

# ABBREVIATIONS

| | |
|---|---|
| AMEC | African Methodist Episcopal Church |
| ANC | African National Congress |
| APLA | African People's Liberation Army |
| APO | African Political Organization |
| AWB | Afrikaner Weerstandsbeweging |
| BAAB | Bantu Affairs Administration Board |
| BAWU | Black Allied Workers' Union |
| BOSS | Bureau of State Security |
| CODESA | Convention for a Democratic South Africa |
| CONTRALESA | Congress of Traditional Leaders of South Africa |
| COSAS | Congress of South African Students |
| COSATU | Congress of South African Trade Unions |
| CUSA | Council of Unions of South Africa |
| ESCOM/ESKOM | Electricity Supply Commission |
| FOSATU | Federation of South African Trade Unions |
| FRAC | Franchise Action Committee |
| GEAR | Growth, Employment and Redistribution Programme |
| GNU | Government of National Unity |
| HNP/NP | Herenigde National Party |
| ICU | Industrial and Commercial Workers' Union of South Africa |
| IFP | Inkatha Freedom Party |
| ISCOR | Iron and Steel Corporation |
| *JAH* | *Journal of African History* |
| *JSAS* | *Journal of Southern African Studies* |
| KZN | KwaZulu/Natal |
| MAWU | Metal and Allied Workers' Union |

| | |
|---|---|
| MK | Umkhonto we Sizwe |
| NAD | Native Affairs Department |
| NEC | Native Economic Commission |
| NEUM | Non-European Unity Movement |
| NP | National Party |
| NRC | Native Recruiting Corporation |
| NUM | National Union of Mineworkers |
| NUSAS | National Union of South African Students |
| OB | Ossewabrandwag |
| PAC | Pan-Africanist Congress |
| Putco | Public Utility Transport Corporation |
| RDP | Reconstruction and Development Programme |
| SAAU | South African Agricultural Union |
| SAAWU | South African Allied Workers' Union |
| SACP | South African Communist Party |
| SACTU | South African Congress of Trade Unions |
| SANAC | South African Native Affairs Commission |
| SANC | South African Native Congress |
| SANNC | South African Native National Congress |
| SAP | South African Party |
| SASM | South African Students Movement |
| SASO | South African Students Organization |
| SPP | Surplus People Project |
| SWAPO | South West African People's Organization |
| TNIP | Transkei National Independence Party |
| TUCSA | Trade Union Congress of South Africa |
| UDF | United Democratic Front |
| UP | United South African Nationalist Party (United Party) |
| WNLA | Witwatersrand Native Labour Association |
| ZANU | Zimbabwe African National Union |
| ZCC | Zion Christian Church |

# CHRONOLOGY

| | |
|---|---|
| 1877–80 | British conquest of Transvaal, Sekhukhuneland, Zululand; rebellions quelled in Lesotho, Transkei, and Bechuanaland. Afrikaner Bond founded in Cape. |
| 1881 | South African Republic in the Transvaal reasserts independence. |
| 1880s | Cape African peasantry flourishes; J. T. Jabavu starts newspaper *Imvo Zabantsundu*; African independent churches founded. |
| 1886–7 | Discovery of gold on Witwatersrand; De Beers monopoly of Kimberley diamond mines under Cecil Rhodes. |
| 1890s | Rhodes Prime Minister of Cape (1890–6); Kruger President of South African Republic; Natal granted responsible government; conquest and annexation of African chiefdoms completed; white settler control entrenched. |
| 1895 | Jameson Raid—abortive forcible takeover of Transvaal. |
| 1896–7 | Rinderpest epizootic—devastating cattle disease. |
| 1899–1902 | South African War. |
| 1905 | Report of the South African Native Affairs Commission—post-war Reconstruction government's programme for segregation. |
| 1906 | Bambatha rebellion in Natal. |
| 1904–11 | Johannesburg overtakes Cape Town as region's largest city; African employment on mines exceeds 200,000. |
| 1910 | Union of South Africa formed including the Cape |

Colony, Natal, Transvaal, and Orange River Colony (Orange Free State); South African Party government led by Generals Louis Botha and Jan Smuts takes power.

1912    Foundation of the South African Native National Congress (later ANC).

1913    Year of crisis: Natives Land Act passed; Gandhi's march to the Transvaal and Indian sugar workers' strike; African women march against passes in Bloemfontein; white workers strike in gold mines.

1914–15    National Party founded under General J. B. M. Hertzog, initially based in Orange Free State; Afrikaner rebellion, coinciding with outbreak of First World War; *Die Burger* newspaper launched.

1918    Influenza epidemic—the only major demographic set-back in the twentieth century.

1919    Botha dies; Smuts becomes Prime Minister.

1918–20    Strikes and boycotts on the Rand culminating in first major African mineworkers' strike.

1922    Rand rebellion of white workers.

1923    Drought Commission Report highlighting environmental degradation; Natives Urban Areas Act tightens urban segregation and controls over movement to cities.

1924    Hertzog's National Party wins election in alliance with white Labour Party.

1925–30    Industrial and Commercial Workers Union, founded in Cape Town 1919, becomes first national African mass opposition movement and spreads to rural areas.

1927    Native Administration Act extends recognition of chieftaincy and forms basis for decentralization of authority to chiefs in African reserves.

1926–30    Imperial conferences enhance South Africa's independence as a Dominion within the British Commonwealth.

1930    White women enfranchised.

1930–1    Livestock numbers peak at nearly 60 million small

stock and 12 million cattle; drought and environmental crisis follow.

1930–4     Depression: gold mines benefit; agriculture hit; poor white problem highlighted.

1932     *Native Economic Commission* report provides guidelines for development of reserves.

1933–4     Hertzog and Smuts form Fusion government and United Party in response to Depression; National Party breaks away under D. F. Malan.

1932–40     South Africa leaves Gold Standard; gold mining expands rapidly and employment exceeds 400,000; manufacturing boom begins.

1936     Native Trust and Land Act passed promising more land for African reserves; remnant African common roll vote in Cape terminated.

1939     Betterment proclamation provides for far-reaching reorganization of settlement and agriculture in the African reserves.

1939     South Africa votes to enter Second World War. Hertzog resigns; Smuts governs as Prime Minister to 1948.

1940     Ossewabrandwag, Afrikaner anti-war paramilitary movement, founded.

1940–6     Wartime industrial expansion; employment in manufacturing industry overtakes that in mining; rising level of African militancy culminating in 1946 black mineworkers' strike and launch of squatter movements on Rand.

1948     Malan's Nationalists win election on *apartheid* slogan.

1950–3     Major apartheid legislation passed: Population Registration; Suppression of Communism; Group Areas and Prevention of Illegal Squatting; Separate Representation of Voters; Bantu Authorities; Bantu Education.

1952     ANC leads Defiance Campaign.

1955     Freedom Charter sets out ANC's alternative vision for a non-racial South Africa.

Chronology

| | |
|---|---|
| 1956 | Tomlinson Commission report on Homelands. |
| 1958 | H. F. Verwoerd becomes Prime Minister. |
| 1958–60 | Black opposition peaks: Pan-Africanist Congress splits from ANC; rural revolts in Sekhukhuneland and Pondoland; Sharpeville massacre; mass urban stay-aways; march on Parliament in Cape Town. |
| 1960–1 | South Africa becomes Republic outside the Commonwealth; ANC and PAC banned and go underground. |
| 1962–3 | ANC leadership including Nelson Mandela captured and imprisoned, or escape into exile. |
| 1966 | Verwoerd assassinated; B. J. Vorster becomes Prime Minister. |
| 1960s | Years of rapid economic, especially industrial, growth; white incomes increase as apartheid entrenched; homelands and forced removals policies implemented; black population growth increasingly outstrips white. |
| 1972 | Black People's Convention launched. |
| 1973 | Durban strikes; independent trade unions formed. |
| 1975 | Relaunch of Inkatha, the Zulu cultural and political movement; Portuguese colonies of Angola and Mozambique achieve independence. |
| 1976 | Soweto students' protest; Transkei becomes first 'independent' homeland; television introduced. |
| 1977 | Steve Biko, black consciousness leader, killed by police. |
| 1979 | P. W. Botha Prime Minister and 'reform' era begins. |
| 1970s to mid-1980s | Rural removals and displaced urbanization peak. |
| 1979–80 | Nationwide strikes, student and community protests; African government in power in Zimbabwe. |
| 1982 | Afrikaner Conservative Party formed. |
| 1983 | Tri-cameral parliament and new presidential government; United Democratic Front initiated in protest. |
| 1984–6 | Insurrection and state of emergency. |

| | |
|---|---|
| 1985 | COSATU trade union federation founded. |
| 1986 | Rescinding of pass laws as population of major cities explodes with informal settlements. |
| 1989 | F. W. de Klerk becomes President. |
| 1990 | Nelson Mandela released; ANC and other movements unbanned; rescinding of apartheid laws gathers pace. |
| 1991 | Convention for a Democratic South Africa meets to negotiate new constitution. |
| 1992 | Boipatong massacre; talks suspended but relaunched at end of year. |
| 1990–4 | Violence in black townships, and between ANC and Inkatha supporters in KwaZulu/Natal, spreads. |
| 1994 | First non-racial democratic elections held; ANC wins 62 per cent of vote; Mandela becomes President in a Government of National Unity including National Party and Inkatha Freedom Party. Non-racialism, reconciliation, and redistribution stressed. |
| 1995 | Truth and Reconciliation Commission appointed. |
| 1996 | Government of National Unity dissolves; Reconstruction and Development programme sidelined as ANC confirms cautious economic policy. |
| 1990s | Formal sector employment in manufacturing and mining declines; unemployment, crime, and violence against women increase. |
| 1999 | Second democratic election; Thabo Mbeki becomes President; African renaissance increasingly stressed; National Party vote collapses. |
| 2000 | National debate on HIV/AIDS as reported incidence reaches alarming heights; international conference on the disease held in Durban helps to highlight its seriousness and government inaction. |

# INTRODUCTION
# Conquest, the State, and Society

By the early 1870s, the area that became South Africa had been washed by successive waves of European expansion, notably the Dutch maritime empire of the seventeenth and eighteenth centuries and British imperialism in the nineteenth. Four settler states had been established. The original Cape Colony, which passed finally to Britain in 1806, boasted the largest area and settler population. It had recently acquired a parliamentary system and a measure of self-government. Natal remained a British colony. The Boer states of the Orange Free State and South African Republic on the interior highveld of the country struggled to maintain their independence from British and Cape influence.

The African people of the region had been deeply affected by colonization over two centuries. In the Cape, the San and Khoikhoi had been decimated and largely displaced; they survived as farmworkers or on mission stations and settlements around the peripheries of white control. The Xhosa on the eastern frontier and the Sotho on the highveld had been conquered and partly incorporated. Yet the colonial impact was uneven. Between the settler states and to their north a number of African polities remained, by reason of their power and size or their geographic position, relatively independent. The Zulu kingdom on the east coast, north of Natal, was the largest; the Swazi, Tswana, Pedi, Venda, Mpondo, and Thembu remained substantial chiefdoms. Within the next couple of decades, however, they were drawn decisively, with more or less force, under British or settler rule.

In the decades around the turn of the twentieth century, South African society was deeply moulded by the British imperial presence. Not only did imperial armies, together with the commandos and cavalry of the settler states, finally complete the conquest of African chiefdoms, but a huge investment of European capital made the mining industry into the new economic motor of the country. Settler and African agrarian economies were fundamentally reshaped. Between 1899 and 1902, Britain fought perhaps its greatest colonial war to annex the Boer republics.

As ox-wagons trundled across the veld, moving Lord Kitchener's giant army, so the tracks were laid for a coherent single state in South Africa. The country was locked together in war. Ox-wagons had carried the Boer settlers into the interior; wagon routes were the sinews of the trading economy that, spreading from the major colonial ports in the nineteenth century, clutched both black and white societies into its grasp. The ox-wagon, so potent a symbol of Afrikaner identity in the twentieth century, was previously a vehicle of imperial conquest.

British power, which had ebbed and flowed in southern Africa through the nineteenth century, projected itself as an essentially peaceful force. Britain honoured its military heroes with graves in St Paul's Cathedral and conceived of violence as provoked by uncivilized 'hordes' and 'tribes', or by semi-barbarized Boers. The British duty to civilize them all both explained and justified conquest. But in nineteenth-century South Africa, empire and its colonial agents were harbingers of a great deal of bloodshed that was not simply incidental to expansion. Most of the major battles were fought on the territory of Britain's opponents. While there were periods of indecision in the conquest of this corner of the Empire, there was no absence of mind. Britain's economic and strategic imperatives made it determined to defend and expand its interests in the subcontinent. This required war with the Zulu, the most powerful remaining African state, and with the Afrikaners. Had the South African War of 1899–1902 not been dwarfed by the First World War, it would have studded world history even more sharply.

British expansion in the nineteenth century had by no means been the only trigger of conflict. The settler states were often themselves key agents of expansion and conquest. African chiefdoms were trying to consolidate their authority and defend their boundaries against black and white challenges. It is very difficult to write nineteenth-century South African history without constant reference to violence and military engagements. All these nodes of power had competed for land, labour, natural resources, and political space. Guns poured into the subcontinent, intensifying its conflicts. But British interventions greatly increased the scale of violence in the late nineteenth century.

Ironically, British intervention also resulted in the imposition of a colonial peace that ended more than century of war. The economic muscle and bureaucratic sophistication of an advanced capitalist country were transferred to the region and helped to bequeath a powerful state structure. Twentieth-century conflicts were civil rather than military. The *impi*, the redcoat regiment, and commando moved to the background; conflict had its locus in the mines, the streets, and on the farms. For seventy years, until the waves of decolonization swept downwards across the subcontinent, and a resurgent mass opposition burst through internally, the state established at the turn of the century held sway and remained militarily secure. Even the guerrilla wars of the 1960s to the 1980s, the rearming of the subcontinent, and internal insurrections of the 1980s did not quite dislodge it.

The very solidity of the state provided the stepping stones for whites, both English and especially Afrikaans-speaking, to take power and entrench a system of racially based dominance that was unique in its rigidity. Segregation to 1948, and apartheid afterwards, were policies aimed not simply at separating white from black, but at regulating the way in which the indigenous population was drawn into a new society. Economically, blacks were essential as peasants, workers, and farm tenants; politically, the settler state tried to exclude them. The country's relative peace for nearly three-quarters of a century was achieved at the cost of deep divisions of power, race, and wealth. White power in South Africa was more efficient and often more uncompromising than in many other colonial contexts.

White power had deep foundations in the region, but, even at its height in mid-century, the settler state was shaped by its African context. In Africa as a whole, colonial rule, though far-reaching in its consequences, was a relatively short-lived historical moment. In South Africa this phase was longer. More radical social transformations—industrialization, urbanization, and agricultural expansion—were effected. Africans have gained power in a country whose people are overwhelmingly urban or wage dependent, yet it is important to understand that South Africa remains part of the African continent.

South Africa differed from much of colonial Africa in that its climate, its diseases, and natural resources allowed for substantial early European settlement. Although this was certainly no 'vacant' land, the Khoisan population of the Cape was politically weak and highly susceptible to diseases such as smallpox. In this area, the colonial experience in South Africa was more like Australasia or the Americas than Africa. But elsewhere southern Africa differed from most 'new-world' colonies of settlement in that the settler thrust was weaker and the indigenous response stronger. The further the settlers penetrated into the interior, or into areas of dense African settlement, the more dilute their influence became. Unlike in North America or Australia, land in South Africa beyond the old Khoisan areas could be taken over only with great difficulty.

The area of modern South Africa was, to a significant extent, shaped by the zones of effective white settlement in the nineteenth century. Yet even in the census of 1904, which was taken when the white population was probably at its highest relative to the black, the country was demographically speaking largely African (**Table 1**). A little under 5.2 million people were counted in the states that became South Africa. By this time the racial categories labelled as European, Coloured, Asiatic, and Native were firmly established. Roughly one-fifth (21.5 per cent) of the total, or 1.1 million people were counted as Europeans and 8.6 per cent as coloured, overwhelmingly in the Cape, descended from the Khoikhoi, slaves, and settlers. About 2.4 per cent were Asiatic, largely Indian workers on the Natal sugar estates and their descendants. Over two-thirds, or 3.5 million people, were counted as Africans. If Lesotho, Swaziland, and Botswana—all part of the same economic and political zone—had been included, the proportion of the white population would have been smaller.

C. W. de Kiewiet, author of the most exciting single-volume history of South Africa, expressed the particularity of the South

African experience by arguing that South Africa was not 'a romantic frontier like the American West' (1941: 48): 'Legend has denied the Pondos, for example, a place besides the Pawnees . . . The stuff of legend is not easily found in a process which turned the Ama-Xosa, Zulus, or Basuto into farm labourers, kitchen servants, or messengers.'

De Kiewiet was surely wrong. It was the very fact that South Africa remained part of Africa, that its black population survived conquest and made the transition from warrior to wage slave, that was the core of the South African black legend. De Kiewiet's romanticization of the Native Americans was a celluloid picture, made in Hollywood, which could be recreated by the dominant culture precisely because the people on whom it was based had been so thoroughly displaced and marginalized. His alliterative choice of the Pawnee, who tended to side with the colonists and still lost their land, was hardly appropriate.

The romance of Mpondo history—or that of the Sotho or Xhosa or Zulu—was that they retained some of their land and their culture. The Mpondo survived well enough to stage one of the last major rural revolts against white authority in 1960. It was the capacity of black peasants and workers to adapt, increase demographically, educate themselves, and strike back politically that was at the heart of twentieth-century South African history. The African experience is now also the subject of celluloid celebration in films such as *Cry Freedom*.

In the early twentieth century a single state was forged but not a single nation. Economic change and new forms of government overlaid but did not fully subsume what went before. The old identities and social geography of African chiefdoms remained partly intact and a dynamic factor in the country's development. Old layers of settler society also continued to exercise a deep influence on the political trajectory of the region.

Liberal and radical historians of South Africa have often focused on the rapidity with which a common economy and society emerged, arguing that the reality of interaction was stopped in its tracks by politically enforced segregation. Mining and industrialization have been the organizing historical themes, together with the rise of new nationalisms, both Afrikaner and African.

These must remain central and persistent historiographical concerns. But we need to find a method that will allow analysis of these forces together with the remnant identities and particularisms that have been so powerful in shaping the ideas of the mass of people in the country. The history of political opposition, for example, cannot be reduced to the rise of African nationalism or the working classes. A means has to be found to express also the vitality of discrete rural localities, the salience of ethnicity, the fragmented patterns of urban social life, the multiplicity of religious expression. These are all forces, both dynamic and destructive, that stalked and enlivened twentieth-century history.

South Africa was part settler state and part African colony in the early twentieth century. It included diverse recently conquered African polities as well as a divided white population. The historical comparison with other colonies of settlement provides only partial insight into its history. In a post-colonial, post-apartheid context, where political power is in African hands, it becomes all the more important to understand African heritages. An understanding of African and other extra-European states, the character of political authority within them, and transitions towards democracy become increasingly necessary as a comparative foil.

The South African government became in 1994 representative of the majority of its people and its constitution a model of democratic values. Although the transition was achieved at considerable cost, thus far relative stability both within the country and in the region has been restored. The divisions of the apartheid era have not dissolved, and the country remains one of extraordinary social diversity, sometimes volatile in its cultural chemistry. But there are signs that a varied, hybrid, and distinctive national culture could amalgamate.

# PART I

# A State without a Nation, 1880–1948

# 1

# African Rural Life and Migrant Labour

### *The Division of Land*

Any author writing a general book on South Africa must decide whether to start with whites or with blacks. For reasons both of accuracy and of ideology, most historians writing recently have abandoned 1652, foundation date of the Dutch station at the Cape, and begun instead with pre-colonial African societies. It is more difficult to begin with African people in a book that starts in the late nineteenth century. Markets, empire, industry, capital, railways, and political union in 1910 were the new motors of change. None of these forces had to do simply with white or black, but in dealing with them the agency of the settler and metropolitan worlds must be emphasized.

One way out of the dilemma is to address the last century initially from the vantage point of the varied agrarian worlds that were being consolidated into a single state. There is a demographic argument for this approach in that the great majority of people still lived in the countryside at the turn of the century. There is also an explanatory logic: by evoking different rural zones it will be easier to keep the diversity of the country in mind as other themes are developed. And by focusing most of the first two chapters on the rural areas, it is also possible to begin with African people. Although a majority (53 per cent) of whites lived in towns by 1904, only 15 per cent of blacks and 10 per cent of Africans, including migrant workers temporarily in the cities, did so **(Table 3)**. The bedrock of settlement and population in the country, well over three million people, were Africans who lived in villages and dispersed homesteads on reserved lands and farms.

The division of ownership and possession of rural land by race in South Africa, which had deep historical roots, was formalized and consolidated in the 1913 Natives Land Act. It is often said that 87 per cent of land was reserved for whites and 13 per cent for Africans. These figures are not quite accurate for the first few decades of the twentieth century. Whites have never owned so much of the land and rather less was initially reserved for Africans. About three-quarters of the country's surface area was demarcated for private rural ownership by white individuals or by companies; around 8 per cent was reserved solely for African occupation, and a little more was privately owned by Africans or for them by institutions such as missions. The rest was urban land and Crown or state land. Much of the latter was demarcated for game reserves, forests, or other uses and only lightly occupied, but some was rented out to tenants. Only after the 1936 Native Trust and Land Act did the area reserved exclusively for African occupation gradually increase to 13 per cent.

Whatever the exact numbers, this was a degree of land alienation unrivalled in any sub-Saharan African context. In neighbouring countries with large areas of private farmlands, such as Zimbabwe, Swaziland, and Namibia, under 50 per cent of the total area fell into the hands of settlers. But these stark South African figures require more detailed explanation. They disguise a pattern of land occupation and distribution that initially allowed Africans to retain a more significant stake in the land than the raw percentages might suggest.

The land area that came to comprise South Africa is divided by the 20 inch or 500 mm. rainfall line, which runs from Port Elizabeth in the eastern Cape through the middle of the Free State into the western Transvaal (**Map 1**). Over half of the country, most of it to the west of this line, receives so little rain that it was very difficult to grow crops. The dense settlements of iron-using, cultivating, Bantu-speaking African people, who had for centuries made up the bulk of the country's population, lived mostly to the east. They did not penetrate into the one better-watered pocket of the west around the Cape Peninsula. In pre-colonial times both the western Cape and the drier parts of the interior were occupied largely by Khoisan hunters, gatherers, and herders. The major exception has been the Tswana chiefdoms, whose territories, based around pre-colonial towns, straddled semi-arid highveld zones. Xhosa communities also penetrated to the dry northern Cape in the early nineteenth century.

The land reserved for African occupation in the twentieth century was largely within the higher rainfall zone. Some of it may have become very poor, but initially it was not the worst land. Africans tended to retain reserves in the heartlands of their old, conquered chiefdoms—the areas most suitable for their systems of agricultural and pastoral production. They certainly lost a great deal of land and were severely disadvantaged in the competition for unexploited areas made possible by new technologies such as ploughs, dams, and windmills. But over 20 per cent of the land that they had effectively occupied was initially reserved for them. Within the eastern half of the country, a majority of African people lived in the relatively narrow strip of land between the Kahlamba (things cast down in heap) or Drakensberg (dragon) mountain range and the Indian Ocean. It was here also around the old Xhosa, Thembu, Mpondo, and Zulu chiefdoms that the bulk of African reserve land was situated. Although the Xhosa suffered particularly in the nineteenth century from the eastward thrust of settler colonialism, most east coast chiefdoms retained far more than 20 per cent of the land they had occupied before conquest; in the case of the Mpondo the great bulk was retained.

Another reason for caution when discussing the racial division of land is that many Africans stayed on white-owned land. It would be a mistake to draw too hard a dividing line between categories of land at the turn of the century. Land alienation was part of the process of military conquest only recently completed and it proved more difficult for whites to assert control over land than to defeat African armies. Private property was sometimes imposed over areas that were still occupied by African communities and held for speculative purposes. In Natal and the Cape reserved land policies were instituted from the middle of the nineteenth century, but even here large numbers of Africans lived or worked temporarily on farms. Boer ideas led them to demarcate private property more generally, whether or not this could be

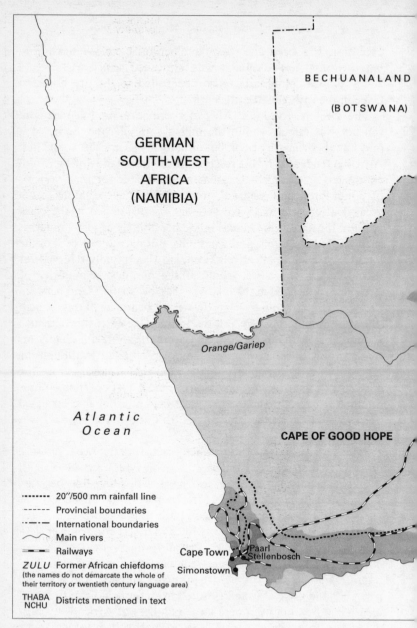

BECHUANALAND

(BOTSWANA)

GERMAN
SOUTH-WEST
AFRICA
(NAMIBIA)

*Orange/Gariep*

*Atlantic
Ocean*

**CAPE OF GOOD HOPE**

....... 20″/500 mm rainfall line
------ Provincial boundaries
-·-·- International boundaries
~~~ Main rivers
=■= Railways
*ZULU* Former African chiefdoms
(the names do not demarcate the whole of
their territory or twentieth century language area)
THABA
NCHU  Districts mentioned in text

Cape Town · Paarl
Stellenbosch
Simonstown

MAP 1. *Union of South Africa, c.1910*

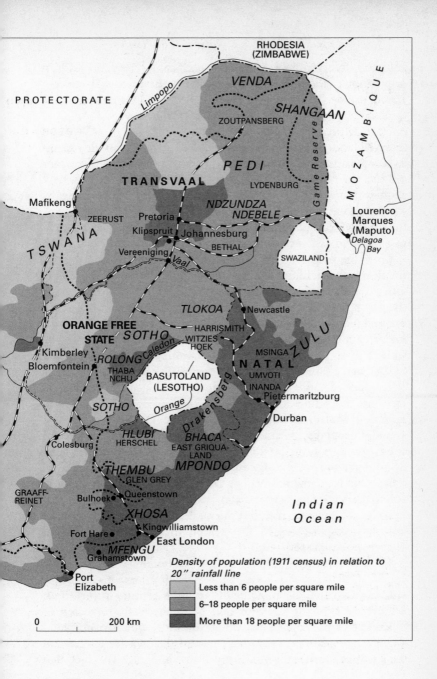

RHODESIA
(ZIMBABWE)

*VENDA*

PROTECTORATE

*Limpopo*

*SHANGAAN*

ZOUTPANSBERG

M
O
Z
A
M
B
I
Q
U
E

*PEDI*

**TRANSVAAL**

LYDENBURG

Game Reserve

Mafikeng

*NDZUNDZA
NDEBELE*

Lourenco
Marques
(Maputo)

ZEERUST

Pretoria

*Delagoa
Bay*

Klipspruit

Johannesburg

**T S W A N A**

Vereeniging

BETHAL

*Vaal*

SWAZILAND

*TLOKOA*

● Newcastle

**ORANGE FREE
STATE**

*SOTHO*

HARRISMITH

WITZIES
HOEK

Z
U
L
U

*Caledon*

MSINGA

Kimberley

*ROLONG*

**NATAL**

Bloemfontein

THABA
NCHU

**BASUTOLAND
(LESOTHO)**

UMVOTI

INANDA

*Orange*

Pietermaritzburg

*SOTHO*

*Drakensberg*

Durban

Colesburg

*HLUBI*

HERSCHEL

*BHACA*

EAST GRIQUA-
LAND

*THEMBU*

*MPONDO*

GLEN GREY

GRAAFF-
REINET

Bulhoek

● Queenstown

*Indian
Ocean*

*XHOSA*

Fort Hare

● Kingwilliamstown

East London

*MFENGU*

Grahamstown

Port
Elizabeth

*Density of population (1911 census) in relation to
20″ rainfall line*

Less than 6 people per square mile

6–18 people per square mile

More than 18 people per square mile

0          200 km

enforced; reserved areas were less significant. The rural African population of the Free State and especially the Transvaal, concentrated around the old Sotho, Tswana, Pedi, and Venda states, was thus scattered in smaller reserves and on white-owned farmlands. African settlements could straddle the boundaries of private and reserved land. Many landowners required Africans on their farms as tenants and workers and had little incentive to expel them. Nor did this need diminish. Throughout the first half of the twentieth century the number of black people on rural land owned by whites increased rapidly. In the 1936 census about 37 per cent of the total African population was counted on farms, 45 per cent in reserves, and 17 per cent in towns.

From the point of view of some African communities, the distinction between different sorts of land was only being more fully infused with meaning at the turn of the century. Many retained their own sense of social geography—the phantom districts of the pre-conquest chiefdoms. Almost everywhere black people were a majority in farming districts where the bulk of land was owned by whites; in some they were a large majority. There never was a 'white man's country' nor 'white farms' in the sense that these were zones of numerically predominant white occupation, only in the sense that whites, through their economic and political power, exercised control over the people on the farmlands. Africans actually occupied, mostly as tenants, far greater swathes of the countryside than the land reserved for them or owned by them. Maps depicting the country around the turn of the century fail to reflect this fundamental reality. They report graphically the new colonial social geography—farm boundaries, towns, roads, and railways. They might mention the names of a few old chiefdoms, but, census maps excepted, they seldom illustrate the distribution of rural population.

These points are not offered in order to minimize the impact of conquest, dispossession, and racial legislation, but because they are central to an understanding of twentieth-century history, both urban and rural. If Africans had been physically restricted to 8 or even 13 per cent of the worst land in South Africa, then a much larger number would have moved to town far earlier and the country's history would have been different. The fact that very many Africans were able to retain some access to land helps explain critical historical issues such as the tenacity of the peasantry in the reserves; the predominance of migrant labour as a form of proletarianization; the importance of tenancy on the white farms; and the character of African political struggles.

## The African Heritage

The African reserves and tenanted farmlands of the eastern half of the country were the most densely populated parts of rural South Africa in the early twentieth century. Although their inhabitants were involved in deeply rooted patterns of agriculture and social life, they found their lives transformed in increasingly fundamental ways: what patterns of authority and power they recognized and how they sought to alter these; what they produced and consumed; how they worked and for whom; and which gods they looked to. The term peasant has been used widely by historians attempting to describe and analyse these broad changes. On the one hand, it affirms the point that most Africans depended on their homesteads, agricultural production, and family labour for subsistence; on the other, it implies that they were no longer part of independent chiefdoms, but incorporated in some way into a broader colonial economy and society.

Debates about the causes and nature of these changes have been central in recent historiography. Bundy's *Rise and Fall of the South African Peasantry*, which suggested a relatively positive African response to the new opportunities, markets, and faiths of the nineteenth century, remains a trenchant text. Some historians, such as Lewis, have emphasized the more coercive elements of incorporation. They have seen fewer economic benefits for Africans in the early stages of colonial rule and a more continuous decline in standards of living after conquest. Others have detected pockets of powerful African traditionalism, and resistance to social and economic change. The idea of a peasantry can be a blunt analytical instrument in distinguishing the experiences and fate of local African communities from different pre-colonial chiefdoms, on different types of land, subject to different patterns of colonization. It nevertheless remains a useful term to describe the general processes involved.

An understanding of African responses to colonization must recognize the powerful social legacies of pre-colonial societies: there was no single African political or economic system. The chiefdoms had been independent and while alliances were possible between them in the face of colonial encroachments, they were not unified politically or militarily. The more powerful African chiefdoms had generally expanded in the nineteenth century, following the rise of the Zulu kingdom, in which the political system had been fundamentally restructured. The Sotho under Moshoeshoe, the Swazi under Sobhuza and Mswati, the Mpondo under Faku, the Pedi under Sekwati and Sekhukhune, amongst others, conquered or absorbed smaller polities and clans by mid-century. The population of most of these chiefdoms grew to over 100,000 people before conquest—and the Zulu state at least twice that. Although it was by no means the only factor, the size and cohesion of the Sotho, Swazi, and Tswana states contributed towards their separate annexation by Britain, and they remain politically independent from South Africa to the present. All of these groups to some degree retained their own territories and political authorities. A common African identity was still to be forged.

The east coast, where Zulu- and Xhosa-related languages predominated, and the Sotho- and Tswana-speaking interior highveld were to some degree culturally and linguistically distinct. Environmental influences, such as the availability of water, combined with social and political institutions to shape different patterns of life. A web of rivers flowed eastwards from the Drakensberg mountains to the sea. Not only was rainfall generally higher on the east coast, but water was widely distributed through the broken, hilly countryside. Settlement tended to be in dispersed homesteads rather than villages, often on ridges above valleys where women collected water from the streams. Homesteads were large, housing three generations, including a number of married men (brothers and sons), their wives and children.

By the early twentieth century, the old wicker 'beehive' huts had been displaced by 'wattle and daub' structures in which a framework of poles and lathes was plastered with mud. Almost everywhere, and especially in the deep reserves of Zululand and Transkei, local materials were still used for building, huts were circular, and their conical roofs were thatched. Many families still arranged their huts in a semi-circle around the cattle kraal where the animals were brought home from the pastures for protection each night. Square houses, usually of mud-bricks, had appeared on mission stations and were a mark of Christianity elsewhere. Pastures, fields, and buildings were the result of centuries of settlement, leaving only pockets of indigenous forest. This countryside of rolling hills, green and lush in summer, brown and dry in winter, had a beauty which was noted by colonial observers. Remnants of this pattern of settlement and efficient local resource use still survive and have lessons to teach.

Across the Drakensberg mountains, in the interior, rainfall tended to be lower and more sharply concentrated in dramatic afternoon storms. In a flatter world, water flowed in fewer streams; large river systems—such as the Gariep (Orange), Caledon, Vaal, Limpopo, and their tributaries—were more important lifelines. Springs and vleis (shallow depressions) were also critical as water sources. Settlement tended to be clustered in villages for both for water and defence. Pre-colonial towns were most developed on the extreme west of African occupation in Tswana territory, where they reached over 10,000 people; some have provided the basis for later urban development in Botswana. Where wood was scarce, as in Lesotho, stone building was developed by mission-trained masons. Livestock could not be grazed so close to home in these chiefdoms and they were often taken to cattle posts for long periods.

Africans' capacity to contain the impact of settler incursions, trade, and demands for labour stemmed from their control of some land and also the strength of their productive systems. All except those in the driest regions had added maize, originally from America, to sorghum as a staple crop in the eighteenth and nineteenth centuries. Cattle were the bedrock of most economic and social systems; they supplied milk, meat, and skins as well as oiling the wheels of marriage and exchange. The grassy, well-watered eastern half of South Africa was particularly suitable for cattle and it was largely free from tsetse fly, restricted to an arc around the north-eastern boundaries of the country. A good herd could be the basis of economic independence after colonization, just as it had been the primary object of accumulation before. Although the resources of individual homesteads were being squeezed, many rural families still produced much of the food they consumed and maintained complex economic and social links between homesteads.

Pre-colonial political hierarchies around the major chiefs, especially in larger reserves of the Transkei, Natal, and the Transvaal, remained significant. Chiefs and headmen had to work under European magistrates and they could no longer command regiments. But they ran courts and their income from fees, fines, and death duties did not immediately disappear. Nor did their capacity to distribute cattle as loans in return for labour service. Chiefs had historically cemented their status, and forged bonds with other royal families and clans, by polygynous marriage alliances. Although a few Christian chiefs now abjured this custom, major chiefs continued to have a number of wives. As guarantors of African land, they had a powerful symbolic standing. Some, such as the exiled Zulu king Dinuzulu, who were associated with resistance to conquest, commanded widespread authority among their people.

African patterns of marriage proved remarkably resilient. Bridewealth was paid by the husband's family to the wife's, often in the form of cattle. Women moved on their marriage to their husband's homestead, where they did the bulk of the agricultural work as well as household labour and care of children. Women carried many of the burdens of rural life, but they could acquire influence, especially when older. Patriarchy was symbolized by avoidance customs (*hlonipa* in Xhosa) that women had to obey: they could not use words that contained the names of their husband's male kin, or handle cattle, or even drink milk in many situations. Cattle were the province of men: boys and youths herded them. The division of labour had never been rigid and taboos were breaking down in the early twentieth century. For example, ploughs, which required the use of oxen, brought men more centrally into agriculture, and on mission stations men were encouraged to work the fields. But women and children were still seen as major productive assets and ambitious men still strove to accumulate the resources to marry, procreate, and extend their lineage and labour force. Polygynous marriages were not prohibited by colonial law.

Hierarchies of age, gender, and rank were the hallmark of the homesteads and villages. As long as patterns of authority were respected, these were inclusive institutions that provided food and security. The size, adaptability, and cohesion of the 'extended family' were a ballast against deprivation. More extensive networks were also recognized and symbolized by the use of clan names (*izibongo* in Zulu/Xhosa) in greetings. Yet the strength of local communities could also be inhibiting. Those without rank who accumulated too much could be perceived as a political threat and accused of witchcraft; other outsiders, not least women, were particularly vulnerable. These beliefs were deeply set, and, although they gradually eroded in the twentieth century, they came into play especially during times of social crisis. African homesteads, and the changing dynamic of the social relationships within them, remained a major force in twentieth-century South Africa.

The term 'communal tenure' has often been applied to African landholding systems. In so far as it indicates that land could not be bought and sold, it remains useful, but it disguises considerable variation in patterns of tenure and control over land. To generalize: African systems involved rights to land that came from membership of a lineage, a family grouping, or a chiefdom. In the nineteenth century, there was enormous mobility between and within African chiefdoms: land was acquired by *khonza*—to use the Zulu term—or by recognition of the political authority of a chief or headman and the obligations that this entailed. Local political authorities would then grant arable plots, usually assigned to married men who had the wives to work them. The number and size of fields were expanding rapidly, as ploughs gave late-nineteenth-century peasants profligate new powers of production. Thus the right to break new fields was as important as the right to keep a field within a family; again it was negotiated through the local headmen and council. Pasturage, the bulk of land in any African territory, was open to all those who possessed stock, subject to local grazing regulations.

Once a homestead had established rights over pieces of arable land, these could be relatively secure, though they were vulnerable in succession disputes or when families moved. Specific arable sites might be removed from families, but chiefs could not generally disqualify their subjects from access to land. Even when individual men were absent as migrant workers, the homestead could maintain its rights. Although there were experiments, especially in the Cape, with more individualized tenure, colonial and Union legislation generally entrenched modified versions of these customary systems of landholding in the African reserves. Africans could purchase land outside the reserves, with varying degrees of restriction, until the Natives Land Act of 1913, but relatively few were able to do so. Within the reserves, both before and after 1913, land could not be bought or sold, nor privately accumulated; by and large, the African people of these areas defended such tenure, which underpinned their remaining social cohesion. While chiefs and other powerful men might have more arable plots at their disposal, and could accumulate significant herds of hundreds of cattle, which were grazed on the commonage or loaned to followers, they could not easily translate their wealth into landed assets.

Tenure in the African reserves thus differed radically from the largely white-owned districts, where land was more rigidly divided into private property. In the nineteenth century, Afrikaners who did not own farms could often get access to land as *bywoners* through tenancy and family relationships. When these came under pressure during the agrarian transformation of the early twentieth century (**Chapter 2**), Afrikaners were driven off the land very rapidly, despite the extensive areas reserved for whites. A far larger proportion of Africans in the reserves, protected by communal tenure, was able to maintain access to land, and this diminished the impact of conquest. Initially, as population increased, arable plots could be found by carving up the pasturage. The cost for African communities over the longer term was that the amount of land available to each homestead declined; while the system did not constrain an early expansion of peasant production, especially of crops, with basic new technology, it did inhibit investment and so also a transition to more capitalist forms of agriculture in the African areas.

## African Peasantries

In many areas, especially in the eastern Cape, coastal and midland Natal, and the highveld of the Transvaal and the Free State, loss of land necessitated changes in the way that African families survived. Resources such as wildlife—hunted out by settlers and Africans with firearms—became scarce by the late nineteenth century. Everywhere colonial taxes were, in Cecil Rhodes's ironic words, a 'gentle stimulus' to labour. Taxes in South Africa were relatively high in comparison to the rest of the subcontinent. The hut tax, favoured in the Cape, and in Natal before 1906, was levied on married men with land and could be met by the sale of produce. Poll taxes levied in the Transvaal, the Free State, and Natal on all men over 18 whether they had rural resources or not were designed more explicitly to push them into seeking waged work.

In the Cape, the Glen Grey Act of 1894 attempted to introduce a new labour tax, a form of individual (but not fully private) land tenure, as well as segregated local councils financed by further taxes. In some senses this law, often cited as a cornerstone in the development of white domination, is a red herring in South African historiography. The labour tax proved so unpopular and difficult to collect that it was dropped; individual tenure spread through only seven districts out of about thirty-five occupied by Africans in the Cape and was not very effective. The most important legacy of the Act was the system of councils in the African districts, gradually extended through the country as a whole, which were later used as a basis for political balkanization.

Taxation and land loss were not the only forces at work in transforming African societies. Trade almost always pre-dated such processes. In the nineteenth century guns had been important imports. Muzzle-loaders in African hands did not delay the forward march of colonialism for very long, but they were seen as vital by African chiefs throughout the subcontinent both to claim a breathing space against settler commandos and as defence against armed African neighbours. By the 1870s, mounted cavalry with muzzle-loaders, even breech-loaders, rather than foot soldiers with shields and assegais, were the spearhead of a number of surviving African armies. However, investment into firearms became very difficult once conquest was completed.

Most ubiquitous of the trade items were cotton and woollen goods. Blankets almost completely displaced hides or *karosses* by the end of the nineteenth century and were in some communities giving way to Western-style clothes. Blankets initially saved time taken in preparation of skins. But they also reflected the flexibility of African taste. Africans used them to create new styles of clothing appropriate to their needs and identities, which later were called traditional or 'tribal' dress. They were thus able to contain and shape if not exclude imperial commercial forces in which textiles were often at the cutting edge.

All the African societies of southern Africa had ironworkers, but the quantity and variety of goods available were limited and the cost high. British-made iron goods, such as three-legged cooking pots, nails, hoes, and ploughs, became central to the life of Transkei peasants and Transvaal tenants alike. Ploughs also demanded an innovation in the use of oxen as draught animals. In the second half of the nineteenth century, African agriculture in southern Africa went through a revolution in technology unique on the continent for its rapidity and scope as tens of thousands of ploughs poured into the country. Further north the scourge of tsetse fly, vector of the disease *nagana* (trypanosomiasis), limited the use of cattle as draught. Oxen, sometimes used as pack animals in pre-colonial times, now in teams transformed the capacity of African farmers to transport their goods. Some of the 'burdens borne on the heads of women' (Bundy 1979: 55) were transferred to sledges, wagons, and carts, though women were still responsible for the collection of water and firewood. Introduced animals, such as wool-bearing Merino sheep, which displaced the fat-tailed, hairy, indigenous variety, provided a further source of income and facilitated exploitation of marginal lands.

Missionaries and magistrates recorded these developments with enthusiasm. Of Oxkraal and Kamastone mission settlements, near Queenstown, one wrote in 1876 of

the very great advancement made by the Fingoes in a few years ...
Wherever I went I found substantial huts and brick or stone tenements.
In many cases, substantial brick houses had been erected, and ... fruit
trees had been planted: wherever a stream of water could be made available it had been led out and the soil cultivated ... wherever a plough
could be introduced. The extent of the land turned over surprised me.
(Bundy 1979: 72)

If mission stations were the first centre of peasant endeavour, they
were by no means exclusively so. In a missionary's words: 'The
heathen Natives, seeing the result of industry ... have followed
the example; so that the possession of a plough or waggon is no
longer the mark of a Christian owner. I have quite lately travelled
through two districts, under notoriously heathen headmen, and
yet the apparent cultivation in them is greater than in some
professedly Christian locations' (Bundy 1979: 90).

Moshoeshoe's Sotho people had experienced dramatic dispossession in the loss of rich arable land in the Caledon valley, which
was incorporated into the Free State as the 'Conquered Territory'.
They had been amongst the first Africans to adopt horses, initially
for military purposes, and bred a hardy mountain pony. They
introduced wheat as a winter crop alongside maize. Together
with woolled sheep and their cattle, these adaptations greatly
facilitated expansion into difficult mountain terrain towards the
Drakensberg. Other Sotho-speakers moved as tenants and sharecroppers onto the farmlands of the Free State. It was not least
Sotho peasants in Lesotho, and tenants in the Free State, who
supplied the bulk of food to the Kimberley diamond fields in the
early years—much of it carried by Boer transport riders. To the
north, Tswana chiefs and notables became involved in commercial
hunting and supplied timber to Kimberley before the railways and
coal arrived in 1884.

The far-flung routes of international trade and empire
impinged on the African peasants of South Africa, whose very
material existence now centred around maize from Latin America,
cloth from Manchester, and imported ploughs. The changes
they experienced were not essentially different from those of
Afrikaners enmeshed in the same expanding networks of trade.
By the turn of the century, Australian gum trees and wattles had

made their appearance around homesteads in Natal and Transkei for fuel and timber; the agave from Mexico was used as fencing for kraals; American prickly pear spread in dryer zones such as Pedi territory, called Sekhukhuneland after their nineteenth-century chief, where its fruit was eaten by people and the large leaves used as fodder for livestock.

An intricate network of trading stations was established through the African rural areas, so that by the early twentieth century few settlements were untouched. In the Cape alone there were probably close on 1,000, usually owned and run by licensed whites. Sales of grain, cattle, wool, or labour had become vital for the purchase of commodities or to pay taxes, rents, and school fees. Traders became the conduit for migrant workers as well. While they facilitated the growth of commerce and provided an outlet for African produce, white and Indian traders also precluded the development of African markets. One striking difference between southern Africa and much of the rest of the continent was the absence of colourful rural markets or of African traders in produce.

South Africa's settler frontier has been contrasted with West Africa, where production was dominated by peasants. Yet South Africa had its moment of peasant expansion. Because of the plough, which was rare in West Africa, the productive capacity of South African peasant and tenant farmers may briefly have rivalled that of West African cash crop producers of palm products, groundnuts, and cocoa. South African black farmers produced very largely local food and fodder crops for internal markets, rather than specialist crops for export, and their success was less visible.

The great majority of African homesteads were incorporated to some degree into the colonial world by the twentieth century, but some resisted the process. Especially in Zululand, the coastal Transkei, and the northern Transvaal, the combination of chiefly power, adequate land, and explicit traditionalism held commercial forces at bay. Those who most fully reconstituted their identities and consumption patterns tended to be most numerous where pre-colonial society was disrupted and along the major routes of Boer and British expansion. Mfengu communities, refugees in the eastern Cape from the conflicts in Zululand in the early nineteenth century, as well as Sotho-speaking tenants on the highveld and mission families of Natal were striking examples. From amongst them emerged the vanguard of the African peasantry, the owners of private land, of wagons, and of square houses.

Colonial and settler intrusion did not simply create new classes. Those Africans called by traditionalists 'dressed', 'pierced', or *kholwa* (believers in Zulu) developed their own sets of ideas about the colonial state and their rights within it. They hoped their loyalty to local magistrates and the ethos of an inclusive British Empire might protect them from the machinations of land-hungry settlers. They provided the loyal headmen to displace recalcitrant chiefs, as well as mission-educated ministers, teachers, and agricultural demonstrators, who became the models and ideologues for a new African identity. Most were Christian, but there was no one version of Christianity. A multitude of denominations, from Anglicans and Methodists to Lutherans and Catholics, had taken root, reflecting the crowded and competitive mission field in South Africa. Although Christianity was still the religion of a minority of Africans in the early twentieth century, it was sufficiently established to become the dominant, and still buoyant, faith of South African blacks as well as whites.

Missionary activity should not simply be equated with British cultural imperialism. Some of the most important and successful societies, especially in the Transvaal, were German—notably the Berlin Mission Society. Both the denominations and the cultural milieu for African Christians here differed from the eastern Cape. Yet as British authority in the region gradually extended, so English was increasingly used by the missions and African elite. When Albert Kropf of the Berlin mission produced a standard dictionary of Xhosa words (1899), it was translated into English, despite the fact that his predecessor Dohne had used German in an earlier compilation. Solomon Plaatje, later to be first secretary of the South African Native National Congress, was educated at Pniel Berlin mission near Kimberley. Teaching was often in Cape Dutch, the children spoke a variety of African languages, such as Tswana, Sotho, or Koranna, and the teachers often spoke German. The schoolbooks were in English, notably the ubiquitous Nelson's *Royal Readers*, and Plaatje emerged with English alongside Tswana as his main language.

Black Victorian and Edwardian Christian culture flourished first in the eastern Cape, partly because it was earliest colonized, and missionized. Mid-Victorian liberalism in Britain had combined with local interests to produce a non-racial qualified franchise in the Colony. Towards the end of the nineteenth century, African voting power became significant in some eastern Cape constituencies, as did coloured in Cape Town. While Afrikaners and English-speaking farmers sought measures that discriminated against Africans, a more liberally minded settler minority of urban professionals, Native Affairs officials, missionaries, and merchants involved in the African trade saw both moral justice and material advantage in trying to protect African civil rights, access to justice, land occupation, and productive capacity.

For much of the 1880s and 1890s, a key figure in the African politics of the Cape had been J. T. Jabavu, editor of the first African newspaper, *Imvo Zabantsundu* (*Voice of the People*), friend of white liberals, and organizer of the African vote. He was reluctant to form a countrywide and assertive African organization, arguing that this would further alienate whites. But African Christians were not simply the dependent clients of missionaries and liberals. Jabavu himself spearheaded a powerful challenge to dominant settler ideas. Many African Christians were rejecting the missionary version of Christianity for a new independent or 'Ethiopian' church movement in the 1890s. The term was used not because of any direct connection with Ethiopia, but in a purely symbolic way, drawn from biblical texts, and to identify with a specifically African Christian tradition in a country that had not been colonized. Methodism, perhaps the denomination with the largest African membership, produced the most dramatic splits when some of the first generation of black ministers affiliated with the American-based, largely black, African Methodist Episcopal Church.

African independent church leaders made no great innovation in the religious sphere and did not attract as many adherents as the mission churches that they had left. Schooling, a major stimulus to conversion and to the black demand for Christianity, remained essentially under mission control and this inhibited the growth of African churches. Established denominations were more financially secure. But independent churches made a powerful political statement about the capacity of Africans to manage for themselves and claim, in a slogan of the time, 'Africa for Africans'. They spread yet further the reach of Christianity and the profusion of churches.

## Mining and Labour Migration

Africans were initially drawn into the colonial world through fighting it, trading with it, worshipping common gods (though not in general in the same churches), paying its rents and taxes, and working on settler farms. By the early twentieth century the mining industry and other colonial enterprises increasingly influenced the pattern of incorporation and domination. The awesome speed with which mining expanded after the discovery of diamonds in 1867 and the golden wealth of the Witwatersrand reef in the 1880s was not an accident. Industrialists and merchants in Europe were looking for overseas investments in the late nineteenth century. The gold standard had been widely adopted in the 1870s as the basis for currencies, and international markets for gold, based in London, were more than usually hungry. It was the age of the gold rush from the Klondike to Australia. A mobile population of prospectors, profiteers, and technicians followed the glint of minerals.

The sparkle of diamonds first attracted large quantities of capital and labour. Within twenty years about £3 million's worth were being exported annually, half of the Cape Colony's exports. Kimberley's 30,000 people made it the second city in southern Africa to Cape Town. When the labour force hit its early peaks, some 18,000 black workers were employed on the mines at any one time. Because the great majority of them were migrant workers from the Pedi chiefdom in the Transvaal, or from Lesotho or southern Mozambique, many more passed through the town annually.

The excitement of 'rushes', the charisma and hubris of Cecil

Rhodes, and the extraordinary big hole covered with an intricate lace of ropes and pulleys, all made Kimberley synonymous with money and wealth. In order to mine the deep pipes in which diamonds were found, capital, technology, and control of water were all-important. Mining of this kind lent itself to amalgamation. By 1888 Rhodes had created an effective monopoly through the De Beers company, which displaced smaller companies as well as white and black diggers. A monopoly was also useful, because diamonds sold on their rarity, and if the market was flooded prices could collapse. Concentration eased the enforcement of a racial division of labour, which set the precedent for gold mining and other industries. When Rhodes claimed that Kimberley was the 'richest community in the world for its size', he certainly did not include its black migrant workers (Turrell 1987: 57).

On the Witwatersrand the gold-bearing rock was discovered in outcrops on the surface, but within a few years it became clear that the deposits followed reefs deep underground sloping to the south. Successful exploitation needed well-capitalized companies prepared to make large investments. Small operators were again elbowed aside and control concentrated in six large mining houses, which attracted between them external investments of perhaps £200 million over the first twenty-five years. The mines required extensive underground works because of the depth and shape of the reef and complex surface works. Large quantities of rock had to be dynamited, taken to the surface, crushed, and then treated by chemical process. In 1899 the Rand produced 27 per cent of the world's gold with over 100,000 workers; by 1913 40 per cent, worth £30 million, with over 200,000 workers. In 1911 Johannesburg's population had reached 240,000 and the Witwatersrand as a whole twice that. Between 1904 and 1911, by contrast, Cape Town's population actually declined a little from a peak of over 200,000 (**Figure 1**).

Such growth should be kept in perspective. American, Canadian, and Australian towns were expanding as rapidly and there were more of them. The 200,000 black workers recruited annually for gold-mining work throughout the whole region of southern Africa were still only twice that captured and shipped annually at the height of the Atlantic slave trade a full century before. But mining was a huge addition to the South African economy, and mining interests asserted themselves forcefully in the political sphere. Rhodes, who controlled the diamond fields, had a major share in one of the gold conglomerates, and organized the colonization of Rhodesia, was the most influential politician of his age. As Cape Prime Minister between 1890 and 1896 he personified these forces.

Despite his blatantly imperial aims, Rhodes sought to realize his goals with the help of Cape farmers in the Afrikaner Bond (**Chapter 2**). Both mining companies and white farmers were more interested in increasing labour supplies than in African peasant production. Elijah Makiwane, a leader of the Cape African Christian community, noted that the influence of these 'money gentlemen', who were for 'repressing the native', was 'beginning to assert itself and sour the native mind all over South Africa' (Beinart and Bundy 1987: 115). Legislation in 1887 and 1892 restricted the potential for growth in the Cape African franchise and disallowed land held in communal tenure from assessment for the property qualification that had to be met. Although the Glen Grey Act of 1894 was not fully implemented, its portents were clear in that it promised to mobilize more labour and sharpen political segregation; both jobs and urban residential areas were becoming more tightly demarcated. This alliance of diamonds, wine, and wool, though shattered by the Jameson Raid and the South African War (**Chapter 3**), was precursor to the 'uneasy alliance between gold and maize' that characterized the pattern of dominance in the first half of the twentieth century.

Mining was central to South Africa's expansion, and black men became the core of its labour force at the heart of the economy thousands of feet underground. Their subterranean and compound existence was far removed from the leafy suburbs of South Africa's towns or the British home counties, where much of the financial wealth from the mines was deposited. Perhaps, in a warped way, the stock exchange in the City of London recognized this contribution by calling South African gold-mining shares 'Kafirs'. In the early twentieth century, they were not, as in the period of conquest, 'restless', but, in stock market parlance, 'firm and active'.

Migrant labour, oscillating between town and countryside, was not unique to South Africa. It was a feature of many industrializing societies, signifying a transition from rural to urban life and agrarian to industrial work, especially where industrialization was in an enclave and not preceded by an agrarian capitalist revolution that destroyed the peasantry. Even in the peasant economy of Ghana, people from the north migrated south to work for African cocoa-growers. What was particular about southern Africa were the scale and longevity of migrancy. For over a century it was the dominant form of labour supply to the mines. It was extended to other industries and enterprises and became central to government policy. The practice of housing migrant workers in huge, single-sex compounds near the place of work, with all the associated controls, tensions, and personal frustrations, was perhaps unique in its extent. In 1911 over 90 per cent of the black population of Johannesburg was male. It remained preponderantly so until the 1940s—with important consequences for African urban culture.

Male-only compounds for workers were initially entrenched in Kimberley, where mine-owners argued that they were the only way to control diamond theft and illicit diamond buying. This most romantic of South African crimes, much favoured by novelists, was regarded as amongst the most heinous by budding South African capitalists, in the same way that real or imagined stock theft traumatized settler farmers. Unlike gold, diamonds could be picked up; perhaps, as stories have it, some stones did get back to Pedi villages. But compounds were also a good way of reducing costs in housing and feeding workers, preventing absenteeism, and increasing oversight. Compounds were introduced during the first major recession on the diamond fields in 1884–5, and they were transferred to Johannesburg, even though gold theft was not possible. 'If the "dark satanic mill" was the abiding image of new social relationships in Britain, it was the repressive role played by the mine compound that came to symbolise the early development of capitalism in South Africa' (Turrell 1987: 45).

One powerful explanation of the prevalence of migrant labour as a core institution of twentieth-century South Africa has concentrated on the demands of mining capital. The argument, developed by Harold Wolpe and others, has rested on the point that mining required large quantities of cheap black labour and that migrant labour was particularly cheap. Employers did not have to pay wages that could meet the subsistence needs of the family as a whole, because workers' families stayed in the rural areas and produced their own food. The costs of social security, or the reproduction of labour, would also be met by rural societies. Compounds enabled mine-owners to put further downward pressure on wages, as they provided cheap food and accommodation. In short, migrant labour gave capitalists a workforce without the full costs of supporting workers and their families in town.

The nature of gold as a commodity, and of the Transvaal gold mines in particular, has been invoked to strengthen this explanation. Gold prices were kept stable for many years from the 1870s to the 1920s as an underpinning for the international financial system. Yet Transvaal gold was expensive to extract and many mines had a relatively low grade of ore. Mine-owners were faced with tight margins, particularly because they had little control over the costs of machinery, supplies, and largely white skilled labour; it was easier to keep down wages of politically powerless unskilled black workers. A further element in the argument is that gold was not sold locally but exported onto markets that had an almost inexhaustible appetite for the commodity. Mine-owners were unencumbered by the problem of domestic demand for their product. As long as they could get a sufficient labour supply, it was not in their interests to increase the purchasing power of their workers. In fact some associated with the industry thought that if they paid workers more, they would make fewer trips to the mines, because Africans had relatively simple, fixed needs.

In the long run, there is no doubt that the mining industry preferred migrant to settled workers and fought hard to maintain this system. However, explanations for the origins of migrancy have shifted. The mines were not the originators of long-distance migrant labour. Migrant 'Mantatees', descended from Mantatisi's Tlokoa people who had fled their highveld homes during the turmoil of the mid-nineteenth century, built walls, fences, dams, and kraals on the nineteenth-century Cape sheep farms. Sheep-shearing was also often done by migrant Mfengu and Thembu men. Pedi workers from the eastern Transvaal walked 1,000 kilometres to Port Elizabeth some decades before they went to Kimberley and the Rand. Mozambicans were established on the Natal sugar fields before they became the predominant group of workers on the mines. Moreover, migrancy was not initially cheap for all employers, because of the costs of recruitment and constraints on the acquisition of skills; in the late nineteenth century, mine wages were relatively high. Employers were primarily concerned to get labour in whatever form it came. The origins of mass migrancy need to be sought as much in the dynamics of African societies as in the demands of the gold mines.

Although African participation in the labour market could from its very earliest phases be linked to dispossession, this was not always the case. When long-distance migrancy began, there were not yet bright lights in the city, nor were the streets of Johannesburg paved with gold, but there were particular commodities that African societies required. Pedi chiefs organized groups of young men to earn money for guns to defend their political independence. Chiefs lost control over labour supply before the end of the nineteenth century. The wages that men received gave them economic power, just as exchange with colonial traders loosened the economic bonds that held chief and subject together. But many migrants remained locked into rural society and determined to return there. Families tended to send out younger sons who were not essential for the maintenance of agricultural production. Fathers tried to control the wages of their sons, or to ensure that cash was invested into what they saw as solid rural assets such as cows, ploughs, and wives. Even where married men continued to migrate to work, as became common in the early decades of the twentieth century, many saw wage labour as a means of establishing themselves more securely in the countryside. The persistence of forms of communal tenure in the reserves made this possible.

Southern Mozambique was the most important source of migrants on the Rand for many decades; 'foreign' workers provided over half the labour force in the first twenty-five years of gold production to 1910 (**Figure 2**). The Transvaal economy faced as much towards Mozambique's Delagoa Bay as to the Cape, and it was President Kruger's intention to use the rail connection there in order to establish independence from British ports. In southern Mozambique, increasing rates of migrancy were accompanied by rising rates of bridewealth (Harries 1982). Young men going out to work were having to stay longer if they were to acquire rural assets. Similar patterns of bridewealth inflation, either engineered by elders in the society, who thus gained more control over wages, or merely as a result of demand, because men could marry younger, occurred in Lesotho.

Elsewhere, as in Pondoland, families arranged advance payment of wages from local traders and recruiters before migrant workers left home. Cattle were given in exchange for a pledge of labour in much the same way as chiefs had cemented relationships with their followers before. This had the effect of drawing migrants home, as they did not have the cash to establish themselves independently in town. Their immediate needs would be met in the compound, while their families might meanwhile benefit from the use and increase of the animal. Rural traders, who often doubled as moneylenders and labour recruiters, also favoured systems of advance payment as a means of increasing their turnover in competition with urban shops. Rural African families, and traders in the African reserves, both had an interest in maintaining a migrant system of employment.

African societies influenced the way in which labour was released to industries in other ways. Male predominance in the mine labour force must largely be explained by the demands of employers. Although women and children had worked in the mines of Victorian Britain, by the turn of the century the British elite had clearer ideas about fit work for women. Yet the mines had little choice but to employ African men. They were not the only employers; there was great demand for domestic servants— probably the second largest sector of employment in early twentieth-century towns. While women were often employed in the Cape, the great majority of domestic servants in more recently colonized parts of South Africa, such as Natal and the Rand, were black men or youths. Whether or not employers thought them appropriate, it was they who offered themselves.

The predominance of men in the labour market of South

Africa in the early twentieth century can partly be explained by the division of labour within African rural society, where women did the bulk of the fieldwork. After boys had completed a phase of herding, they tended to have fewer responsibilities, especially as the calls of military service declined. Some African women, especially from Christian and tenant families, did themselves go to town, but this was a muted social development until the 1920s. Bozzoli (1983) has argued further that the strength of rural African patriarchy helped to ensure that women stayed at home and worked the land. Patriarchy may not have been the only influence. Evidence from rural women's political movements (**Chapter 4**) suggests that many were committed to the rural areas. Whatever the case, the division of labour in African families meant that it was least disruptive to send out youths.

By the early twentieth century, African peasant families were coming under increasing economic pressure in many districts—squeezed for land on which to expand agriculture, beset by taxes, disadvantaged in markets for agricultural produce and in access to credit. Two devastating cattle diseases, rinderpest in 1896–7 and East Coast fever, which moved slowly through the country from 1904 to 1913, each killed as much as 80 per cent of the herds in some districts. The diseases were not an intended cause of colonization, though some Africans believed them to be; rather they were part of a broader spread of new plagues consequent on more rapid mobility and international exchanges of people, plants, and animals. Cattle numbers recovered but at the cost of increasing rates of labour migrancy to pay for restocking. By the 1920s African small-scale farmers in the reserves and on the white-owned farms still produced nearly a quarter of the maize and held nearly half the cattle in the country. The Transkei—the largest single reserve area—probably imported only 10 per cent of its food by 1930. But few peasants were able to produce much surplus. Perhaps 30–40 per cent of the economically active men in rural reserve areas were away at labour centres at any one time. The character of migrancy also changed in that married men were having to migrate over a long period in order to help meet the subsistence needs of their families. An increasing number were interested in moving to towns permanently and the state's role in controlling urbanization through wide-ranging pass systems became far more explicit.

Even then the drive to maintain a rural homestead was often important for Africans. One of the greatest ironies of early twentieth-century southern Africa was that both the country's major industry and many rural communities favoured a system of labour mobilization in which male migrants worked for a limited period and then returned with their wages to their homes. What became a highly exploitative pattern of employment appeared initially to many Africans to be less disadvantageous than a move to town. Both parties also came to share an interest in maintaining reserved areas with inalienable or communal land tenure where Africans would be free from the threat of further dispossession. For the mining industry, this was perceived to guarantee migrant labour in the longer term, as further land alienation would drive more rural families to town. For rural Africans and their chiefs, this underwrote a last haven in which they could protect some of their old culture and identity. In some senses, there was agreement on this aspect of what became segregation policy. But by fighting to maintain reserves, rural Africans did not generally accept the terms of segregation as laid down in the 1913 Natives Land Act, nor their exclusion from other rights in society.

# 2

# Economic and Social Change on the Settler Farmlands

*Agrarian Worlds in the Cape*

In the early twentieth century commentators on the history of the white-owned parts of the South African countryside—roughly three-quarters of the country's surface area—emphasized their backwardness. Colonial land policies and settler predispositions, so historians argued, combined to produce an extensive rather than intensive form of agriculture: pastoralism remained widespread, investment low, and improvement rare. The prevalence of systems of African tenancy in which large numbers of African families actually lived on white-owned farms seemed to retard modernization and efficient use of labour. White impoverishment in the early twentieth century was seen as a result of isolation and outdated ideas, a barrier to economic growth, and a strong spur to racial protection and segregation. Their comparative foil was the settler Dominions such as Australia, as well as the USA and Britain itself, where agriculture seemed to be modernizing more rapidly.

There is some substance in this view. South African farmers were not generally highly efficient and technical innovation lagged behind. But what is striking in retrospect is just how rapidly agricultural production grew in the late nineteenth and early twentieth centuries. Settlers had to confront severe ecological problems, and they did not have the freedom that the near genocide of the indigenous population had given those in North America and Australia. With the support of the state, they nevertheless wrought changes unique in their scale on the African continent. Moreover, in parts of South Africa, production grew initially because of, rather than in spite of, African sharecroppers and tenants.

In the 1970s and 1980s revisionist and Marxist historiography, deeply influenced by a comparative model of the transition from feudalism to capitalism in Europe, reinterpreted this period and highlighted the transformation of agriculture especially in the more densely populated, higher rainfall arable zones of the high-veld and Natal. The growth of internal markets, especially around mining and urban centres, was seen as one critical motor of change; another was the intervention of the state after the South African War (1899–1902). Rich and detailed studies on rural social history have explored especially the consequences of an emerging capitalist agriculture: on the one hand, poor whiteism; and, on the other, the rise and subsequent destruction of the relatively independent African tenantry, who were so important in the first phases of market-oriented production. Tenants found it was their labour, rather than produce or rent, that landowners increasingly demanded; this was a slow process, not completed till the 1980s, but momentous in the numbers affected and the social costs involved.

This writing remains a major advance in the understanding of twentieth-century South African history, and a rich source for comparative analysis. But it also has its limitations. It is intriguing that in a country with so small a percentage of arable land, compared to Europe or even the USA, historians have neglected settler pastoral history or have understood it primarily in terms of the frontier and trekboer experience. Especially in the Cape, pastoral farmers, specializing in sheep and ostriches, intensified their operations quickly in the late nineteenth and early twentieth centuries, largely in response to external world markets rather than internal urban growth. If the Cape is drawn fully into the new agrarian history, the periodization of change requires modification. Overall, regional differences in environment and production regimes have been underemphasized.

This chapter attempts to capture the variety of experience for both whites and blacks on the farmlands. It is worth emphasizing, at the outset, that although claims to distinct and unique nationhood have been a powerful strain in twentieth-century white South African politics, the whites who found themselves on the land came from very diverse backgrounds. The settler population was deposited in layers, as successive waves of development in the world economy left their traces on the shores of the subcontinent. The Dutch Empire brought officials, burghers, and slaves to its Cape station; South Africa picked up Huguenots fleeing from France; the nineteenth-century post-slavery British plantation system supplied both planters and indentured workers. In the nineteenth century, when European imperial power made free international movement possible, Britons, Irish, Germans, Jews, and others poured out of their homes. People from all these groups found their way onto the land in South Africa.

There were a number of discrete settler agrarian worlds at the turn of the century, each radiating out from a colonial port, each shaped by its ecology and climate, its pre-colonial heritage, distance from markets, and its particular mix of products. The longest established, in the western and southern Cape, was distinct from the rest of South Africa in its winter rainfall, 'Mediterranean' climate, indigenous *fynbos* vegetation, and historical roots in the Dutch seaborne empire. Its climate favoured the importation of European plants: oaks were a symbol of Dutch settlement; and Cape Town's hinterland became the centre of wine, wheat, and fruit growing, supplying what was the largest city in southern Africa until the first decade of the twentieth century. Despite the opening of the Suez Canal in the 1860s, it remained an important supply station for ships travelling east from Europe.

The western Cape was also distinct because the displacement of Khoisan peoples necessitated slave imports—many from Indonesia—as a source of labour. By the turn of the twentieth century, the working class, largely of Khoisan and slave origins, was called 'coloured' rather than 'native'. The predominant language of the farms and streets, the Cape vernacular, was a form of Dutch and a progenitor of Afrikaans. Islam, carried by those sections of the slave community that came from Asia, survived in the face of a dominant Christianity. Though there were pockets of peasant settlement, mainly around old-established mission stations, the western and midland Cape had no reserves for black people. Coloured farmworkers shared the same agrarian and social world with Afrikaners, although they were generally segregated by race and power. Most were agricultural labourers, rather than tenants.

The agrarian zone around Cape Town was losing its leading role by the mid-nineteenth century to the eastern, sheep-rearing, parts of the colony. But it by no means stagnated. Its Dutch gentry was sufficiently well rooted to withstand the transfer of the colony to the British, the emancipation of slaves in the 1830s, and the advent of representative government in 1854. Only a minority of Afrikaners joined the Great Trek to the highveld (1836–8) and most of them were from the eastern and northern frontier districts. Ensconced in their whitewashed, Cape Dutch homesteads, the best of them beautifully gabled, some western Cape families were able to hold onto their land and labour supply through successive economic fluctuations. They did so with the help of elaborate legal controls and the 'tot' system—partial payment of wages to their workers in cheap wine, which instilled alcoholism and indebtedness. After the Cape received responsible government in 1872, its revenues swollen by wool and diamond exports, the region's Dutch-speaking farming lobby formed the Afrikaner Bond under J. H. Hofmeyr. Though Hofmeyr refused to offer himself as Prime Minister, he became the most influential broker in the Cape parliamentary system.

In the late nineteenth century, the growth of railways, ports, and mines all sucked labour from the western Cape farms. Recession in the 1880s was compounded by phylloxera, which swept aside not only vines but many poorer farmers. Some of those who displaced them had money from land speculation, commerce, the law, and mining. They included John X. Merriman, the eloquent Cabinet minister and Cape liberal, as well as Rhodes himself, who bought twenty-nine farms worth £250,000 in 1897, a year after he had ceased to be Prime Minister. Both believed strongly that a modern, progressive, and scientific agricultural sector was essential for the colony's development. Wheat and dairy products were in strong demand for growing urban communities. Cape brandy held its own as a basic South Africa rotgut to be found in colonial clubs and drink cabinets, in the hovels of workers on western Cape farms, and in the huts of African chiefs. Though wine production did not expand between 1891 and 1910, Cape fruit, benefiting from the inverse southern-hemisphere seasons and the new availability of refrigerated transport, was exported to Covent Garden in London from 1893.

The western Cape remained not only an important agricultural region but a political and intellectual centre. Some of the earliest protagonists of Afrikaner nationalism came from these old agrarian heartlands, which had lived longest in the imperial shadow. It was around Paarl and Stellenbosch that intellectuals defined the Afrikaans language as separate from Dutch and the first *Geskiedenis van Ons Land in die Taal van Ons Volk* (History of the Country in the Language of our People) was written in 1877. S. J. du Toit, its author, helped to found the Afrikaner Bond at this time, but was ousted by the moderate Hofmeyr and went north to become Kruger's Secretary of Education in the Transvaal. Hofmeyr was more pragmatically concerned about empowering farmers in the colonial economy and content to achieve this in alliance with the arch-imperialist Rhodes until the Jameson Raid (1895). Subsequently he worked with anglophone politicians and Cape liberals opposed to British jingoism.

Pragmatic Afrikaners were by no means immune to nationalist ideology, nor unmindful of its potential economic advantages. Led by men such as Hofmeyr and Jan Marais, who had profited from diamonds as well as agriculture, they founded their own financial institutions, providing credit to farmers when British banks proved tight with loans. They also invested in educational and political ventures, launching *De Burger* newspaper in 1915 as the leading voice of Afrikaner nationalism in the Cape. Soon afterwards the inappropriately named Victoria College became the 'Dutch-Afrikaans' Stellenbosch University, a centre of Afrikaner education, following a bequest of £100,000 in Marais's will (Giliomee 1987). In 1918 Afrikaner insurance and trust companies were founded and wine-growers formed themselves into one of the earliest and most important agricultural cooperatives, the KWV.

Eastern and midland Cape agricultural expansion followed the in-migration of both British settlers after 1820 and Mfengu in the 1830s. Wool-bearing merinos shouldered aside the Khoikhoi fat-tailed varieties adopted by the early trekboer colonists. The large white-owned farms of the interior, in the semi-arid Karoo mid-lands with rainfall between 250 and 500 mm., supported an essentially pastoral economy, exporting wool, later supplemented by ostrich feathers and mohair from angora goats. Key innovators were often British settlers, but Afrikaners, still the predominant landowners, were drawn into the commercial pastoral economy. The least promising agricultural land became the new engine of colonial growth. In the early decades of the twentieth century, probably over a third of South Africa's land area was dominated by sheep.

Port Elizabeth, the major wool port, and East London—100 miles further up the coast, which also serviced the African districts—together overtook Cape Town as entrepôts. Graaff-Reinet, the only pre-British village in the east, became a busy commercial town with the largest concentration of Cape Dutch buildings outside the western districts. Imperially named Grahamstown, Kingwilliamstown, and Queenstown grew alongside it as centres of administration, transport, and trade away from the coast. Wool greatly intensified land-use. In 1865 a third of the Cape settler population of about 180,000, considerably more than the whole of the Transvaal, lived in the main Cape sheep farming districts. The settler population faced less towards the sea.

The history of sheep is often left in the 1870s, when the value of wool exported peaked at over £3 million. Subsequently the rise of diamonds and gold are seen to have overshadowed agriculture in general and wool in particular. It is true that wool producers, beset by falling world prices and livestock diseases, experienced considerable difficulties in the final decades of the nineteenth century. But the spectacular rise in demand for ostrich feathers provided an alternative in the semi-arid districts until the First World War killed off flamboyant fashions and hats in Europe. Markets for mutton and skins were not negligible: in the 1910s around 1.5 million carcasses were processed annually at the Johannesburg and Cape Town abattoirs alone. If the pastoral economy is considered as a whole, including the value of animals for meat, dairy, and transport, it exceeded diamond production, and the income was more widely distributed.

Pastoral production did not achieve its full economic potential

for the Cape. By the late nineteenth century wool washing, formerly a thriving coastal industry that doubled the value of the
materials exported, had declined precipitately. Wool was a truly
colonial product; the great bulk of it went to Britain. Although
South Africa was one of the largest fine-wool producers in the
world, the country was not able to translate this advantage into
manufacturing; the first blanket factory was established only in
the 1920s.

Nevertheless, commercial livestock farming transformed the
frontier economy that depended initially on the plunder of rich
resources of wild animals and the establishment of a mobile pastoralism. The trekking routes and outspans—a term derived from
unyoking a team of oxen—became major channels of communication into the interior. Farmworkers in the pastoral districts were
drawn from the old Khoikhoi population, effectively a rural proletariat, or from African families displaced by colonization. Most
were wage-workers living on the farms, though peak demands for
labour—for example, during shearing season—were met by
migrants from coloured mission villages or African districts.
Sheep did not 'eat' people, as in the Scottish Highlands. This zone
had been sparsely inhabited beforehand and its overall population
continued to grow well into the twentieth century. The land of the
Khoikhoi became thirty or forty administrative districts, each
with its small town, its church, magistrate, jail, police post, shops,
and services.

The Dutch Reformed Church had been involved in the laying-
out of new villages so that it could reach its increasingly scattered
membership which came together for *Nagmaal*—the quarterly
religious and social trek of far-flung Afrikaner farmers to a
common meeting point. As in African districts, Christianity and
commerce were intertwined. Migrant traders or *smouse* who
moved from farm to farm were displaced by small-town wholesale
and retail outlets linked to merchant firms such as Mosenthals in
Port Elizabeth. Wool gave farmers cash, and patterns of consumption changed as the need for self-sufficiency diminished.
Country banks proliferated. Sixty newspapers were published
outside Cape Town by the turn of the century, mainly in English
but also in Afrikaans—from the *Graaff-Reinet Herald* to the

*Colesberg Advertiser and Boerenvriend.* Newspapers helped to create a local civic identity and break the isolation of dispersed farmers, instilling, on the one hand, English-speaking ideas of progress and, on the other, the ethnic nationalism that enthused Afrikaners. The down-at-heel migrant tutor, or *meester*, immortalized in Olive Schreiner's *The Story of an African Farm* gave way to schools regularly inspected and staffed by trained teachers. In 1905 the Cape parliament legislated for compulsory primary education for whites.

By no means all whites were able to accumulate on the land. Many farmers succumbed to drought or debt; white poverty was evident in the rural Cape well before poor whiteism was defined as a major cause for concern in the 1890s. An anonymous Afrikaans poem, 'Die Arme Boer' (The Poor Boer), published in 1885, captured their helplessness.

> Our sheep have *brandsiek* [scab]
> Our wheat has the rust,
> the cattle have redwater
> and the horses die of *droes* [glanders].
> The money is scarce
> and the coffee so dear,
> the foreign banks are our *baas*
> and the interest eats like fire . . .
>
> The locust and the drought
> are heavy on our land,
> what's going to become of us
> I cannot comprehend.
> (*Groot Verseboek*, 25)

Commercial stock farming left its imprint on the rural environment in other ways. Unlikely stylish Victorian buildings dotted the semi-arid districts. Their open verandahs, sash windows, and gardens proclaimed a post-conquest settler security and ease. Water rather than markets was a great constraint in expanding animal numbers. Dams were one solution, both to slake the thirst of livestock and to feed patches of green lucerne for ostriches. Oudtshoorn became the primary centre for feather production, not least because of its combination of dry atmosphere and abundant water supply. In the twentieth century, boreholes, their pumps powered by wind, became a vital and popular addition. Clanking metal windmills, originally imported from the USA, became a feature of the South African landscape. Prickly pear, adopted as supplementary fodder in dry districts, became a weed, subject to desperate eradication programmes. Poor people, both white and black, were reluctant to stop its spread. With their skills at home brewing, they turned its fruit into a particularly intoxicating liquor. These apparently isolated districts of South Africa were, like the African reserves, a crossroads for new animals, techniques, and plants.

The spread of a more intensive pastoral economy had important ecological effects. It spelt the end of wild life. Elephants had been hunted out of most of the country by the 1860s for their ivory; so too the major predators, such as lion and leopard, because they threatened both people and livestock. Antelope were shot for their meat and skins and also because they competed for pastures. The last great migration of more than half a million springbok 'as beautiful as it was wondrous' crossed the sparsely populated lands of the northern Cape in 1896. 'The Boers mounted a huge hunting operation to prevent them damaging the veld and hundreds of thousands were shot . . . the skin selling for 5d or 6d and the meat converting into large quantities of biltong [dried meat]' (Mackenzie 1988: 116). The springbok became so powerful a symbol for whites only when it had been displaced and came under threat. The South African rugby team adopted the name early in the twentieth century when rugby was replacing hunting as a major sport.

Wool production drew civil authority into the countryside to police private property and settler accumulation. Farmers always perceived stock theft to be rife, just as they thought labour was always short. The state was also called in to deal with stock disease, especially scab—a major constraint on wool production. Veterinary officials enforced sheep-dipping, and controls on the movement of animals, initially against considerable opposition from both white and black stockowners. Some Afrikaner farmers disputed scientific interpretations of the disease; those in the drier districts were particularly reluctant to accept restrictions on their mobility in search of pastures and water. Transhumance was in their eyes both a necessity and a way of life. Social improvers and self-consciously progressive English-speaking farmers, by contrast, influential in Jameson's Progressive Party government (1904–8), advocated a system of agriculture that prioritized investment in the land and a settled lifestyle where children could go to school. Cattle-dipping was imposed after 1904 when the tick-borne East Coast fever devastated herds. The colonial state took shape in the rural areas not least through the regulation of animals, their diseases, and the environment.

Cattle and sheep were grazed largely on the open veld well into the twentieth century. As in African societies, animals on white-owned farms were usually kraaled each night to safeguard them from predators, straying, and theft. Vets condemned kraaling for spreading disease because large numbers of animals were huddled together nightly. Progressive farmers and officials argued that millions of livestock, which had to be driven long distances to and from pastures every day, 'tramped out more than they ate', thus causing soil erosion. Dongas (eroded gulleys) scarred the South African countryside, raising fears of a 'newly created South African desert' (Union of South Africa 1923). They wanted farmers to adopt improved grazing techniques by fencing paddocks or camps where animals could be left overnight.

Legislation facilitated fencing so that barbed wire—used both on the American prairies and in late-nineteenth-century warfare—snaked across the countryside. Fences were not only a means of improving pastures. They were a physical mark of private property, defining boundaries between farms and also between black and white. As they restricted the movement of people and animals, they were widely disliked by rural Africans. Fence-cutting, like stock theft, could be an expression of resistance. The state also acted against predators. Jackals, thought of as the epitome of stealth and wiliness, were estimated to take nearly the same number of sheep as were delivered to Johannesburg's and Cape Town's abattoirs. A high bounty on 'vermin' from 1918 brought in over 300,000 jackal and wildcat pelts in the Cape alone during the next six years.

It was the cumulative impact of these interventions that salvaged struggling wool producers, underwrote technical improvements in agriculture, and enabled livestock farmers to increase their flocks dramatically. Mining was by no means the only sector of growth and modernization. In the Cape alone, the number of woolled sheep increased from less than 10 million in 1904 to over 23 million in 1930. Small stock peaked nationally around that year at about 45 million woolled sheep, and over 10 million others (mainly goats). The value of wool exports rose from £4 million in 1904 to a peak of £20 million in 1919, then fluctuated around £15 million annually. While this expansion was achieved not least through environmental controls, it put great pressure on natural pastures. When drought and depression hit in the early 1930s, nearly a third of the country's small stock was lost. Wool production recovered but never regained its former economic importance. The depression also pushed more poor whites into the cities and highlighted their plight. They became subject of one of the most intensive sociological studies yet undertaken in the country, the Carnegie Commission, and increasingly significant in the white politics of the country.

## *Natal and the Highveld*

On the subtropical eastern coast, the British settlement at Port Natal (later Durban), founded in the 1820s, depended initially on trade with Africans and settlers in the interior. Subsequently sugar, successfully established in the 1860s, fuelled Natal's growth. In the years up to 1911 British planters, unable to secure or coerce sufficient labour from local Zulu people, turned to imperial labour-supply networks. A total of 150,000 Indian indentured workers came to Natal. They were followed by Muslim 'passengers'—traders and merchants who could pay their own fares. A significant Indian population became established.

By the turn of the twentieth century Natal sugar production, with about 30,000 acres under cane, was relatively modest in international terms. But acreage expanded dramatically to 90,000 in 1920 and doubled again by 1940. Output rose even more rapidly from under 30,000 tons in 1900 to about 150,000 tons in 1920 and nearly 600,000 tons in the peak year of 1940. As in nineteenth-century Europe, sugar found favour with the growing urban and working-class populations, white and black, and the internal market underpinned expansion. Some was also exported. Natal's agricultural economy diversified rapidly, including dairying, bananas on the coast, and stock-farming inland. Wattle plantations provided timber, and their bark was used for tanning leather, one of South Africa's early coastal industries. Quick-growing wattles and eucalypts (gum trees) spread through the country for a multitude of uses on farms, mines, and railways and became a mark of habitation.

Sugar, unlike wool, was a crop that required relatively little land but a great deal of capital and labour both for agriculture and processing. By the late nineteenth century, sugar mills were concentrated in the hands of a small number of concerns—some of which also ran the biggest estates—such as Tongaat and Natal Estates on the north coast, Reynolds and Crookes to the south of Durban, and Huletts in Zululand. A tight hierarchy of property, wealth, and skills evolved, which reflected the social divisions of British colonies in general and South Africa in particular. Sugar brought diverse people together in a single productive enterprise and ruthlessly divided them by colour and class.

The sugar barons were English-speaking, influenced both by the Indian Empire and 'home'. The richest of them carved out the role of a gentry around landownership, clubs, polo, horses, and elite private schools. Generally supporters of Smuts's South African Party, they tilted to pro-imperialism when their interests were threatened and acquired the reputation of being amongst the most conservative English-speakers in the country. Supervisory control was usually exercised by whites. On the big estates, some technicians were Mauritians, while skilled mill-workers were often Indian. Once the importation of indentured Indians ceased in 1911, Zulu-speakers took over much unskilled work in the mills. Many of the poorly paid cane-cutters were long-distance migrants from the Transkei or Mozambique. All tended to be housed separately: like the mines, the estates were a microcosm of the evolving pattern of segregation in the country.

The sugar fields were notorious through the early decades of the twentieth century for their conditions of employment. Youth and child labour was common on all the farms of South Africa; on the estates children were expected to perform at an almost industrial intensity and live in barracks without the minimum regulation of conditions that were enforced on the mines. Rates of desertion were high. The political power of the estate-owners helped to fend off state intervention in their activities.

Outside the Cape and Natal coast, in many other white-owned areas of the country, farmers depended more directly on the growth of internal markets for food and on mobilizing a labour supply from African rather than imported workers. Treks by the Dutch-speaking Griqua (remnants of Khoisan and slave communities) and by Boer communities and their servants had penetrated the interior in the first half of the nineteenth century. Although they were called Boers, the Dutch word for farmer, it would be a mistake to think of all the Afrikaner trekkers and their descendants essentially as farmers. As in earlier phases of frontier expansion, they were supported not least by hunting, dispersed pastoralism, and booty from war. During the first thirty years after the Great Trek, till the 1860s, ivory was the major export from the Transvaal. When settlers did secure control of large areas of land, many depended on their African tenants. And by the early twentieth century, poorer Afrikaners worked as transport riders or left the land completely.

The frontier experience in the Cape and then on the highveld was identified by an early generation of historians as an explanation for the Afrikaner mentality, forged in isolation and conflict, and for racial prejudice and segregation in the twentieth century. The argument has been countered by historians, who point to the fact that, even in the interior, trekkers had connections with the outside world, depended on imported commodities, and drew merchants with them. Moreover, they developed trading, sexual, and military relationships with Africans. The origins of more rigid racial divisions, Legassick (1980) suggested, should be sought in the slave-owning Cape and in zones where agrarian capitalism and industry displaced the relatively loose relationships of the frontier with racially based hierarchies of ownership and labour.

Though these points are important, there is room for a restated argument about the significance of the frontier. It is true that the early Transvaal state, like some African states in the interior, was relatively weak and unable easily to control or tax its subjects. To some degree it replicated the precedents set in Mozambique, which might have become an alternative node of European expansion into the interior of southern Africa. The Portuguese struggled to establish their presence in the interior, and authority was exercised by partially Africanized *prazos*—land concessions that became small chiefdoms trading in slaves and ivory. Some trekker groups, hostile to the British abolition of slavery, reconstituted servile forms of labour, including the capture and exchange of *inboekseling* (indentured) African children; the British authorities regarded this practice as akin to slavery. Boer polities traded and treated with African chiefdoms. In these respects the Boer experience bears out arguments about the fluidity of the frontier. But in others even early Transvaal trekker groups differed from the *prazos* in that they retained their racial and cultural identity. Boer churches and governments in the interior were racially exclusive from the start. The frontier did contribute to the formation of racial ideologies, even though these were not precisely the same as those elaborated in industry during the segregationist era.

Boer relationships with African people in the interior involved both interdependence and exploitation. In a hostile world, they accumulated partly by force. Hunting, fighting, and coercing a labour supply lent themselves to a hard and sometimes violent masculinity, as well as a strong patriarchalism, which were later available as cultural reference points. Compared to those who benefited from agricultural expansion and schooling in the more settled areas of the Cape, some Transvaal frontier families did live a rough life. And, while isolation is a relative term, it is difficult to dismiss the conviction with which investigators into the poor-white problem in the twentieth century dwelt on this social legacy in trying to understand the difficulties that dispossessed rural Afrikaners experienced in an urban and industrial world.

The settler impact was most powerful on the highveld of the Free State and southern Transvaal. Inland Natal, the eastern Cape, and much of the Transvaal remained divided zones, where settler land was interspersed with large pockets of African settlement in a complex patchwork. In all these newly colonized areas occupation and control of the land remained an issue of contestation and political struggle in the early decades of the twentieth century. In the Transvaal it seemed briefly possible that Africans might retake some land during the South African War, when the devastation of Boer farms by British scorched-earth tactics gave tenants an opportunity to reassert their claims. But Boer and Briton united in repossessing the farms—an understanding that was as important for the future of white domination as the section of the peace treaty of Vereeniging (1902) in which the British victors left the question of the African vote to be decided by the local white parliaments.

The highveld proved suitable for rain-fed, dryland grain production, especially of maize. Maize stored well, gave a high yield per acre, and did not require guarding against birds, as did the older African crop sorghum. It could be used for oil and fodder as well as food. Internal demand was fuelled both by the problems of the peasantry and by the growth of the compounds. Wider national markets were coalescing in the early twentieth century. The population of the urban areas increased from 22 per cent of the total (1.1 million) in 1904 to 31 per cent in 1936 (3 million). Given that townspeople had on average far greater per capita income, the urban markets were even more important than population figures suggest. By 1936, nearly two-thirds of the white and Indian population lived in towns (**Table 3**).

As in other agrarian systems, transport was a major constraint on the expansion of grain farming. Commodities with higher value for their bulk such as ivory, skins, and wool could be moved more profitably; sheep and cattle could walk themselves to market. In a tsetse-free zone, where all sections of society adapted quickly to the use of animal draught, South Africa had a great transport advantage over many other parts of the continent that were dependent on humans for porterage. But even then 'the sheer immobility of produce' made it difficult to reach new markets from grain producing districts (Keegan 1987: 98).

Wagons, commonly drawn by sixteen oxen, were adequate if slow for the transport of small quantities from field to farmstead and farm to mill. They were less efficient when large volumes, requiring tens of thousands of oxen, had to be moved long distances to the towns. War and cattle disease undermined the supply of animals. When there were enough oxen, the pressure on dirt roads and outspans was enormous. Imported American, Argentinian, or Canadian grain, rushed through the ports and by rail to the mining centres, undercut local produce and depressed prices. It was cheaper to transport grain 6,000 miles by ship and 1,000 by rail than a few hundred miles by wagon. Marketing of grain was hardly regulated at the time; good seasons produced gluts and depressed prices. During 1904–5, there was a glut of grain in some parts of the Free State, but more maize was imported than exported.

Railways resolved these problems quite rapidly, although unevenly, facilitating the switch towards arable production. When Lord Lugard argued in his *Dual Mandate* (1929: 462) that 'the development of the African continent is impossible without railways, and has awaited their advent', he expressed a view shared by many South African farmers, businessmen, and politicians. Railways were the sign of progress; heated debates were conducted in newspaper columns and parliament about their routes. By 1900 all the major ports were linked by rail to the Rand; over 4,000 miles had been constructed in South Africa. In the next ten years another 3,000 miles, much of it rural branch line, was completed. The hub of the Rand provided links between railway systems lacking in other African colonies. Grain-producing areas of the highveld benefited particularly and farmers secured favourable rail rates. African reserve areas, by contrast, were largely bypassed.

Railways absorbed the largest element in Cape government expenditure in the early twentieth century, a third of its annual budget (averaging nearly £3 million), not including interest on debts. Receipts from the railways were also the single largest item of government income in both the Cape and Natal. Taken as a whole, the railways of South Africa returned a good profit in the decade before Union, even if interest payments on loans are included. So successful was the improvement in transport that maize could be exported in significant quantities by 1907.

By the 1920s a state-subsidized system of grain elevators, silos, and storage at railheads helped to ease the cycle of glut and scarcity. Early pictures of the elevators show them surrounded by ox-wagons. These were gradually replaced by lorries. Afrikaner nationalists organized a wagon trek to Pretoria in 1938 to celebrate the centenary of the Great Trek and lay the stone of the Voortrekker monument. Like the springbok, wagons were loaded with heavy symbolism when their commercial significance began to decline.

Farmers received direct state assistance in numerous other ways. Generous loans were made both to English settlers and to Boers after the South African War. Restocking, fencing, boreholes, and seed were all part of the package. The Land Bank established in 1907 in the Transvaal, and expanded in 1912, has often been cited as a primary example of differential assistance to white agriculture. In fact, financing from other institutions offering credit and mortgages, including family networks and rural trading stores, was initially of greater importance. Further subsidies were available for fencing and irrigation. The introduction of limited liability cooperatives in 1922 and increasingly systematic price subsidies in the 1930s transferred even greater resources to farmers. Especially after the First World War, governments were committed to food self-sufficiency based on white commercial agriculture.

State financing of research and agricultural schools assisted rapid diversification. Veterinary scientists made their names in South Africa and their debates took on great political and social importance. The discovery that redwater and East Coast fever in cattle, as well as heartwater in sheep, were carried by ticks and not directly contagious like rinderpest, entrenched dipping as a major prophylaxis throughout the country. New scientific ideas—not always practicable—were applied across a whole range of agricultural problems and disseminated through the publications of the Agriculture Departments. The well-illustrated *Agricultural Journals* are a treasure trove of official thinking at that time. Blacks were not entirely excluded; they shared in the costs and benefits of dipping. In 1904 an experimental farm was established in the Transkei, which was probably the first in the country to train agricultural demonstrators. But state services mainly served large farms, and when new techniques were applied in African areas, official prescriptions tended to ignore local systems of tenure and knowledge as well as land shortage.

The state also entrenched legislation that reflected changing white attitudes to wildlife. By the end of the nineteenth century, influential figures both in Britain and South Africa recognized that predatory hunting and clearing of wild animals threatened a number of species. While some attempted to conserve animals for hunting as a socially exclusive pleasure pursuit, a more scientific conservationist ethic evolved alongside such ideas of sport. New methods of protection entailed not simply enforcement of existing hunting laws, but the establishment of game reserves, including a large area of the far eastern Transvaal, bordering Mozambique.

In 1926 this land was renamed the Kruger National Park. The first warden felt that Kruger himself 'had never in his life thought of wild animals except as biltong' (Carruthers 1994, 1995). But the Transvaal republican government had reserved some of this area in 1890s, and protagonists of protection used Kruger's name to win Afrikaner support for the project. Wild animals became powerful symbols of white nationalism. Although the area was not densely populated before, those Africans who had formerly lived or hunted there were excluded and became poachers. In the 1930s they lost their battle over rights of access, as tourism (over 30,000 annually) and police posts provided the Park with the resources for tighter control. Forests reserves, some fenced, had also been gradually extended since the late nineteenth century. Capitalist land-use patterns entrenched a sharper division in the functions of land than had been the case in pre-colonial society.

## The Fate of Tenants

In the early decades of the twentieth century, at least one-third of Africans in South Africa lived on white-owned farms. Especially in Natal, the Free State, and the Transvaal, they were tenants rather than agricultural workers: they had some access to land and pastures. Their fate was of central importance in the African experience and must be considered against the backdrop of agricultural improvement and intensification on the farmlands.

Tenancy arrangements varied greatly. It is useful to distinguish between three main forms found on the white-owned farms: rent tenancy, sharecropping, and labour tenancy. In general, white landowners were not short of land, but the capital and labour to work it. Where land was held for speculative purposes by companies—perhaps 20 per cent of the farms in the Transvaal in 1905—African tenants often paid rent in cash. Such tenants formed part of larger communities, even sub-chieftaincies, who were relatively free to control their own systems of production. As on the African reserves, youths would migrate to work in the mines.

Sharecropping became a means by which landowners could respond to new internal markets with little investment, and without the difficulties of procuring and controlling workers. African tenants contracted to pay one-half, later more, of their crop to the landlord for the right to cultivate and graze their cattle. They had to attempt to produce at least double their own subsistence needs. Sharecropping offered a viable option for African families with implements and oxen who preferred to escape the constraints of crowded communal reserves or the demands of chiefs. The system reached its apogee in the Free State and southern Transvaal between about 1880 and 1913.

It was usually the more resourceful and more incorporated black rural families that took this route. Some of those on the Vereeniging Estates, prize landholding of early Transvaal industrialist Sammy Marks, produced hundreds of bags of maize a season, when they needed perhaps twenty for their food supply. Kas Maine, most famous of black sharecroppers, was a highly skilled agriculturalist. Afrikaans-speaking and adept at finding good contracts, he was sufficiently confident and proud to move when he felt he had been sold short by a farmer. These Christian families were a black yeomanry in the forefront of the peasant revolution. Insecurity taught them how to get the maximum out of the land in a short period and they had to remain mobile. One route of migration took sharecroppers from the Sotho-speaking areas around lowland Lesotho to the north-eastern Free State and southern Transvaal. When such areas, well placed for transport to new markets, became more intensively capitalized, sharecroppers moved further north and west.

While the interests of tenants and landowners could intersect in the sharecropping relationship, this could also be tense, particularly at the moment when the crop was divided after harvest. Tenants made two piles, and landlords then chose one. Sharecropping ultimately benefited farmers in that they could accumulate through the sale of surplus and eventually dispense with such independent tenants. Those white highveld farmers who survived rinderpest, the South African War, and East Coast fever, did so partly by offloading the costs and risks of production onto African sharecroppers. One tenant's daughter recalled of her father many years later: 'Naphthali was a hard worker. Indeed, he worked very hard in his fields. He produced a lot from the soil. Hundreds of bags, half of which he gave to Theuns [the farmer], who in turn would proceed to sell them and get a lot of money from the labour to which he had never contributed anything' (Matsetela 1982: 227). The family had by then moved to Soweto, victims of the rise of the mealieboer—archetype of white dominance on the platteland (countryside; literally flat land)—whose success often depended first on black tenants, then on black workers.

Tenants' survival depended on their capacity to control their own family's labour for more intensive agriculture. Here the legacy of African society proved important. Women and youths, as well as men, were expected to work. This gave black tenants a competitive edge over white families, where it was not easily accepted that women and children should work in the fields. Boer urbanization in the early twentieth century was so rapid, not only because of disease, indebtedness, and private land tenure, but also because some were reluctant to work as families for white masters. Farmers preferred black tenants who produced more on less land.

As successful farmers accumulated more capital, they required labour rather than crops from their tenants. Some were able to retain 'servants' (or wage labourers) on their farms. But relatively few African families were prepared to accept this relationship while any alternative remained open. Labour tenancy was the most common compromise reached. In this relationship, members of tenant families worked for part of the year in exchange for the right to stay on a farm, run animals, and grow crops. Where possible, tenant families would attempt to meet the farmers' demands by providing youths and children to work as herds, domestic servants, or fieldhands. Even if African men worked themselves, they hoped to keep their wives' labour for the family's subsistence. 'I must work for the baas', argued a Transvaal tenant, 'but not my wife . . . . I buy a woman to work for me' (Bradford 1987: 37). As late as 1930, when sharecropping had been abolished, Africans on farms still held 1.5 million cattle, 14 per cent of the total in South Africa. (Those in reserves held a further 37 per cent.)

It was not least in regard to labour that farmers asserted their interests in the political sphere. Few farmers could compete with the mines for migrant labour from the reserves or Mozambique. Their concerns found one focus in opposition to 'squatters'— African tenants who paid largely rent. Squatters were seen to be responsible for stock theft; rented farms were seen to bottle up labour. As a countermeasure in the Transvaal, legislation limited the numbers of tenants on any particular farm to five. If it had been enforced, the tenant population would be more evenly dispersed through the farmlands. In the Cape, a different strand of early twentieth-century legislation tried to enforce registration of 'private locations' on farms with large numbers of tenants. Inspectors were appointed and farmers had to pay fees for their tenants. In neither territory were such measures effective.

In the early twentieth century, various interests coalesced to demand tighter controls on tenancy. Whites forced to leave the farms increasingly saw African sharecroppers and tenants as responsible and they found willing defenders in Afrikaner churchmen and politicians. Powerful groups of farmers were now prioritizing labour procurement. They wanted a general change in the form of tenancy so that there were no bolt-holes for tenants who wished to avoid more onerous contracts. These provisions were written into the 1913 Natives Land Act. The Act did not only attempt to demarcate land that would be reserved for Africans. It also disallowed residence by African tenants on farms unless they provided a minimum of ninety days' labour annually to the landowner. Forms of tenancy, such as sharecropping and cash rental, that did not involve a transfer of labour to the farmer were thus to be outlawed. As important, Africans were to be prevented from buying land in areas designated as white. Given that most areas scheduled for African occupation were held in communal tenure, the long-term effect of this provision was to curtail any extension of private landownership for Africans. Successful peasants and tenants could not transform themselves into capitalist farmers.

The Land Act became a major issue for African politicians. Solomon Plaatje's scathing indictment of its effects, *Native Life in South Africa* (1916), was perhaps the first major political polemic by an African author—it is still in print and a central text of South African history (**Chapter 4**). Plaatje was especially influenced by personal acquaintances amongst the struggling Baralong landowners of Thaba Nchu in the Free State. He also travelled widely, and *Native Life* includes a harrowing description of the broader fate of sharecroppers who, given no option but to become labour tenants or trek, found themselves in thousands along the roads, their cattle dying. The African was becoming a 'pariah in the land of his birth' with nowhere to bury his dead. Plaatje blamed the Boers for the Act. He noted that not all Afrikaners supported it: the paternalism of poorer Afrikaners still dependent on their sharecroppers was evident in 'the kindness of Boer women' to individual families. More specifically, he felt that the repressive Free State spirit epitomized by General Hertzog, then still in Botha's South African Party (**Chapter 3**), infused this legislation.

It is true that the Afrikaner members of parliament supported the Act almost to a man, while many English-speakers did not. But Plaatje, in trying to secure British intervention, glossed over the forces behind the Act. While a few English-speaking liberals opposed the Act in principle, most questioned its detail. Plaatje tended to overlook the role of accumulating English-speaking farmers and officials committed to segregation on the land, who also saw agricultural improvement as dependent on a switch to wage labour. The details of the Act were evolved not least by English-speaking Native Affairs officials. They drew on precedents both in the Cape and Natal—where the idea of reserves for Africans had been developed—as well as segregatory recommendations of the imperial South African Native Affairs Commission (1905).

In order to get his point across, Plaatje romanticized life on the farms before the Act. Yet, as one black leader had noted, 'barbarities' had long been practised 'and no one intervened' (Keegan 1987: 148). Plaatje also exaggerated the immediate effects of the Act. For the most part, its provisions were not enforced in courts. The government accepted that the promise of extra land for African reserves should be fulfilled before farm removals were sanctioned—a task hardly begun until the 1936 Native Trust and Land Act was passed. In the Cape, the Natives Land Act was declared *ultra vires* by a court in 1917, as it impinged on the capacity of Africans to qualify for the franchise by gaining a property qualification. Sharecroppers and rented farms could be found in rural districts, especially in the Transvaal, for at least another few decades. By the late 1920s it was estimated that nearly a quarter of a million Africans in Natal either hired ground from absentee white owners, or were tenants on Crown land. Some also worked for wages, but not necessarily on the farm that they occupied.

Nevertheless, grain-producing Free State farmers did treat the Act as a charter to narrow options for their tenants. It signalled a changed trajectory for tenants, their mobility restricted by passes and permits, and increasingly vulnerable to demands for servile labour. In some districts labour tenancy terms became more onerous by the 1920s and 1930s. The social revolution imposed by landlords and the state, as well as rapid technical improvements, set the scene for a further sustained increase in output on the white farms; by about four times between 1918, when the first annual statistics were collected nationally, and the 1950s. Segregation on the land was therefore not about keeping Africans off white-owned farms, but about regulating the conditions under which they remained on them. As mentioned above, the number of black people on farms increased significantly up to mid-century, although not as quickly as the urban population.

By the 1920s white farmers in South Africa were a highly differentiated group. Despite state aid and overall increases in production, many farms were unprofitable and indebtedness widespread. Labour tenants, intent on salvaging some of their status as peasants, were often reluctant workers. Youths resistant to the authority of both their fathers and white farmers tried to find some means of escaping to town. Volatile agricultural prices induced farmers to rush into particular commodities and thus flood the market. By 1930 many farms were heavily mortgaged. While wealthier farmers were able to accumulate land, subdivision was simultaneously common and the number of farming units increased.

Cheque-book farmers, to use Macmillan's coinage, with other interests and other sources of income, could do well from poor whites' plight. Lawyers and agents secured quantities of land on a rising market by foreclosing on debts owed to them; some white and black landowners were barely literate and easy prey for those skilled in the complexities of land law and contract. The state subsidized a number of resettlement schemes for poor whites, but they hardly reversed the flow from the land. Poor whites, in turn, demanded protection from the state in labour markets.

Agricultural capitalism in the interior of early twentieth-century South Africa was still in its brutal youth. The farms were wellsprings of white reaction and racism. Paternalism allowed limited interactions—white children were nursed by black nannies and could play with black children. Surprisingly close social contacts were possible on western Transvaal farms in the inter-war years where sharecropping survived, van Onselen (1990, 1997) argues, but even these took place within tight constraints. If Afrikaner politicians did not concentrate their efforts primarily on racial issues, in the sense of a formulated national policy by which to segregate and control Africans, they clearly expressed white rural feelings about appropriate racial relationships that exerted a powerful influence on national policy. These ideas were shaped by the received scientific notions of Social Darwinism (**Chapter 3**) but not caused by them.

Few white farmers supported the extension of African reserves, since this implied giving up land and providing escape routes for labour tenants and workers whom they wanted to tie to their farms. They could not compete with the mines in wages for migrant workers from the reserves. Some were against the idea of

African reserves at all, but in many districts farmers were more ambivalent. They were perturbed about the juxtaposition of farms and land occupied by Africans. 'When they have a beer drink they go though your fences, their dogs are worrying one's sheep continually and destroying your game: whenever you are adjoining a location they have their rams, their bulls and their horses, and they are continually breaking through your fences and getting at your stock' (Beinart *et al.* 1986: 300). Many farmers therefore came to support more stringent segregation of Africans who were not under their direct control.

The language of the farms could be harsh—it was the language of insecure landowners, many of whom had only freshly acquired property through conquest. 'Native rebellion' remained a pervasive fear in recently colonized rural districts, even when military power had been decisively demonstrated. Poor whites, who saw African tenants and workers as unfair competition, played on racial fears to win support and protection. Priests and politicians took little persuading that miscegenation was the ultimate consequence of economic degradation. It was a world where terms like 'kaffir' were everyday currency. Slaves in the Cape had sometimes been called by months of the year—there are still families with the surnames February, April, and September. Whites distanced themselves and dehumanized their workers by calling them after coins, kitchen implements, or animals: Sixpence and Shilling; Saucepan or Bobbejaan (baboon). (Many workers also took Afrikaans or English Christian names.) Mature men were called 'jong' or 'boy'; women 'meid' or 'girl'.

Power relationships were not expressed only in language. Farmers tended to be armed, tenants unarmed. Violence may not have been an everyday occurrence, but it was frequent enough—not least in the more intensive farming zones like the sugar fields. It would be misleading to see violence simply as the result of some frontier hangover. As in the case of the American South or Italian rural Fascism, the efforts being made to extract labour in the 1910s and 1920s tended to produce a particularly harsh system of control. On occasion, the state had to step in to contain settlers who had exceeded the law in what they perceived as their own domain. The intermediaries and supervisors—mostly but not all white—in this process could be the most careless in their violence. Poor whites who joined the police or drifted to small towns could be quickest to defend their racially arrogated status.

The intensity of social division in the countryside had many roots. For whites, *baasskap* (domination) on the land was legitimized at the national level by the rise of exclusivist Afrikaner nationalism and segregationist ideology that undermined more liberal paternalist sentiment. The legacy of the frontier was reshaped by the new antagonisms between those undergoing dramatic social changes. Ultimately, as on the Rand, racial divisions did not preclude rapid economic growth in the countryside and in certain contexts coercive controls facilitated capitalist development.

# 3

# War, Reconstruction, and the State from the 1890s to the 1920s

*War, Reconstruction, and the Logic of the Mines*

John X. Merriman, long-serving and acerbic Cape politician, regarded Johannesburg, 'its Stock Exchange, and its prostitutes and prize fighters', with a combination of fascination, horror and disdain. His failure to succeed either in diamonds or gold perhaps led him to appreciate and assert the more legalistic and genteel traditions of the Cape. The brash new city seemed to lack natural beauty. Mine dumps were its mountains; the contours of race were harshly drawn. His wife, Agnes, wrote of the Exchange on a boom day: a 'scene of mad excitement—men taking their coats off and shrieking like maniacs—fortunes were made and lost in hours; St John Carr, an ex-clerk .... made £20,000 in a day' (Lewsen 1960–9: xli. 277). Nor was it only those from the Cape who found that the 'struggle for wealth' was 'at no time an edifying spectacle' (van Onselen 1982: i. 1). But money spoke; Carr became the first mayor of Johannesburg's new city council in 1901. Mine-owners who made even more money did not hesitate to use their influence.

By 1895 the fast-amalgamating Randlords knew that the future of the gold mines lay securely with the deep levels that required large and long-term investment. It took the cavalier ambition of Rhodes to translate this realization into the Jameson Raid, which tried to use the growing *uitlander* (foreign) population in the Transvaal to help bounce out Kruger's republican government in a *coup*. In 1895 Rhodes's colleague Dr Jameson—fresh from colonizing Rhodesia—was to ride into the Transvaal at the head of a small force that would be met by cheering supporters. The plan failed. It was not a very British *coup*, but had more of the mark of settler politics. True, Britain's military adventures in South Africa had not all been successes, but they were usually better organized if a great deal more costly.

Merriman, who was by no means unwilling to work with the titan Rhodes up to the Jameson Raid, then developed a clearer critique.

Those who compare him with Clive or Warren Hastings are those who take their history from the *Daily Telegraph* or *Tit Bits*. He is a pure product of the age, a capitalist politician . . . In Australian or English or, I conjecture, American politics he would have made no figure, as he cannot stand up to his equals in debate and has neither moral courage nor convictions, but he has the sort of curious power that Napoleon had of intrigue and of using men . . . for his purpose which is self-aggrandisement under one high-sounding name or another. (Lewsen 1960–9: xliv. 254–5)

Merriman was surely underestimating Rhodes's idealism and wrong about politics elsewhere, but he was right to identify a new 'mixture of Imperial politics and Stock Exchange' (Lewsen 1960–9: xliv. 255). Son of the Bishop of Grahamstown and educated in England, he, like most English-speaking South Africans, valued the imperial connection. But he was alarmed that the political direction of the subcontinent was apparently being shaped, not by order, bureaucracy, and the civilizing mission, but by massive share deals in London's City offices, nods and winks in gentlemen's clubs. In particular, the logic of the gold mines seemed to rule supreme.

The logic of gold mines was, their owners argued, that they operated within particular constraints shaped by the fixed price of gold and the low grade of ore. Mine-owners had to draw in large quantities of machinery, supplies, and labour to a spot remote from transport links and they saw Kruger's South African Republic government to be less than sympathetic to their requirements. Explosive issues such as his policy of granting a monopoly concession for the supply of dynamite confirmed their belief. About 200,000 cases of dynamite were used annually between 1894 and 1899, between 10 and 20 per cent of working costs. The capacity of the industry to organize itself in the Chamber of Mines (founded 1889) and propagate its position in newspapers such as

the *Star* was important in establishing the logic of gold production in the public mind. Afrikaner leaders did increasingly
recognize that the mines were the Transvaal's golden egg and
tried to come to terms with the giant in their midst. But to the
mining industry, the Republican government represented an
essentially rural community incapable of managing capitalist
industrialization.

Kruger was also faced with the demand for *uitlander* rights—
votes for thousands of foreigners, including the skilled workers
required to establish the mines. They came from Australia,
America, Eastern Europe, and especially Britain, where the
decline of the Cornish tin mines coincided with the rise of gold.
Pro-imperial newspapers and political groups felt that rapid
enfranchisement of immigrants to the Rand could swing the balance of power in the Republic to favour the mining industry. But
even if Kruger had given way on *uitlander* rights, this may not
have been enough. Britain had long sought to retain an exclusive
sphere of influence over the Boer republics and had annexed the
Transvaal before (1877–81); now the Transvaal's new wealth
seemed to threaten British interests in the region as a whole. Other
European powers, such as Germany, were spreading their wings
and extending their interests. Kruger had established a rail link
with Portuguese-held Delagoa Bay in Mozambique. And if
Britain did not need to control the gold-producing areas directly,
its commitment to an international gold standard and gold backing for sterling made privileged access to this major new supply
highly advantageous.

Iain Smith (1996) has reasserted an interpretation of the South
African War that focuses on imperial strategic visions rather than
gold and its effects. The two explanations are not mutually
exclusive: on the one hand, minerals transformed the social geography and politics of the region as well as its international significance; on the other, war also required a failure of diplomacy.
The war was probably unnecessary in that some kind of political
accommodation could have been reached between mine-owners,
the Republics, the colonies, and Britain that would have facilitated
the development of the mines. As long as Britain did not wish to
impose political rights for blacks in South Africa, which it showed

no signs of doing, many other issues were negotiable. But it was difficult for the most important power in the world to negotiate with lesser states controlled by Boers or blacks. Even though the most aggressive phase of the Scramble for Africa was over, military mobilization to protect interests, make labour work, avenge slights, or maintain face was still an option for British policy-makers when the stakes were so high.

Afrikaners harboured an enormous sense of injustice about British intervention, which helped to make them impervious to any criticism about their style of control in the Transvaal. Boer self-righteousness comes through powerfully in books like *A Century of Wrong* (Reitz 1900), in which Jan Smuts, youthful Attorney-General in the Transvaal after graduating at Cambridge, had a hand. It feeds on the version of nineteenth-century history increasingly propagated by nationalist intellectuals that asserted unquestioningly the depth and unity of the *volk* and perfidy of the British who seemed to favour Africans. Afrikaner history became a search, sanctioned by God, for independence and identity against the combined forces of Mammon and Ham. Such ideas about morality and justice were powerful spurs to political action in turn-of-the-century South Africa, not least because of the violence of the nineteenth. These moral issues subsequently recurred in political debate between Boer, Briton, and African: who got there first; who invaded whose land; who ignored whose rights; to whom did the wealth and resources of the country belong? There is nothing so dangerous as people who feel they have been deeply wronged, and are blinded by their own sense of injustice. Afrikaners fed on that sense, and the scale of British intervention was partly responsible.

The issue for Britain was not so much whether it was capable of winning the war but whether it was committed to doing so. That commitment was displayed in the tactics used finally to suppress waning Boer military capability. Unable to compete in set-piece battles after their initial successes in 1899, Boer generals resorted to guerrilla warfare. British generals responded with a scorched-earth policy, burning farmhouses and collecting women and children into concentration camps, where the death rates from disease were very high. About 28,000 Boer civilians died; Boer losses in battle, at about 7,000, were light in comparison. (British forces lost three times this number.) But perhaps one-tenth of the Republics' Boer population lost their lives. This was not a 'gentlemen's war'.

Nor was it simply a 'white man's war'. Hundreds of thousands of black people were drawn into the conflict on both sides as suppliers of produce, as auxiliaries who manned the vast British transport networks, as grooms and servants. Many lived on the farms that became a terrain of battle, or were victims along with pro-British populations in sieges such as that of Mafikeng. In the latter stages of the war, some became armed combatants, and at least 14,000, probably more, died in camps in similar conditions to Boer civilians. The black role, initially explored by radical historians such as Warwick and Nasson, was extensively discussed during recent centennial commemorations of the war under the new ANC government. There was even 'an emphasis on mutual suffering' by Afrikaner and African at the hands of British imperialism, suggesting that the war could become 'the crucible of a common identity' (Cuthbertson and Jeeves 1999: 7). This is problematic, both as interpretation and as expectation, not least because of the pattern of post-war reconstruction, in which a magnanimous imperial power reached an accommodation with defeated Afrikaners. Most blacks had in any case supported Britain.

Despite persisting till the Republics surrendered, Britain did not have a clean slate on which to reconstruct them, nor did it wish to shoulder aside all Boer claims. White dominance over Africans on the land was reinstated at considerable cost. Moreover, Milner, High Commissioner in South Africa from 1898 to 1905 and the main architect of British policy, could not directly control the Cape and Natal. Their governments had been a critical source of support in the war, but they had strongly established self-government, which, although constrained in the war, soon had to be fully restored. Reconstruction in the former Boer Republics involved extending the governmental system of the Cape as much as imposing a new one from Britain. Though it fell into a deep recession in 1904 after the removal of imperial troops, the Cape was still the biggest and most populous of the colonies, with the most sophisticated bureaucracy and parliamentary system. Cape officials were influential throughout South Africa and Rhodesia. And in the Cape, pragmatic Afrikaners in the Bond had worked both with Rhodes and with explicitly South African-minded English-speaking politicians such as Schreiner (Prime Minister 1898–1900) and Merriman (Prime Minister 1908–10). This alliance—forged after Rhodes's demise—took the name South African Party, which was adopted by the white coalition that came to power after Union in 1910.

Nevertheless Britain's brief period of direct rule (to 1905) in the Transvaal was significant in shaping South Africa's future. Merriman scathingly labelled Milner's officials—young, unrepresentative, and from Oxford—a Kindergarten. But he underestimated the extent to which apparently untamed capitalist imperialism also held by a philosophy of order and planning. The infant bureaucracy anxiously set about creating the conditions for the mining industry to expand—reshaping transport and customs, abolishing concessions, initiating improved housing for workers, reforming municipal government and agricultural services, and policing Africans more assiduously. The mines also benefited from a favourable tax regime. Up to the early 1930s, the state usually took well under £2 million annually in revenue directly from the mines, although the value of gold produced rose from £20 million in 1905 to £45 million in 1930 (Yudelman 1983). Reconstruction bound the state and the mines together in many different ways, some officials moving freely between them.

Perhaps the major problem facing the industry was its labour supply. While the exact balance between white and black workers had not been settled at the time of the war, mine-owners were convinced that they required a very large proportion of cheaper black workers. Key mining houses such as Wernher, Beit, and Eckstein (the Corner House group), which controlled about 50 per cent of production, committed themselves to maximizing output by mining lower-grade ores that intensified the requirement for unskilled workers. Radical historians revising the understanding of South African history in the 1970s and 1980s did not simply invent the idea of a colonial obsession with labour; it springs out of the documents and archives of the time. 'The dignity of labour' was a catchphrase of the 1890s, and, if politicians seemed preoccupied by war, peace, and Union, then labour recruitment and control were increasingly the meat of everyday 'native administration'.

While the war was still in progress, the Chamber re-established the Witwatersrand Native Labour Association (WNLA) to recruit workers. In 1901 Milner renegotiated an agreement with the Portuguese colonial government in Mozambique to allow recruiting there in exchange for direct payment in gold and preference for Delagoa Bay as a port. Mozambique supplied 60 per cent of the total black labour force (about 50,000 annually) from 1903 to 1907 (**Figure 2**). Although the percentage gradually dropped to 35 per cent over the next couple of decades, Mozambican numbers increased to peak at 80,000. One of the ironies of the early twentieth-century Transvaal is that, despite conquest, its economy faced increasingly east to Delagoa Bay, rather than south to the British sphere. Cape ports were not easily able to compete for the Transvaal trade because of Milner's agreement and their distance from the Rand. By 1909 their combined share of Transvaal trade had fallen to 13 per cent, while Durban had 22 per cent and Lourenco Marques (now Maputo) 65. This greatly contributed to the Cape's recession; customs revenues declined by more than half between 1902 and 1908.

Despite the depressed state of the Cape and Natal, the mines could not initially win back labour supplies from their densely populated African reserves. Cape workers complained of the danger, high death rates, and the ruthlessness of discipline under white overseers and 'Tshaka guards'—the Zulu-speaking mine police. Black workers in the Cape benefited from high wages in the ports, on the railways, and in British army employ to 1903. When these options closed, tens of thousands went as far as German South West Africa (Namibia) to find similar work during the devastating German war against against the Herero and Nama from 1904 to 1907.

In response to the perceived shortage of workers, Milner set up the Transvaal Labour Commission. The majority report (1904), reflecting the position of the mine-owners, concluded that 129,000 workers were lacking and a further 196,000 would be required in the next five years. It saw both South African and imperial interests at one with rapid expansion of mining. A minority group of commissioners, expressing the views of white labour and some commercial interests, suggested both that these figures were inflated and that the number of white workers could be increased instead. It presented an alternative vision of the future where growth would be less rapid, wealth more widely spread within the settler community, and less attention paid to the clamour of foreign shareholders. The minority report recognized that low wages were a major cause of the shortage of black labour.

Milner and the mining houses ignored clear evidence that a reduction of mine wages for Africans to 35 shillings a month had caused the labour shortage and that an increase in 1903 to 45 shillings attracted Mozambicans back. (A 'month' involved 30 daily tickets, which would take more than a month to complete.) Instead they tried to hold down wages by extending recruitment to China. Many nineteenth-century British settler enterprises, including Natal's sugar estates, had drawn on the international market in Asian indentured labour after the abolition of slavery. Wages in South Africa for unskilled labour were relatively high in international terms, and between 1904 and 1906 over 60,000 Chinese workers came. Although they were expensive to import, they stayed longer than most African migrant workers and therefore had the opportunity to become more efficient.

Together with Mozambicans, Chinese workers carried the mines through a period of rapidly expanding output to 1907. Unlike Indians in Natal, however, they did not become another minority in South Africa. Their contracts forbade this and the Transvaal's new responsible government (1907), intent on protecting whites, and the British Liberal government, uneasy about imperial overreach and 'Chinese slavery', were determined that they should go. Subsequently, as mine wages increased to about 60 shillings a month, Cape workers replaced them. Between 1904 and 1910, their numbers on the Rand increased from 6,000 to 60,000, from 7 per cent to 29 per cent of the total labour force in the mines.

The labour shortage was effectively solved. Despite the evidence that the supply of migrant workers was linked to wage increases, the Chamber developed an argument to suggest that if Africans earned more, they would work less. It was based on the assumption that migrant workers with land had only a very limited desire for 'luxuries' or consumer items: 'the only pressing needs of a savage are those of food and sex', so the Labour Commission opined, 'and the conditions of Native life in Africa are such that these are as a rule easily supplied' (Great Britain 1904: 71). If wages were higher then consumer requirements would be met more quickly.

Although it is true that some African men did not have to work continuously at the turn of the century, poverty pushed many onto the labour market while others tried simultaneously to expand their agricultural production and wage income. Moreover, in West African colonies British officials saw fair prices for African-grown cash crops as an incentive to increased peasant production and the expansion of African consumer demand. The self-serving Chamber argument, which ran counter to its own experience and resonated with white racial ideas, was used in justification of both the low wage regime, and the closing of opportunity for Africans, in later years.

Recruitment of workers in the first twenty years of gold mining had been a relatively haphazard process, a sub-industry in itself of contractors, agents, touts, and runners. By 1910 some 200,000 black workers had to be found each year. The Chamber of Mines was keen on a single recruitment agency in order to limit competition between different employers, which had the effect of driving wages up. They also wished to diminish the number of middlemen involved, as each wanted a cut. WNLA, the initial vehicle for this policy, succeeded in Mozambique but failed in South Africa, where there was more competition. It was only by about 1920 that all the major mining houses recognized the new Native Recruiting Corporation (NRC) as sole internal recruiter. In later years, the blue and white buildings of Kwa-Teba—the place of Taberer, first head of the NRC—dotted rural districts alongside the magistrates' offices and trading stores.

Colonial and Union governments attempted to control the worst features of recruiting at the same time as facilitating the flow of workers. Acts and regulations dealing with touting, desertion, recruiting licences, written contracts, pre-contract medicals, child labour, and large advances squeezed out smaller and more unscrupulous operators. Desertion rates, over 10 per cent in 1909, dropped to insignificant proportions by 1920. Controls were consolidated in the Native Labour Regulation Act of 1911, for many years the cornerstone of industrial legislation for black mineworkers. It established basic standards for compound accommodation, food, and medical services, but gave few rights to Africans as workers and retained criminal sanctions for breach of contract.

## Social Policy and Urban Growth in the Reconstruction Era

'Native policy', though deeply influenced by the imperatives of labour supply, was far broader in its scope and aims. The incorporative elements of Victorian liberalism were being jettisoned in British and colonial thinking, replaced by the loose amalgam of ideas sometimes called Social Darwinism. Race became an increasingly important category of social thought and races were ranked in a supposed hierarchy of civilization. Biological ideas of supremacy justified European pre-eminence and there were fears that this might be diluted or corrupted by intermingling with 'lesser' races. John Buchan's adventure story *Prester John* (1910) is a highly revealing account of British attitudes at the time. Later Governor-General of Canada, Buchan was a middle-ranking official in the Reconstruction Transvaal. His novel has as hero a young Scotsman, Davie Crawfurd, who goes to trade in the rural Transvaal and quells an African rebellion led by the Revd John Laputa. The book reflects a still pervasive fear of 'risings', fuelled by discontent amongst tenants in the Transvaal, by the 1906 Bambatha rebellion in Natal (**Chapter 4**), and by new racial anxieties about the 'black peril'—whether male servants in the kitchen or 'swamping' in the towns.

Buchan depicts the Transvaal along strict lines of racial hierarchy. Davie is the model of efficiency and heroism. Women hardly feature in the novel at all; colonialism is portrayed as a male enterprise. Earlier settlers are cruel and violent, unable to understand the white man's burden in Africa or the value of fairness and bureaucracy. The 'half-caste' Portuguese character, who sides with the Africans and deals illicitly in diamonds, is the quintessence of evil; 'miscegenation' and social degeneracy are explicitly linked. Africans are represented as 'hordes', without individuality or rationality, impervious to pain and available for rousing emotional appeals. Laputa alone has a personality, biologically represented in his aquiline rather than squat nose. A Christian with a classical education, he was also a subtle manipulator of traditional magic, invoking the power of a legendary black king, Prester John. His ability to straddle both worlds, as in part a creation of empire, made him a particular threat. Laputa's name is surely taken from the island in *Gulliver's Travels* where self-regarding philosophers are shown to be incompetent in practical affairs. Although he had to be crushed, the dilemma of dealing with him illustrates British uncertainty about the 'civilizing' mission.

Davie not only quells the rebellion but finds his fortune—a clear statement about who has rights to the wealth of a colony. He is sufficiently cognizant of his imperial duties to sell his diamonds to De Beers, 'for if I have placed them on the open market I should have upset the delicate equipoise of diamond values' (p. 200). The rest he takes home to Britain. The novel ends with the establishment of a 'great native training college . . . no factory for making missionaries and black teachers' but a 'technical workshop' (p. 202). Civilization increasingly meant different things for different 'races'.

What Buchan expresses in popular fiction comes through in a more considered way in the *Report of the South African Native Affairs Commission* (Great Britain 1905). The assembled English-speaking experts aimed to arrive at rational and socially beneficial solutions to the 'native problem'. The Report tried to subsume the differing heritages of the Republics, the Cape, and Natal into one policy, to arbitrate competing interests, as well as pay some attention to the evidence from African witnesses. SANAC affirmed that the Cape franchise should not be extended. Conferring on blacks political power 'in any aggressive sense, or weakening in any way the unchallenged supremacy and authority of the ruling race', was out of the question (para. 442). The Report assumed—despite evidence to the contrary in Cape politics (**Chapter 4**)—that all Africans would behave in essentially the same way and 'voting of the future may proceed upon race lines'. Racial mixing and squatting on the land were seen to be undesirable both for whites and for blacks, making it 'far more difficult to preserve the absolutely necessary political and social distinctions' (para. 192).

Chiefs, now under colonial control, were less frowned upon than they had been in the nineteenth century when they led rebellions. The black Christian elite were no longer seen as loyal allies, but a potential threat—'precocious' and 'troublesome'. Education could give 'an exaggerated sense of self-importance', while 'the stolid good sense of the more experienced but less lettered men seldom if ever finds expression in print' (para. 328). SANAC did not completely jettison the rhetoric of 'civilization'. It was one of the last major government reports that saw some future for educated Africans 'uplifting' themselves and their people within a common national context. 'Responsible' expressions of opinion through newspapers and independent churches were considered legitimate safety valves. But SANAC proved to be a powerful source for the ideas of what was becoming known as segregation. The Cape, Natal, and the Republics had already imposed various elements of that policy; these were now being reworked to meet new social circumstances and pressures.

Many historians agree that the edifice of the modern South African state and racial domination were definitively erected during the period from 1901 to 1910 and that Milner's policies set the design. They underestimate the Cape heritage. And they have also misjudged another issue: that of white immigration or anglicization. Historians tend to agree that Milner failed in this central aim.

On the political side [he wrote], I attach the greatest importance of all to the increase of the British population . . . If, ten years hence, there are three men of British race to two of Dutch, the country will be safe and prosperous. If there are three of Dutch to two of British, we shall have perpetual difficulty . . . We not only want a majority of British, but we want a fair margin, because of the large proportion of 'cranks' that we

British always generate, and who take a particular pleasure in going against their own people' (Thompson 1960: 7).

Milner arranged state-sponsored settlement schemes on the land to supplement the flow of immigrants. Women were given assisted passages, both to replace black men in domestic service and, by providing marriage fodder for white male mineworkers, to help establish a settled English-speaking white working class.

While it is true that settlement schemes and immigration projects directly sponsored by the state were of limited success, the white population of the area to become South Africa nearly doubled between 1891 and 1904, from 621,000 to 1,117,000—the last period in which the rate of white population growth significantly exceeded that of the black. The growth rate averaged nearly 5 per cent per annum, compared with an average of around 2 per cent per annum, including immigration, for whites between 1904 and 1936. Without immigration, the white population was unlikely to have topped 800,000 in 1904. Perhaps 350,000 immigrants and their progeny were added to the population in these thirteen years, roughly 70 per cent of them British and many of them men. South Africa attracted a significant proportion of the voluntary emigrants pouring out of Europe in an era of high population mobility.

The mining industry, which employed some 14,000 white workers by 1904, was only one attraction. Many soldiers stayed on after the war. Natal's largely English-speaking white population nearly doubled. English-speakers dominated commerce, professions, and municipal government in most of the rapidly growing towns of the interior, which only became Afrikaner bastions in later decades. An estimated 40,000 East European Jews arrived between 1880 and 1914, about half moving to the Rand. They hawked, speculated in livestock, opened shops, hotels, liquor outlets, wholesale and manufacturing businesses, and moved into the professions. Considerable numbers of other European immigrants arrived, some absorbed into Afrikaner society. They included the Dutch parents of one of the strongest Afrikaner nationalists of the twentieth century, Hendrik Verwoerd. The rapidity of immigration and movement within the country set the

scene for culture change and reaction. Judged against the longer
term of South African history, this period saw a startling anglicization, if that term is taken to mean more immigration. This
legacy of imperial policy was in any case changing. Anglophone
politicians, including Milner's successors, increasingly turned
their attention to a common white South African identity as they
worked towards Union.

Although Dutch-speakers remained more numerous, Milner's
miscalculation was not so much about the potential for immigration as about the congruence between culture and class. His
assumption that 'race' or culture determined political interest and
behaviour was a very powerful one amongst imperial thinkers
at the time and has flawed many analyses of South Africa
since. Milner was wrong to think that English-speakers, barring
a few cranks, would share his view of the world. Many of the
working class and some in the commercial world backed the
anti-imperial Responsibles in the Transvaal, later absorbed in
the South African Party led by Botha and Smuts. Some were
responsible for trade-union and worker organizations that shook
the mining industry to the core in the next few decades; a few even
made contact with blacks in socialist organizations. Conflicts
between essentially English-speaking social groupings, the mine-
owners and white workers, became a critical nexus of early
twentieth-century politics. Even if there had been a majority of
English-speakers, they probably would not have united politically.

White immigrants landed up in the towns at the same time as
poor whites and blacks were beginning to drain more rapidly from
the land. There was also a significant movement of whites north
from the other colonies. In 1891 well over 60 per cent of those
classified as white still lived in the Cape, less than 20 per cent in
the Transvaal. By 1904 the figures were 52 and 27 per cent respectively and, by 1921, 42 and 36. Turn-of-the-century governments
had to confront the problem of how to house this diverse new
population. The mining towns that grew so rapidly at this time
were a third layer of urban settlement, following the ports and
subsequent inland administrative, market, and transport centres
such as Pietermaritzburg, Bloemfontein, and Pretoria.

Kimberley, Johannesburg, and the Rand towns were all sited

primarily because of their proximity to mineral deposits. The same applied to the coal towns of northern Natal such as Newcastle. Like other mining enclaves, the Rand was boisterous and rough, with a preponderantly male population demanding more than the usual quota of liquor, sexual services, and boarding-house accommodation. There were 153,000 more men classified white than women in the country in 1904 and 59 per cent of the white Transvaal population was male. The reconstruction government's aim was to encourage a stable white working-class community, which included family housing for whites on the mines and in new suburbs. Large brick and cement works, which displaced the small-scale operations of Afrikaners who had moved to town, reduced building costs, and tram transport to the new white suburbs was rapidly installed.

This was also a period when Cape Town's working-class suburbs expanded around the lower slopes of Devil's Peak. The railway line down the eastern side of the peninsula to Simonstown created new pockets of suburban settlement. Victorian colonial houses with balconies and delicate ironwork, now much valued as 'broekielace', gave way to more prosaic single-storey buildings. Suburbs and roads were given British names, so that it was possible to live in Fulham Road, Brixton, Johannesburg. City-centre development followed in the British architectural mould. Office blocks, banks, public buildings, and shops of four to five storeys with ornate gables and cupolas lined the streets of central Johannesburg, Cape Town, and Durban. The British architect Herbert Baker was influential in developing a distinctive style of public architecture manifest in Rhodes's mansion at Groote Schuur, the majestic stone Union Buildings in Pretoria that housed the new government offices, and the University of Cape Town on a prime mountainside site. He adapted and developed Cape Dutch motifs such as shutters and gables, reflecting a more general desire by anglophones to acclimatize to their surroundings and forge a British–South African identity.

Rapid migration by women from both Europe and the country-side reduced the preponderance of white men in the cities to negligible levels by 1921. To the great relief of those concerned about enforcing segregation, the incentive for white men to marry or cohabit across the colour line was reduced. In 1902, at a period of heightened racial anxiety, the Cape parliament outlawed the sale of sexual services by white women to black men; the Transvaal had already done the same. The legislation was extended in 1927. Surprisingly, marriage between whites and others was not then made illegal. Such marriages were rare and segregationists believed that public opprobrium would be an adequate safeguard.

Urban space and racial mixing became fraught issues. Market forces and municipal regulation had laid the basis for partial segregation in most towns by the late nineteenth century. But poorer districts near the fast-growing city centres tended to reflect the very diverse origins of the country's working class. Where there were separate African locations, they were often centrally located, and freehold property rights were usually allowed. Bubonic plague, which arrived on board ship from India in 1901, galvanized white communities to change this pattern. Cape Town was packed with highly mobile people in the latter phases of the South African War and could have been an ideal location for the disease to spread. Following the Indian example, the Public Health Department laid down stringent plague rules. It was known that rats spread the plague, but it was also associated with squalor, poverty, and, in the colonial mind, with Africans.

Public Health legislation provided the means to push Africans out of town, and the growing demands for urban segregation could now draw on the 'sanitation syndrome', a powerful language of disease and purity (Swanson 1995). Legislation in 1902 provided for central government funding of new African locations in Cape Town and Port Elizabeth. In 1903 Johannesburg followed suit; Klipspruit was founded to the south-west of the city near the sewage works. Urban segregation cannot be explained simply by anxieties over public health; nor was it fully enforced for many decades (**Chapter 5**). Indeed, the continued presence of resident black servants in many white households might be construed to negate the apparent health benefits of segregation. (Blacks in this context were seen as sanitized by their surroundings and inferior status.) Africans were also resistant to such regimentation—as Swanson notes, they were 'like quicksilver under the thumb of "native policy"' (1995: 407).

## Afrikaners Re-Emergent

By 1905 Britain, bowing to Boer pressure, began the process of decentralizing authority in the Transvaal and the Free State. Settlers who paid taxes had everywhere shown themselves determined to have political control, even if Britain maintained that it bore the costs of their defence. Moreover, the Liberal Party, which came to power in 1906, believed 'that liberty, not force, was the cement of Empire' (Thompson 1960: 23). It had been less committed to the South African War and included a pro-Boer group. As agreed at the Peace of Vereeniging, whites were able to restrict the franchise to themselves when local self-government was installed by 1907. To African political leaders, Britain seemed to be selling out the interests of blacks to its bitter enemy, the Boers.

The two Boer generals, Louis Botha and Jan Smuts, who emerged at the head of Transvaal politics, opted for conciliation between the English and Afrikaners. The fact that both had heroic war records and the authority of military leadership helped them to take a wounded Afrikaner population in this political direction. Botha was a highveld Afrikaner with limited education and patriarchal demeanour, more charismatic and popular than the clinical and efficient Smuts. But both recognized the primacy of ensuring favourable conditions for the gold-mining industry and efficient agriculture as the foundations of a modern state and both accepted that some kind of union of the South African colonies was desirable.

The reconstruction administration had worked towards this goal and most English-speaking politicians agreed. Jameson, Prime Minister of the Cape from 1904 to 1908, claimed with some justification that his mentor Rhodes advocated cooperation between the white 'races'; here his views accorded with Merriman's. His Progressive Party administration worked closely with emerging regional institutions, and there were major advantages that could accrue in spheres such as railways and customs. Union was achieved in 1910, after lengthy negotiation about its exact form. A racially exclusive, British-influenced parliamentary system was agreed, though liberal Cape politicians managed to salvage and entrench a non-racial qualified franchise in their province. The only other clause entrenched in the South Africa Act was that there should be equality between the two predominant white languages: English and, at this stage, Dutch.

The South African Party (SAP), which took power after Union, though dominated by Afrikaners, included anglophone politicians. The main opposition Unionist Party, largely English, did not prove a parliamentary threat. Despite this apparent political accommodation, Afrikaner nationalism increasingly became a major force in fleshing out the contours of the Union's body politic. The demographic calculus of white South Africa, which offered the possibility of Afrikaner ethnic power through the franchise, provided a lodestone for exclusivist leaders. But Afrikaners were no 'chosen people'. Unity was not natural or self-evident, and, in the first half of the twentieth century, they proved just as incapable of maintaining a single political front as English-speakers, despite economic and cultural movements that tried to weld an Afrikaner identity.

Afrikaners were not the sole carriers of the language. They shared this, their history, and even some of their ancestry with people of colour, especially in the Cape, who had long been part of colonial society. Although the possibility of incorporating coloured people into the ethnic camp as 'bruin [brown] Afrikaners' was occasionally mooted, it was never seriously pursued. Not only was colour of overriding importance in the early twentieth-century white ideology, but many Afrikaner intellectuals and rural leaders perceived coloured people through the eyes of masters, as poor people who should be servile. The most educated group called coloured tended to be Muslim, and those who did have the franchise were not usually sympathetic to Afrikaner parties. Racial boundaries in the poorer suburbs were often fluid, but this alarmed rather than encouraged the Afrikaner elite.

On this point, Afrikaners were largely agreed. Their divisions stemmed partly from the differing experiences of the Cape and the former Republics. Ironically, Botha and Smuts aligned themselves with a pragmatic white South Africanism, while the Cape continued to produce radical intellectuals who gradually turned to republicanism and led the language movement to replace Dutch with Afrikaans. Divisions between *bittereinders*, who fought to the bitter end in the war, and *hensoppers*, who surrendered, also cut across other boundaries. Above all, the stress laid by Botha and Smuts on a new white South African identity, which might include all those who sought their future in the country, made many Afrikaners uneasy. Dutch Reformed ministers, who played a major role in social reconstruction after the war, opposed Smuts's secular attitude to education and his lack of commitment to the future of Dutch in schools. They started Christian National Dutch-medium schools. Afrikaner women who drew on the suffering experienced in the concentration camps were amongst the most insistent on resisting cultural compromises.

J. B. M. Hertzog, like Smuts a former general and ambitious lawyer, took up the fight to extend Dutch in schools and enforce full bilingualism in the civil service. The leading politician in the Free State, he was not explicitly Republican but advocated more tenuous links with empire. His insistence on language equality would greatly facilitate Afrikaner access to the expanding bodies of state. It was the clarion call for the long Afrikaner trek into the bureaucracy. Botha tried to contain Hertzog within the SAP, but their disagreements were sufficient to split them asunder at the very moment that Afrikaners achieved control of the country. Hertzog formed a separate National Party in 1914.

Political unity was further tested when South Africa went to war as part of the Empire in 1914 and invaded German-held Namibia. Afrikaner opponents of the invasion rebelled. They included Boer generals and *bittereinders* in the South African War, some of whom had been exiled, nursing a nostalgic republicanism. Some Afrikaner members of the newly formed South African Defence Force were uneasy about the demise of the old Commando system and the imposition of 'colonial training methods, uniforms, ranking systems' and 'disciplinary codes' (Swart 1998: 751). Their support was largely from poorer whites, in rural areas such as the Western Transvaal, marginalized by the changes sweeping through the agrarian world. A prophet, van Rensburg, emerged to articulate rebel anxieties in the folk language of dreams and visions. Although the threat of a split in the army made the rebellion potentially dangerous, it was controlled by Botha and Smuts at the head of Afrikaner troops. They then led their forces against the Germans in Namibia and East Africa. It had been part of their aim to win control of the former territory; they were given the Mandate to rule it at the Treaty of Versailles.

Hertzog did not rebel, but his party became more closely associated with Afrikaner cultural movements and rural demands throughout the country. Botha's death in 1919 left Smuts and the SAP very vulnerable. The 1920 election was indecisive: Hertzog's Nationalists became the largest party with 44 seats to the SAP's 41; the Unionists retained 25, while the largely English-speaking white Labour Party peaked at 21. Smuts, now being absorbed into the highest councils of the British Empire, was pushed into an alliance with the Unionists, who had shed their most ardent pro-imperialists. Although Smuts was able to retain some Afrikaner support, Hertzog won a close election in 1924 in alliance with the white Labour Party. Nationalists and Labour formed the Pact government.

Nationalist politicians won support not only because they espoused Afrikaner causes, but also because they took up the issue of white poverty. The closing of the frontier, rinderpest, the South African War, indebtedness, and agrarian change all contributed to increase rural poverty after the turn of the century. Especially in the Cape, where the boundaries between white and coloured could be fluid, poor whites were seen to be losing their identity. Afrikaners were found to intermarry or cohabit with English-speakers or, in non-racial zones of the towns, with black women. In an era of intensified racial ideology, poverty was increasingly defined in racial terms as poor whiteism, requiring particular attention. New social explanations of poverty and the role of the state in combating it placed the issue high on the political agenda.

White poverty found its main expression in urbanization, though the process often involved a move to small towns first. Some rural skills proved valuable. In turn-of-the-century Johannesburg, van Onselen (1982) demonstrates, Afrikaners ran small brick-making works and animal-drawn transport. Many were again marginalized by large-scale industries, as well as trams and railways. Unskilled or supervisory jobs on the railways and mines were an alternative, but here they had to compete more directly with blacks. Many saw great advantage in defining themselves as white and seeking protection from the state. English-speaking white workers, some in craft-based trade unions, did not work to include the Afrikaner poor in their organizations. Afrikaner politicians, by contrast, saw both the potential of harnessing, and the danger of ignoring, this group, who, unlike poor blacks, had the vote. Smuts was portrayed in cartoons sitting alongside Hoggenheimer, symbol of capitalist greed, or spoken of as too *slim* (wily) and untrustworthy. He could not compete with Afrikaner exclusivists, despite his legislation effectively restricting apprenticeships to whites (1922) and intensifying urban segregation (1923).

Afrikaner churchmen and politicians were adept at turning social deprivation to the national cause. But even the religious field had to be fought for. Louis Leipoldt, medical man, writer, and author of cookbooks, documented Afrikaner beliefs in witchcraft, ghost stories, healing, and prophecy in his *Bushveld Doctor* (1937). Less-educated rural Afrikaners weaved these ideas, some derived from Africans, into their version of Protestant Christianity. In town, some were attracted to fundamentalist churches. Johanna Brandt, daughter of a minister, organizer of resistance in occupied Pretoria during the South African War, and co-founder of the women's section of Hertzog's party, was one such unconventional religious leader; her philosophy included millennial beliefs. Orthodox Dutch Reformed ministers preached against such manifestations of popular consciousness. One of the victories of Afrikaner nationalism in these years was both to incorporate and partly to conquer popular folk beliefs with a modernizing nationalist message. African ministers and politicians were less successful in this task.

Hertzog was able to ally with English-speaking workers and win power in 1924, not least because they were so bitter about Smuts's role over a period of intense industrial conflict from 1907 to 1922. South African white workers had to replay nineteenth-century European struggles for trade-union recognition, shorter working days, and reasonable conditions. Death rates from silicosis, miners' phthisis, and tubercular diseases were very high on the Rand. White miners were initially perhaps even more susceptible than black, because they tended to stay for longer continuous periods on the mines. Research into Cornish miners who had worked in Johannesburg and died in Cornwall between 1900 and 1902 revealed an average age at death of 36.4 years old (Richardson and Burke 1978: 151). Of the eighteen leaders on the 1907 strike committee, fourteen died of phthisis before the next major strike in 1913 (Yudelman 1983: 93).

While working conditions were initially critical to the white miners' struggle, the issue that became central in the early decades of the century was more particular to South Africa: the protection of jobs on a racial basis. Although skilled workers from Europe had been required for the initial development of the mines, demand for them gradually declined. The fact that African workers also acquired some skills allowed a dilution of tasks. An increasing proportion of whites worked above ground or in supervisory rather than skilled roles. Mining companies knew that they could employ black miners for less. In this context, white workers wanted to defend their access to certain tasks such as blasting. They also wished to control the intensity of work. The 1907 strike was triggered by a dispute over how many drills should be under one supervisor. Afrikaners were drawn onto the mines to replace strikers. Over the next decade, the proportion of South African-born white miners steadily increased—from 17 per cent in 1907 to 50 per cent in 1918. They tended to rely even more than immigrant workers on racially based agreements and legislation.

In 1907, the new Afrikaner government of the Transvaal brought out the troops against strikers. Free-born Englishmen, the former *uitlanders*, proclaiming their civil rights, found no imperial support. Government intransigence and the imposition of martial law during the 1913 strike helped to transform it rapidly from a more limited action to a general withdrawal of white labour from the gold mines. After a mass meeting, the offices of the Johannesburg *Star*, owned by mining interests, were set alight. The government deployed British troops from the imperial garrison left in the country after Union, killing over 100 strikers. Botha and Smuts were forced to negotiate, but, when labour leaders tried to push their advantage in 1914, Smuts made pre-emptive arrests. Facing 70,000 troops in a reorganized army, the miners stood down; Smuts illegally deported the leaders. The Riotous Assemblies Act, subsequently often invoked against blacks, was passed to control white strikers.

White workers did succeed in achieving some of their industrial aims, including Union recognition, an eight-hour day, and further protection of some categories of employment in the 1911 Mines and Works Act. The principle of a job colour bar was not seriously in dispute. Though white workers cost on average about twelve times more than black, mine-owners found advantages in maintaining racial divisions and using established lines of domination. It was the exact proportion of whites in the labour force that remained contested. In the period of high inflation after the First World War, companies feared that their lower-grade ore would become uneconomic to mine. Although their wages were under pressure, white miners did not come out on strike during the peak years of industrial action, locally and internationally, between 1918 and 1920. They did not support the black miners' strike of 1920. But, after a concerted effort was made to reduce white mine employment, they struck again in 1922. Socialist ideas spread, a broader revolt developed, and a workers' government seemed momentarily possible. Strikers, including Afrikaners, also drew on their military experience in the First World War—they developed an insurrectionary 'commando structure' even mobilizing cavalry-like 'horse-borne formations' (Krikler 1999: 238).

The suggestion that the 1922 Rand rebellion could have changed the face of South African politics underestimates the remaining significance of the white rural population and the armed forces. The strike was suppressed by Smuts with even greater ruthlessness than he had previously demonstrated. Radical historians have also argued that the white working-class movement was finally defeated after 1922. The subsequent Industrial Conciliation Act (1924) sought to incorporate trade unions, restrict their capacity to initiate industrial action, and lay down tight legal control over disputes. If this was a defeat, it was hardly a devastating one. The percentage of whites in the mine labour force dropped temporarily from about 11 prior to the strike to 8 in

1922, but by 1926 it was back to 10 per cent. During the great expansion of the 1930s, white employment kept pace with black, so that by 1937 there were over 37,000 white miners, more than 11 per cent of the workforce. Real wages rose again from the mid-1920s and differentials between whites and blacks were maintained.

The idea of a defeat perhaps stems from reading too much into the political aims of these strikes. Although a radical syndicalist leadership emerged both in 1913 and 1922, the primary demands of many white workers over the longer term seem to have been security of employment and wages. Certainly there were socialists amongst them, such as Bill Andrews, who were initiators of a political tradition in South Africa that has survived to the present day. In some industries, where they were less threatened by black workers, trade unions were less concerned about statutory colour bars. But miners used their political strength to secure segregation and preferment in the labour market and colonial society—hence the slogan 'workers of the world unite and fight for a white South Africa' at the height of the Rand rebellion.

If, as Yudelman (1983) argues, there was a symbiotic relationship between the mining industry and the state, then the Pact election victory brought greater convergence between these two interests and white workers. The colour bar was entrenched and broadened during Hertzog's period of government from 1924 to 1933, partly through further legislation and partly in the 'civilized labour policy'. Civilized in this case unambiguously meant white. The compromises made by white workers in the mining industry were relatively insignificant, given the scale of protection elsewhere. Afrikaners, in particular, gained favoured access to employment in state-run enterprises such as the railways on a scale far greater than before and were paid at higher rates than blacks.

Although the contribution of agriculture should not be underestimated, mining provided a major basis for economic growth during the early decades of the twentieth century. Unlike Kimberley, the Rand did not become a single monopoly surrounded by a company town that ceased to grow. Its sheer size and range of demands stimulated developments in other sectors. Yet mining interests were not strongly in favour of broadly based domestic industrial development. Mine-owners wanted cheap food, cheap labour, and the capacity to import what manufactures they needed in an open colonial economy. They were answerable in part to foreign shareholders. Until the 1920s the logic of the gold mines pervaded economic and political policy. The mining industry was taxed lightly and domestic manufacturing industry was not significantly protected.

Such free-market approaches were not, however, uniformly applied. Liberal critics such as W. M. Macmillan in the 1920s argued that South Africa was effectively one country with one economy and that a freer labour market would increase national efficiency and development. Rising wages for blacks would hasten the growth of the internal market. Whites would no longer be threatened by undercutting if blacks were not so poor; all would benefit from a larger national cake.

Few South African whites recognized the degree of economic integration that had been achieved. They saw blacks as different rather than poor and most supported racial protection. The nature of industrialization, based around exports of primary products, diminished the interest of the major industrial and agricultural producers in their domestic consumers. Black workers were unlikely to buy gold, however generous their wages. With respect to labour, the mine-owners were not prepared to insist upon their supposedly free-market approach.

South Africa was not exceptional at this time in the degree of state intervention that began to characterize policy, only in the degree of segregation. While industrialization seemed to create the potential for social fluidity, it ultimately resulted in hardened racial divisions. That is why the radical historians of the 1970s and 1980s emphasized so strongly that capitalist growth was not a harbinger of liberal government or an inclusive political system. Economic growth interacted in intricate ways with the legacy of the frontier, changes in the countryside, and new racial thinking to produce increasingly systematic segregation. No one segment of the white population achieved all its aims, but most found some of their interests served under the segregationist umbrella. In the competition for shelter, immigrants became white and

Afrikaner identity was reinforced rather than diluted. The legacy of the war and intensity of impoverishment helped to ensure this outcome. The compromises that characterized late-nineteenth-century Cape parliamentary politics were undermined and the Transvaal's counter-conquest of the Cape was beginning.

# 4

# Black Responses and Black Resistance

## *The Black Elite and African Nationalism*

Solomon Plaatje, destined to be the first secretary of the South African Native National Congress (SANNC) in 1912, arrived in Kimberley in 1894. His Tswana-speaking forebears, some of whom had been Christians since the 1830s, acquired their Dutch surname when living with Griqua people. Plaatje was brought up on Lutheran missions near Kimberley and the town was an obvious place of employment for a promising product of their school. He joined the Kimberley Post Office, which in a late Victorian liberal gesture had staffed its telegraph department with graduates of Lovedale, the most prestigious black school in the colony. In 1898 Plaatje moved to Mafikeng as the court interpreter. He played an important role in the South African War, supplying the British forces with intelligence about Boer combatants and African communities.

Living at a German mission station on the periphery of a British colonial town peopled by Africans from different backgrounds, Plaatje became familiar with a range of cultures and languages. But it was the culture of the imperial outposts, Kimberley and Mafikeng, that most coloured his experience. Amongst the 20,000 or so African inhabitants of Kimberley were a small minority of several hundred more educated people, many of them English-speakers from leading Xhosa and Mfengu Christian families in the eastern Cape. Bound together by the churches, they created a distinct community vividly evoked in Brian Willan's biography (1984) of Plaatje. Some of the men held the franchise and were involved in the 1898 election contest between Henry Burton, a young liberal lawyer, and Cecil Rhodes for the Barkly

West parliamentary seat. They organized a South Africans Improvement Society, holding fortnightly debates on subjects historical and moral. Plaatje attended Shakespearian performances by a visiting British company at the Queen's theatre. A few of the black American Jubilee singers, who toured South Africa in 1895, stayed on in Kimberley and helped form a Philharmonic Society. An eclectic musical culture included the new African church choral music as well as adaptations of traditional songs, British ballads, and American spirituals. African cricketers formed The Eccentrics and Duke of Wellington teams.

This African elite was partly forged in the colonial world and claimed a place in the colonial order. But their position was anomalous. Though segregation was not yet rigid, many of their activities were restricted to their own community. Everywhere the barriers seemed to be moving up against them. Plaatje's perception that opportunities for mobility within colonial society were declining helped persuade him to leave the civil service in 1902 and start a newspaper in English and Tswana. As their capacity to influence policy declined, the elite looked for wider political constituencies. One turning point was in 1902, when British and Boer signatories of the Treaty of Vereeniging agreed 'to secure the just predominance of the white races'. Africans sensed they would not be rewarded for loyalty in the War. J. T. Jabavu's *Imvo*, expressing his gradualism, was challenged as the leading black newspaper. Jabavu had allied himself with those Cape liberals, such as Merriman and Burton, who jettisoned Rhodes in 1896 and worked with the Afrikaner Bond. Rhodes responded by funding a new eastern Cape black newspaper *Izwi Labantu*. *Izwi* editor A. K. Soga, son of the first black Presbyterian minister in South Africa, increasingly projected a more independent radical position, critical of big capital, segregation, and Jabavu's dependence on white politicians.

Together with Plaatje's paper, *Izwi* was associated with the foundation in 1902 of a Cape-based South African Native Congress (SANC), which aligned itself neither with the Bond nor with Jameson's Progressive Party, inheritor of Rhodes's mantle. A network of local organizations known as the *Iliso Lomzi* (eyes of the nation), or vigilance associations, proliferated alongside

Congress. In 1903 a Transvaal Native Congress was launched. Walter Rubusana, an SANC member, was elected to the Cape Provincial Council in 1910 in the Thembuland (Transkei) constituency, where almost half the registered voters were black. He was the only African ever to gain a seat in the Cape. The antipathy between him and Jabavu was such that Jabavu opposed his candidacy in 1914 and Rubusana failed to hold the seat.

In the western Cape F. Z. S. Peregrino, a West African who had lived in Britain and the USA, launched the *South African Spectator*, broadly aligned with the SANC. The African Political Organization (APO), founded in 1902, was less certain of its direction. Dr A. Abdurahman, from a Muslim family and British educated, led the APO from 1904, edited its newspaper, and organized missions to England in 1906 and 1909 to claim rights for coloured people in the former Boer Republics. By 1910 he was sharing political platforms with African leaders and calling for unity in opposition. But the APO was split on the issue of African membership and his constituency remained largely coloured and Cape based. The APO also maintained an uneasy relationship with the populist politicians of 'the stone', a large boulder on the slopes of Table Mountain that served as a Sunday meeting-place. And they all distanced themselves from the riots that exploded in Cape Town in 1906 at the height of the depression. Poor and unemployed people of all origins, clustered around District Six, participated. Mountain vagrants rushed into town looking to loot.

African leaders also arranged frequent deputations to England—notably in 1909, to oppose the terms of Union, and in 1914, following the promulgation of the Natives Land Act. It was not entirely clear that Britain had abandoned black interests to the settlers, nor was there much alternative. Chief Bambatha's brief rebellion in Natal in 1906, which was brutally suppressed, clearly demonstrated the hopelessness of violence. These appeals to the 'sense of common justice and love of freedom so innate in the British people' all failed, but the pro-imperial sentiments of the elite died hard.

John Dube was one of the most important early Congress diplomats. An American-educated minister who became the leading spokesman of the Natal *kholwa* (Christians), he laid particular stress on self-improvement through education. Influenced by the American model of Booker T. Washington's Tuskegee College, he founded a similar Ohlange Institute in Natal. He emphasized industrial as much as academic education, but placed less reliance on the goodwill of whites, more on the realization of black aspirations. Links with the USA were forged more widely by independent churches such as the African Methodist Episcopal Church. For those few who could raise the funds, university education at black American colleges was highly prized; it was not then obtainable in South Africa.

As the segregationist direction of white politics became clearer, Plaatje, Dube, and others were convinced that the time had come for them to be 'race leaders' (Odendaal 1981). A growing sense of South Africanism amongst whites had its mirror image in a more explicit attempt to create a more assertive African national identity. In 1912 various regional African organizations met in Bloemfontein in 'tophats and tails' to form the South African Native National Congress. Dube (President), Plaatje (Secretary), and Seme, a Transvaal-based lawyer, initially shaped its policies. A nominated upper house of chiefs did not function effectively but was important as a statement about Congress's all-inclusive ideology. Some chiefs were involved; Seme married into the Zulu royal house and the Swazi royal family provided funds for the first Congress newspaper *Abantu Batho* (Our People).

Although Congress leaders were redefining their role, they still tended to be suspicious of mass politics. Nevertheless, they were drawn into broader protests. At a local level, *Iliso Lomzi* groups were becoming involved in passive resistance against taxes and state intervention. As the Cape franchise became progressively diluted, so its defence became less of a preoccupation. Land issues, which potentially affected a far wider range of African people, became more central, and national leaders had the skills to assist in representing popular demands. J. T. Gumede, later president of the ANC, was long involved as a lawyer in the case of Tlokoa people in Harrismith, who were asserting claims to ancestral lands. The Natives Land Act galvanized Congress. Some of its leaders were personally affected as landowners or potential purchasers, but they also took up the general cause of African tenants. Plaatje was only one of the politicians who spoke widely against the Act and its implications (**Chapter 2**).

Jabavu initially supported the Land Act. He was certainly constrained by his loyalty to white liberal politicians, shareholders in his newspaper company. They argued for the protective elements of the Act in safeguarding and extending African reserves in a context where Afrikaner politicians, now in control of the Union, might alienate even more land from blacks. Jabavu and some rural communities echoed such views, prioritizing the entrenchment of reserved land rather than the right to compete on the land market. A spokesman in the Transkei noted: 'Supposing the whole of South Africa were today cut up into farms, and offered for sale to both white and blacks, what native millionaire would secure land for these millions of natives? . . . South Africa would at that moment become absolutely "A White Man's Country" and natives hurled headlong will-nilly into the mines' (Beinart 1982: 123). Congress politicians did not oppose African reserves and communal tenure, nor a degree of segregation on the land. They wanted to retain reserves plus the right to purchase and rent elsewhere. Some liberals and rural chiefs felt that, as there was no possibility of winning both, it was better to settle for the promises implied in the Land Act, despite its unfairness.

In 1913, the year of the Land Act and the Rand Strike, another issue that was to become a central to black politics—urban rights and passes—was highlighted by a major protest of African women in Bloemfontein. African women had not yet migrated in large numbers to the cities, and most municipal authorities did not attempt to impose restrictions on them. Bloemfontein was one of the few cities where the number of African women was nearly as high as men, and the Free State authorities demanded that women carry urban residential passes. Following the SANNC's foundation meeting in the city and an address by Charlotte Maxeke, its leading woman member, 5,000 signatures against passes were collected and a deputation sent to Cape Town. When arrests increased in 1913, women tore up their passes in the centre of town while police watched—thus starting a long tradition in South African protest politics. Imprisonment was met by passive resistance; the example of Gandhi's campaigns was invoked. Free State women, dubbed by papers 'our local black suffragettes', with cautious Congress support, eventually won one of the few victories by black political activists in these years.

Unlike Afrikaner nationalists, early African nationalists did not become strongly anti-imperial. They retained a liberal belief in multiracial civilization and citizenship in South Africa. Aside from some white liberals and socialists, they were the only political grouping at the time to articulate this goal. Their interpretation of non-racialism and their strategies for achieving it were often uncertain, as was their view about incorporating the uneducated masses. But they were not offering a black version of exclusive white South Africanism—whites as well as blacks were part of the nation. They opposed, at least in frequent rhetorical flourishes, the ethnic concerns beloved of Afrikaner politicians. Their politics was born in the optimism imbued by partial incorporation into an imperial world; their political edge came from the shattering of that optimism.

Far more so than their Afrikaner counterparts, the African elite was hampered by having to conquer divisions of language; they were having to create a new cultural identity rather than remould an old one. English seemed the most appropriate medium for their movement, but was not widely spoken and was the language of the conqueror. Despite new opportunities for mobility, problems of travel as well as communication were immense. Widespread illiteracy made it very difficult for educated leaders to transmit their ideas and develop a national political discourse. African newspapers were important in the formation of a new identity but had a relatively small circulation: *Imvo* at its height perhaps 4,000; the others all less than 2,000.

Indian political leaders, even more so than coloured, worked within their own diverse communities, attempting to weld them together and challenging the state to protect sectional rights and interests. Nevertheless, the political position of the Indian elite in the early twentieth century was in many ways similar to that of Africans. The literature concentrates on Mohandas Gandhi, who lived in South Africa from 1893 to 1914. Trained in London as a lawyer, Gandhi was employed to represent a firm of Durban Indian traders in a major legal case. He arrived in South Africa wearing a suit and a turban, believing he could bridge the European and Indian worlds. He left, at least metaphorically speaking, in a *dhoti*.

In some respects, Gandhi's political development paralleled that of African leaders. He started learning his politics shortly after arrival, when Natal settlers, flexing their political muscles on receipt of responsible government in 1892, were determined to undermine what few voting rights Indians had. Gandhi also claimed to have been thrown out of a first-class railway coach, an indignity that exactly expressed the ambiguous position of the black elite. Merchants in the Natal Indian Congress (1894) and the Transvaal British Indian Association led the defence of these rights. It was their position as traders and property-owners that initially concerned Gandhi. At this stage, he was still a supporter of imperial authority and assisted British forces in the South African War and the Bambatha rebellion. Like African leaders, he hoped to win moral authority and use this in bargaining for a better deal.

The British had been the shopkeepers and merchants of South Africa in the nineteenth century and resented Indian competition. Indians were well established in Natal and the Transvaal, but Britain upheld the Boer ban on their entry into the Free State. Indian traders were also prohibited by the Cape authorities from the Transkeian Territories. Attempts were made to register and control Indian traders in the Transvaal, the most valuable new retail market, between 1906 and 1909, and this provoked passive resistance protests led by Gandhi. Like African leaders, he recognized the centrality of the press in politics and worked through the newspaper *Indian Opinion*.

Gandhi's *satyagraha*, soul force and passive resistance, drew on Western and Hindu ideas and was a method—already employed by African peasants—suited to the constituency that he wanted to mobilize: a relatively powerless group in a political context where settlers had a monopoly of coercion. *Satyagraha* also offered ideas of community and identity in a fragmented Indian population. Although Swan argues that Gandhi's role in mass protest has been exaggerated, his campaigns undoubtedly attracted attention and provided a cathartic focus for Indian politics.

A new generation of colonial-born Indians, children of indentured workers, launched organizations that took up broader issues such as the £3 tax on ex-indentured workers designed to push them back into work or return to India. In 1913 a strike on the Natal coal mines was followed by a march to the Transvaal and massive withdrawal of labour on the sugar fields—probably the largest strike there had been on the estates. Gandhi did not play a major role in mobilizing sugar workers, but their strike gave him a lever when he met Smuts and negotiated a withdrawal of the tax. Indian politicians and the Viceroy ensured that for once the Imperial government did not turn a blind eye to events in South Africa.

More so than educated African leaders, Gandhi was immersed in the racial language of the time, and it clearly appealed to some members of his constituency of Indian merchants. 'If there is one thing which the Indian cherishes more than any other,' he said, 'it is the purity of type'. His political language made clear distinction between 'British Indians', 'coolies', and 'Kaffirs', and he did not try to win African support (Stone 1990). Nevertheless, Gandhi's political thinking did broaden dramatically in South Africa; his political skills guided Indian protest and provided a model for others. The techniques of resistance that he forged were to have a major impact in India. He did also have wide political contact with Jewish and Christian intellectuals and with African leaders such as Dube, whose Ohlange Institute was close to Gandhi's Phoenix rural settlement in Inanda, Natal. It was very difficult for any leader to organize across ethnic lines at the time in South Africa.

## Chieftaincy, Ethnicity, and Rural Protest

The problems of nationalist and elite politicians were not simply those of transmitting their message. Though the ANC became the major vehicle for African political expression, there is no simple continuity from Plaatje's time to Mandela's. Nationalism was not the predominant response to colonization at the time. The history of black political opposition is certainly rich, but more diverse, less predictable, and less united than has been supposed. The fact of oppression did not necessarily determine the trajectory of responses.

One aspect of this diversity was the very different social roots and experiences of African, Indian, coloured, as well as poor-white subject communities. As important, any analysis of African political responses must start with an understanding that the chiefdoms were discrete and neither politically nor culturally united. Subsequently, colonization was piecemeal and responses to it localized. Colonial forces were frequently able to find African allies or levies, such as Mfengu people in the eastern Cape or Swazi in the Transvaal. Within chiefdoms there were often divisions as to how to respond to missionaries, or settler encroachments. Early colonial rule through 'loyal' intermediaries shaped local political conflict and left a deep legacy in many rural areas that their opponents did not find easy to forget. Political thinking and action grew out of real and self-conscious local rural communities, where the great majority of African people still lived. In particular, the political processes surrounding the remnant chieftaincies remained important.

Conquest, white rule, common experiences on the land and in towns began to define general political issues, but people from different rural areas were absorbed into the labour market in different ways. Whereas the urban world and workplace could provide the basis for new identity and action in the early twentieth century, these were also contexts for ethnic redefinition as communities competed for employment and space. The dominant colonial obsession with race and racial distinctions of all kinds sometimes fed into the ideas of the dominated. Ethnicity has had a bad name amongst opponents of apartheid, and understandably so, as the South African state systematically used divide-and-rule strategies founded on ethnic categories. But it is important to recognize the salience of cultural as well as class divisions amongst the dominated.

Moreover, local identities and associations could be unifying social forces for the multitude of pre-colonial societies and immigrant groups that made up South Africa's population. Sometimes they were critical in defending the interests of the weak, enlarging their political horizons and enabling them to establish leverage in a new context. Indian and coloured people, Zulu and Mfengu, poor whites and white workers were defining themselves as such as well as being defined in the early twentieth century. Coloured people in Cape Town instituted a popular carnival in the late nineteenth century; it became an annual event in which they temporarily claimed the city centre. Such identities were not necessarily exclusive and they were often fluid. People could conceive of themselves as clan member, Zulu, and African; as coloured, Malay, and South African.

The politics of Plaatje, Dube, Gandhi, and Abdurahman were of limited relevance to the great majority of Africans who remained on the land. Rural political struggles tended to be defensive, though they were often also innovative. They were geared to maintaining access to resources such as land, forests, and grazing, which were critical to the survival of peasant families. New impositions and taxes or tighter controls over the way people managed their environment or livestock were often the spur to mobilization. This could take many different forms from polite petitioning to rural riot. Age-old peasant strategies of delay, demands for consultation, refusal to listen, silent boycott, and attempts to restrict the state's knowledge were frequently deployed.

The fact that chieftaincy remained an important focus of politics did not mean that all chiefs received support. The institution itself had many layers, from paramounts of large, recently conquered chiefdoms to local headmen of distant royal descent. Claims to office were often disputed, the more so because the state recognized, paid, and extended limited powers to many members of chiefly lineages as government headmen. Disputes over genealogy and succession were often intertwined with broader political issues. Chiefs who attracted popular following were likely to be those who resisted colonial instrusions, but 'loyals' might have strong support in particular locations where there was a tradition of cooperation or Christian influence. Chieftaincy could be a focus both of resistance and of ethnic expression.

Bambatha's rebellion in Natal in 1906 was the most dramatic incident of rural protest in the first decade of the century—as much for the intensity of white reaction as for the degree of black mobilization. Conquest and annexation of Zululand was completed only in the 1890s. Natal's colonial government was dominated by white farmers and in 1903 a Commission was set up to carve coastal land out of Zulu territory for the expansion of settler sugar farming. Elsewhere, African tenants, especially those on the best-placed farms near railway lines, bore the brunt of social pressures. When the post-war recession began to bite in 1904, the Natal government decided to ease its revenue problems and labour shortages by levying a poll tax on all those who did not already pay hut tax. 'If Natal liked to revert to medieval methods of taxation,' a British Colonial Office official commented, 'I do not see that it is any business of ours' (Marks 1970: 142).

There was a new focus, as well as new causes, for dissent. Dinuzulu, the Zulu king, returned from exile in St Helena in 1897 when Zululand passed from British to Natal rule. His Usuthu royal house became associated with a revival of 'national feeling and the desire to remain one people under English rule' (Marks 1970: 98). The term Zulu itself, more strictly applicable to those who had been part of the Zulu kingdom rather than Africans of different origins in Natal, began to be used more widely by both officials and Africans to refer to both. Whether he wished it or not, Dinuzulu's name was invoked as a symbol of resistance.

It also became associated with other rumours—that Africans should kill white goats, pigs, and fowl and destroy tools of European manufacture. Pigs and lard were thought to attract lightning, and people were told that, if they deposited lard on hillsides, they would be saved and lightning would strike those who attempted to collect the £1 poll tax. Whites feared that the killing of animals was a warning to them, but this is unlikely. Episodes of mass animal slaughter had a long history in South Africa. The best known of these, the Xhosa cattle-killing of 1857, was perhaps an extension of the sacrifices that were so central in African religions—a search for purity and rebirth through mass communication with ancestors. There were a number of mass pig-killings in east-coast African districts until the 1920s, following prophecies aimed at cleansing society by purging an introduced animal. Such millennial or purificatory ideas were a persistent feature of rural politics in the early twentieth century, but they were not universal nor did they preclude more instrumental political behaviour at the same time.

Many Zulu chiefs refused to cooperate in paying the tax, provoking dispersed confrontations and arrests. Bambatha, a deposed chief in Umvoti district, was a farm tenant already subject to court action over rent demands. In an encounter with the police, his people used the royal cry of Usuthu. Shula Marks, historian of the uprising, sees it as a 'reluctant rebellion' and largely restorationist. An African witness to the subsequent enquiry explained that Bambatha 'went to extremes simply because he was tied hand and foot by the network of troubles in which he found himself . . . like a beast which on being stabbed rushes about in despair' (Marks 1970: 208) If the rebellion was reluctant, its suppression was not: twenty-four whites died and perhaps 4,000 Africans. After his capture, Bambatha's head was cut off. Dinuzulu was exiled again, this time to the Transvaal. The limits of armed resistance were demonstrated, but the reputation of the royal house, uncorrupted by having to work within the system, was enhanced.

The issues surrounding the Bambatha rebellion were echoed in other parts of South Africa. In the Cape, the state's attempts to extend the Council system, based on the Glen Grey Act of 1894, became a major issue. Some self-consciously progressive rural Christians thought that the system offered hope of rural improvement. But an additional ten-shilling levy on all hut-tax payers guaranteed the councils' unpopularity. Many traditionalists also feared that appointed councils would be 'puppet governments' dominated by those 'who had sold themselves' to the state (Beinart and Bundy 1987: 229). Educated radicals argued that councils were the basis of a segregated system of local government, with only advisory capacity, which further threatened common political rights. Although councils were generally implemented by 1930, it was around their extension that some of the most important new political alliances formed between dissident Christians, chiefs, and people.

For people in the countryside, new laws such as those governing access to game or forests could criminalize what had been everyday activity. The introduction of cattle-dipping to combat East Coast fever, a tick-borne disease, was equally fraught. At issue were different perceptions of disease and how it should be dealt with. Restrictions on the movement of cattle struck at the heart of rural life, hampering transhumance, sales, and cattle transfers for marriage. Some educated rural men who were substantial livestock-owners appreciated the arguments for dipping and saw it as beneficial. Many other rural Africans felt that such regulation truly made them subjects of the state by extending the government's reach over one of their most prized assets.

Protests were essentially about the extent of control and fines levied for breaches of the regulations. In three districts of East Griqualand between 1914 and 1917, men took to the hills with rusty rifles retained from anti-colonial wars and blew up dipping tanks with dynamite abducted from road construction parties. Trading stores were looted and telegraph wires cut. These were local riots that fizzled out quickly rather than rebellions. But disputes about how to respond to intervention continued to feed political tensions within African communities throughout the country. The violence that characterized Msinga district, northern Natal—so that the area became a byword in South Africa for revenge killings—had roots in nineteenth-century conflicts, overlaid by disputes over land and state intervention in the twentieth.

African people who lived on farms faced different impositions from those experienced in the reserves. Isolated and unprotected, their direct action, such as ham-stringing cattle, cutting fences, and going slow at work, tended to be dispersed and individual. Mobility was often the best defensive strategy, though difficult where large communities tried to maintain their social cohesion. For some on the farms the best option seemed to be in playing the segregationist game and seeking restoration of land. The African tenants of Harrismith district in the Free State, whom Gumede helped to represent, were on prime maize territory. They claimed their land had been sold from under their feet by an unscrupulous Afrikaner official in the nineteenth century. When legal cases and a deputation to Britain failed, they identified themselves as a tribe with a chief to claim reserved land. They were unsuccessful and many ended up 'everlastingly moving from one place to another ... a nation sorrowing for our country' (Beinart *et al.* 1986: 247).

Redefining ethnic identity on the farmlands was not simply an instrumental way of trying to acquire land. People identifying themselves as Ndzundza Ndebele in the southern Transvaal were best known in the twentieth century for their elaborate 'traditional' patterns of dress and house decoration—highly attractive to photographers. Yet they suffered a particularly brutal experience of dispossession. A small chiefdom of perhaps 10,000 people in the 1870s, based around a strongly fortified village, the Ndzundza sided with the British and Swazi in the conquest of the Pedi in 1879. In the 1880s they came into conflict with the newly restored republican Transvaal government: their capital was burnt down, their chief imprisoned, their land largely turned into farms, and many people indentured to Boers. The South African War provided some of the Ndzundza, scattered on farms throughout the Transvaal, with an opportunity to escape and regroup. Their traditionalism grew out of their quest for identity and attempts to reconstitute families split by conquest. Most remained as farm tenants, but after some decades succeeded in registering themselves as a recognized 'tribe' and competed successfully for a reserve. Their decorative traditions, a reworking of pre-colonial motifs, were partly an expression of individual artistic skill, partly a collective assertion.

At Bulhoek in the eastern Cape, resistance was framed by fierce religious rather than ethnic commitment. Enoch Mgijima, from a Mfengu Methodist family, had formed his own church of Israelites in 1912. Guided by visions and prophesying the end of the world, he established a religious community in 1919 who saw themselves as chosen and awaited the coming of the Lord. Settled on land to which they were not legally entitled, and refusing to pay taxes, the Israelites soon came into conflict with the authorities. They asked, unsuccessfully, to be left alone 'for the purpose of praying and fearing God's wrath which is coming upon the whole world' (Edgar 1988: 15). In 1921 a police contingent was sent to disperse the 3,000-strong community. After protracted negotiations, white-robed Israelites ran towards the police and were mown down by gunfire, leaving nearly 200 dead.

## Popular Struggles in the 1920s

Although rural responses and political movements appear fragmented and localized, difficult to incorporate into regional or national struggles, it should not be suggested that peasants were simply backward looking, ultra religious, and unable to make broader political linkages. In order to discern more general trends it is important to turn again to the large towns. The Rand was the biggest centre of African urban population; by 1920, nearly 100,000 blacks were employed in non-mining activities and a further 200,000 on the mines. Though many of these were migrant workers, housed in compounds and barracks, urban slumyards and locations were growing rapidly. East Rand mineworkers, faced with declining real wages as prices inflated after the First World War, boycotted mine stores in 1918. Participants were largely migrants from Mozambique, then still the most numerous and well-established segment of the workforce and most dependent on wage income.

Soon afterwards, white power workers plunged the city into darkness for five nights and were awarded a large wage increase. Their action was followed by African municipal employees working in the sanitary services who asked for a more modest rise. Johannesburg, sited for its gold, had no natural channel for effluent, and the municipality, slow to develop underground sewage systems, operated nightsoil collections. By 1918, some 6,000 Africans were employed as 'bucket boys', mostly Bhaca migrants from the Transkei and southern Natal. A distinct urban presence, innovators in dress and urban magic, they were probably originators of the gumboot dance where teams of men stamp and slap their boots in complex rhythms. This kind of ethnic specialization by particular groups of workers—other examples include Zulu washermen and rickshaw-pullers—was not unusual nor did it preclude organization. It could provide the kind of solidarity that men at work required to launch united action in the era before trade unions.

The 'bucket boys' were dealt with harshly and their punishment sparked renewed urban protest. The Transvaal leadership of Congress was drawn into a more radical working-class politics and in 1919 organized a campaign to boycott and destroy passes. In 1920 black mineworkers staged a major stoppage following the arrest of two miners. Led by Pedi and Shangaan workers, the strike had wide support—a figure of 71,000, or one-third of the total, is often quoted. Again it was largely self-organized migrant workers, drawing on networks of compound solidarity, who led the strike, and it was difficult for them to coordinate and sustain their action. Nevertheless, it encouraged mine-owners in their determination to ease the job colour bar that in turn helped precipitate the 1922 white Rand revolt.

In addition to a more explicit worker consciousness, ideas of black self-assertion suffused urban communities. Black American influences, already widespread in independent churches and in music, were extended by advocates of Garveyism. Marcus Garvey's radical black consciousness and back-to-Africa movement, which had found widespread support in US cities, did start branches in South Africa. But it was more significant in adding muscle to the language of black unity and protest. 'Amelika' became a symbol of freedom.

The South African African National Congress (ANC) was formally renamed in 1925, when it also adopted the anthem 'Nkosi Sikel' i-Afrika' (God Bless Africa) and the green, black, and gold flag. Symbols of unity made it no easier to steer a path, in a segregationist era, between liberalism, rural traditionalism, and urban radicalism. Regional organizations tended to go their own way. Transvaal leaders were drawn briefly into workers' issues, the eastern Cape remained more concerned with older questions of the vote and land, while western Cape leaders espoused Garveyite ideas. A breakaway independent Cape ANC tried to organize rural farmworkers. Dube in Natal was equivocal about segregation policy and, ousted from the presidency in 1917, cemented his links with the Zulu king. The movement could not establish a role as intermediary with the state; officials preferred to deal with rural chiefs and headmen or members of the new councils. Although the national leadership swung in a radical direction in

1927 under Gumede, the ANC soon reverted to a more conservative position and, lacking national coherence, failed to attract a mass following. White liberals and the mining industry worked hard to moderate black leadership through the Joint Councils movement, where whites and blacks met together to discuss social and political issues.

The ANC was partly supplanted in the 1920s by the Industrial and Commercial Workers' Union of South Africa (ICU) and its various offshoots, which attracted those who sought a more radical political vehicle. An analysis of the rise and fall of the ICU helps to clarify some of ideas and strategies necessary to create a mass movement at the time, but also the problems of doing so. Launched in 1919 in the Cape Town docks, the ICU drew on the heritage of trade unionism in the Cape, which had been less sharply divided by race. Ports and railheads have often been the crossroads for people, ideas, and political organization in colonial Africa.

The ICU rapidly became a general rather than a craft or industrial union, highly adaptable to the demands of disparate groups of workers, tenants, and peasants throughout South Africa. Clements Kadalie, a mission-educated migrant worker from Malawi 2,000 miles to the north, became leader. While it drew some support from the same communities as the ANC, the ICU's reach was greater and links with Congress soon faltered. Early successes included a major strike of both African and coloured workers in Port Elizabeth in 1920. As so often in this period of Smuts's premiership, the episode ended in tragedy; police fired upon a crowd, killing twenty-four.

From the mid-1920s the ICU took up the cause of rural tenants and spread rapidly through the countryside. Membership perhaps briefly exceeded 100,000 by the late 1920s—far outstripping the ANC—and the movement reached to Zimbabwe and Malawi. Its leaders could talk the language of trade unionism, workers' rights, and wages; they also stressed black unity and nationalism, and advocated black commercial opportunity and an African Christianity. Members of the Communist Party, founded in 1921, briefly became involved in the mid-1920s, when they ceased to prioritize white workers. But Kadalie, anxious about his control and uneasy about communist ideas, expelled them in 1926. Kadalie was charismatic and ambitious, a rousing if sometimes bombastic speaker, who did not easily work in a collective or subordinate position.

ICU influence in the rural areas was strongest in the regions undergoing rapid transition towards capitalist agriculture, such as the eastern Transvaal. It also attracted a following in Umvoti district, Natal, former home of Bambatha, where African labour tenants were being evicted or squeezed for more work. Local ICU leaders married Zulu nationalism with claims for the rights of tenants to land. Despite the highly dispersed rural workforce, wage claims were advanced by work stoppages. Violent incidents studded the conflict that exploded when gravestones were desecrated in Greytown's white cemetery and the ICU offices were razed to the ground in response.

The ICU's mushroom growth was not sustained. It fragmented into regional groups in the face of state repression and amidst accusations of corruption against the leadership. Kadalie launched an Independent ICU in East London and in 1930 the city was rocked by a major strike. When Kadalie was arrested (and tried to call off the strike), local organizers sustained the action for nearly six months, drawing in not only dock and railway workers, but domestic servants and women beer-brewers in the locations. They mobilized in support of their right to brew, which had been severely curtailed by the municipal council. In this phase of radicalism, Independent ICU leaders espoused a powerful anti-white rhetoric, invoking separatist Christianity and, in a striking image, a black Jesus.

None of the ICU successor groups was able to cement a lasting organizational framework. The depression, unemployment, failure to deliver on promises, ideological differences, and personal squabbles rendered the movement moribund by the early 1930s. Some historians have argued that populism and lack of an industrial strategy were its downfall. But it was the one black movement that was able simultaneously to develop some national organization and to secure, on occasion, mass local support amongst disparate and divided communities. Industrial unionism was in its infancy amongst black workers and was not an alternative as a means of attracting a mass following. The ICU's flexibility enabled it to bridge town and countryside, although it was sometimes captured by its diverse rural constituencies and could become a catalyst for protests that were not essentially union struggles.

The ICU was not the only movement that attempted to fuse rural idioms and nationalist politics. In Herschel district, bordering Lesotho and the Free State, state attempts to enforce Councils radicalized the peasantry. In 1922 local women, inspired by events on the Rand, boycotted trading stores. When the magistrate tried to register their land in 1925, they boycotted mission schools, because the teachers were seen to be sympathetic to the government. Many joined African churches and some independent schools were started; for rural Christian women, one recalled, age-old taboos such as the prohibition on handling cattle were breaking down. Protestors formed themselves into a religious and political front called the *Amafelandawonye* (people who die together in one place) and called for local self-rule under a popular chief.

The *Amafela* were sufficiently organized to sustain a movement over some years, develop their own political ideas, and call in help from the ANC in Cape Town. Wellington Buthelezi, a product of Lovedale school, was another of their champions. He made his living as a itinerant populist politician, evangelist, and vendor of patent medicines in the Cape and Natal. His Garveyite ideas, celebrating black pride and self-help, resonated well with militant rural anti-colonialism; he helped to set up schools and churches. Elsewhere, his movement was associated with millennial and purificatory messages, including pig-slaughter. In some versions, it was said that non-believers would find their homes burnt by bombs dropped from aeroplanes flown by American blacks come to liberate South Africa. Buthelezi identified strongly with the widespread rural sense that help would come from 'Amelika' and was far more attuned than ANC leaders to the separatist impulses in rural politics. The idea of liberation by aeroplane imaginatively inverted control of that new instrument of power that Smuts had used to quell protest.

Christianity was one of the binding forces of 1920s radicalism and Africanist thinking. It was still not the majority black religion, but its language reached far beyond the old mission communities. Some of the early independent African churches had fragmented further by the 1920s. They were joined by a new religious force—fundamentalist Apostolic and Zionist churches. Most of these had their roots in the USA but adapted rapidly to the South African context incorporating African symbolism and practices. As charismatic leaders jostled for members and churches were absorbed in local communities, many split again. A bewildering array of denominations emerged; Sundkler listed nearly 1,000 African churches by 1945.

The attractions of Christianity were many and complex. For early converts missions had often been a refuge; conversion was also a route to literacy and education. Christianity provided universal belief and networks as well as a more individualist moral alternative to the bonds of rural African communality. Christians themselves established self-concious communities with a strong associational life and new modes of interaction. The Bible had been translated into a number of African languages in the nineteenth century, was widely available, and an important means of basic instruction. In the 1920s messages of political as well as religious redemption were often drawn from it. Historians are increasingly emphasizing spiritual as well as instrumental and social factors in the remarkably rapid spread of diverse churches amongst the poor. As a religion of sacrifice, blood, saints, spirits, purification, and redemption, Christianity had much in common with pre-colonial African beliefs. The biblical world, evoking a pre-industrial and patriarchal society, clearly resonated with African ideas. Increasingly, Christianity was moulded by African people into forms they found useful. Women, in particular, were the backbone of many churches.

By this time women were the majority in most rural reserve districts, because so many men were migrants. By contrast, they were a minority in town. Last off the land, they found it most difficult to secure niches in the urban labour market. Some did move as wives, while others came to escape conflicts and restrictions at home, or as migrant workers themselves. Women in town had to earn money either for themselves or because the wages for

African men were so low. Domestic service increasingly opened up to them; those nearer the white suburbs took in laundry. But many African women earned their keep on the peripheries of the urban economy, renting out rooms, selling sexual services, or more especially, brewing home-made maize and sorghum beer for sale to the large number of urban men. Beer was central to African rural life: a means of using grain; an important part of the adult diet; a lubricator of ceremonies and celebrations. It was also the medium of payment for labour after communal work parties. African women carried their rural skills into the urban areas, much as Afrikaner brick-makers and transport riders had done, and adapted their practices to sell beer for cash, sometimes making it stronger and more quickly.

The authorities generally frowned upon such sales. Manufactured alcohol, especially spirits, which were thought to be destructive of industrial discipline and moral fibre, was banned to all but a few exempted middle-class Africans. Only weak maize beer, incorporated into the compound diet for nutritional reasons, was allowed on the mines. Durban municipality tried to raise money from monopolizing production and sale in beer halls; elsewhere domestic brewing for consumption was allowed, but brewing for sale was widely restricted. Urban women were thus deprived of potential income, and police raids, searches, and conviction for petty criminal offences became everyday experiences. The right to brew and the politics of liquor were key issues, a trigger of riots in Natal in 1929 and important in the 1930 East London strike.

The majority of workers in the cities and mines were still male migrants who retained a strong attachment to their rural homes. Migrant workers did take part in strikes, in the ICU, even in Congress politics. But this type of politicization was not their central experience and many were involved in other kinds of associations. Youths and young men predominated in some spheres of employment, such as domestic service in Natal and the Transvaal. Those from the same rural districts sometimes congregated in towns or compounds. At home, many were involved in dance, stick-fighting, and courting groups, which met regularly. These were transposed to town, where they took on a new form.

*Amalaita* groups in Natal and the Transvaal were one of the most striking examples. The name came into use soon after the turn of the century in Durban to describe unruly African youth gangs. It was probably derived from English, perhaps from the idea that violence was like lighting a fire. An African newspaper suggested that youthful miscreants would ask for money to light their way, in the same way as African doctors called for their fees. The *amalaita* were not one group, but a name given to a range of street gangs and youth associations. Accounts tell of them marching four abreast through the streets of Durban, colourfully dressed and playing mouth organs, ready to beat unprotected lone youths.

The *amalaita* were Zulu-speakers in Natal, but, in Johannesburg and Pretoria, Pedi youths from the eastern Transvaal formed similar associations. Some were simply dance and sport-fighting groups for domestics on their days off. Some developed a more elaborate hierarchy of *Morena* (chief), captains, and sergeants. Up to 100 strong, gangs wore knickerbocker trousers and red cloth badges: the 'servile "boy" during the day' became the 'virile, manly, aggressive "Sergeant" of the night' (van Onselen 1982: ii. 59). It was the alleged rape of a white woman by such a gang that gave rise to a 'black peril' panic on the Rand in 1912.

In Natal competitive dances, called *Ngoma*, and pitched stick battles expressed a 'tightly-bounded sense of rural identity', a popular culture 'infused with military symbols and rituals drawn from a pre-colonial past' (la Hausse 1990*a*: 101). *Amalaita* gangs were anti-authoritarian and powerfully masculine but not easily available for broader political enterprises. They could, however, be mobilized. In Durban around 1929–30 the *amalaita* were absorbed into ICU activities and the beer-hall riots. Regimental anthems were sung at Union meetings, and cries of Usuthu, the Zulu royal praises, accompanied demands for the right of women to brew beer. Migrant culture differed from that of the more established urban Christian communities. For example, football, which was eventually to replace stick-fighting, made some impact on the Rand and in Durban but had limited following amongst migrant youth.

Masculinity was expressed not only in gangs and violence. In the 1910s and 1920s, most of the 200,000 African men employed in gold-mining lived in vast single-sex compounds. It was difficult for them to form relationships with urban women, expensive and dangerous for them to buy sexual services. Venereal diseases were, along with tuberculosis, amongst the most rapidly spreading in the subcontinent and in part followed the routes of long-distance migration. 'Mine marriages' and homosexuality emerged as a response, initially probably amongst Shangaan workers from Mozambique. Harries discusses widespread homosexuality, usually between established mineworkers and young new recruits, as including 'strong ties of affection' (1994: 200–8). For youths it could become an alternative rite of passage to manhood and introduced them rapidly to 'an influential network of male friends and fictive kin'. Amongst Mozambican workers, the relationship was often expressed in paternal terms, although in particular contexts youths displayed femininity in dress and behaviour.

Such relationships, however, also grew from coercive encounters and became locked into the hierarchies of the compound. Well-established older men would be in a position to threaten new recruits or offer *amankotshane* ('wives') gifts and favours in return for physical comforts. Some youths 'agreed to play the part of "women" in sexual activity in order more rapidly to become "men" at home' (Moodie 1994: 139): the quicker they improved their position in the harsh world of the mine, the sooner they could afford bridewealth and cattle at home. Compound managements generally colluded in these practices, although it was possible for youths to refuse.

Criminal gangs, distinct from the looser *amalaita* youth associations, spread in prisons and compounds in the early decades of the twentieth century. They boasted complex hierarchies, drawing both on Zulu regimental terms and those of colonial armies. Major mine and prison gangs, such as the largely Zulu Ninevites and the Isitshozi, mainly from Pondoland, also played some part in regulating homosexuality. They preyed on migrant workers returning home with cash as well as mine stores. They armed themselves with a range of dangerous weapons such as battleaxes and knives deployed in frequent fights for control and authority in and around the mining complexes. Criminal gangs drew in relatively small numbers, but they added to the harshness of the compound environment and provoked others to form defensive groups.

Male associations were a particular feature of the South African social landscape; in the absence of trade unions, these were the predominant forms of self-organization. They drew on rural influences but these were adapted in the mine and urban contexts. Control on the mines was exercised by white compound managers and supervisors through African *indunas* and *isibonda* (room reprentatives). *Fanakalo* (probably from *enza fanakalo*—do it like this), a restricted Zulu-based hybrid language of command and work, provided one general means of communication. Patterns of violent discipline in a 'world without women' (Breckenridge 1998: 675) tended to reinforce the development of a rugged masculinity. Ethnic housing in the mines was reflected in associational life. Wild-cat strikes or protests could result if too autocratic an approach was adopted; as in 1920, these could transcend ethnic boundaries, with workers negotiating between themselves and officials. But male solidarities could also take on an explosive ethnic character in compound 'faction fights', especially when established workers felt threatened by large numbers of new arrivals.

African political and social responses included many oppositional features, but the South African state was not without allies. Rural headmen took on major responsibility for maintaining order. African levies fought in nineteenth-century wars; there were black members of anti-stock theft units and, over a long period of time, a significant number of black policemen. The mines were seldom short of 'boss boys' and compound police. An African undercover constable reported in detail the proceedings of the meetings of the International Workers of Africa, the first socialist organization on the Rand to incorporate blacks. Similarly, records of ICU meetings in East London between 1928 and 1932 survive in the archives because they were reported by both white and black policemen. (Kadalie knew they were there and tried unsuccessfully to convert them.) Such 'loyalists' provided state officials with a constant if uneven stream of material, which has also been, ironically, an important source of information for historians of protest. They were of some significance in providing a ballast to the state as it implemented restrictive policies or segregationist measures.

Perhaps more important were the attempts made to reach accommodation with chiefs. Traditional authorities at various levels had been given some recognition in the Cape and Natal before Union; in effect they retained significant local judicial and administrative powers. Leading paramount chiefs were given substantial stipends by the state, more than a magistrate's salary; headmen received smaller amounts of about two or three times a migrant worker's earnings. The Native Affairs Department (NAD), which sought to enlarge its own powers by monopolizing the administration of Africans, and separating these functions from other state authorities, advanced this strategy in the Native Administration Act (1927). Appointment of chiefs and recognition of their courts was to be extended throughout the reserved areas. It was an important step in consolidating the system of state authority around a conservative rural hierarchy. Segregationist politicians sought to 'retribalize' African society in order to defuse national political organization.

By no means all chiefs supported the government. However, many sought to augment their authority, notably the Zulu king Solomon ka Dinuzulu and his supporters. Men like John Dube, former president of the ANC, became increasingly involved in the politics of the Zulu chieftaincy in the 1920s and helped launch a first version of *Inkatha*, the Zulu cultural movement. Dube was concerned by the radicalism of the ICU and thought that Solomon might provide an alternative political focus. A number of rural popular movements had focused on demands for chiefs who could protect their interests. Some Zulu workers and farm tenants had shown themselves to be sympathetic to ethnic appeals associated with the royal house. Even George Champion, ICU leader in Natal, whom Solomon had called 'irresponsible', 'dangerous', and 'an exploiter of "poor Native workers"', made his peace with the Zulu king (Marks 1986: 88). Segregationist ideologues and officials fed off and directed these varied rural political impulses with some success. The uncertainty of the African elite, which was under great social and economic pressure, and the failure of the ICU, helped undermine national movements by the early 1930s. Radical nationalist rhetoric so characteristic of the 1920s found fewer organizational homes or charismatic leaders to take it forward.

Historians have increasingly emphasized that Africans were not passive victims of colonization, oppression, and segregation, but were involved in a wide range of inventive political responses and innovative forms of action. The protests of African women in such diverse locations as Herschel, East London, Durban, and Potchefstroom are especially striking. At the same time, the limits of nationalist and working-class organization have been recognized. Africans could not mount any coordinated political action that might challenge the state. In many senses, the rural areas rather than the cities were the primary locus of political conflict in the 1920s. There were signs, albeit faint, in the ICU and similar organizations that a revolutionary or nationalist movement linking urban activists to the rural masses might have been possible, as in China or India. But this was not to be. State control was more far-reaching in South Africa. And the incomplete transformation of African societies, together with the thrust of state policy, opened areas of compromise in the reserves, where opportunities for African advance sometimes seemed more tangible. Some popular movements were actually separatist in character. The accommodations reached ultimately helped to defuse conflict in the inter-war years at the height of segregation.

The origins of the homelands can certainly be detected in this period. But other powerful influences were forged that influenced black politics in South Africa over many years: on the one hand, radical Africanist ideas and a shared sense of new African identity; on the other, a non-racial and non-violent political ideology, which took up the legacy of the Victorian Cape and developed the idea of black people as an oppressed majority in a white-dominated state.

# 5

# The Settler State in Depression and War, 1930–1948

## *The Settler State and Afrikaner Politics*

White authority was securely established after the tumultuous decades of the early twentieth century. Union was given political and administrative content and the challenges of popular protests were seen off by ruling groups. The great depression of the early 1930s signalled a sharp break in South African history. Hertzog's National Party, victorious in the late 1920s, succumbed to the economic whirlwind. As a result, Afrikaners lost their relatively united political front between 1934 and 1948. Smuts and the South African Party were brought into a national government that presided over a period of rapid economic expansion. From 1939 to 1948, Smuts again ruled as Prime Minister. Despite Afrikaner demographic preponderance, white party affiliations remained fluid. The broad accommodations that had been reached by different white interest groups under the umbrella of segregation did not preclude bitter divisions. White dominance was assured but its pattern was by no means predictable.

Hertzog's first five years in office were highly successful from the point of view of the specific groups he represented. Afrikaans rather than Dutch was installed as an equal language in 1925 and bilingualism introduced into the civil service—measures that favoured the employment of Afrikaans-speakers. The Bible was now available in Afrikaans. Hertzog was an important architect of a more independent status for the British self-governing Dominions, following the agreements at the Imperial Conference of 1926. A compromise was struck on the troubled issue of the national flag. Based on bold blue, white, and orange stripes, last used in the Dutch East India Company period, the agreed design was even more syncretic than the British flag: it included at its centre miniature Transvaal and Orange Free State flags and a Union Jack. An Afrikaans national anthem 'Die Stem' (voice) was adopted formally in 1934, to be played alongside 'God Save the King'. The new medium of radio facilitated its popularization.

Hertzog could also feel satisfied at the success of his policy of job protection for poor whites. To the cost of both African and coloured workers, the South African Railways became the single largest employer of Afrikaners. The figure climbed to 77,000 by 1942, perhaps one in eleven adult male Afrikaners (O'Meara 1983: 90). At small country stations throughout the land, processions of wheeltappers rung the victory of protected employment on the wheels of countless trucks and engines. Though the state had less direct influence on industry, white employment in mining recovered and most manufacturing and commercial enterprises employed a far higher proportion of whites than did the mines. Hertzog was also able to finalize the plans for national Electricity Supply Commission (ESCOM) and Iron and Steel Corporation (ISCOR), as well as increase protection for infant consumer-oriented industries. The entrenchment and renaming of the Kruger National Park provided a strong set of symbols for both English and Afrikaners. In addition to Afrikaner nationalism, a broader South African white identity seemed to be flourishing.

Although Hertzog was not able to move as fast as he would have liked on legislation regulating African rights, he successfully made race domination into a major issue in the 1929 election. The scale of his victory allowed him to drop his sometimes uneasy alliance with the English-speaking Labour Party. In 1930 the franchise was extended to all white men—qualification was still necessary for blacks in the Cape—and to white women. Up to this time, gender had been a more rigid category of exclusion from the vote (if not from other legal rights) than race. The women's suffrage movement in South Africa was led mainly by English-speakers from leading families, such as Lady Rose-Innes, and professionals. It was weaker than in Britain and abandoned its commitment to the Cape's qualified colour-blind franchise in the mid-1920s. 'Sex loyalty', Walker comments, 'stopped at the heavily guarded boundaries of white privilege' (1991: 314). Hertzog's

Cabinet saw white women's enfranchisement not least as a means of further diluting the influence of black voters and increasing the predominance of Afrikaners.

The National Party looked well set to ride out the depression. Its failure to do so resulted both from the severity of the downturn and from the government's inability to manage the crisis, even in the interests of Hertzog's own narrow base of support. This is the more surprising because South Africa had decisive advantages in the depression in that gold production prospered. After Wall Street crashed in 1929, prices in general deflated. South African gold producers found that their costs declined. With gold at a relatively fixed price, their profits increased. Demand for the metal nevertheless remained high because of financial instability.

In order to reflate its economy, Britain abandoned the gold standard in September 1931 and sterling was devalued. Hertzog's government, however, stayed on a gold standard for over a year. It was initially attracted by the prospects of cheap imports, which would lower the costs both of production and of consumption—a strategy with which the mining industry concurred. He also construed his refusal to follow the British lead as an assertion of economic independence and nationalism. As a result, the highly valued South African pound made life very difficult for agricultural exporters in already depressed markets. Hertzog's Cabinet therefore resolved to tax the profitable mining industry in order to support agriculture till these markets recovered, but his immediate political calculus proved wrong.

Wool producers, the most dependent on international markets, were hit hard and early. Australia had also abandoned the gold standard and deflated its currency, making it even more difficult for South African wool to compete. The wool clip increased, but its value plummeted and pastures came under enormous pressure as farmers tried to maintain their income by increasing sheep numbers to unprecedented heights. This made them particularly vulnerable to drought and environmental degradation; by 1935, nearly 15 million sheep had been lost. The price of maize, the major agricultural commodity on the internal market, declined by more than half from 1929 to 1933.

Hertzog was eventually persuaded to abandon the gold standard only in December 1932. Afrikaner politicians, and the mining industry, which now sought to free the gold price, both supported this. But his popularity had suffered, and, insufficiently confident to call an election, he was driven into Smuts's arms in 1933. With the economic tide turning, their 'Fusion' coalition won the great majority of seats when elections were held. In 1934, the SAP and National Party amalgamated to become the United South African Nationalist Party (UP). Hertzog stayed on as Prime Minister and Minister of External Affairs while Smuts became his deputy and Minister of Justice.

Despite their rhetoric, Smuts and Hertzog had a good deal in common. Smuts agreed to safeguard a 'sound rural population' and a white labour policy, as well as to respect the constitutional devolution Hertzog had achieved. Hertzog had already expressed a desire to halt further demands for constitutional change. 'After what has been achieved at the Imperial Conferences in 1926 and 1930,' he argued, 'there no longer exists today a single reason why, in the constitutional and political fields, Dutch- and English-speaking South Africans cannot feel and act in the spirit of a consolidated South African nation' (O'Meara 1983: 40). Smuts was a super-bureaucrat as much as a politician, far more effective in office than in opposition. While he and Hertzog differed on the details of segregation, Smuts was prepared to compromise in order to stay in power.

South Africa's economic recovery in the 1930s was fuelled by gold. Following the demise of the gold standard, the metal's price doubled within a decade. Lower-grade ores could be exploited on a scale previously impossible. Although gold production increased only 33 per cent from 333,316 kg. in 1931 to 448,128 kg. in 1941, the tonnage of rock processed leapt from 29 million to 63 million and total income from gold increased 2.5 times to £120 million in 1941. Employment reflected the tonnage figures: the African workforce, at about 200,000 in 1929, peaked at over 383,000 in 1941, and the number of white miners rose from 22,000 to 41,500. South Africa was again the beneficiary of a windfall gain blown by forces unleashed in the international economy.

The mining industry had not been a major direct source of state revenue prior to the depression. But economic thinking was changing in the post-depression world, especially in Franklin D. Roosevelt's 'New Deal' USA. Hertzog and the Fusion government broke with precedent and imposed an excess profits tax on gold. State revenue from the industry increased from about £1.6 million annually between 1925 and 1930 to over £12 million in 1933 and £22 million in 1940—from 6 per cent of total revenue to around one-third. With resources on this scale, the government could conceive of projects that had not been possible since the days of reconstruction after the South African War.

White farmers, who had been a major casualty of the depression, were the greatest beneficiaries. Considerable sums were transferred through Land Bank loans and, for example, the £2.5 million distributed under the 1932 Soil Erosion Act for dams, bore-holes, and contour works. Support came to farmers not primarily from direct grants or loans but via a complex system of price protection. The process of stabilizing and protecting prices, begun with wine and tobacco in the 1920s, spread to almost every agricultural commodity in the 1930s. Following the trend in Britain, Control Boards were established to manage the markets. In 1937 the system as a whole was regulated by a Marketing Act under which Boards would work with white farmer cooperatives as sole purchasers of a number of commodities. By 1950 over 90 per cent of white farmers belonged to at least one cooperative. Afrikaner financial institutions benefited greatly from the cooperative accounts that they held. De Kiewiet argued in a memorable if not accurate aphorism that South Africa 'came . . . to be farmed from the two capitals, Pretoria and Cape Town' (1941: 253).

Manufacturing industry, also deeply affected by the depression, received less overall support but grew more rapidly than the agricultural sector. Agricultural development was in itself one stimulus as dips, fertilizers, windmills, machinery, and fences were required for more intensive production. Internal urban and mining markets were more important. During the First World War, a number of local consumer-oriented and engineering industries had been able to take advantage of the protection arising out of disruption to international shipping. The fact that the major concentration of population and industry was on the Rand, well away from the ports, provided some further protection from overseas commodities. Hertzog was prepared to back this advantage with tariffs though they may not have had a great effect in themselves.

Industries such as clothing, textiles, and food-processing all expanded rapidly, so that their workforces grew even more quickly than in mining. Employment in metal and engineering trebled to over 50,000 between 1932 and 1940. Some white women had already been absorbed into secretarial and factory work, and many more, mostly Afrikaners, now joined them in the industrial workforce. Unlike African women, who did the bulk of agricultural work in the reserves, young white women tended to come off the land first while their families tried to hang onto a rural livelihood. They were also paid less than men and considered dextrous in using machines.

In the light of these advances for whites, the reasons for the headway made by D. F. Malan's *Gesuiwerde* (purified) National Party, founded in 1934 in protest over Fusion, are not self-evident. Three times in the twentieth century, in 1913, 1934, and (following a small 1969 breakaway) in 1982, a sizeable group of Afrikaner exclusivists split away from Afrikaner leaders attempting to cement a broader ruling alliance. Each phase involved a battle for the hearts, minds, and pockets of Afrikaners. But despite the cyclical pattern and some intriguing similarities, it cannot simply be assumed that there was always a bedrock of uncompromising ethnic opinion seeking a political outlet. Each split requires a different kind of explanation.

Ironically, the constituencies to which Malan's party appealed—Afrikaner farmers, civil servants, teachers, workers, and poor whites—benefited from the economic boom after Fusion. Economists and ideologues for the gold mines certainly thought so and objected strongly to the level of taxation and state intervention. Yet there were not only economic issues at stake. Malan, first editor of *Die Burger* and formerly in Hertzog's Cabinet, had his base in the well-financed Cape provincial organization of the National Party before Fusion. It was here that he received his initial backing. He could attract disillusioned communities in the wool districts, savaged by the depression, drought, and dead sheep. He also found support amongst young intellectuals, some nurtured in Stellenbosch University, some trained in German universities, who believed in the primacy of the Afrikaner *volk*. The term was given additional content and system as ideologues developed the idea of *Nasionalisme as Lewensbeskouing* (a total outlook on life).

The 'civil religion' offered by Dutch Reformed Churches also gave moral and social security to highly mobile and disoriented people. It was a means of recreating communities disrupted by migration from the countryside. The language of Christianity was far more important to ex-*predikant* Malan than to the religiously agnostic Hertzog. Keeromstraat in Cape Town—centre of the Party offices and literary production—was also at the heart of the movement. Its arteries now included not only the far-flung rural districts but sprawling white suburbs. The Burger Boekhandel publishers produced 1,100 Afrikaans books, which sold 3.25 million copies over the period 1917 to 1940 (Hofmeyr 1987: 112). Afrikaans magazines like *Die Huisgenoot* spoke across the divide of town and country. Profusely illustrated, it became probably the most popular publication in the 1920s.

Such material dwelt on women's role as bearers of cultural tradition and language. Afrikaner women were newly empowered by more extensive literacy and the franchise. The Carnegie Commission on poor whites laid great stress on the deleterious effects of isolation and impoverishment on rural women and children. Its authors, largely Afrikaner academics, felt that these women no longer had the knowledge and support to fulfil their role as mothers. They argued strongly for education and social welfare in order that women might play their role as *volksmoeders* of a new and modern Afrikaner nation.

Hertzog initially won the northern provinces for Fusion. For some northern Afrikaner intellectuals, however, the compromises he had made were too much to bear. The Afrikaner Broederbond, formed in 1919 by a small group of largely urban exclusivists in the Transvaal, expanded significantly, incorporating white-collar workers and professionals. More so than the Freemasons, widespread amongst English-speakers, the Broederbond was a secret organization restricted to carefully chosen white Protestant men. Its influence behind the scenes of Afrikanerdom was fully revealed only later. A major foundation of Malan's Transvaal support, it became a font of Christian national, republican, and sometimes pro-Fascist tendencies.

The Broederbond concentrated on winning influence in educational institutions, the bureaucracy, and white trade unions. It sought specifically to unite Afrikaners across class barriers and opposed political alliances with non-Afrikaner organizations. The railway union was the first to espouse this position. Working closely with Afrikaner cultural organizations, the Bond was responsible for a major cultural *coup*—an ox-wagon trek in 1938 from the Cape to Pretoria to celebrate the centenary of the Great Trek and lay the foundation stone of the Voortrekker monument.

The rhetoric of Malan's *Gesuiwerdes* drew on a century of treks, conflict, and warfare. His movement sought purification and cleansing from old enemies such as mining capital, the Empire, and Smuts. These new ethnic nationalists confronted the poor-white problem energetically. They included Hendrik Verwoerd, youthful professor at Stellenbosch who became editor of *Die Transvaler* newspaper in 1937, a key mouthpiece for Malan's party. They were critical not of capitalism, but of foreign capital. Indeed, O'Meara (1983) argues that *Volkskapitalisme*, ethnic capitalism, and economic organizations designed to enlarge the Afrikaner stake in the economy were central projects. And to an even greater extent than Hertzog, they argued for racial protection against the rising black tide as much as cultural protection from the tentacles of empire.

The political loyalties of Afrikaans-speakers nevertheless remained divided. Many stayed in the United Party. Some Afrikaner women on the Rand were successfully organized into trade unions, notably the Garment Workers. Its radical leaders such as Hester Cornelius and Solly Sachs advocated socialist ideas and tried to encourage activities that might provide its members with an alternative social focus. Malan's Nationalists gained steadily but were not yet close to electoral victory when the Second World War broke out. By a narrow majority, parliament decided in 1939 to enter the war on the allied side. Aware of the deep opposition amongst Afrikaners to fighting a war with Britain and against Germany, Hertzog first advocated neutrality, then resigned as Prime Minister.

### Segregation and Urbanization

In addition to protecting whites in the labour market, establishing controls on African political organizations, and restoring chieftaincy, Hertzog had begun to address the future of the African reserves and African political rights. He appointed a Native Economic Commission (NEC, 1930–2), whose report proved critical in formulating policy. The Commission's terms of reference explicitly linked the poor-white problem to black urbanization and the deterioration of the reserves. Its report distilled much of the segregationist thought of the 1920s and, like SANAC in 1905, projected a far-reaching policy programme. Incorporating the ideas of liberal segregationists in the 1920s, it sought to find a 'middle way between tying him [the "native"] down and trying to make of him a black European, between *repressionist* and *assimilationist* schools' (Dubow 1989: 36).

The report was organized around a cluster of concepts evoked in the idea of 'tribe'. Africans, so the report argued, had a different mentality from Europeans, shaped not only historically but racially. They were essentially rural and their way of life emphasized continuity, subsistence, and security. The colonial peace inhibited Africans' supposed natural propensity to violence and was thus leading to a large increase in population. Africans were also perceived to suffer from a 'cattle complex', recently defined by anthropologists, which led to hoarding of cattle for religious purposes and the payment of bridewealth. Uncommercial use of cattle caused overstocking, soil erosion, and 'desert' conditions. The Commissioners felt that the tribe, the cattle complex, environmental decay, and population increase were the cause of rapid African urbanization that threatened to swamp the white population.

The Commission's conception of Africans not only explained the problems of the reserves but led them to a solution that was compatible with white interests. Most Africans should stay in the reserves, but these had to be developed and made ecologically safe to facilitate increased agricultural production. Development and social modernization should come from within the 'tribal' system under the chiefs. The Native Economic Commission (NEC) also expressed widely held white suspicions of educated Africans, arguing that those in town were 'exiles' who had abandoned their true role of uplifting their people in the rural areas.

The report worked with the idea of racially based cultures that should now become more congruent with separate territorial zones. Its solutions sat easily with the system of large-scale African male labour migrancy, although it was not an ardent proponent of the system. The NEC underestimated the extent of social change and the implications of urbanization. It minimized the effects of dispossession and lack of land for Africans and failed to recognize that it aimed to concentrate future African population growth in what were already the most densely inhabited rural districts of the country. Other observers of the reserves noted their poverty, malnutrition amongst children, and the spread of diseases like tuberculosis from the cities and mines. Although wage income and the rural trading network appear to have solved the problem of famine, constraints on peasant agriculture tended to restrict the range of foods available—not least milk for children.

Segregationist thinking materialized in the Native Trust and Land Act and the Native Representation Act, passed in 1936 after ten years of tortuous negotiation within the white body politic. Political groupings that differed little about the broad parameters of segregation nevertheless haggled long about the detail and language of 'native policy'. Many Afrikaners emphasized protection of whites and exclusion of Africans from the central political system. Liberal segregationists prioritized development in the reserves. Conservative Natal English-speaking MPs, like the influential Heaton Nicholls, adamantly opposed any African franchise and took this view to its logical conclusion. He was a powerful protagonist of African communalism—of going 'back to the native kraal, to the native family, to the tribe, to the tribal council'—in order to counter both African demands for representation and the threat of communism (Dubow 1989: 145). Positively formulated in this way, segregation was conceived to have ideological and moral justification and would shield Africans against further expropriation of land, the corruption of urban life, and alien ideologies. Proponents argued that it was similar to indirect rule and trusteeship, which characterized British colonialism in Africa.

The crux of the new legislation was that some additional land and development funds would be made available for the reserves, but Africans in the Cape would finally be removed from the common voters' roll. African political rights were envisaged in a segregated context. A new Native Trust was empowered to purchase and administer farmland with funds from the central legislature and thus make good the unfulfilled promises of the 1913 Land Act. As in that Act, any extension of reserved land for Africans came with costs. The Trust and Land Act also further tightened provisions governing tenancy on farms: the labour required from African tenants in specific districts could be increased to 180 days, although this measure was not immediately implemented in many areas.

The loss of the Cape vote was of limited significance by the 1930s. Enfranchisement of white women had further diluted it and the number of African voters had declined absolutely to little over 10,000 (1.2 per cent of the national total). But the issue remained important in white politics as a reminder of an alternative political route and the old Cape liberal tradition. Some Cape UP representatives, and African political groupings, wished to preserve a vestige of central representation. As a concession, Africans in the Cape were allowed to elect three white MPs on a separate voters' roll. A partly elected Native Representative Council was established at the apex of the now widely implemented African local council system. Although prominent African politicians joined it, including ANC leaders, it was restricted to an advisory role and after a decade was condemned by one of its most active members as a 'toy telephone' (Benson 1966: 104).

In addition to parliament, the South African bureaucracy was of great significance in shaping the policy, the legislative details, and everyday administration of segregation. As in many other countries, both the size and the functions of the bureaucracy increased dramatically after the depression. The way that government revenues were expended in assisting white farmers was critical in sharpening divisions between farmlands and reserves. State aid to African farming, though it did increase through the programme of agricultural demonstrators, was organized separately through branches of the Native Affairs Department (NAD) and Transkeian Council. Africans were largely excluded from the cooperatives and marketing controls that soaked up so much state funding.

The scope for African employment above menial positions, except in Native Affairs and the Police, diminished as the Afrikanerization of officialdom proceeded. The NAD gained authority and became more centralized. Officials governed by proclamation and government notices that could not easily be challenged in court—one of the last refuges for constitutional opposition. Municipalities also expanded their own separate Native Affairs sections to administer urban segregation. (Education, although segregated, still remained under the same provincial inspectorates.) Other state institutions, such as Provincial Councils, the Post Office, forestry, and railways, developed their own practices, which often intensified segregationist tendencies.

The 1920s and 1930s can be seen as a high point of segregation. Formal ideologies and policies were underpinned by widespread everyday racial prejudice in the language and behaviour of whites and sometimes others. Political accommodation in the rural areas, together with the difficulties of organization, stalled black national opposition. But state policy was by no means uncontested. There were alternative visions within the black and white population. Moreover, at the very moment that segregation seemed entrenched, social and demographic processes undermined it. Rapid expansion in mining and industry in the 1930s, which may also have helped to defuse discontent, drew more African workers to the cities. Economic demands and social fluidity during the Second World War further undermined controls over African urbanization.

Urbanization has been a continuous process in the twentieth century, but an uneven one. Censuses suggest that, in stark contrast to the second half of the century, overall white demographic growth matched that of black between 1904 and 1946 (**Table 2**).

The percentage of the white population living in urban areas increased more sharply from 50 to 75 per cent, trebling from about 600,000 to 1.8 million people by 1946 (**Tables 2 and 3**). The Indian population also became largely urban as indentured workers left the sugar estates.

African urbanization was relatively slow, increasing steadily from about 10 to 23 per cent of the African population (including migrant workers) between 1904 and 1946. In numbers, however, this represented growth from about 350,000 to 1.8 million; for the first time, the African urban population equalled that of whites. Especially between 1936 and 1946, the predominance of men in the urban African population declined noticeably. The percentage of women amongst Africans in Johannesburg rose to 36 (140,000 out of 390,000). While the African population of Durban and smaller Rand mining towns remained mainly male, about half the Africans in Port Elizabeth, Bloemfontein, and East London were now women. Up to the 1936 census the major movement to town seems to have been from the farms, but in the next decade, from the reserves. In some reserve districts, numbers remained almost stable between 1936 and 1946. For whites, it seemed that the urban areas were increasingly overtaken by blacks and that African families, rather than migrant men, were establishing themselves securely.

The 1923 Native Urban Areas Act, passed during Smuts's first premiership, gave municipalities greater powers to segregate housing, to police African communities, and to control movement by imposing passes. The Act and its many subsequent amendments proved difficult to implement. As the census figures indicate, while passes hampered African freedom of movement, they did not prevent urbanization. Moreover, municipalities might have wanted segregation, but the Act specified that alternative housing should be built for those removed and neither ratepayers nor government proved enthusiastic about funding this. City slum landlords could make money from African tenants and city traders had an interest in maintaining lucrative custom. Some employers, especially in smaller businesses without compounds, were uneasy about restrictions on housing for their workers.

The result was that by the early 1930s legislative intent was not matched by social reality; many African people in the cities still lived quite centrally, rather than in peri-urban townships or locations. Domestic servants were dispersed through the white suburbs in backyard quarters or *kayas*. Migrant workers lived in barracks and compounds, some of which, such as Crown mines and the Municipal compound in Johannesburg, were centrally located. Slumyards abounded precisely because they diminished the cost and trouble of getting to work and provided economic opportunities for those servicing the large black working population. If women were going to make a success of brewing, they had more chance of doing so in Doornfontein's Rooiyard than in far-flung locations. By the late 1920s, there were perhaps 40,000 Africans living in central Johannesburg slumyards. The population of older locations nearer to the city centre, such as Alexandra and Sophiatown, where home ownership was allowed, also increased rapidly.

New peri-urban locations were initially less popular. Orlando, established in the early 1930s south-west of Johannesburg next to Klipspruit, was the node around which Soweto (acronym for South Western Townships) grew. It set the style for soulless municipal housing and could not be filled, despite the crush of the slumyards. But by 1940 Johannesburg's slum-clearance campaigns were under way and the flood of migrants to town had little alternative; Orlando's 5,000 properties then housed 35,000 people. By the end of the Second World War, illegal squatter settlements on the urban peripheries were also absorbing large numbers of people. Urban segregation was being imposed, but it was proving very difficult to keep people out of the cities.

## African Urban and Rural Life

Black urban life in this pre-apartheid period inspired evocative novels and autobiographies. Modikwe Dikobe, one of the first black working-class novelists in South Africa, based his *Marabi Dance* on a slumyard in Doornfontein in which he had lived: 'when it rained, the yard was as muddy as a cattle kraal, and the smell of beer, thrown out by the police on their raid, combining with the stench of the lavatories, was nauseating' (1973: 1). In its buildings, cockroaches and rats abounded; whole families and sometimes their visiting relatives or tenants lived in single rooms. Peter Abrahams's *Mine Boy* (1946) and Alan Paton's *Cry the Beloved Country* (1948) also etched images of urban squalor.

Hellmann's *Rooiyard*, one of the first systematic exercises in urban anthropology, documented the economic base of a slum in great detail. She demonstrated the importance of women's contribution to urban survival through brewing for consumption and to supplement wages. As an informant explained to her, Africans 'eat from beer' (1948: 39). African families were not nuclear in the rural areas and the nuclear family was only one form of reconstituted family life in the cities. Many women fended for themselves and brought up children as single mothers. Powerful women who provided both financial and emotional strength in these transient communities feature strongly in writings on the slums. Unlike in prohibition Chicago, individual women rather than criminal gangs controlled much of the illegal brewing. This gave them a degree of authority, but it also meant that women lived in an enforced state of criminality.

While the details of urban poverty are clear, interpretations of its causes and implications differed. Like many white liberals and rural blacks, Paton did not support segregation but despaired of the slums—'the garbage heap of the proud city'. The power of his heart-rending novel derives not least from the contrast he drew between the romanticized decaying beauty of the countryside in rural Natal, where people could live an apparently simple moral life, and the city, which corrupted those who came within its grasp.

Dikobe, unlike Paton, did not see the slums from a distance; his novel evoked the vibrancy and permanency of city life. In Paton's novel, liquor, the lifeblood of the slumyards, breeds crime, vice, and violence. In contrast, Dikobe can celebrate the Marabi culture of music and dance that grew around the yards, the powerful *skokiaan* beer, and shebeens (an Irish word which slid easily into urban black argot). Dikobe's heroine, in so far as he has one, is a young woman finding her feet in town and impatient with traditions such as arranged marriages. While Paton, Hellmann, and others see urban Africans caught between two worlds—a city life that they cannot have and a rural life that they do not want—Dikobe projects a specifically African urban culture into which many people had made a transition. For Hellmann, the piano in the slumyard is an example of Westernization and conspicuous consumption—a consumer item that people could not understand. For Dikobe, the piano was a cultural instrument for Africans and a means to an income for the Marabi jazz pianist in his novel.

All these works suggest a rather introspective and defensive African inner-city culture, symbolized by the necessity to post guards continuously to warn of police liquor raids. Dikobe's book is not explicitly political. Unlike Abrahams, he offers no optimistic socialist view of white and black workers united, rising up to throw off the shackles of oppression. His characters interact individually with whites, some good and some bad. He describes a world of conflict. The young, turning away both from rural custom and from churches, challenge the old. Christianity, witchcraft beliefs, and materialism vie with one another in the minds of his protagonists. Newly urbanized people are uncertain as to how far they should share in a consumer society where some blacks, as well as most whites, identify manufactured commodities as 'the white man's things' (Abrahams 1946:63). Yet Dikobe's world is a powerful statement about the vitality of urban black communities in a segregationist state that was trying to destroy them.

The Second World War stimulated internal industrial growth in an economy that was already diversifying rapidly. Even though the gold mines contracted somewhat after their peak of 1941, overall demand for labour grew dramatically. Of the 300,000 men mobilized for the armed forces, 186,000 were white. This was a significant proportion of the white labour force and it had to be replaced, especially in industry. When manufacturing and construction employment doubled to 330,000 between 1932 and 1939, 33 per cent of the increase was white, but only 15 per cent of the further 125,000 people absorbed during the war (Wilson and Thompson 1971: ii 34–6). Africans in manufacturing industry found their real wages to be rising.

In the early years of the war, manufacturing overtook mining both in its share of the country's GDP and in employment. The concerns of manufacturers about new markets and a more settled labour force impinged on state policy. Smuts's UP government (1939–48) was unique in the history of the Union in that it was more English- than Afrikaans-speaking. It was certainly conservative and in broad terms committed to some form of segregation. But it was more pragmatic and more closely linked to manufacturing, commerce, and the professions than its predecessors. Jan Hofmeyr, who acquired considerable power as Smuts's deputy, was particularly open to the relatively well-organized white liberals in the South African Institute of Race Relations and those few who served, especially as Native Representatives, in parliament. During the Second World War, pass controls were relaxed and, with so many white servicemen away, Smuts was concerned to defuse African industrial unrest. Prices for key foodstuffs were held down. His government also began to confront the reality of planning for a large urban African population.

South African politicians and bureaucrats were by no means immune to international trends in their pursuit of more systematic planning in the post-depression era. Government commissions, long important in shaping policy, were now supplemented by a Social and Economic Planning Council that explored many aspects of society. Deep concern was expressed about African poverty, crime, delinquency, and the effects of migrant labour. Hofmeyr pursued the cause of African education and moved considerable new central funds in this direction. In 1944 a Commission on National Health advocated a health system on a non-racial basis that would have had enormous implications for state spending and social welfare. By 1946 the Minister of Native Affairs, no liberal, was publicly articulating the desire of manufacturing industry for a more settled labour force. This willingness to recognize some of the implications of mass urbanization was reiterated in the Fagan Commission report of 1948. Smuts did not seriously envisage extending African political rights, but state responses implied the possibility of new directions.

African protest both reflected and influenced these economic and social changes. In the early 1930s, the ANC was small and the ICU had fragmented. The Communist Party, which in 1928 had committed itself to a 'Native Republic' as the first stage of the revolution, was severely weakened by internal purges. But Hertzog's Land and Franchise bills stimulated new attempts at organization. D. D. T. Jabavu, son of J. T., coordinated with the ANC to establish an All Africa Convention in 1935. While this failed in its immediate goals of halting the legislation, it prodded the ANC, including Communist leaders such as J. B. Marks, into calling their own national conference in 1937. Cape politicians meanwhile developed the Convention into a Non-European Unity Front.

Communists such as Gana Makabeni, and other socialists such as Max Gordon, revived trade unions in the service and small-industry sector when the economy picked up after the depression. The African Clothing Workers, the Broom and Brush Union, and the Native Laundry Workers laid the foundations of a renewed industry-based unionism as opposed to the mass approach of the ICU. They were particularly successful in organizing Indian workers in Natal from the late 1930s, attracting committed leaders like Dr Y. Dadoo. A Wage Board established in 1925 to set minimum wages in certain sectors allowed some access for representatives of black workers. Most unions were organized on a racial basis, but there were a few coordinated strikes by black and white sections. Although the Communists committed themselves to the war effort after the end of the Nazi–Soviet Pact and were therefore hesitant to support strikes, they met with particular success in launching unions amongst migrant workers in large industries such as the African Mineworkers Union under J. B. Marks.

By the end of the war, the Council of Non-European Trade Unions claimed 119 affiliates with 150,000 members. The number of hours lost in strikes, many of them illegal, between 1940 and 1945 increased from 6,000 to 90,000 annually. Durban dock-workers staged sustained actions and the crest of the new wave of unionism was reached after the war in 1946, when inflationary pressures intensified and over 70,000 African mineworkers struck for higher wages. It was the largest and longest strike experienced in this key industry. The Union was able to initiate and coordinate networks of migrant workers across a wide area in a way that had never before been possible. Smuts, his attention less diverted by war, resorted to his time-honoured tactic of calling in the army to break the strike.

The cutting edge of black politics was moving to the large cities, and unions appeared to be a powerful vehicle at the vanguard of a black working class. But they suffered severe setbacks after 1946. The wartime shortage of workers ended. Unions came under strong pressure from the state and the Communist Party decided to shift its priorities away from mass labour organization. The Mineworkers Union still faced enormous difficulties in retaining support amongst a transient and fragmented workforce; it had not struck sufficiently deep roots to survive state repression. White workers in the Trades and Labour Council, who had maintained some support for new African unionism during the war, now again prioritized racial protection. The 1946 mineworkers' strike turned out to be the end of a phase of militant unionism, rather than the beginning.

Wartime political activity had many other facets. In 1943–4, the Communists directly addressed the issue of controls over black urbanization in initiating mass anti-pass protests. In 1944, one of the first major bus boycotts was launched in Alexandra township in the north of Johannesburg. The costs of transport had been an issue since the beginning of urban segregation that pushed Africans further from city centres. In the 1920s and early 1930s African bus-owners dominated the urban routes and competition between them had driven costs down. But the state introduced a licensing system in 1930, which was gradually enforced to the advantage of white entrepreneurs. When fares were put up in the war, African commuters responded with boycotts and many walked to work. Black transport entrepreneurs supported the protests and this alliance brought some gains in 1944.

Squatter movements also flourished. In the rural areas, the word 'squatter' was applied to tenants on farms or state land, including those initially within the law, who gave little labour to their landlord. In town, the word referred to those who illegally took possession of land on the urban peripheries. Perhaps 90,000 people settled in squatter camps on the outskirts of Johannesburg by the late 1940s, 20–25 per cent of the city's African population. James Mpanza, a Zulu-speaking member of the Orlando Advisory Board, led backyard subtenants in the location onto fresh ground nearby in 1944. His *Sofasonke* (we die together) movement, which included many recent immigrants from the rural areas, was able to secure recognition from a hostile municipality and some finance for new settlements.

A spate of related movements tried to emulate Mpanza's success. As one leader commented: 'the Government was like a man who has a cornfield which is invaded by birds. He chases the birds from one part of the field and they alight in another part of the field . . . We squatters are the birds' (Stadler 1979: 93). In 1947 municipal attempts to establish control over trading in these areas precipitated a riot. In 1948 some squatters moved onto land controlled by the council and attempted a rent boycott through the *Asinamali* (we have no money) campaign. Ultimately provision of new settlements and tighter legislation undermined the squatter leaders' authority, though Sofasonke survived as a party in Soweto politics.

Mpanza was a charismatic populist who started his own church—a 'Messiah-cum-Chief-cum-Gangster Boss' (Hirson 1990: 151). Called *magebula* (slicer of land, from a word used for cutting through enemy lines, clearing forest, or, metaphorically, opening eyes), he governed his settlement with little attention to the state. He controlled entry, issued residence permits and trading licences for a fee, administered justice, and punished misdeameanours with fines and beatings; beer brewing was permitted. Mpanza went about on horseback, hailed as chief; his speeches, dense with biblical allusions, included comparisons of himself to Christ. Urban squatter movements of the 1940s in many ways resembled rural movements of the 1920s, such as the *Amafela* and the ICU. Leaders intertwined political and religious, traditionalist and newly forged ideologies and symbols. They were particularly successful in mobilizing women.

The ANC, reviving in the late 1930s, received new impetus under the Presidency of Dr A. B. Xuma from 1940. Although it developed some contacts with the unions and bus boycotts, its leadership was still uneasy with mass politics and the powerful language of deliverance 'in the midst of hessian sacks' and corrugated iron of impoverished shack settlements (Hirson 1990: 154).

However, the 1946 strike and the squatters' movements galvanized younger men, recently moved into ANC politics on the Rand, into forming a radical group within the Congress Youth League. Initially led by Africanist lawyer Anton Lembede, they included Nelson Mandela and Oliver Tambo, former students at Fort Hare. They were deeply aware of the progress of international events: the promises of the war for democracy, the moves towards Indian independence, and the surge of nationalist protest in other colonized countries such as Ghana and Nigeria. By the late 1940s a plan of mass protest was being formulated.

While the urban areas were increasingly at the cutting edge of radical politics, the rural districts were not quiescent. The Native Affairs Department, looking to work through chiefs and headmen, intervened more systematically to appoint cooperative men, sometimes precipitating conflict or storing it up for the future. In Pondoland, Transkei, where the state had reached a working relationship with the paramountcy, the government intervened in a succession dispute in 1937 and appointed Botha Sigcau, a progovernment chief, against popular feelings. Conflict over the role of chiefs remained central in rural politics and became bound up with rural protests against state intervention into African patterns of cattle-keeping and landholding.

Concern about environmental degradation in the African reserves, expressed for example by the NEC, permeated official thinking, which also linked the success of segregation policy to ecological recovery. Evidence suggests that the number of cattle and sheep in the reserves increased sharply in the 1920s, after the introduction of dipping reduced deaths from disease. Human population growth increased the demand for livestock, as each rural homestead aimed to acquire enough cattle for milk and draught. While rising livestock numbers underpinned the fragile maintenance of peasant production, they also took their toll on the land. As on the white-owned farms, animal numbers peaked around 1930 and severe losses were experienced in the subsequent droughts. The multiplication of scattered fields was seen as an equally serious problem. By this time, officials had identified African districts that they felt required urgent attention. Programmes were instituted to fill dongas, build contour banks, and promote contour ploughing. Officials argued for a reduction in livestock and (following the Drought Commission) proposed fenced paddocks where herds and flocks could be rotated through the year to increase carrying capacity and save the veld. They believed that this in turn would necessitate the removal of scattered African homesteads into villages.

These proposals were developed into a comprehensive 'Betterment' proclamation (1939), which included villagization, fencing, the separation of arable land from grazing, and provision for livestock culls. Betterment planning changed through the years—and affected highveld communities in different ways from those on the coast—but it is not an exaggeration to say that officials planned to move millions of people. Any new Trust land purchased for African occupation under the 1936 Act was to be planned before it could be settled. Betterment constituted perhaps the most far-reaching intervention into rural life since annexation, the introduction of taxes, and dipping.

When the state began to implement these policies, rural people claimed that contour banks traversed their fields, diminished their plots, and were washed away during storms. They complained that they were not consulted and that interventions, sometimes technically inadequate, were insensitive to rural social life. Little compensation was paid when people were moved into villages— the government assumed that the labour and materials that went into African hut construction were free. More than anything else, the threat of stock reduction or culling (largely through enforced sales) persuaded many reserve-dwellers to resist the whole range of agricultural policies. Cattle were still a key resource in the rural economy and any measure that threatened a family's capacity to build up an adequate herd for draught, milk, meat, and bridewealth would dig deep into the remaining, and waning, independence of the homesteads. Despite official arguments that stock reduction would benefit the population as a whole, individual interests were too deeply affected for it to be acceptable. Spokesmen argued that the solution was more land, not less cattle.

In the Transvaal, protests against Betterment became linked with battles by farm tenants to resist labour demands on the farms. In Lydenburg, eastern Transvaal, where the ICU had been active, tenants successfully countered farmers' attempts to use the 1936 Native Trust and Land Act to impose six months' unpaid labour on them as rent. Alpheus Malivha, a migrant factory worker from the northern Transvaal, joined the Communist Party and in 1939 launched a Zoutpansberg Cultural (later Balemi or Ploughmen's) Association to make representations on such issues. In the 1940s it directly challenged the environmental controls imposed on new Trust farms allocated for African settlement. Implementation of Betterment was largely delayed till after the war and was met in the late 1940s with a wave of new, largely uncoordinated, protests rippling through the countryside from Middledrift in the Ciskei, Mount Ayliff in the Transkei, to Witzie-shoek, north of Lesotho. Rural resistance significantly delayed the Betterment and culling programme. Officials believed that their strategy for the African rural areas was in the best interests of the people themselves, but they had to confront a large gap in the understanding of their actions. Despite its attempts to redirect 'native policy' along slightly less authoritarian routes, and to pay some attention to African opinion, Smuts's government found it difficult to maintain control in city and countryside.

### The Demise of Smuts

Had it not been for the war, the compromises that Hertzog and Smuts hammered out under the Fusion agreement might have lasted. While Afrikaner exclusivist thinking, the tight equation of ethnicity with nation, certainly found enthusiastic support, the survival of a more broadly based white party may have provided sufficient Afrikaans-speakers with an alternative political home. Hertzog's resignation from the UP in 1939 sent him into the political wilderness and undermined the claims of that party to represent Afrikaners. Hostile to what was seen as Smuts's war, many swung into extra-parliamentary politics, including various paramilitary groups that were either pro-Fascist or opposed the war effort.

The restaged trek in 1938 provided the symbolic springboard for the largest of these—the Ossewabrandwag (OB) or ox-wagon guard. Launched in the Free State in 1939, the OB spread through the country to draw support from Afrikaners across regional and party lines. At its peak in 1941 it claimed 300,000 members, many of them urban and about 60,000 on the Rand; railway workers were one strong source of support (Marx 1994: 195, 209). Smuts's commitment to the war touched the raw nerve of Afrikaner anti-imperialism and the OB organized terror groups and sabotage, including bombing, of South African army targets.

OB members wore uniforms, developed a militia, and incorporated *skietvereenigings* (shooting associations) in an echo of the commando military tradition. OB members directed a great deal of energy into the Afrikaner cultural revival: resurrecting the game *jukskei* originally played with yoke-pins from the ox harness; organizing *braaivleis* (barbecue) evenings; celebrating the Trek and Afrikaner motherhood. Again, such activities drew dislocated urban communities together and provided new scope for male solidarity. While the OB paralleled aspects of European Fascist movements, its form was distinctly local. After a period of uncertainty about party loyalties, most OB members were absorbed in Malan's Nationalists after the war.

In 1943 Smuts, at the head of the UP, was able to win a wartime 'Khaki' election. Subsequently strikes, squatter movements, urban crime, and rural protests frightened many whites, who felt that the government was being too liberal in its approach. The flow of Africans to the towns stimulated the fears of 'swamping' that Hertzog had fed so assiduously in earlier years. Whites in Natal became obsessed with protecting what they saw as their urban space by restricting expanding Indian trade and city-centre property ownership. When Smuts took on the issue of Indian representation and rights, he found even his plans for limited concessions along the lines of the Native Representation Act were widely criticized as too generous. A segment of the white population did emerge from this war for democracy, believing that black aspirations had to be taken into account. But many responded to the wartime challenges from blacks by moving ideologically in the other direction. Economic stringency after the war reinforced this reaction.

In this context, the UP narrowly lost the 1948 general election.

Smuts's defeat was not inevitable, nor was there any landslide swing against him, even amongst Afrikaners. Afrikaans-speakers made up about 60 per cent of the white electorate; an estimated 40 per cent of them voted for the UP and its allies. Indeed, the Nationalist victory was probably dependent on a protest vote of perhaps 20 per cent of English-speakers. Even so the United and Labour parties won 53 per cent of the votes in 1948, while the Nationalists received only 39 per cent (Heard 1974; figures include estimates for uncontested seats.) Malan's victory was possible because Smuts had allowed rural and some peri-urban constituencies, where the Nationalists won a number of narrow victories, to retain their disproportionate weighting in the electoral system. By contrast, the UP won some large majorities in urban and English-speaking constituencies.

The UP lost support on the Rand and in white working-class areas where the threat from blacks was perceived to be especially acute: Afrikaners had been extending their trade union support; whites returning from military service found jobs that they considered their sphere occupied by blacks. Even more important was the swing in the rural areas of the Transvaal and Free State. Despite the government's generosity in the 1930s and rising agricultural prices from the mid-1940s, farmers began to doubt the UP's commitment to their interests. Smuts seemed to favour urban consumers, holding down commodity prices in order to defuse urban militancy. Labour supplies were also a central issue. Mechanization increased the land under cultivation, but farming remained highly labour intensive. Legislation such as the Native Service Contract Act of 1932, which gave farmers further legal powers to constrain African mobility, was insufficient to hold their workers when higher urban wages beckoned. The UP seemed unable to solve the farm labour shortage or to impose stringent controls on black urbanization.

Those who felt threatened found solace in the Nationalist election slogan of apartheid (apartness). Though this had not yet been closely defined, it was well known that Malan stood for more rigid segregation and white protection, as well as undiluted nationalism. Perhaps the Nationalists would have won power soon afterwards, playing to white fears and Afrikaner cultural fervency. Smuts was old, preoccupied with international affairs, and uncertain in his policies. In contrast to the efficient Nationalists, the UP was a loose and inadequately funded coalition with few tightly organized branches. But Afrikaner unity had been difficult to achieve in the past and, without the victory of 1948 and the power that this brought, may have proved to be so again. Only in 1958, when coloured people had been removed from the common roll, did the Nationalists win a majority of the vote, and even then, if estimates for uncontested seats are included, the UP and its allies may still have secured a slight majority of white support.

Despite many biographies, Smuts remains an elusive figure. Except for interludes in the South African War and in opposition (1924–33), he was close to the heart of power continuously from 1898 to 1948 and a central architect of the new state. But, on the one hand, he was extruded from the Afrikaner nationalist galaxy and, on the other, was too compromised a figure to be taken up later by white liberal or African movements. He seemed to speak with a forked tongue, articulating to some audiences clear racial and segregationist ideas, while projecting the role of an eminently reasonable Commonwealth statesman to others. He appeared more interested in efficient administration than political direction. Despite his sense of legality, he could resort to dramatic displays of armed might and air power to quell internal opposition with literal overkill.

Yet some of his legacies may yet be valuable: a personal simplicity and asceticism; incorruptibility; broad (if still racially-based) South Africanism; a love of nature and environmental concern; a capacity to motivate his bureaucracy; and efficiency in government if not always in party organization. His very capacity for political compromise permitted a period of relative openness during and after the Second World War, when the country's more liberal whites and welfare planners briefly had greater influence than at any other time till 1990. Even African political leaders felt they could make some impact. With Smuts's demise, his white cross-ethnic, centrist, and armed forces constituency gradually eroded.

State power in South Africa came to be dominated by a group of whites who used the term nation narrowly to mean an

ethnically defined segment of about 12 per cent of the population.
Their ruthless determination to entrench themselves over the next
four decades left a bitter legacy of suffering and social division.

# PART II

# Afrikaner Power and the Rise of Mass Opposition, 1948–1994

# 6

# Apartheid, 1948–1961

## The Nationalist Mission

Striking documentary film footage records the ageing but wiry Jan Smuts descending the steps of the Union buildings in Pretoria in 1948 to take his leave following his election defeat. His place on the hill of power, in the building designed by Baker on a koppie overlooking the valley of Pretoria, was taken by D. F. Malan—for over thirty years a 'solid, conservative' nationalist. This was a moment when white politics mattered deeply. For fifty years South Africa had been ruled by men who had cut their political teeth at the turn of the century in the politics of the South African War and the compromises of Union. In retrospect, they appear relatively pragmatic. But the age of the generals was over and that of the ideologues and technocrats had begun. These were men who came of age in the inter-war depression years—a time of extremes.

In very many areas, Malan's now *Herenigde* (reunited) National Party (NP) built its policy on the foundations of the segregationist legacy laid by Rhodes and Milner, Kruger and Shepstone, Hertzog and Smuts. But the Nationalist government contained new elements. It aimed to reverse the relaxation of authority by Smuts and to meet new challenges with a tighter set of racial policies. Moreover, although Malan was committed to the parliamentary process based on a white franchise, the Nationalists were increasingly prepared to stretch the system to it limits. If Smuts had been too prone to compromise, the new rulers of South Africa pursued their aims with conviction and self-righteousness. There is a book to be written about unimplemented legislation in the country, but the Nationalists were, at least

143

initially, more determined and more confident of state power than most of their predecessors.

Apartheid became so dominant a feature of life over the next forty years that it must be intrinsic to a description and understanding of this period. It gave South African society a distinctive profile and a long shadow. Although segregationist attitudes in earlier decades may have been more stringent than in many other colonies, or in the USA, they were not vastly different. Apartheid was a more intense system and increasingly jarred in an era of decolonization and majority rule. The South African government was by no means the only authoritarian regime in the world, but it rejected an all-embracing nationalism and enshrined racial distinctions—anathema in the post-holocaust and post-colonial world—at the heart of its legislative programme and political projects. Despite many articulate exiles, it took more than two decades for international criticism to make an impact; when it did, apartheid was the issue.

Yet it is wrong to conceive of South Africa in this period simply in terms of apartheid. At its height in the 1960s, Verwoerd so closely defined his goals and so systematically attempted to engineer them that they were often mistaken for reality. Angry black autobiographers and anguished white liberal academics highlighted racial prejudice, poverty, the formidable legislative programme, and the contorted social results of apartheid. Nevertheless, important changes were taking place that, though influenced by state policy, should not simply be subsumed in a discussion of apartheid.

African population growth, for example, which had major social and political implications, must be considered in a wider context. And apartheid could not reverse African urbanization. The related erosion of old communities and ways of life on the land was traumatic, but it was hardly new or unique to South Africa. With ever greater finality, the bulk of the population was sucked into modes of living that demanded new forms of consumption. As blacks lost their rural ballast, so the social and class divisions within both their communities and the society as a whole were further recast. Despite apartheid, South Africans remained relatively open to global economic and cultural influences. These processes were all intrinsic to the apartheid era and ultimately played a major role in the demise of that policy.

Although the classic colonial commodities of minerals, raw materials, and crops continued to dominate South African exports, the country was becoming a medium-sized industrial power, like Australia, Korea, Mexico, or Brazil, with a great range of domestic manufactures. It was served, sometimes savaged, by an elaborate and ever more diverse bureaucracy. Ox-wagons had given South Africa an enormous advantage in communications over the rest of Africa at the turn of the century. Now road, rail, telecommunication, and air networks—though they were not universally accessible—continued to distinguish it on the continent. The Nationalists liked to think of the country in these terms: a conservative but modern industrial, capitalist, Western-oriented nation. It was not only that: the government did not fully admit that a large part of the population could not share in the benefits of modernity. Yet many of the features of the social and economic landscape delineated in the apartheid era might survive its demise.

At issue for many historians and social scientists considering this period has been the link between industrialization, modernization, and the repressive racial order (**Chapters 7 and 8**). This chapter focuses on the more immediate impact of the Nationalist government. A powerful strand in the writing about Afrikaners emphasizes their preoccupation with their own nationhood and identity, rather than their policy towards blacks.

If there was any dominant ideology, it was one that stressed the values of *volkseenheid* (unity), which transcended class or regional (the North–South antagonism) differences, and *volksverbondenheid*, the notion that the realization of the full human potential comes not from individual self-assertion but through identification with and service of the the *volk*. (Giliomee and Adam 1979: 116)

Malan and his successors were indeed deeply committed to unity, anti-imperialism, and anti-communism. But the rhetoric of cultural solidarity sat easily with racial exclusivity and the use of ethnic power for economic gain.

Nationalist politicians did not have a complete blueprint when they arrived in office in 1948. The way in which their legislative programme unfolded over the decades was influenced by contending interests in the party, by contingencies, crises, and the pattern of opposition. From the outset, the meaning of apartheid was disputed. Some intellectuals held by the chimera of total separation, including economic separation, dispensing as far as possible with black labour. More pragmatic views, not in themselves uncontested, always dominated. Farmers, for a start, could not conceive of managing without black workers. But the purists were influential in maintaining ideological goals and justifications. These tensions were often creative—contributing to a complex political ideology that could both be a creed for followers and remain attuned to the changing interests of support groups and opponents.

Succeeding Prime Ministers also modified policy. D. F. Malan, the architect of revived Afrikanerdom, was rooted in the Cape movement. He is usually characterized as a man concerned most with Afrikaner identity and culture. Nevertheless, his commitment to segregating coloured people in the Cape and other early racial legislation set the parameters for apartheid and resulted in acute political tension in his period of office. He was also pressed by more extreme interests in the party to appoint Verwoerd as Minister of Native Affairs in 1950. Malan was succeeded on his death by J. G. Strydom (1954–8), the 'lion of the north', an adept politician and skilled populist speaker, representing powerful Transvaal factions including white workers and farmers. He was less cautious in articulating the ideology of race and republic.

Apartheid in its broader conception has increasingly become associated with H. F. Verwoerd. As Minister of Native Affairs from 1950 and Prime Minister from 1958 to 1966, he dominated policy towards Africans. Partly educated in Germany, Verwoerd had been a professor of Psychology at the University of Stellenbosch before he moved north in 1937 as editor of *Die Transvaler*. Fiercely ambitious and inexhaustible, he became a republican and Broederbonder, but retained the sociological analysis and language honed in his academic years. His concerns for logical explanation, systematic theory, comprehensive planning, and social engineering were the hallmark of his approach. He was one of those ideologues who had shifted away from the language of *baasskap* to mould apparently more justifiable notions of separate cultures, nations, and 'homelands'. 'Natives' became Bantu, a word derived from Xhosa/Zulu for 'people'; apartheid became 'separate development'.

Whatever apartheid came to mean, party statements and documents over many years agreed on the irreducible aims of the 'maintenance and protection' of Afrikanerdom, white power, and the white race. Even if biological racism was not explicitly part of Nationalist rhetoric, its crude assumptions suffused everyday white language. NP politicians were far more ready to exploit white fears of what was called 'miscegenation'. The killing blow in a white political argument was, put delicately: would you let your daughter marry a black man? A staunch Afrikaner admitted 'that he was better able to raise money for the party by mentioning the fact that white women were dancing with black men in Cape Town, than by stressing the republican issue' (Moodie 1976: 250). Hostility to 'miscegenation' distilled unspoken racial reflexes. It played on deeply set white notions of purity, especially that of white women, and Social Darwinist fears that mixing would result in racial decline. It also addressed formal political anxieties about racial electoral power, which might be diluted by the long-term arithmetic of mixing.

Such concerns quickly materialized in legislation: the Mixed Marriages Act (1949) and the Immorality Act (1950), which prohibited marriage and extramarital sex across racial boundaries. It was not unusual for white men, including Afrikaner men in the rural areas, to have sex with black women. These relationships often expressed patriarchal domination over servants and other subordinated women rather than mutual affection. Legal controls in this sphere partly reflected a desire for social discipline of whites who strayed from the fold. But black women could also suffer harshly and unfairly from conviction. Court cases attracted wide publicity, especially from English-language newspapers, which ridiculed snooping policemen who sought evidence for conviction by feeling beds (for warmth) in early morning house raids. Relationships across colour lines were a central theme for critical novelists because they encapsulated in a personal narrative some of the country's most dramatic social tensions.

In 1950 the Population Registration Act provided for compulsory racial classification on a national register. Documents would be issued to all stating their racial group; a Race Classification Board would adjudicate disputed cases. This insistence on ascription by race, which increasingly determined public and private rights, as well as highly intrusive state regulation, seemed to epitomize the archaic imperatives of Afrikanerdom.

## Legislation and Reaction

The NP's apartheid edifice, drawing on segregationist precedents, can be conceived as resting on seven pillars: starker definition of races; exclusive white participation and control in central political institutions (and repression of those who challenged this); separate institutions or territories for blacks; spatial segregation in town and countryside; control of African movement to cities; tighter division in the labour market; and segregation of amenities and facilities of all kinds from universities to park benches. Politicians insisted that there were only two alternatives: integration and the submersion of whites; or the increasingly elaborate system of apartheid.

In the early stages of their legislative journey, the Nationalists had very real concerns about their capacity to maintain power. They rapidly Afrikanerized the state, both to provide jobs and to ensure a pliant bureaucracy. Key English-speakers in spheres such as the army, military intelligence, the South African Railways and Harbours, broadcasting, African administration, and the economic bureaucracy were sidelined or retired. An explicit attempt was made to fill Native Affairs posts with Broederbond members or party supporters. Increasingly excluded from top posts in the rapidly expanding civil service, fewer English-speakers saw this as a possible career. The ethos of public service became more closely identified with the Nationalist project.

Neither was their parliamentary position, resting initially on a minority of the white vote, secure; in 1953 the vote for the opposition parties, at about 54 per cent, remained stable. A variety of manœuvres was designed to entrench control, including new white seats in Namibia and, in an echo of Krugerite politics, delays on citizenship for immigrants. Most important, the Nationalists removed coloured voters—at about 50,000, far more than the total of African voters in 1936—from the common roll. Few coloured voters supported the NP and their numbers were growing.

Coloured people, perhaps the most likely potential allies had whites offered them full political rights, were amongst the primary victims of the early apartheid years. In poorer Cape suburbs, racial barriers remained relatively porous; coloured people occupied common residential areas along the Peninsula's long Main Road. Nationalists had agitated for their segregation since the 1930s. Classification under the Population Registration Act caused enormous confusion and misery, with many uncertain cases and split families. There was no possible geographic 'homeland' for coloured people and it was difficult to develop a discourse of separate nationhood for the Cape's working class. Nevertheless, the Nationalists were so obsessed with making 'race' and nation congruent that they explicitly set out to intensify coloured self-awareness: 'one can only hope to succeed if one develops that sense of national awareness and that sense of pride in himself and his people' (Goldin 1987: 168). They aimed to win support by giving preference to coloured people over Africans in the employment markets of the western Cape.

The policy of separation was driven especially hard down the long and tortuous route to disenfranchisement. Malan argued that South African parliamentary sovereignty was no longer restricted by the entrenched status of the Cape franchise clause in the 'imperial' South Africa Act; a simple majority would be sufficient to remove it. In 1951, the Separate Representation of Voters Act passed through parliament. Coloured people were to elect four white representatives rather than retain their common roll vote for white candidates in all Cape constituencies. With typical insensitivity, given the severe problems of alcoholism amongst the Cape working class, the Minister of Interior, Donges, likened this to four full bottles of wine rather than fifty-five empties.

The Act sparked a wave of protest amongst both whites and blacks that, alongside the Defiance Campaign, was perhaps the most widespread in the early apartheid years. Mass white opposition may seem surprising in that the UP had proposed only to protect, not extend, the existing vote and did not allow coloured people to become full party members. But the UP clearly had some electoral self-interest in defending the franchise. Moreover, many of its supporters were ex-servicemen who had fought the war for democracy against fascism. Even if their version of democracy for blacks was etiolated, they saw the 'rule of law' and constitutionalism as part of a civilized heritage. They were defending what they saw as the constitution, and especially the requirement for a two-thirds majority in parliament to revoke entrenched clauses. Many Nationalists had opposed the war effort. They were now, in the words of opposition spokesmen at the time, going beyond 'constitutional political conduct' and 'solemn promises' made to coloured people at the time of Union. They were the compromises that salved the consciences of more liberal English-speaking white South Africans.

White anger found its outlet in the War Veterans' Torch Commando, which organized motorcades, rallies, and dramatic torch-light processions in 1951. The symbolism of the movement was peculiar in that it evoked the commando and Fascist torchlight parades rather than dominion parliamentarianism. Perhaps this was one last attempt to capture icons that might appeal to the mass of Afrikaans-speaking South African whites. The Torch Commando agreed to put its efforts into the re-election of the UP in 1953, and, when that failed, the movement dissipated. The white opposition was soon to fragment. The UP, uncertain and compromised in its policy, lost Afrikaner support to the NP, and in 1959 its liberal wing broke away as the Progressive Party. In 1953 a more radical Liberal Party had been formed, while some of the white left allied with the Congress movement. The white Labour Party faded away along with its English-speaking working-class constituency.

Black protests were more splintered. A Communist Party and Congress-linked Franchise Action Committeee (FRAC) did organize large rallies in Cape Town, as well as a strike. FRAC aimed to extend the franchise, not simply to defend the 'constitution', and the Torch Commando refused to coordinate activities with it. The ANC and its allies soon shifted their energies into the Defiance Campaign. The Cape-based Unity Movement, with a strong following amongst both coloured and African teachers, pursued a strategy of total boycott rather than confrontation. Although their influential local paper, *The Torch*, maintained a scathing commentary on South Africa's 'herrenvolk' rulers, they were also unable to find sufficient common ground for an alliance with FRAC.

Representatives of coloured voters, acting with the UP and sympathetic white lawyers, challenged the Act in court and succeeded in having it invalidated by a relatively liberal Appellate Division. An unprecedented and bitter constitutional crisis was resolved only when Strydom succeeded in passing the Act with a two-thirds majority in 1956 after packing the Senate with nominated supporters. New Afrikaner judges were appointed to the Appellate Division. In the 1960s the government pushed coloured representation further towards the African pattern by removing the four white representatives and creating a separate Coloured Council with some control over local government. The euphemistically named Prohibition of Improper Political Interference Act (1967) outlawed most political activity across racial lines.

A parallel issue peaked in the Nationalist drive finally to segregate the railways in the early 1950s. While effective separation on mainline long-distance passenger trains was long entrenched, station platforms and suburban trains in the Cape were not so tightly controlled. Increased usage of first-class carriages by black people at a time when some suburbs were being Afrikanerized irked Nationalists, who decided to bring Cape Town into line. The language of racial inferiority and exclusion was used as unselfconsciously in this debate as it was on the franchise question. One politician argued that mixing on the railways might make South Africa like another Brazil. Brief encounters at railway station cafés were unlikely to have produced many 'mixed' marriages, but the sentiment expressed the stark alternatives in Nationalist thinking. Blacks were excluded from the main concourses of the new Johannesburg and Cape Town stations; ticket offices, platforms, subways, and bridges as well as carriages were racially reserved.

Railway segregation was significant beyond the station gates. Challenges to these rules in court, coordinated by the ANC, produced another anti-apartheid legal victory. In 1953 the Appellate Division asserted the principle (not enforced before) that while separation of facilities was legal, this should not result in substantial inequality. The government restored its freedom of action with the Reservation of Separate Amenities Act (1953), which allowed separate and unequal public facilities. The resulting 'petty apartheid' came to symbolize the Nationalist project in South Africa: the highly noticeable reservation of swimming pools, buses, park benches, beaches, post office counters, and much else for whites. Signs saying 'whites only/*blankes alleen*' multiplied, a favoured target of opposition cartoonists and foreign photographers. Intriguingly, while some shops such as liquor outlets were segregated, many remained unregulated and served a mixed clientele.

Spatial division of urban residential areas was central to Nationalist aims. Africans had been effectively removed from many city centres, but some suburban freehold areas such as Sophiatown in Johannesburg remained under black occupation. Coloured and Indian communities were dispersed widely through city-centre zones. To the metaphors of disease and racial purity were added the justifications of slum clearance, urban planning, and strategic control of internal enemies. Post-war planning was nearly as ambitious in the urban as in the rural areas (**Chapter 5**). As in Europe, where modernist visions and Second World War bombs ravaged inner cities, the poor were to be rehoused in purpose-built accommodation on city outskirts. There they were seen to be more easily controlled and would impact less on sanitized business centres remodelled for the car.

Durban had been wracked by conflict over Indian property ownership in the 1940s. Its growing Indian population found that sites were available near the centre, as whites moved to the suburbs and their commercial success enabled them to purchase land. White protests led to the Pegging Act (1943), which restricted Indian purchase, and Asiatic Land Tenure Act (1946), which envisaged strict racial zoning for urban expansion, using rivers and ridges as buffers. In the 1940s, Cape Town's planners recommended the wholesale demolition of the centrally located District Six, by then a largely coloured area, to be replaced by roads, commercial zones, and new housing.

These initiatives prefigured the policies pushed through under the NP's Group Areas Act (1950) and Prevention of Illegal Squatting Act (1951), which allowed racial zones to be defined and people to be moved between them. Moving people about became a major preoccupation of apartheid planners. Once the Group Areas Board was established, its enormous powers to expropriate property and enter the real-estate market provided a new momentum to urban segregation. Building firms and developers, some with inside knowledge, could purchase expropriated houses cheaply, improve them, and sell them off as whitewashed cottages to whites. Elsewhere, land was cleared and sold for new housing and office developments. Escalating from the mid-1950s, Group Areas impacted most on coloured and Indian people—an estimated 600,000 were removed over three decades as Cape Town, Durban, and others cities were pulled apart and reassembled to conform to the new pattern. District Six lost around 60,000 people and many Victorian buildings were destroyed. By the 1970s it was a city-centre wasteland dotted with a few churches and mosques and fringed by new highways; its reoccupation remains a politically charged issue.

Some of the most dramatic early removals, such as the destruction of Johannesburg's Sophiatown, also affected African people. As an area of freehold tenure, established for decades, it was not subject to the same array of regulations as the municipal locations. A wide cross-section of people lived there, including politicians and writers, such as Dr Xuma and Can Themba. Sophiatown was the stamping ground of Trevor Huddleston, the Anglican minister who became a central figure in the British anti-apartheid movement and initiated the musical career of Hugh Masekela. It was a crucible of new black urban music, influenced by American jazz. Like District Six in Cape Town, it was also a world of shebeens and gangs.

Sophiatown's racy, hard-drinking urban style, which attracted many of the young writers and intellectuals of the 1950s, was captured in *Drum* magazine. A weekly, financed and edited by whites, *Drum* nevertheless had 'the black hand upon it'—a focus for a black journalistic revival and 'for readers who thought and spoke in jazz and exclamation marks' (Sampson 1956: 24, 27). Sophiatown epitomized the urban African culture anathema to apartheid. It was displaced by the new brick bungalows of the white suburb Triomf. In the longer term, most black people came to live on the outer peripheries of cities, separated from white areas by industrial zones, open spaces, or highways. As in so much of apartheid practice, justified in that it would reduce 'friction' to the benefit of all, whites were beneficiaries; in the first two decades of Group Areas, only an estimated 2 per cent of those moved were white.

Successive pieces of legislation impacted on an ever-wider circle of people. Dr Xuma, who had helped place the ANC on a more stable organizational basis but remained cautious in his approach, was voted out of the presidency in 1949. The Congress Youth League pushed through a Programme of Action, which aimed to generate a mass movement through confrontational protests, boycotts, and passive resistance. Communist activists, their party banned in 1950, put their weight behind mass action through the Congress movement. The Communist Party was especially important in cementing ties between the ANC, the Natal Indian Congress, and white radicals in the Congress of Democrats— partly as a response to the Durban riots of 1949, when Indian traders were attacked by Africans.

The Congress movement, although it evolved through separate racial groupings, emerged as the most effective national non-racial leadership in the early 1950s, deeply conscious of the need for greater unity, a wider support base, and the identification of popular issues. Its new strategy found focus in the Defiance Campaign of 1952 where unjust laws were to be breached by groups inviting arrest. The campaign did not fill the gaols, as was planned, in that little over 8,000 people were arrested. It did greatly enhance solidarity amongst committed supporters and gave Congress a sharper public profile. Gandhi's strategies of controlled confrontation by symbolic challenges to entrenched hierarchies and restricted spaces—including white-only railway carriages—were revived. Congress membership, probably less than 5,000 when Xuma left, soared to about 100,000, and the regional committees succeeded in working better together.

For the first time, the ANC seemed capable of becoming a mass movement. Its ideologues reflected the central concerns of anti-colonial struggles about freedom and began to instil the idea with meanings appropriate to its varied South African constituencies. In 1955 an Assembly of the People met in Johannesburg to agree on a Freedom Charter after widespread consultation. This committed the Congress movement to a non-racial democracy, equal opportunities for all people, and some redistribution of wealth. The programme remained at the heart of Congress campaigning for many years.

### Apartheid, Labour Control, and the Homelands

In addition to the spatial division of the urban population by racial category, apartheid planners saw it as essential to translate into policy long-identified connections between protecting white workers from competition and controlling African movement to town. The government greatly impeded radical worker organization through the Suppression of Communism Act (1950). Separate procedures were formally set up for disputes involving Africans, and strikes by African workers were banned.

Tighter 'job reservation' for whites was a feature of the early apartheid years. Racial protection in manufacturing had generally not been as far-reaching as in the mining industry. But white workers found their monopolies of skill eroded in the post-war period. Both their trade unions and the government responded to their dilemma. The Trades and Labour Council, which had been the most significant non-Afrikaner trade union federation, had retained a degree of openness to cross-racial cooperation. In a series of splits and re-amalgamations, at a time when anti-communist rhetoric was especially strong, white unions broke away from it and moved increasingly towards a policy of racial definition of jobs. A new, largely white, Trade Union Congress of South Africa (TUCSA) emerged, although it did attempt to keep some contact with other unionized workers, particularly in coloured unions. The Congress movement set up its own South

African Congress of Trade Unions (SACTU). Legislation in 1956 and 1959 reserved a far wider range of jobs for whites only in the private and public sector: Africans could be barred from skilled work in the clothing industry or prevented from becoming traffic cops. Black workers were not allowed to have authority over whites. Unions with white and coloured workers were required to have separate branches and a white executive. There is no doubt that, together with rapid economic growth and the availability of state employment, job reservation went a long way to resolve remaining white unemployment and poor whiteism.

Some academics in the 1970s saw the maintenance of the migrant labour system as a centrepiece of apartheid. Migrant labour, they argued, had proved cheap for the mining industry because employers did not have to pay a wage that would support a whole urban family. Now the government hoped to extend its benefits to the growing manufacturing sector. In order to do so effectively, Wolpe suggested, the Nationalists wished to restore the crumbling economies of the African reserves, but this was insufficient in itself. Tight 'influx' controls were designed to check urban growth and inhibit the development of a black urban working class. Industrial decentralization of factories to areas near the African reserves would take the pressure off labour requirements in the big cities. Labour-hungry commercial farmers would benefit, as workers would be bottled up in the rural areas. An extension of migrancy would also help protect white workers.

It is certainly true that mine-owners remained committed to migrancy. Their labour supplies were threatened as the economy grew after the 1930s depression and as competition with industry and agriculture became more intense. In response, the Chamber of Mines adopted its previously favoured strategy of extending the geographic range of recruiting activities rather than increasing wages. From 1932, when 'tropical' recruitment was again permitted, WNLA developed its activities in Zambia, Malawi, Angola, Tanzania, Zimbabwe, and Botswana, all lower wage areas than South Africa. William Gemmill, the Chamber's labour 'czar', pursued a long-term strategy of investment in road and air networks, rest camps, and medical facilities in these territories (Crush *et al.* 1991).

By 1960, the mines employed about 75,000 'tropical' workers as well as 80,000 from southern Mozambique and 50,000 from Lesotho and Swaziland, so that well over 60 per cent of the black labour force were foreign migrants (**Figure 2**). The Chamber's South African black workforce, though declining slightly, was also employed on a migrant basis from African reserves and continued to live in giant single-sex compounds. The mines were clearly committed in their policy documents to maintaining the role of South African reserves as labour reservoirs and to the restoration of traditional African authorities within them.

The test for the government, however, was the manufacturing sector, where total employment had overtaken mining in the 1940s. By the 1950s, African employment alone in industry exceeded that in mining (**Chapter 7**). It is true that some factories drew on rural migrants, whom they saw as cheaper. The large market for domestic servants was also increasingly supplied by African women from the rural areas, although many contrived to stay on in town even if this meant dodging apartheid regulations. Migrant workers themselves continued to shape the labour market—for example, in the way that networks from particular districts tried to ensure that they were replaced in their jobs by men or women from home.

The state, however, faced a dilemma. Important industrialists associated themselves with the view that migrant labour inhibited productivity and that low wages constrained the growth of an internal market; they wanted a more skilled and stable workforce with lower job turnover. Unlike the mines, the bulk of industrial establishments, many of them small enterprises, were not geared to receive migrant workers. Yet the areas in which industries expanded—the Rand, Durban, Cape Town, and Port Elizabeth— were precisely those that the government hoped to protect from further African urbanization. Moreover, the proportion of women and of black families in these cities was rising.

In examining the government's response to these problems, scholars have diverged from the argument that apartheid simply involved an extension of the migrant labour system and industrial decentralization. They have detected a more compromised policy involving an attempt to divide urban African 'insiders' from rural migrant 'outsiders'. Section 10 of the 1952 Urban Areas Act (one of a number regulating African movements and urban rights), which specified who was permitted to live and work freely in towns, became a critical instrument of this policy.

In order to qualify, Africans had to show either that they had been born in town; or that they had worked continuously for one employer for ten years; or that they had lived in town for fifteen years. Spouses, unmarried daughters, and sons under 18 could also qualify. Those who did not qualify and new work-seekers had to register with the authorities and, if they were not employed, they were liable to be 'endorsed out'. For the first time a systematic attempt was made to incorporate women on a national basis in the web of legislation controlling African movements. State-regulated labour bureaux were established in the rural areas and smaller towns to oversee the flow of workers.

While these laws made it difficult for new families to establish themselves legally in town, they did not remove rights for those who had come before or even during the war. Those who qualified could benefit from preferential access to housing, services, and employment. Thus apartheid policy in its earlier years was partly intended to ensure that many African workers remained migrant. But in effect it was an attempt at 'labour differentiation', in which established urban Africans had relatively secure rights as families, rather than a wholesale drive to extend migrancy (Hindson 1987).

Enforcement of these laws required a huge bureaucratic and police effort. Xuma protested that 'flying squads, pick-up vans, troop-carriers, and mounted police are all abroad irritating and exasperating Africans by indiscriminately demanding passes . . . handling them in an insulting and humiliating way' (Posel 1991: 123). Resentment at the 'dompas' was powerfully expressed in a march of 20,000 women, organized by the Congress-linked Federation of South African Women, on the Union Buildings in Pretoria in 1956. Nevertheless, by the early 1960s nearly 600 labour bureaux had been created. Four million men and 3.6 million women had been issued with new pass books. Convictions under the influx control laws increased from 164,324 in 1952 to a staggering 384,497 in 1962—a total of three million in ten years—with hundreds of thousands of foreigners deported. Pass raids were stepped up in politically sensitive areas or after riots and protests.

It is also important to stress that influx control was only very partially successful and had limited effect on the rate of growth of the African urban population. Between 1936 and 1946, the annual average increase was 3.4 per cent. Between 1946 and 1951 the rate averaged 6.6 per cent per annum, though this figure is probably exaggerated, because the definition of urban areas in the latter census was extended. From 1951 to 1960 the rate of increase fell slightly to 4.5 per cent annually; that of African women fell from 8.5 to 5.4 per cent. But the pace of urban growth was still faster than the heights reached under previous governments, which had been less restrictive in their approach. Influx control was no more than a partial holding operation. The number of Africans in urban areas increased from 2.3 million to 3.4 million in the 1950s, from 27 to 32 per cent of the total African population (**Table 3**). Many people braved arrest and continued to come to town illegally.

The government hoped that it would achieve relatively full employment amongst those Africans permitted to live as families in town. They would therefore simultaneously meet the demand of industry for a more settled labour force and address the acute problems of urban poverty, crime, and delinquency that had been so marked in the 1940s. In the longer term, the Nationalists aimed to externalize population growth and unemployment to the reserves, where, in theory, 'separate development' would absorb them. Expenditure on services and education would also be concentrated as far as possible in the reserves. These aims were not realized: high unemployment persisted; urban gangs such as the *tsotsis* and the Russians, as well as delinquency, flourished. The ANC's expansion was also partly rooted in the burgeoning city population.

Another piece in the complex jigsaw of social engineering—closely related to employment—was the Bantu Education Act (1953). Funding and administration of African education was removed from missions and provincial authorities and taken under the iron hand of Dr W. Eiselen, Verwoerd's Secretary of Native Affairs. Education at the 5,000 or so mission schools had produced, in Nationalist eyes, an academic training with too much emphasis on English and dangerous liberal ideas. It was seen as the foundation of an African elite that claimed recognition in a common society. Now African vernacular languages, which would cement ethnic awareness in African children, would be more extensively used as the medium of instruction up to Standard 6 (the eighth year of schooling). In higher classes, Afrikaans as well as English was to be used. Bantu Education also confirmed pre-apartheid tendencies towards more technical education and greater central control over syllabuses. Condemned as 'education for barbarism', it hit at the beneficiaries of the old system, the most articulate section of the African population. Critics saw it as a measure for retribalization, which would produce a cheap but not entirely illiterate labour force. The large gap between expenditure on black and white children confirmed their worst suspicions.

Defenders of the old mission-based system may have been exaggerating its effectiveness. Hyslop argues that, 'far from thriving', it was 'in a state of near collapse' (1993: 394). It could not cater for the growing urban population and officials felt that the lack of educational provision in the major cities exacerbated problems of urban crime and delinquency. A striking feature of the new system was the increase in overall educational provision for Africans from about 800,000 school places in 1953 to 1,800,000 in 1963; numbers expanded even more rapidly afterwards. By 1958 Bantu Education was so large an enterprise that it became a separate department of state.

Even though there was gross underfunding, inadequate teacher training, and very many pupils still did not get beyond the first four years of schooling, the proportion of students at secondary level gradually rose. Employment for teachers expanded, and, as there was little alternative for African families, they made what they could of the opportunities offered. Some schools were able to dilute central directives—for example, by not teaching in Afrikaans. The quality of education offered and the funding per capita were inadequate. But the consequences of Bantu

Education and more widespread literacy were to be far less predictable than either its planners or its opponents expected.

Territorial separation became increasingly central to NP policy in the 1950s. For the more far-seeing nationalists, no longer satisfied with the half-measures of segregation, the alternatives seemed to be giving Africans separate territories, or seeing Africans gain power in a single state. In 1951 the Bantu Authorities Act prepared the way for a new system of local and regional government in the reserves that remodelled the old councils and elevated chiefs. The Tomlinson Commission (1956) examined ways of developing the homelands economically within the parameters of apartheid: 'there is no midway between the two poles of ultimate total integration and ultimate separate development of the two [racial] groups', its report concluded; hence 'sustained development of the Bantu Areas on a large scale' was 'the germinal point' (Union of South Africa 1956: 194).

Tomlinson strongly supported the implementation of Betterment as a first stage in the rehabilitation of the reserves in order to combat soil erosion and underpin agricultural expansion. But it also advocated 'economic farm units' with freehold title for a limited number of African farmers who would become an 'agricultural class' (Union of South Africa 1956: 194–6). This implied moving large numbers of people off the land. As apartheid policy precluded their absorption in established cities, they would be housed in urban zones within the homelands. Decentralized industries in the homelands, or on their borders, would provide employment. Fragmented reserves would gradually be consolidated into larger contiguous homeland units through the purchase of land under the Trust. Thus while Tomlinson retained the old concerns of the NEC about agricultural development and retribalization, the proposals for territorial consolidation, economic units, industrialization, and urbanization in the homelands went beyond earlier thinking. The report was less concerned with underpinning migrancy than with creating 'viable' homelands and preventing movement to cities.

Verwoerd, as the Minister involved, accepted only limited parts of the strategy. While rehabilitation would proceed, he rejected concentration of landholding within the homelands, because it would undermine the chiefs, on whom the homeland strategy depended, and might precipitate even more rapid urbanization. Forms of customary land tenure were still widely supported by rural African people, who felt it was their best guarantee of access to resources. Direct investment by white-owned firms into the homelands was disallowed so that Africans could develop separately 'at their own pace'. Not only would this protect communal resources and local African entrepreneurs, but it answered critics who feared that homeland industries might undercut those employing white workers in established industrial areas.

By the late 1950s, with three election victories under its belt, the government's hold on power was more certain. The idea of separate development was espoused as a central element of NP rhetoric, and increasing amounts of the Native Affairs budget were directed towards the reserves. Ideologues in the Broederbond who advocated more thorough separation were in the ascendant. Verwoerd himself was deeply perturbed by the forces of African nationalism on the continent and resolved to push through the homeland policy as a means of promoting internal decolonization. Despite the rapid growth of urban townships, these were now increasingly conceived as outposts of the homelands, the latter being the base of new nations.

Whatever the language of the government, its strategy clearly aimed to defuse the growing challenge of African nationalist and urban political movements. Whites from very diverse backgrounds were to be one group with one territory, while blacks with similar recent histories were to become a series of separate minority nations. There was to be no English homeland in Grahamstown and Durban; no Jewish in Sea Point or northern Johannesburg. But there were to be separate Xhosa-speaking homelands in the Ciskei and Transkei, a Zulu homeland in Natal, Tswana in the fragmented zones that became called Bophuthatswana, Pedi in Lebowa, Shangaan in Gazankulu, and others in more minuscule pockets of land (**Map 2**).

The partial survival of old chiefdoms with land in communal tenure and distinct languages did provide some basis to the proposed balkanization. In attempting to restore African chieftaincy as a means of decentralizing power to a conservative rural elite, officials were rebuilding and extending rather than inventing the institution. Through the 1950s, government anthropologists and black information officers scoured the reserves collecting genealogies to establish the legitimate incumbents of new Tribal Authorities. As Harold Macmillan was talking about the winds of change in parliament in Cape Town in 1960, other winds were blowing through African reserves. Bowler-hatted, dark-suited ministers were helicoptered in to wax eloquent in deliberately archaic language about the virtues of progress through tradition.

Whatever other interests it had in the restoration of chieftaincy, the state took the symbolic side quite seriously and sought some consistency on this question. 'Dear Mr' or 'Dear Sir' had already been abolished by the Native Affairs Department in letters to Africans before the Nationalists came to power, to be replaced by 'Greetings!'. Chiefs were addressed by their African praise names. Leopard skins, neo-traditionalist insignia, made frequent appearances at the installation of chiefs. The Minister of Bantu Education instructed his officials 'not to greet Bantu people by shaking hands'. Part of the reason was to protect officials 'against tendencies towards social equality', but part was also due to a belief that Africans did not traditionally shake hands—an issue that had confused whites since the nineteenth century. (Bishop Colenso was instructed not to shake hands with the Zulu.)

The state's obsession with African chieftaincy fitted quite neatly with the peculiar mix of ideology that characterized Afrikaner views of themselves: a celebration of the *volk* married with a determined sense that this could prosper along with technical advance in an industrial state. Segregationists in previous decades, and particularly those involved in the NEC of 1930–2, had done much of the ideological work necessary to square developmentalist and modernist ideas with traditional forms in relation to African societies. Now the government was taking these insights and prescriptions to their logical conclusion. While most British colonial states began broadening the range of African representation at the centre instead of narrowing it, and sought to court and contain the new urban elite, the South African state seemed to be moving in the opposite direction, even though its African urban classes were proportionately larger than in British colonies.

Governor Arden Clarke was handing over to Nkrumah in Ghana at the moment that Verwoerd was discovering Kaiser Matanzima in the Transkei.

The government was not totally isolated in its mission. As in the 1920s, some chiefs and ambitious local politicians pushed officials hard to deliver on their fulsome rhetoric about the virtues of African self-rule. There was considerable promise for them in large homelands, with growing budgets, such as the Transkei or KwaZulu. They espoused alternative versions of African modernism that could bypass, at least temporarily, the difficult route of African nationalist struggle for a single South African state. Taking hold of such decentralized authority was a means of coming to terms with white power, of getting whites off their backs, and of participating in the scramble for expanding political and economic resources on the South African periphery (**Chapter 8**).

In the late 1950s the Bantustan strategy, which the government increasingly used to justify restrictions elsewhere, became central to opposition as well as government politics. In Sekhukhuneland, later the eastern Transvaal homeland of Lebowa, rural resistance to rehabilitation and Bantu Authorities found support from the ANC-influenced migrant workers' movement *Sebatakgomo*. In Zeerust, western Transvaal, women led a sustained protest against passes; women again took a central role in the protests that swept through rural Natal in 1959 and 1960. In such areas, support was mobilized in favour of popular claimants to the chieftaincy against those seen to collaborate with the government. Though some rural people were renouncing chieftaincy, most still saw the institution as having the potential to represent them and stave off unwanted interventions. Disputes often focused on the legitimacy of particular incumbents. Rural movements still reflected some anti-modernist ideas, which would prove a difficult inheritance for the ANC and the state.

Probably the most sustained rebellion took place in Pondoland, Transkei, in 1960—a reserve area with close to half a million people that was divided into eastern and western zones under different paramount chiefs. Victor Poto, who inherited the western paramountcy as a youth in 1918, learned how to cope with the political brinkmanship that the role demanded. He was in favour of elements of tradition but a strong Christian. He supported enhanced powers for chiefs, but opposed balkanization of the country. Although he agreed to Betterment in his area, he managed to retain popular support through the troubled 1950s.

In contrast, Botha Sigcau's chieftaincy in eastern Pondoland had been disputed since his installation in 1938. In the 1950s he sided with the authorities in their homeland policy. Disputes escalated about popular access to reserved forests and coastal grazing lands, as well as plans to implement Betterment and impose Bantu Authorities. As power was devolved to the unpopular paramount, so his opponents argued that he had 'sold the people to the government'. His councillors were burnt out and a few killed. The rebels met on hilltops to avoid surveillance and used the term Ntaba (the mountain) for their movement. When the government sent in the police and army, at least eleven were gunned down at a mass meeting on Ngquza hill, on the borders of Lusikisiki and Bizana districts. Their leader, Solomon Madikizela, was a peasant farmer, small trader and Methodist evangelist for whom legitimate chieftaincy, a measure of local independence, and control over rural resources remained central aims. He and others were tried and sent into internal exile. The rebels linked up with Congress in Durban and were driven to a position where they began to ask for arms. There seemed again to be the potential for an anti-colonial struggle linking nationalists and peasants, town and countryside.

### Sharpeville and the Republic

Rural rebellions alerted African Nationalist politicians such as Govan Mbeki, who later wrote *The Peasants' Revolt* (1964), to the potential of this neglected constituency. The new President of the ANC, Albert Luthuli, was himself rurally based. But the largely urban leadership did not always find it easy to harness localized and sometimes particularist impulses in these movements. The late 1950s had in any case been a difficult period for the ANC. Attempts to extend its political strategies through boycotts and worker stayaways were hampered by bannings and imprisonment. SACTU, the Congress-linked trade union federation, remained relatively small. Though it organized successful strikes, such as at the Amato textile factory on the East Rand where it was particularly strong, these were an insufficient platform for a powerful national presence. The lengthy treason trial staged by the government, for which many Congress politicians were arrested, sucked in the energies of its leaders and lawyers despite their eventual acquittals. Luthuli's balanced leadership and moral authority could not secure unity. Just as a broad political front incorporating urban workers, women, and rural rebels seemed attainable between 1958 and 1960, the Pan Africanist Congress (PAC), impatient with white and left-wing influences in the Congress alliance, broke away, dividing the opposition and tearing at popular loyalties.

Formed early in 1959 under Robert Sobukwe, the PAC, espousing a militant Africanism, attempted to inject new urgency into campaigning and upstage the ANC in mass mobilizations. In March 1960, the PAC put its weight behind an anti-pass campaign; one centre of activity was Sharpeville, the African location of Vereeniging, south of Johannesburg. A crowd converged on the police station, and, despite the security of their Saracen armoured cars, nervous policemen opened fire, killing sixty-nine and wounding many more. Sharpeville sent a shudder through white and black communities alike. As the former responded with self-justification, the latter were galvanized into further action. Africans in Cape Town launched a march into the city centre that seemed momentarily to threaten parliament. The government declared a state of emergency and sent the armed forces into dissident areas. Following mass arrests, the ANC and PAC were banned.

Nelson Mandela's dramatic life delineates the phases of black nationalist politics in these years. Born in Thembuland, Transkei, in 1918 his father, a minor chief and headman, was a traditionalist but his mother a Christian convert. When he was 9, his father died and he was adopted into a chief's homestead, where he attended school. Mandela retained fond memories of his childhood in the Transkei, where he learned 'to knock birds out of the sky with a slingshot, to gather wild honey and fruits and edible roots . . . and to stick-fight—essential knowledge to any rural African boy'

(Mandela 1995: 11). He attended circumcision school, but the main influences at the great place were 'chieftaincy and the [Methodist] Church'. In retrospect, he formed a romantic view of rural African life as 'democracy in its purist form', where all men—but not, he admits, women—were 'equal in their value as citizens' and free to speak at meetings (Mandela 1995: 24).

Great emphasis was placed on education by the Transkeian Christian elite and Mandela's status and abilities led him to Fort Hare, the major higher educational institution for Africans. His political horizons broadening, he was expelled over a relatively minor clash with authority. He subsequently rebelled against an arranged marriage and fled to Johannesburg in 1941. There he trained as a lawyer, lived in Alexandra township, and was caught up simultaneously in a multiracial political world and in the radicalization of the ANC. Mandela moved to the heart of the ANC Youth League in the 1940s and was co-opted onto the National Executive in 1950 in place of Dr Xuma. It was the early years of National Party rule that finally confirmed the 'birth of a freedom fighter': he became deeply absorbed as a key organizer of the Defiance Campaign and First Deputy President of the ANC in 1952 (Mandela 1995: 108). Despite his initial doubts, Mandela committed himself to non-racial participation in the civil disobedience campaigns and to the alliance with the Communist Party. He adhered to these positions consistently and became a major protagonist of a non-racial political struggle.

Banned on and off through the 1950s, and an accused in the Treason Trial, Mandela, like many black leaders at the time, found his freedom of action severely constrained. But his legal practice with Oliver Tambo was a lively centre for Congress political networks and he became a core figure in the transformation of the ANC from a nationalist protest movement to a national liberation movement after Sharpeville in 1960. 'Of all that group of young men,' Tambo argued, 'Mandela and his close friend and co-leader Walter Sisulu were perhaps the fastest to get to grips with the harsh realities of the African struggle against the most powerful adversary in Africa' (Tambo in Mandela 1965: p. xi).

While mass action was not immediately abandoned by the ANC and PAC, both developed underground structures, espoused the idea of armed struggle, and sent representatives abroad. Mandela stayed in the country and operated from hiding—a 'creature of the night'—initially planning the mass stay-at-home of 1961 (Mandela 1965: 317). With Sisulu and Joe Slovo of the South African Communist Party (SACP), he then formed the High Command of Umkhonto we Sizwe (Spear of the Nation, later MK), the new armed wing of Congress. The ANC argued that it had exhausted the potential for non-violent protest; the state itself was illegitimate and rested on violence. Rural rebellions as well as mass urban protests suggested that the people were ready to fight. Fuel for armed struggle seemed to be there, if only a spark could be found to light it. Anti-colonial movements from Algeria to Cuba had shown what was possible and African politics in Zimbabwe and Mozambique were beginning to move in the same direction. In 1962 Mandela travelled secretly to Tanzania, Ethiopia, as well as West and North Africa, to seek solidarity and assistance—his first experience of independent African countries.

Government control was sufficient to stifle any early success. By 1961 Verwoerd was reaching the height of his confidence. Internal opposition was neutralized and he wished to redefine South Africa's international position. Through the 1950s, South Africa's relationship with Britain had been renegotiated across a range of issues such as control of shipping and the Simonstown naval base. In 1957 the Union Jack and 'God Save the Queen' were finally abolished from official ceremonies. In 1960 a new decimalized currency of rands and cents replaced sterling. In the same year, Verwoerd held a referendum on the long-promised republic, which the Nationalists won narrowly.

The British response was ambivalent. In some respects, Britain tried to rein in Afrikaner ambitions. Renewed South African efforts to annex the High Commission territories of Botswana, Lesotho, and Swaziland in the early 1950s were rejected. (The Nationalists soon abandoned this strategy when they recognized that it cut across their homeland policy.) One of the British aims behind the Federation of Rhodesia and Nyasaland, created in 1953, was to establish a relatively strong and independent colonial nexus north of South Africa—an echo of late-nineteenth-century politics. But British and other Western countries with extensive interests in the country deflected early attempts at isolating South Africa internationally. For all the unease about Afrikaner power, South African was a signficant centre for investment and commerce; critically, it represented a regional bastion against communism as the cold war intensified.

International attention was sharply focused on the country at the time; Luthuli was awarded the Nobel Peace prize in 1960. Powerful criticism from newly independent Commonwealth countries, shocked by the Sharpeville shootings, led to the formation of the Republic of South Africa in 1961 outside the Commonwealth. Verwoerd remained Prime Minister and a largely ceremonial, non-executive presidency was established.

NP victory in 1948 marked the beginning of an elected racial autocracy. This version of the Westminster system, in which a simple majority could enact such far-reaching legislation, had struck with a vengeance in South Africa. Though Nationalists took the institution of parliament seriously, checks and balances in the judiciary and the civil service, as well as criticism by the opposition and mass protest, had been brusquely elbowed aside. Many commentators were seduced by the power of the Afrikaners' own myths—their preoccupation with apparently archaic ethnic concerns about *volk* and the obsessive ideology of race. Yet the Nationalists had also succeeded in taking rapid command of a complex bureaucracy, further developing a modern technocratic state and providing economically for their followers. Though they had provoked a potentially powerful opposition nationalism that defined South African citizenship in a non-racial and inclusive manner, they had also controlled it.

# 7

# Economy and Society in the 1960s and 1970s

## *Apartheid and Economic Growth*

Many opponents of apartheid in the 1950s and 1960s argued that it was not only morally unjust but economically inefficient. Yet the first two decades of Nationalist rule were distinctive as a period of rapid economic growth—in particular of new manufacturing industries. From the late 1960s, a new generation of radical historians and social scientists attempted to reassess the relationship between apartheid and economic growth. Elements of this reinterpretation have been discussed in preceding chapters, but it is worth summarizing here. It was a debate of the high apartheid years and, although analyses are more fluid now, a good deal of academic literature was influenced by it.

English-speakers tended to see apartheid as a peculiarly Afrikaner policy. Some, taking Nationalist ideas about their past at face value, felt it was a hangover from the frontier and the Boer republics; 'the present Government's policies are acting out the same sick, violent drama as those of their ancestors' (Desmond 1971: 22). Some gave more emphasis to the recent political role of special interest groups like farmers or white workers. But they tended to dissociate apartheid from the major capitalist enterprises in the country. Even though they recognized that segregation had its roots in the British colonial era, as in Natal, and that migrant labour was central to the British-owned mining, nevertheless they suggested that Afrikaners had made such policies their own and developed them to a point far beyond earlier practice.

Apartheid, in this view, had become economically irrational and increasingly inimical to capitalist growth—an idea that was lent cogency by an increasing shortage of skilled labour in the

1960s. Labour migrancy was seen not only as socially destructive of both rural and urban communities but as leading to high turnover, acute difficulties in training, and low productivity. Unequal education as well as the racial bars on apprenticeship and many categories of work skewed the labour market. Black poverty limited the growth of internal markets. Drawing on a whiggish understanding of British history, some suggested that ultimately growth would undermine or 'explode' apartheid and result in a more open society along the lines of the established industrial democracies.

To radical scholars in the early 1970s, these ideas seemed unconvincing. They argued that, except for a brief hiccup around the political crisis of 1960, growth rates were impressive on an international scale. The fact that few blacks had benefited did not seem to set the process back. 'White prosperity and white supremacy' appeared not to inhibit economic growth (Johnstone 1970). Both agriculture and extractive industries such as mining certainly seemed to benefit from a cheap, controlled, black labour force; manufacturing industry, the fastest growing sector, could at least live with this political dispensation. Drawing on Barrington Moore and other social theorists of modernization, Trapido pointed out that democratic systems were by no means the only outcomes of industrialization. Extensive state intervention and 'Prussian', even totalitarian, regimes often characterized late industrializers.

Segregation and apartheid could thus be construed as the product of a particular type of capitalist development, in a post-conquest context, rather than a system at odds with capitalism. White workers and poor whites certainly played their part in its development but were not the main agents of the many regulations governing black workers and communities. It was perhaps on this point—the imperatives of capitalism, especially manufacturing industry—that the radical interpretation differed most from liberal positions.

The debate took many forms, intensified by its relevance to opposition political strategies such as sanctions. Those supporting boycotts and disinvestment emphasized that economic growth was unlikely in itself to bring change. They questioned the motives of those who argued for continued trade, investment, or 'constructive engagement' in the hope that growth would explode apartheid. This seemed an excuse for business as usual: foreign firms making fat profits from cheap black labour. Some radical academics, strongly influenced by the exiled movements, or by socialist currents in European and American universities in the late 1960s and early 1970s, suggested that capitalism as much as apartheid was the problem. Blacks were an oppressed working class, rather than just the subject of racial laws. The political transformation of South Africa, it was implied, would also require major economic restructuring.

This debate is further explored at the end of this section and again at the end of **Chapter 9**. In examining patterns of economic and political change in the 1960s and 1970s, the mid-1970s should be kept in mind as a turning point. The oil crisis of 1973, the collapse of the Portuguese colonial empire in 1974, the rise of black worker militancy and the Soweto students' revolt of 1976 all combined to slow growth and jolt the government into reconsideration of its direction—especially after P. W. Botha succeeded B. J. Vorster as Prime Minister in 1978. A cycle of insurrection, reform, and repression began.

South Africa benefited from economic growth on a number of fronts. Although the post-Second World War agricultural boom should not be underestimated (**Chapter 8**), manufacturing, commerce, and finance were the most rapidly expanding sectors of the South African economy at this time—averaging over 7 per cent annually from 1946 to 1975. The value of manufacturing output outstripped mining in the 1940s and employment rose more quickly than in any other sector, at 4 per cent annually from 855,000 in 1951 to 1.6 million in 1976 (J. Nattrass 1988). Profits, size of firm, and productivity all increased. South African manufacturers produced very largely for the internal market, substituting locally made goods for imports in very diverse spheres.

Although food and clothing, the two best-established industries at the end of the Second World War, more than doubled in size by the 1970s, they had become far less significant. The textile industry, still in its infancy with less than 10,000 workers in 1948, employed 50,000 workers by 1962 and 90,000 by the mid-1970s.

Loans from the state's Industrial Development Corporation (1940) and foreign investment fuelled this expansion; small-scale entrepreneurs, some of them Jewish immigrants, became major industrialists with thousands of employees. Britain's biggest textile company, the Lancashire Cotton Corporation, established a plant in Natal with local tycoon Philip Frame.

Heavier industries such as metal products, machinery, and chemicals also expanded rapidly. South Africa produced an increasing amount of its steel and mining equipment, tools, explosives, fertilizers, and chemicals, as well as consumer durables such as washing machines, stoves, and cars. Production was protected where necessary by tariffs or, as in the case of the motor industry, the requirement that a proportion of parts should be locally manufactured. Demand for vehicles took off in the post-war years, and by 1960 South Africa produced 87,000 cars, more than most developing countries, including Brazil, which was much larger, and all the South East Asian countries together. With less than 20 per cent of parts and components locally made, the eastern Cape car factories were primarily assembly plants; fewer people worked for them than for motor dealers (32,000) and garages (20,000) (Andrews *et al.* 1962: 117). But by the end of the 1960s, the industry was being transformed: production doubled again to 195,000 vehicles annually and a 66 per cent local content programme was introduced.

South Africa was very much part of the post-Second World War globalization of multinational investment. Its efficient communications and financial sector, the lively Johannesburg stock exchange, a well-educated local white management and professional class, as well as relatively cheap labour, all made it attractive. There was a significant withdrawal of capital when slower growth in the late 1950s was followed by political crisis in 1960. But the government acted decisively to block the export of foreign exchange, increase interest rates, raise protectionist barriers, and crush opposition. Foreign investors responded by rewarding the reimposition of political authority rather than penalizing the intensification of repression; rates of profit were especially high in the 1960s.

Britain remained the largest source of investment and trade, but German involvement increased dramatically in the late 1960s, as did French, especially through military and related contracts. Japan became the second most important market for South African goods as early as 1964, though it was not until the 1970s that Japanese products made an impact. American influence was evident especially in high-profile consumer products: Coca-Cola signs were emblazoned on city-centre buildings and corner cafés. While the proportion of capital generated from overseas had declined since the early days of mining, foreign capital poured into manufacturing and commerce as never before.

The gold-mining industry, powerhouse of early twentieth-century growth, was constrained by the restitution of a fixed price for gold against the dollar ($35 per ounce) after the war. The industry contracted a little in the 1940s, but recently discovered gold in the northern Free State and West Rand underpinned renewed expansion. Between 1955 and 1970 gold production doubled to over one million kilograms; mining employment rose to new peaks in the 1960s (**Figure 2**). Uranium, first exported in 1952, was in particular demand for western nuclear programmes: a profitable by-product of gold mining, it became a major resource for some West Rand mines. Uranium not only increased mining income, but proved of great strategic value, cementing government links with Western powers and providing a bargaining counter for South Africa to import the foreign technology for a domestic nuclear industry (Christie 1984: 188).

In 1968 events outside South Africa's control presented another of those windfalls that, de Kiewiet (1941) noted, have been so important in shaping the country's history. As in the 1930s, the gold price was freed. By 1973 international demand drove the price to over $150 per ounce and, in these years of the oil crisis and a weakening dollar, to a brief peak of $800 in 1980. Profits in gold mining increased dramatically; so did state revenue from gold—from under R1 billion in 1970 to over R10 billion in 1980. As manufacturing growth faltered in the late 1970s, mining provided some economic ballast and remained a critical source of foreign exchange. Gold paid for large quantities of imported machinery and, after 1973, offset the increase in the price of oil, which would otherwise have retarded South Africa's economy more severely—as it did other African countries. To some degree, the revenues from gold also paid for apartheid and homeland development.

The Anglo-American Corporation dominated expansion into the Free State and Far West Rand goldfields. Ernest Oppenheimer, who established the group in South Africa and masterminded the takeover of De Beers, Rhodes's old diamond company, in 1929, was succeeded by his son Harry in the 1940s. Initially, Harry followed in both Rhodes's and his father's foot-steps in trying to marry business and politics: he became UP MP for Kimberley in 1948. Although politics remained close to his heart, Oppenheimer's taste was for cautious understatement rather than titanism; white politics did not look promising for a man of his relatively liberal views. He withdrew from parliament and played a role behind the scenes as a major influence in and funder of the opposition Progressive Party.

In raising large sums for the Free State goldfield developments, Anglo-American remained a major interlocutor between London's City and South Africa. By the late 1950s it became the largest single gold producer, benefiting from the efficiency of new mines. By 1976, with a third of the country's gold mines, the company was by far the most powerful group in the industry. It also had a major stake in uranium, coal, Zambian copper, and mining operations worldwide; De Beers controlled over 80 per cent of world diamond production.

Anglo-American's growth into South Africa's largest corpor-ation helps to illustrate the links between mining and manufactur-ing; together with other successful mining groups, it diversified energetically. When Anglo took over De Beers, it had acquired African Explosives and Chemical Industries, the biggest explo-sives, fertilizer, and later plastics producer in South Africa. Anglo developed a major presence in the metals industry, launched a merchant bank, and had an interest in the Nedbank consortium—the third largest in the country. Nor did it neglect public opinion: its newspaper company controlled the two largest selling daily papers, the Johannesburg *Star* and *Cape Argus*. Newsprint requirements made it advantageous to develop a paper and pulp concern and Anglo controlled Central News Agency—

South Africa's major newsagent and retail stationery chain. By the late 1970s over 150 Anglo-linked companies covered almost every sphere of mining, industrial production, finance, property, and agriculture, including the old Rhodes fruit farms. It was said that over half of the shares traded on the Johannesburg Stock Exchange were in Anglo companies. Other successful mining groups bought large brick, forestry, and paper concerns as well as the Cape's major fishing and freezing company.

Aside from mining capital, the savings derived from agriculture, and foreign investment, state involvement in heavy industry took on a new importance. It is often noted that, despite the Nationalists' hostility towards socialist ideas, state control of the economy was extended on an unprecedented scale. Post-war public-sector growth in South Africa reflected that in many industrial economies with social democratic governments. State-owned monopolies continued to control electricity and water supply, railways and harbours, broadcasting, air transport, and much steel production. (Coal mining remained private.) Manufacturing capital generated by the state increased from less than 10 per cent in the 1920s to 25 per cent by the 1970s. But public-sector spending as a proportion of the GDP—at about 30 per cent in 1975—probably did not rival that in Western Europe at least till the early 1980s. Unlike many Western democracies, South Africa operated a relatively low tax regime and offered very limited health and welfare provision, especially to blacks. The most rapidly growing area of expenditure was defence.

The government pursued a policy of economic nationalism, especially with major new ventures in oil and armaments. While South Africa had large and relatively cheap supplies of coal, it lacked natural oil. Anxious about sanctions and energy security, the state sponsored an oil-from-coal plant using a process developed in Germany before the war. The Sasol corporation, launched in 1951 in the northern Free State, became especially significant after 1973 when OPEC raised prices and banned trade with South Africa. Iran continued to be a safe source only until the Shah's fall in 1979. Although South Africa could always purchase oil, and multinational refiners and distributors such as Caltex, Mobil, BP, and Shell kept supplies flowing, the country's vulnerability was clear. In 1974, massive expansion of Sasol was planned at Secunda in the eastern Transvaal in close proximity to coalfields and electricity generating plants. Sasol produced around a third of oil supplies in the early 1980s and soon after consumed perhaps a quarter of coal production. Most of ESCOM's electricity generating capacity was also underpinned by coal.

After the UN Security Council imposed a ban on weapon exports to South Africa in 1963, Armscor was established as a parastatal company. By 1982 it had become one of the largest industrial enterprises in the country and probably the largest arms manufacturer in the southern hemisphere. Whereas in 1966 perhaps 70 per cent of arms expenditure was on imports, by 1982 over 80 per cent of a hugely increased budget was spent within the country. As in the case of oil, it proved possible to circumvent embargoes. French-style armoured cars and Mirage fighters, as well as Italian-designed Impala aircraft, were made locally; access was maintained to some Israeli and American technology. Nevertheless, South African military hardware could be distinctive: armoured vehicles such as Ratels, Hippos, and Casspirs, dramatically deployed when the army moved into the townships, epitomized local military style. (Casspir was an acronym derived from its joint developers, the South African Police and the Council for Scientific and Industrial Research, the major state-funded research institute established in 1945.) Armscor's contracts provided a major boost both to engineering plants and to the small local microelectronics and computer industry. In this latter area, however, as in sophisticated airforce equipment, the country remained dependent on imports. Nuclear power and weapons capacity was developed with French assistance.

Urban, industrial, and agricultural expansion all combined to place enormous demands on relatively scarce water resources, and dam construction was a major preoccupation. The Vaal dam completed in 1938 secured Rand supplies. In the apartheid years, the Orange River Project, designed for irrigation as well as water (to Bloemfontein) and hydroelectric power, was a key undertaking. The main Hendrik Verwoerd dam, completed in 1971, was linked by a long water tunnel to eastern Cape valleys, where irrigated land was put under crops and fruit. South African consortia were also involved in the Cabora Bassa hydroelectric power scheme on the Zambezi. These new megadams demonstrated conquest and control of nature's most unpredictable element; drought had etched the Afrikaner experience. They were a metaphor for social change in which Afrikaner corporate society had displaced the uncaptured frontier and resolved the poor-white problem. Dams proved photogenic for newsreel film with resounding commentaries and bombastic music. They celebrated a specifically Afrikaner contribution to industrial society and the modernization of agriculture. Yet they have also left a different legacy: the basis for relatively secure water supplies for South Africa's increasingly urban black population.

It is important to appreciate the scale of these developments. South Africa's role as an economic sub-metropole and regional entrepôt expanded in the post-War period. Although this was constrained from the mid-1960s by sanctions and escalating regional conflict, South Africa's position as the industrial powerhouse of the continent was confirmed. The pattern of growth was also a major factor in reshaping the country's social geography. To the original Witwatersrand was added an arc of satellite towns from the Far West Rand goldfields to the huge coal, electricity, and oil plants of the eastern Transvaal. In the 1970s these new heavy industrial zones ranked only behind the six major cities in their size. The Free State goldfields' population, for example, grew temporarily bigger than Bloemfontein's by 1970—though they in turn were soon to be outstripped by urban settlements that had little industrial base (**Chapter 8**).

But even in the boom years, there were signs of weakness. Some economists now argue that, while growth during this period was impressive, it was not as spectacular in international terms as suggested at the time. While both liberal and left commentators saw economic performance as exceptional, they tended to compare South Africa with mature industrial economies, rather than with other similar developing countries. If the latter are taken into account, South Africa probably did not rank in the top ten from 1950 to 1985, behind countries like Brazil, Mexico, South Korea, and Taiwan (Moll 1991: 278–9).

Economy and Society, 1960s–1970s

Although new patterns of consumption permeated many levels of society, manufacturers relied heavily on a limited white market. The shortage of skills raised the cost of white workers, favoured labour intensive operations, depressed productivity, and perhaps hampered innovation and the expansion of more sophisticated sectors. Not many industries were able to export competitively and there were costs to protection and the high degree of monopoly in public and private sectors. South Africa remained dependent on imports for most sophisticated machinery—more so than some other industrializing economies such as India and Korea. The country's import bill rocketed at the height of its boom. These weaknesses, some but not all linked to apartheid policies, were revealed when manufacturing growth slowed between 1975 and 1980 and subsequently stagnated.

## White Society and Culture

The images of Verwoerd, Prime Minister from 1958 till his assassination in 1966, and Balthazar Johannes Vorster (1966–78), brood over the high apartheid years. Vorster rose to prominence as Minister of Justice responsible for much of the repressive political apparatus of the 1960s. His craggy features, glowering eyes, and impassive public face were the epitome of *kragdadigheid*—the uncompromising face of Afrikaner power. He had been interned in the Second World War for sabotage as a member of the OB, a point often made by his critics as he tightened security arrangements. His brother, conservative Moderator of the main Dutch Reformed Church, reinforced his image.

Reassessments of his premiership suggest he was not only less of an ideologue, but far more of a 'chairman', even pragmatist, than either his forceful and visionary predecessor or his imperial successor, P. W. Botha. The beginnning of his period of rule saw the NP at the zenith of its power. In the 1966 election, it collected many English-speaking as well as the vast majority of Afrikaner votes. But Vorster had to respond to new challenges both to white supremacy and within Afrikanerdom itself. By the mid-1970s the remarkable success of the party and related organizations in controlling Afrikaner ideas and identity, as well as containing other social groups, was beginning to wane.

It was the best of times, materially, for white South Africans. This was reflected in demographic trends. By the 1950s over 80 per cent of them lived in urban areas and small towns; by the 1980s, over 90 (**Table 3**). White annual rates of population increase declined from around 2 per cent before 1950 to under 1 per cent by the 1980s, somewhat to the consternation of the government. These figures take account of a net gain of white immigrants of over 20,000 a year between the early 1960s and 1984—peaking at 40,000 in 1975, the year of Mozambican independence, when many Portuguese-speakers fled to South Africa. Birth rates dropped as the population became more urban and wealthier. Like Europeans, white South Africans had fewer children, smaller families, and more disposable income.

Afrikaners benefited particularly from economic growth. The capital accumulated in farming flowed into financial institutions, which helped greatly to diversify the range of Afrikaner commerce. New state investment in education, especially at university level, expanded Afrikaner involvement in the whole range of professions. Those in agricultural occupations dropped from about 30 per cent in 1946 to 8 per cent in 1977 on the eve of the reform era. Afrikaners in blue-collar and unskilled work dropped from 40 to 27 per cent, while those in white-collar employment increased from 29 to 65 per cent (Giliomee and Adam 1979: 169). Of half a million whites in public-sector employment, the great majority were Afrikaners. In the private sector, the job colour bar floated upwards, as whites reaped the benefits of improved training and full employment.

Afrikaner women finally moved out of industrial employment, where significant numbers had worked up to the 1950s. They were largely replaced by black men at lower wages. By 1970 only 3–4 per cent of employed white women worked in factories. Nevertheless, the number of white working women increased overall; benefiting from protection, they were absorbed in clerical, sales, and secretarial jobs, as well as nursing, teaching, and other professions. The fragile social base for pre-war radicalism and worker organization, reflected in the Garment Workers' Union, was rapidly eroded. In major areas of women's employment, such as nursing and teaching, white women were largely separated from black. Black nurses, for example, could not work in segregated white hospitals, although the senior posts in black hospitals were largely taken by white women. Up to 1980 white nurses were numerically predominant, their position safeguarded by the Nursing Amendment Act of 1957 and by apartheid practice. Nursing associations were also racially segregated (Marks 1994).

Afrikaner entrepreneurs such as Anton Rupert, head of the tobacco multinational Rembrandt, spearheaded upward social mobility. Sanlam and Trustbank, amongst others, gave Afrikaners a better footing in a commercial world dominated by English corporations. Anglophone mining houses made space for Afrikaner-controlled corporations, notably *Federale Mynbou*, to buy into this sector. Per capita income amongst Afrikaans-speakers, less than half that of English-speakers in 1946, had risen to 80 per cent in the late 1970s and was heading towards parity. The government not only filled the expanding state corporations and civil service with Afrikaners, but used state patronage to promote Afrikaner firms. Some analysts argued that whites came to enjoy a standard of living equal to that of the richest countries in the North. This statistic is a little misleading in that it compares the top 20 per cent of South African earners not with the top 20 per cent in Europe or the USA but with the whole population of Western industrialized countries. Nevertheless, white South Africans had never had it so good.

Whites are often analysed in this period as agents of a repressive society, but they too have a complex social history. Images of them at the time are conflicting: they are portrayed as religious but militarized, racist but rich, narrow but hospitable. It is their otherness that is often stressed. But for all peculiarity of this 'strange society' (Drury 1968), it was often familiar to Europeans and Americans. The apartheid period was one of suburbanization and the spread of a rather derivative consumer culture spliced onto the gnarled old settler stock.

White English-speaking middle-class culture still looked partly to Britain; a spate of English immigrants arrived after the war. Although new white settlers notoriously adopted apartheid ideas quite quickly, many retained strong links with their countries of origin. Afrikaners were getting richer and the English-speaking working class smaller, but class as well as cultural divisions remained significant in urban social networks. University education was one dividing line and universities themselves were sharply divided between Afrikaans and English. Afrikaners could isolate themselves socially because of their large range of cultural and educational institutions and their dominance of state employment. The strength of the Broederbond encouraged them to do so. Afrikaners who strayed politically or became anglicized could be the object of opprobrium, although ironically educational opportunities increased familiarity with the English language.

White living standards were most manifest in their houses and cars. Low-density suburbs with modern detached houses in gardens, some with swimming pools, proliferated. Vehicle numbers nearly doubled every decade from 370,000 in 1940 to 1.3 million in 1960 and 3.8 million in 1980 (**Table 4**). At about 21 people per vehicle in 1950 and 12 in 1961, South African ownership exceeded that of many European countries, even if the black population—which owned only around 10 per cent of the total—is included (Andrews *et al.* 1962: 25). Per capita car ownership in West Germany overtook South African only in 1958. In the mid-1970s car ownership amongst whites, at 386 vehicles per 1,000 people, was exceeded only in the USA, the most motorized country (507 cars per 1,000), and ranked roughly level with Australia and Canada (South African Information Service 1979). The car culture in the apartheid years greatly facilitated the development of the suburbs and helped whites to insulate themselves from a common urban life.

From the 1960s British and American models were increasingly displaced by German. At the upper end of the market, successful Afrikaner businessmen and farmers bought Mercedes Benz, often white in colour. A small-town funeral, when a procession of cars followed the hearse to the cemetery, could be an extraordinary display of wealth that far exceeded the wildest pretensions of the small Wabenzi classes in independent African states. By the 1980s Japanese manufacturers captured much of the market. They were especially successful in sales of bakkies (pick-ups).

Jeremy Taylor's satirical hit song 'Ballad of the Southern Suburbs' in the musical *Wait a Minim* captured the essence of consumer culture and the primacy of the car in the less fashionable parts of Johannesburg. It started: 'Ag Pleez Daddy won't you take us to the drive-in?' In another verse children asked: 'Won't you take us off to Durban, it's only eight hours in the Chevrolet?' The celebrated chorus ran: 'pop-corn, chewing gum, peanuts and bubble-gum, ice-cream, candy floss and eskimo pie.' Cars and consumer spending reshaped South African shopping. The OK Bazaars (founded 1927), started by Cohen and Miller, introduced mass retailing to South Africa. Now supermarkets, many developed by Jewish entrepreneurs with their fingers on the pulse of international marketing, proliferated. Chains such as Pick and Pay (founded 1967) initially catered for a white suburban clientele. Some were later located near key transport spots and became accessible to blacks. Supermarkets were not segregated.

Consumerism brought with it new cultural influences. The USA did not become South Africa's primary trading partner, nor its main source of investment capital. Nevertheless, post-war American consumer icons and lifestyles had great appeal for both whites and blacks. Sophisticated American advertising provided reference points to what was perceived as an international culture—an escape from both colonial British and Afrikaner heritage. Drive-ins, takeaways, hula hoops, and radio jingles all contributed to Americanization. For South Africans, also, things went 'better with Coca-Cola'. To compensate, you could 'Brush your teeth with Colgate, fight tooth decay all day'.

Hollywood releases dominated the cinemas—Tarzan, Westerns, and the great epics. These were hardly threatening to white patriarchal culture and censors screened out material they thought politically suspect. Soweto gangs took their names from films: the 'Dirty Dozen', 'Bandidos', and 'Jaws' (Glaser 1998*a*: 726). White children played cowboys and crooks rather than Boer and Zulu. When they were bought bows and arrows, the reference point was native American rather than the indigenous San. American country and western styles—drawing on social experience similar to Afrikaners—seeped into local ballads, a market supplied by the smooth tones of Ge Korsten in 'Die Hartseerwals' (Heartache

Waltz). Jim Reeves's lugubrious small-town sorrow struck a specially deep chord. Beach holidays became increasingly popular; white women valued their suntans as evidence of leisure and style. The climate was suitable for adventurous youths, male and female, to develop their version of the Californian dream. The consumption of dagga (marijuana), long grown and smoked by blacks, increased significantly; it was one of the few expanding markets for homeland agriculture. British and American pop music and clothing fashions were dominant. These were all cultural borrowings that to some extent crossed racial boundaries.

In broadcasting, however, the government was determined to retain a monopoly. Hertzog had nationalized broadcasting in 1936 with the specific intention that there should be Afrikaans radio channels. The Nationalists were concerned that untoward 'liberalist' political messages might seep through and exercised tight control over the content of programmes. Largely for these reasons, the introduction of television was delayed until 1976, when the local film industry was more developed; in this respect at least, South Africans were unusually isolated from global consumer culture. The South African Broadcasting Corporation transmitted two national radio channels, one Afrikaans and the other self-consciously English, including imports from the BBC. In 1950 Springbok radio, a less sober bilingual national commercial channel, was launched. Current affairs and news on all these, as well as local FM and African-language programmes, toed the government's line. Radio was an important means by which the government could communicate its position to African people, many of whom were not literate.

White men were the major but not exclusive participants in a culture of smoking, drinking, and sports. Smoking was hardly new: the seventeenth-century Dutch became the most fervent tobacco consumers in Europe, even growing the crop in Holland. Pre-colonial African societies in southern Africa had widely adopted tobacco, although snuff was probably more popular than pipes. The tablecloth in Cape Town, a blanket of clouds blown down the front of Table Mountain, was explained by an old tobacco folk tale: a pipe-smoking contest between the Devil and Mynheer van Hunks, which probably reflected the guilt in a

Calvinist Dutch culture about the centrality of the weed. After the Second World War, cigarettes—including the ubiquitous Springbok brand—increasingly ousted pipes and chewing tobaccos (*twak*). Rupert's Afrikaner tobacco company's name for its brand leader, Rembrandt van Rijn, was particularly appropriate; it evoked a Dutch rather than British masterpiece and Rembrandt's seventeenth-century Dutch culture was wreathed in tobacco smoke (Schama 1988). Life cigarettes appealed to the classically educated with their punning motto *Vita Magna Est*—though they were also advertised in Soweto football stadiums. Popular downmarket brands such as Texan and Lucky Strike were unashamedly American in their marketing reference points. Heavy smoking and high meat and alcohol consumption provided one reason why, in addition to sharing the demographic features of Western countries, white South Africans also came to share their health profile, with high rates of heart disease and lung cancer.

White South Africans could not easily compete in the international cultural stakes; in addition to political exiles, some of those with professional and artistic ambition left. But they could hold their own in sport—a means of male expression and self-fulfilment. It also provided a social cement in new urban communities. Horse-racing, a nineteenth-century sport, remained popular with whites and blacks in town; in the rural districts of the Transkei regular informal race meets were held. For middle-class English-speakers, tennis afternoons, swimming in private pools, golf and bowls at country clubs became central social events. Freed from much household drudgery by black domestic servants, white women could participate in many of these activities.

No serious attempt was made to revive Afrikaner pre-industrial pastimes. *Jukskei*, an old farm and trek game, was kept alive on the beaches of Strand, where farm families came for holidays, and spread at the time of the OB, but remained a minority activity for devotees. Rather, Afrikaners adopted British and international team games. In particular they made rugby their own. Stellenbosch, for many years crucible of Afrikaner intellectual life, also became cradle of South African rugby. It appealed as a 'sport for pioneers' that also allowed Afrikaners to beat the English at their own game. Rugby called for physicality, bravado, and team solidarity. Adopted as the main winter game in many educational institutions, it spread as new communities coalesced around schools, suburbs, police, and other urban networks. The 1951–2 tour to Britain, when the Springboks won thirty out of thirty-one games and beat Scotland 44–0, confirmed the game's central status through the early apartheid years. As Afrikaner wealth grew and self-image modified in the 1960s and 1970s, they increasingly embraced more genteel pursuits such as cricket, tennis, and golf— Vorster very publicly espoused the latter to soften his profile. Motorsports of all kind dispersed with the car culture. Football, king for most black South Africans, was more the game of British and European immigrants and of the older established white working-class areas. Apartheid was rigidly enforced in sport during Verwoerd's years.

In his book *Modernizing Racial Domination* (1971), Heribert Adam, commented: 'one of the most striking features of South African cultural life is the relative isolation and ignorance about the changing world of ideas, which whites in particular hardly seem to notice' (1971: 55). The idea that Afrikaners were inward-looking, had missed out on the first Enlightenment and most since then, was an old one. Certainly, censorship deprived white South Africans of much written and visual material that might have challenged their views. They defended their position with extraordinary vehemence both in public political argument and in everyday behaviour.

The imperative to stand alone, despite being the 'pole cats of the world', was broadcast through the media, political speeches, and the Afrikaner churches with insistent regularity. Though 'overseas' was still a place many wanted to visit, it evoked an increasing defensiveness. Most whites were unable to see black South Africans during this critical period of the country's history. Homelands, passes, group areas, social amnesia, and powerful ideologies put them out of sight, literally and metaphorically. Whites believed that they knew 'their' Africans, and this justified their system against the attacks of ignorant outsiders. Many of them came across Africans only as servants and workers. Their school history taught them that whites had got to this part of

Africa first. They believed that they were guarantors of Western values, technological society, and civilization; that they had invented the wheel and blacks had not. Events in Africa such as *coups*, wars, and one-party states were grist to their self-justificatory mill.

The political and cultural brokers of Afrikanerdom wished to deliver wealth to their people as well as insulate them. To an extraordinary extent they did succeed. But there were greater paradoxes in their achievement than Heribert Adam might allow. It was not only racial domination that was modernized. Afrikaners chose modern architecture for public buildings and churches, proclaiming a desire to be international and forward-looking. Wealth brought the capacity to share in a Western culture of work and leisure, which in turn provided a myriad routes out of the cocooned world. The church, racial ideology, the Broederbond, and *braaivleis* (barbecue) remained anchors for different segments of society. But by the 1970s a cultural secularism based on consumption, sport, leisure, travel, and personal freedom was beginning to fracture Afrikaner ethnic identity. It is an irony that television, launched only when the National Party felt it could control the medium in 1976, coincided with this gradual dissolution of unity and probably contributed to it.

Such paradoxes might be illustrated by growing divorce rates. The Dutch Reformed Churches, overwhelmingly the most important amongst Afrikaners, had long propagated a conservative view of the role of women, marriage, and the family. But in the 1960s, one white marriage in five was ending in divorce and by 1978, one marriage in 3.3 (Burman and Huvers 1985). The demand on the courts was considerable and divorce laws were relaxed in 1979, despite the churches. White women had achieved a degree of security in their access to property and employment as well as some of the sexual and economic freedom characteristic of capitalist societies. Although the state remained staunchly opposed to permitting abortion, contraception was widely available. Feminism was not strongly developed as a movement, but the combination of high levels of education and relative freedom from domestic labour allowed white women to assert a degree of independence in a patriarchal world.

Domestic service created its own anomalies at the height of apartheid. Group Areas achieved apartheid in ownership rather than by preventing African entry into white zones. Growing white wealth drew more black domestic servants, largely African women, into the suburbs, many living on their employers' premises. The sharing of space and functions within households was governed by hierarchies of authority, and domestics were amongst the most poorly paid and insecure workers with the longest hours. Yet domestic employment also sometimes perpetuated complex interactions that went beyond exchanges of wages for labour: charity and, occasionally, racially constrained forms of affection. On Sunday afternoons, when workers often had some time off, the suburban streets seemed more black that white. In the 1980s and 1990s, when political change led to greater self-examination, these paradoxes and uncertainties were captured for anglophone whites by the successful cartoon strip, *Madam and Eve*, which satirized white attitudes and (optimistically) emphasized the bargaining power of domestics.

Even in the apartheid years, many different international currents of thought were being refracted through the complex prism of South African society. A minority white opposition survived and developed. The Liberal Party, which had also attracted a small black membership, dissolved in the 1960s. Some of its support was absorbed by the Progressive Party. Although their commitment was only to a qualified non-racial franchise, this was a challenging concept to whites. Helen Suzman, the redoubtable Progressive MP for the wealthy Johannesburg constituency of Houghton, maintained a relentless criticism of government economic policy, breaches of human rights, and apartheid. Suzman was particularly effective in highlighting the excesses of government security legislation and its disregard for the rule of law; the government retained some concern about legality in its actions, at least up to the 1970s. 'Vorster', Suzman (1994: 73) recalled, 'once paid me the "compliment" of saying I was worth ten United Party MPs; I thought this was an understatement'. She was joined by six others after the 1974 election as the UP fragmented.

The Black Sash, a white women's movement launched at the time of constitutional protests in the 1950s, switched its attention to issues such as passes, influx control, and forced removals. Its Advice Offices provided a useful resource for African people trapped in the web of apartheid controls and created a further direct interface between black and white women. The experience and knowledge generated proved significant in the longer term for mounting legal challenges to apartheid legislation. Organizations such as the South African Institute of Race Relations, Church groups, the Christian Institute, and English universities sustained a strong network of white anti-apartheid activists and a degree of inter-racial contact. Nadine Gordimer's novels and stories, some banned, captured the intense self-criticism and guilt of whites who recognized the immorality of their society. A number of whites were detained, or harassed; their status and visibility gave some, but by no means all, a degree of protection from arbitrary state reprisals.

The restrictive political atmosphere was leavened by an English-language press that could be deeply critical of the government. Banned organizations and people could not be quoted and the scope for reporting was constrained by legislative controls—for example over promoting communist ideas or revealing information on prisons. It was difficult to report on the exiled political movements and illegal to distribute most books about the ANC. Media radicalism was tempered by the fact that the mining industry had a large stake in the two consortia that owned most of the English-language press (and the papers serving African readerships), as well as the conservatism of the bulk of its white readership and advertisers. But it was possible to live in South Africa and read a variety of publicly expressed opposition views on a daily basis.

Individual editors and journalists on newspapers such as the Johannesburg *Rand Daily Mail*, the *Sunday Times*, and the East London *Daily Dispatch* were at times prepared to test the limits of government control. Under the editorship of Donald Woods (1968–77), for example, the *Dispatch*, owned by an independent trust, became a crusading liberal paper. Not least as a result of his personal contacts with Steve Biko (see **Chapter 9**), Woods went further than most in providing space for radical black consciousness views in the mid-1970s. His paper was highly effective in publicizing Biko's death and the police cover-up that followed in 1977. By this time, probably a majority of its readership were black. While the English press may not in itself have formed black opinion, it did help shape what educated black people read and influenced the construction of news in communities starved of independent information.

There were always alternative views available even to Afrikaners, and not only through the English media. Dissident writers associated with the *Sestiger* (Sixties) movement, some of whom had worked in France, experimented with new literary forms; subsequently authors such as André Brink and Breyten Breytenbach explored dangerous themes of cross-racial relationships, Afrikaner self-doubt, and the history of violence and expropriation. At the height of Nationalist control, in 1964, the *Akademie vir Wetenskap en Kuns* (Science and Art), guardians of Afrikaner culture, awarded their annual Hertzog prize to Etienne le Roux's surrealist novel, *Sewe Dae by die Silbersteins*—a 'parable of the failure and corruption of the nationalist mission' (O'Meara 1996: 124). Their decision unleashed a conservative backlash against 'liberal and communistic infiltration' which as in racial matters, sought to purify Afrikaner life. Such disputes fractured the cultural hierarchy.

Social change and political challenges divided Afrikaner *verligtes* (the enlightened) from *verkramptes* (cramped conservatives) on an increasing range of issues during the 1970s. *Verligte* opinion to some degree grew out of newspaper wars and received prominence in the press, which was always more difficult to control than broadcasting. Editors such as Schalk Pienaar of *Die Beeld* challenged the established conservative papers and were increasingly explicit in revealing the bitter politics of Afrikaner division. Piet Cillie, editor of *Die Burger*, and Willem de Klerk of *Die Transvaler* were mainstream nationalists but tried, from their influential positions, to shift Afrikaners from a narrow self-absorption. *Verligtes* questioned the details of petty apartheid. They were the voice of modernizing and expanding Afrikaner business enterprises. They advocated a broader white nationalism, expressed greater desire for international acceptability, and were uneasy about the repressive security apparatus. *Verligtes* certainly felt that they could initiate reform from above and within the parameters of racial separation. Nevertheless, some Afrikaner as well as English intellectuals remained open to a surprisingly wide range of influences drifting in from 'overseas', which gave focus to a variety of social tendencies.

## Social Change in African Urban Communities

In the 1960s and 1970s banned groups and people could not express themselves publicly. It was particularly dangerous for African people to associate themselves with the ANC and PAC. Yet there was a long legacy of highly diverse associations, especially fragmented community and church groups. The homelands produced their own local and ethnically based political parties. Black-consciousness and trade-union movements sprang up to fill the vacuum at a national level and take advantage of the limited openings afforded by government policy. It is important to record what was in fact possible at the height of apartheid—how people compromised, came to terms with their powerlessness, and expressed their interests.

The contours of African life through the relatively quiescent decade after 1963 were moulded by demographic and social change as much as by repression. Political movements are discussed further in **Chapters 8 and 9**, but black people did not live by politics alone. Massive expansion of black employment in industry and, to a lesser degree, in white-collar and educational institutions meant that economic benefits of a kind did accrue to a significant minority, especially urban 'insiders', during the post-Sharpeville boom. In manufacturing alone, the number of African employees more than doubled to about 770,000 between 1960 and 1980 and their real wages increased significantly. Similar patterns are evident in commerce, transport, and construction. There were probably barely 70,000 African professionals and white-collar workers in 1960—notably about 14,000 nurses and 25,000 teachers; by 1980 these figures had roughly quadrupled.

Although they were a tiny percentage of the total black labour force, and although they were greatly disadvantaged compared with whites, the upper echelons of African urban society experienced a sharp increase in income and spending power. Urban unemployment was relatively low. Social scientists investigating fast-growing African urban communities at the time were struck by the growing class of professionals, traders, clerks, and businessmen (especially in building, butcheries, tailoring, and taxis), who had access to higher salaries and tended to intermarry.

The title of Kuper's study of the Durban locations in the early 1960s, *An African Bourgeoisie* (1965), was misleading, as only a small minority of the African elite controlled substantial businesses or properties. They were tightly restricted by licensing controls and racial zoning. Amongst the few very rich were herbalists and medicine manufacturers, who had a protected business on account of their specialist knowledge. 'Dr' Alexander in Durban rented city offices and employed forty African typists to deal with his mail-order herbal medicine business. Khotso Sethuntsa, based in Lusikisiki, Pondoland, claimed to be the son of President Kruger's personal servant and was the source of much rumour both as a diviner, and as an African millionaire with large properties, Cadillacs, extensive cattle holdings, two dozen wives, and 200 travelling salesmen to distribute his remedies (Becker 1975). He was buried in 1972 in a coffin that replicated President Kennedy's.

A wider range of people identified themselves self-consciously as elite or middle class. Awareness of social differentiation was reflected in the language of the townships, which became a biting commentary on such divisions. In Cape Town and Durban, the respectable were labelled 'ooscuse-me'. Though many were from a Christian background, a sense of class behaviour was overlaying the old rurally based distinction between Christians (Zulu *kholwa* or Xhosa 'school' people) and traditionalists. Vilakazi detected a 'concern with individual rights and individual responsibility', as well as 'a high degree of "privatism" among the new *elite*' (1965: 139). While national political leadership tended to come from this social stratum, by no means all were able or willing to identify with nationalist movements. Urban Location Advisory Boards, though they remained weak in the early apartheid decades, were an important focus of activity.

In the gregarious, congested, pre-apartheid inner-city locations like Sophiatown, wealthier families lived together with the poor and it was difficult to maintain social exclusivity. But in large, dispersed new peri-urban townships, members of the middle class were beginning to live in identifiable areas. One such neighbourhood in Lamontville, Durban, where a rare home-ownership scheme survived, was dubbed 'Nylon', possibly because it was built at the time when nylon stockings became available but also apparently because of its social transparency. (Nylon was one of the terms for lies and for police cars.)

As elsewhere, careful choice of consumer goods signified the aspirations of the upwardly mobile. For blacks pushed into far-flung locations, just as for whites moving to the suburbs, cars were highly valued. An African anthropologist noted that 'a car is a very important badge of prominence ... it's no use saying you have money if you can't produce a car' (Kuper 1965: 112). New location houses were furnished with distinctive modern furniture, and hire-purchase arrangements escalated. A limited number of exempted, educated men could legally purchase manufactured liquor; others with resources 'frequented elite shebeens, furnished with plush furniture, where brand names spirits and beers were served' (Crush and Ambler 1992: 32). Urban communities switched to cigarettes rather than pipe tobacco or snuff, although African women were slower than white to take up smoking.

Black middle-class urban communities shared some social pursuits and patterns of consumption with white, though they did not replicate them. Church activities, mostly in established denominations or orthodox independent churches, occupied much leisure time, especially of women. Methodism, a badge of respectability and discipline, had been the most active mission denomination and probably retained its hold as the most widespread group of churches. Red-jacketed women from the Methodist *manyano* (women's union) proclaimed their presence forcefully every Thursday. In this church as in others they were a key nexus of women's organization. The Independent Order of True Templars, a non-denominational Christian organization, attacked the destructive effects of drunkenness in urban society by advocating temperance and self-improvement; it also attracted factory workers. Choirs, often based around the churches, hospitals, and educational institutions at the core of elite networks, were a major social expression, combining a specifically African vocal tradition, church music, and other forms such as black American spirituals.

Nursing was one of the few opportunities available for African women to earn a salary and establish themselves professionally. Given the very limited educational opportunities, nursing was a demanding path that required discipline and set them aside in African society. Their income gave them unusual status and respectability. Nurses could also be influential shapers of style. For example, ballroom dancing had been popular in the Cape cities after the war. The Zimbabwean political leader, Maurice Nyagumbo, later Secretary General of ZANU, was a devotee as a migrant hotel worker in Port Elizabeth; in East London, there were a number of professional dance teachers. It was an avenue for upwardly mobile working-class men in Durban in the early 1960s and 'a key, an invitation card, to the nurses' home' (Kuper 1965: 114).

Sociologists working in this period did not see a simple progress to 'Westernization'. They remained alert to the specifically African characteristics of urban society. Middle-class marriage ceremonies intricately intertwined Christian, traditional, and secular forms. Church weddings in white were frequently accompanied by bridewealth payment (though more in commodities and money than cattle) and elaborate gift exchanges between the families of the bride and bridegroom. Celebrations could include large open parties with beer, samp or *ngqushe*, and meat, private cocktail parties for friends, and receptions that provided material for the society pages of the *Golden City Post* or the *World* in Johannesburg. To a surprising degree, male initiation and circumcision were retained as a statement of Africanness in an urban environment.

Although they were growing, wages remained very low for the bulk of urban workers; they could not emulate middle-class lifestyles. Especially on the Rand, the stokvel, vividly described by Hellmann in inner-city slums in the 1930s, prospered across a range of social classes. It could take the form of a rotating credit society for a small group who pooled their savings regularly to provide one member with a payout at intervals. As always, it was difficult for poor people to accumulate sufficient to make large purchases. These types of savings association could shade into burial societies, which reflected a deep concern for a decent death and well-attended funeral. But perhaps the most common form of stokvel amongst both rich and poor were weekend parties for which entry sums were paid. In the late 1960s at one of the frequent parties in a Rand location, a popular hostess could make a substantial profit of up to R300 on a Sunday. 'The patterns of the Stockfel and the reciprocity on which they were based pervaded all other ... organizations and all forms of entertaining and hospitality' (Brandel-Syrier 1971: 307).

Soweto had become the largest African township in the country and increasingly set the cultural and social tone. Both inner-city removals and rapid urban migration swelled its population. Barely established in the 1930s, it probably housed half a million by the late 1960s and close on a million by 1980. Soweto generated a working-class, popular following for football, increasingly the leading black sport. Initially played at mission schools, it caught on amongst the urbanized core in all the major cities. Like the stokvel, the game then crossed class boundaries. Squatter leader James Mpanza had been a keen player at school, and football spread in the post-Second World War Johannesburg squatter settlements. It required few facilities and gradually displaced stick-fighting as the major sport of urbanizing black youth. Soweto-based Orlando Pirates and Moroka Swallows attracted mass followings in the 1960s, with crowds up to 45,000: it was 'accessible to us as children in the ghetto, and we grew to love it; it was a culture in Soweto' (Bonner and Segal 1998: 64). Leading players became celebrities as the press and magazines expanded their coverage.

Following the establishment of national, increasingly professional leagues for whites in 1959 and blacks in 1970, these were amalgamated into a multiracial league in 1977. Although some forms of 'multinational' sport had been sanctioned under Vorster's regime, it was an extraordinary development at the height of apartheid. Cricket, which had been popular at Cape black schools at the turn of the century, faded with the heyday of these institutions. Rugby did take root. When Steve Biko was portrayed in the film *Cry Freedom* playing rugby, this may have seemed out of place, but it was an accurate observation of the sports preferences of the black eastern Cape elite, even though it would not have been for much of the rest of the country. Eastern Cape black rugby networks penetrated into the working class and were one source of support in a major Port Elizabeth motor-factory strike in 1981. Coloured communities in the western Cape had also long adopted both rugby and cricket; they later provided the first black representatives when the national teams were deracialized.

In 1962 Africans were allowed to purchase manufactured liquor following a long period in which this was prohibited to the great majority. The relaxation reflected the strength of alcohol producers in the country, anxious to extend their internal markets. With an estimated 10,000 shebeens in Soweto alone by 1960, the police were unable to enforce highly contentious liquor controls and some now wished to decriminalize consumption of manu-factured alcohol (Mager 1999: 371). The government saw the lift-ing of this social restriction as an opportunity to diminish tension in the urban areas at a time of political repression.

Some Africans were opposed to this apparent liberalization of control, either because of their concerns about consumption, or because black people were still to be denied licences to sell liquor. Both municipalities and later Bantu Affairs Administration Boards attempted to extend their income by running beer halls for profit, and brewing mass-produced 'Bantu Beer' (a version of traditional beer). The pattern of African drinking gradually changed, as bottled malted beer and spirits became established. Even though it was illegal, some unlicensed shebeens now sold an increasing amount of manufactured liquor, as well as home brew produced by women. Many were controlled by women who, as in earlier years, found themselves on the wrong side of the law. The giant South African Breweries, which increasingly monopolized bottled and canned beer production, found ways to supply these major new outlets for its products, despite discouragement by the state. Shebeens remained key gathering places and sites of convivial drinking, and drunkenness, for many urban Africans. Shebeen-owners also bought into football.

Musical styles for a mass audience evinced a similar eclectic amalgam of African and American influences. *Mbaqanga*, with its instantly recognizable driving guitar rhythms, came to epitomize township music at this time. The most popular Soweto artist was Simon 'Mahlathini' Nkabinde, whose groaning, 'deep goat's voice' (as he called it), offset by the intricate harmonies of the Mahotella Queens and the Makgona Tsohle band, dominated the musical scene in the 1960s and 1970s. *Mbaqanga* was sufficiently neo-traditional to be heavily promoted on the new Radio Bantu (1960), but it was an urgent, urban style born directly out of the townships. Mahlatini was brought up in Alexandra and lived in Soweto. His vernacular lyrics and forthright message cemented a working-class audience. *Bayasazi*, one song from the 1970s, proclaimed: 'they know how good we are . . . they know we're the best, the originators of the music.' *Kwa Mfazi Onge Mama* was a gritty celebration of the city: 'we are going to where things are happening, where women have no mothers; we are going to the big city, where only the tough survive.' By the late 1970s new influences were penetrating: on the one hand, disco music; and, on the other, Bob Marley and reggae music, which became one widespread accompaniment to youth protest.

A range of black women with access to cash income could remould themselves in an urban context. Some spent heavily on clothes. The 1960s was 'the time when we girls used to relax our hair . . . straight, straight, straight; we used to look up to the girls who relaxed their hair as our role models' (Bonner and Segal 1998: 60). Skin-lightening cream, advertised in the press, was also widespread. Herbs had been used for this purpose in Zulu society, but the new fashion spoke about the aspirations of an emerging class of urban youth. Folk singer Jeremy Taylor joked that, while white people wanted to tan themselves black, black people wanted to be light. However, there was a dark side to these heavily advertised creams, which contained dangerous chemicals and could discolour the skin.

Despite the massive increase in employment and in education, by no means all were able or willing to find employment. White employers sometimes preferred migrant workers, whom they saw as more pliant, to urban youths. Gangs proliferated in Soweto and other townships; from the 1940s they were no longer mainly the associations of migrant workers but streetwise and often ruthless urban tsotsi groups. Soweto youth gangs in the 1960s and 1970s were powerfully territorial. They competed between themselves for women, harassed school youths who were seen as key rivals, and organized robberies in other areas. The Hazels, based in Mzimhlope, who dominated criminal activity on the rail routes, were widely feared. Deaths were not unusual in gang fights, and, by the mid-1970s, concern about intensifying crime provoked a generational backlash from Soweto men in the Makgotla. Generational conflicts became increasingly important in urban African societies, as they had been in the rural areas when mass migrancy became established.

Many African workers were still labourers, living in compounds and hostels, or domestic servants on their employers' premises. The Mayers' study of East London, *Townsmen or Tribesmen* (1960), demonstrated that migrant workers continued to be 'encapsulated' in their rural networks and attempted to hold aspects of urban and consumer culture at bay. In the next couple of decades, this type of labour migrancy became less significant, not least because fewer men had prospects of accumulating rural resources. But some migrant workers did guard their identities, their home groups, and their habits of consumption (including sorghum beer) jealously. They were clearly perceived as different by urban township people and this social cleavage became an explosive point of tension in the 1970s and 1980s.

Amongst the most striking of the plethora of African associations were the independent churches, which numbered an estimated 3,000 by the early 1970s with millions of members. About 900 were found in Soweto alone. In general, they were the churches of the working class and of poorer, more rurally oriented people with limited education. They were especially strong amongst women domestic servants. Zionist and Apostolic churches practising healing, river baptism, dancing, night communion, and drumming, grew and fragmented rapidly, throwing up a wide range of bishops, some claiming prophetic powers. While most churches had just a few hundred members, a few, such as the Zion Christian Church (ZCC) of Lekganyane, based in the

Transvaal, and Shembe's Nazarites in Natal, did coalesce under leaders who could combine financial with prophetic skills. The ZCC had perhaps 200,000 members in 1970 and over a million by 1980.

Zionist churches originated in the late-nineteenth-century USA, but their religious forms were adapted in the African context. Church membership clearly provided an arena for social interaction, discipline, and belief in a world of rapid mobility, urban insecurity, and abrupt social change. Most churches had uniforms and developed a strong sense of identity. ZCC men donned oversize white boots with which they ceremonially stamped evil underfoot; Nazarites made extensive use of *izibongo* (praise poems), adapting them to new contexts. Aside from providing scope for intense religious expression, these churches were vehicles for the release of tension and frustration, 'comforting the uncomfortable', and some provided small material benefits in mutual aid and burial societies.

Middle-class black people could be disdainful of 'escapist' churches and uneasy with their fundamentalism. They were seen as politically conservative, concentrating on 'things celestial and heavenly'. Indeed Zulu Zionists were involved with homeland leaders in the development of Bantustan strategies. ZCC mass rallies at its headquarters near Pietersburg, northern Transvaal, attracted extensive publicity for their invitations to leading Nationalist politicians, including P. W. Botha, in the 1980s. But Zionist churches were not least attempting to defend an enclosed and inward-looking spiritual world for their followers, so that they, like their predecessors in the 1920s, could keep the impact of white domination at arm's length and to some small degree shape the pattern of their incorporation.

Middle-class aspirations among the educated, gangs and religious fundamentalism among the poor, were amongst the associations that, given the repressive atmosphere, provided an alternative social focus in the 1960s and early 1970s, a phase of black political fragmentation. The expansion of employment and rapidity of black urbanization created the social conditions for a new consumer culture. Whites expected deference from blacks and to a significant degree received it—at least in face-to-face relationships. Apartheid separated black and white communities more effectively than segregation had beforehand. But these outcomes did not preclude political reorganization and the rebirth of a powerful black popular politics (**Chapter 9**).

# 8

# Farms, Homelands, and Displaced Urbanization, the late 1950s to the 1980s

### *The Demography of Change*

In 1948, when the Nationalists came to power, South Africa was still, demographically speaking, a predominantly rural society. The previous century had witnessed vast movements of population in the region, which greatly modified its distribution but had not finally changed its balance. True, the people classified as white, Indian, and coloured were becoming fundamentally urban: at around 78, 78, and 65 per cent respectively in the 1951 census. It is also true that the epicentre of political conflict between white and black was moving to the cities. But to a significant degree white power still lay in the countryside and the small towns. About half of the urban Afrikaners lived in smaller towns and, politically, faced the country as much as the cities. Most important, perhaps three-quarters of the African population were still rooted in the rural areas, some 39 per cent in the reserves, and 35 per cent on the farms. This surviving rurality, it has been argued, had important implications for an understanding of social change, African political responses, and the nature of the state at the time.

During the next few decades the character of settlement again changed dramatically. By 1990 over 90 per cent of whites and Indians lived in towns. The constituencies behind white domination and the electoral base of the NP had shifted to the cities. And whereas in 1960, after more than a century of urbanization, the percentage of Africans living in towns reached 30, it probably doubled again within the next thirty years (**Table 3**; see Appendix 1: 351). In absolute terms over the same years the number of Africans living in urban conditions increased from under

3.5 million to perhaps somewhere between 18 and 20 million. Hidden beneath the statistics are a multiplicity of stories of dispossession, forced movement, urban treks, and 'crying for land'. Yet they also reveal the attractions, for some, of urban culture and the extension of a mass urban identity rare on the African continent (**Chapter 7**). For African people, like Afrikaners in the previous half century, this was a decisive phase of social change and it fuelled a radical politics that has been a major factor in recasting South African history.

Demographic change has been one of the most important but least explained phenomena in South African history. These figures can be more easily understood if they are considered in the light of long-term population growth. Some census counts of African people are thought to be underestimates, but the general trends are clear (**Table 2**). The years of high immigration between 1891 and 1904 were the last in which the white population grew much more rapidly than the black. In the first half of the twentieth century both white and African populations increased at an annual average of about 2 per cent; up to the census of 1951, the white population remained at over 20 per cent of the total. Thereafter, demographic patterns diverged dramatically. White rates of increase fell to less than 1 per cent annually by the 1980s. The white component in the total population declined to 19 per cent in 1960, 16 per cent in 1980, perhaps 13–14 per cent in 1990, and 11–12 in the first post-apartheid census of 1996—where racial classifications were retained (**Table 1**; see **Chapter 11**). Growth rates for those classified as coloured and Indian were considerably higher than those for whites, so that the decline in their percentage share, at about 8 and 3 per cent respectively, was not as marked.

By contrast the African population mushroomed. Rates of increase probably peaked at over 3 per cent per year in the 1960s and 1970s. The total African population grew from about 3.5 million in 1904 to 8.5 million in 1951, over 20 million in 1980, and perhaps 29 million in the 1991 census. It also became far younger. By 1980, roughly 46 per cent of Africans were under 15 years old, as compared with 26 per cent of whites (**Figure 3**). The children of the black baby boom of the 1960s hit their teens and early twenties in the 1980s, years of recession and youth insurrection. South

African demographic patterns have been similar to those in Latin America and Africa. Overall growth rates, including whites, were about the same as in Brazil after 1960. Trends for the African population alone initially resembled Zimbabwe's (3.1 per cent annual growth from 1960 to 1990), but were lower than Kenya (3.6 per cent). South African rates ebbed from the 1980s, probably more quickly than in most other African countries; the demographic impact of AIDS is as yet unclear.

High rates of population increase can be linked historically in Europe with food security and industrialization. Although malnutrition may have spread, South Africa has been free from serious famine since the early twentieth century. In recent decades, however, third-world population explosions have been more closely associated with high infant mortality, poverty, rurality, and low levels of women's education. Poor rural people sought social security and labour power through having more children. Many African societies have, in the past, valued large families. Moreover, there is strong evidence that, in South Africa, social controls over young men and women eroded—resulting in high rates of teenage and premarital pregnancy. Fewer African women were able to space their children widely. Previously widespread forms of non-penetrative sex (*metsha* in Xhosa) became unfashionable and men placed young women under considerable pressure to have sex. Alternative contraception was not easily available and abortion was illegal.

There may be a profound irony in these figures. A central element of apartheid planning was to stabilize the African population in the countryside and this had the effect of intensifying rural poverty. There were also pockets of high infant mortality, especially in the homelands. Many African families who might otherwise have migrated to the cities tried to hold on to some rural productive base. Simultaneously, it seems that they perceived a need for more potential workers and income-earners as resources declined, and therefore had more babies. It is striking that African population increased most rapidly from the 1950s to the 1970s at the height of the apartheid years. We should be cautious in attributing too much to specific government policies, in that other African countries experienced similar population explosions under very different regimes. Yet, in the specific conditions of South Africa, apartheid may have helped to swell African numbers—which was certainly not the intention of its planners.

African population increase may have been fairly rapid, even if urbanization had been facilitated. But comparative evidence suggests that, as people concentrate in cities, and as services and welfare become available, they tend to have fewer children. In a world where everything has to be purchased, too many children can be a liability and they are less likely to provide security. The South African figures seem to bear this out. Declining rates of increase coincide with the breakdown of apartheid controls over urbanization from the late 1970s. Social advancement was increasingly conceived to lie in smaller families and contraception was also more widely available and acceptable in urban areas. African women have been able to gain access to education on a far larger scale and, often at some cost, to assert their independence. Overall figures for under-5 mortality halved between 1960 and 1990, from 192 to 90 deaths per 1,000 live births—another factor that might have contributed to a slowing of the growth rate. Up to the 1990s life expectancy for African people also increased; HIV/AIDs might change this.

One other reason for rapid population increases may have been migration into South Africa by foreign workers from the region. Despite the government's considerable success in deporting large numbers, many contrived to stay on and the foreign-born black population continued to grow. As in earlier years, foreign migrants established themselves in particular zones of employment: in the mines until the 1970s; as poorly paid workers on the farms; in the hotel and catering trade where the skills and cordiality of Zimbabweans and Malawians were valued. In the 1980s, South Africa absorbed many illegal Mozambican refugees from the war.

Rapid urbanization in these years resulted not least from massive population growth. The numbers of people settled in the rural areas actually increased over the same period, at least until the 1980s. Having been a relatively empty country, parts of South Africa became crowded. At the turn of the twentieth century the USA, even including Alaska, was twice as densely populated as

South Africa; since about 1980, South Africa has become more densely populated. One-eighth the size of the USA, it has one-seventh the population. South Africa still has some wide open spaces in the arid zones, and on the white-owned farms, but it cannot any longer be conceived as sparsely populated nor geographically and culturally as a rural society. Enormous pressures for housing, welfare, education, and employment have been released.

The government's first response to its failure to contain urbanization was to tighten influx control in the 1960s. Between 1962 and 1967 convictions under the pass laws nearly doubled again to 693,661 annually. Statistics show that the African population of major urban areas grew less quickly from the late 1960s to the early 1970s. In Cape Town, where apartheid measures were more strictly enforced to protect both a 'white' city and a coloured labour preference area, the number of African people may have stabilized briefly in the mid-1960s. However, this evidence should not be taken to signify a decline in rates of movement from the countryside. Rather, when the impossibility of enforcing rurality became clear, government strategy changed to one of displacing African conurbations outside the major metropolitan areas. Boundaries were changed and urban growth was contained within extended homeland zones. In order to understand the new social geography of the country, it is essential to turn first to the white-owned farmlands from which many of the millions of Africans leaving the countryside initially came.

## The White-Owned Farmlands

In most industrializing countries, the contribution of the agricultural sector to the national economy has tended to diminish rapidly. This was certainly the long-term trend in South Africa, but three qualifications must be made. Firstly, from about 1945 to 1960 commercial farmers experienced very favourable conditions internationally and domestically. Global prices for primary products soared after the war; urban growth provided new markets at home. Whereas the proportion of gross domestic product contributed by agriculture slipped from over 20 per cent in the 1920s to under 10 per cent in 1945, it increased to 18 per cent in 1950.

Although it gradually declined again to 12 per cent in 1960 and 7 in 1980, these were years when mining and manufacturing were booming; farming output continued to expand fast.

Secondly, the falling share of agriculture in the GDP disguises the significance of farm products in other sectors of the economy: for example, processing of crops such as the milling of wheat, maize, and sugar; transporting farm commodities; or refining the multitude of products that found their way onto supermarket shelves from bread and biscuits to sweets and spaghetti. South African companies, as well as African women brewers, concocted an unusually large array of alcoholic beverages, very largely from local produce: fine wines, powerful brandy and rough sweet plonk from grapes; rum and cane spirits from sugar; vast quantities of beer from barley, maize, and sorghum; skokiaan from pine-apples. The manufacture of goods for farming, such as wire and fertilizers, was a significant element in industrial production.

Thirdly, changes in agriculture had a disproportionate influence on population distribution and social developments. The white-owned farms probably absorbed a greater proportion of the black labour force than any other sector, whether mining, manufacturing, or domestic service, until the 1970s. In addition, homeland-based smallholder agriculture still drew in very large amounts of labour. The way in which African people were first held on farms, then dispelled from them, profoundly affected South African society in the apartheid era.

During these years, commercial agricultural land owned very largely by whites made up about 70 per cent of the total area of South Africa; output increased on a stable area of land. It is sometimes suggested that the key feature of agricultural intensification was a switch from pastoral to arable farming. Surprisingly, the value of livestock farming did not decline as rapidly as might be expected up to the mid-1980s. Through the 1950s, livestock still brought in roughly half of agricultural income; by the 1980s the figure was about 44 per cent. But the era of sheep and wool exports was passing, and the growth areas were in dairy and meat, especially beef and poultry, to feed the urban masses. Battery chicken farms, owned by large companies with optimistic names such as Rainbow, sprouted through the countryside.

Between 1945 and 1960, maize production increased by 50 per cent, wheat a little more. Sugar production nearly doubled; fruit and groundnuts did so. Bananas in Natal, citrus and avocado pears in the Transvaal, pineapples in the eastern Cape all became subject to intensive large-scale commercial farming and greatly diversified the range of crops for domestic consumption and export. Between 1947 and 1961, the number of tractors increased from 22,000 to 122,000 (**Table 4**); by 1980 it had reached 300,000 or about four per farm. Combine harvesters, first introduced in the wheat belt of the Cape, became common in the larger highveld maize districts from the late 1960s. The number of farming units declined from 117,000 in 1950 to about 66,000 in 1980. Land prices increased dramatically and so did the availability of credit. Agriculture was concentrated in larger enterprises and in fewer hands.

Crop production was facilitated by the expansion of irrigated lands, following widespread dam construction. By the 1970s the proportion of South Africa's channelled water supply used for irrigation—rising to roughly 75 per cent compared with under 50 per cent in the USA—was amongst the highest in the world. One of the many inequities of this period was that production on white farms was prioritized over domestic water supplies for black families, most of whom did not have access to tapped water.

The results of intensification for black tenants and workers, by far the majority of the farm population, were complex; it is difficult to generalize comfortably across all regions. In the initial phases of the process, up to about 1970, more rather than less labour was needed, so that the number of farmworkers increased to about one and a half million. Mechanization allowed greater areas to be cultivated more intensively, but it was not yet so complete that machines displaced people across the whole range of agricultural activities. Large gangs were still required especially at harvest for picking fruit or maize, cane-cutting, transporting, and packing. From the 1960s the labour shortage, which had been so central a grievance for white farmers, gradually turned into a surplus. Population growth on the farms was more than enough to supply labour needs, which gradually declined to perhaps 1.2 million in the 1980s. Labour requirements also changed. Farmers wanted a core of permanent workers available all year round, including skilled tractor drivers, dairymen, and others who worked with machinery. But some preferred migrant seasonal workers at times of peak labour demand for harvest and packing.

Most skilled workers on the farms were black; agriculture was one of the few areas to which a systematic colour bar was not applied. Thus some of the staunchest supporters of apartheid were the least interested in protecting white labour on the farms. Farmers were even exempted from the provisions of an Act reserving skilled building work for whites. White tenants and workers drained from the farms even at the height of the apartheid era. In 1960 a Commission of Enquiry raised alarm about the *beswarting* (blackening) of the farmlands; it was largely ignored. By 1970 there were less than 20,000 white farm employees left. The number of whites living in the rural areas fell; the white population of Pretoria, which absorbed many rural Afrikaners, grew more rapidly than Cape Town or Johannesburg. Government promises to 'whiten' the white-owned countryside did not include featherbedding smaller farmers or white workers, both of whom were sacrificed on the altar of costs. As the number of rural whites declined, skilled black workers could find themselves in managerial-type roles, though few had any formal training. The wages of core black farm families actually increased, and, as groups of more progressive landowners organized themselves in bodies such as the Rural Foundation in the 1980s, old-style authoritarian farm paternalism began to change—in some areas—to a more modern managerial approach (du Toit 1993).

Highly capitalized agricultural enterprises such as the sugar estates had long used African migrant workers. Intensive maize and potato farmers began to follow suit in the inter-war years and by the 1960s the fruit farms of the western Cape also employed a large number of migrants, despite official discouragement of Africans in a Coloured Labour Preference area (**Chapter 6**). The labour bureaux, nearly 800 by 1970, and fully supported by the South African Agricultural Union (SAAU), were not least designed to channel migrant workers from homelands to the farms. Those who were less keen to compete for migrants could resort to convicts as casual labour.

The use of migrant and prison labour could result in atrocious working conditions. Despite occasional attempts at regulation by the state, agricultural employers were amongst the least controlled, so that child labour persisted. Henry Nxumalo, writing for *Drum*, and Ruth First, in the Congress paper *New Age*, exposed abuses in powerful muck-raking journalism in the 1950s, concentrating especially on the eastern Transvaal district of Bethal. Long an intensively farmed district, Bethal was a centre for some major maize producers who had pioneered the use of a migrant labour system that 'sold alien blacks to large farmers at a substantial profit' (Bradford 1987: 117). It also became one of the potato-producing centres of South Africa and acquired a wide reputation for brutality: workers, clothed in potato sacks, were regularly flogged. The reports had some impact, precipitating a (suppressed) government inquiry, increasing the circulation of *Drum*, and placing farm labour far higher on the ANC agenda. One of the first ANC commodity boycott campaigns in 1959 was of potatoes.

The result of these processes was that the government, the SAAU, and many leading farmers became far less concerned to immobilize labour on the farms in order to compete with mines and industries. Rather they relied on influx control and labour bureaux to ensure that they benefited from the pool of workers in the homeland areas. Homeland agriculture had long been unable to absorb more people. Foreign migrants, some illegal, also boosted labour supply. The abolition of the Masters and Servants Act, which had criminalized breach of contract, in 1974 facilitated labour mobility. By the early 1980s, as African unemployment increased, many farmers found even the labour bureaux unnecessary. While their perception of the corrupting influences of town and the lack of 'good boys' persisted, larger farmers, like urban industrialists, supported arguments for a freer labour market.

This had a direct impact on the remaining tenants. Labour tenancy, it will be recalled, had been entrenched in the 1913 Natives Land Act as a way of trapping Africans on farms (**Chapter 2**) but reducing their scope for independent production. Legislation illegalizing forms of 'squatting' was strengthened in 1951 and more systematically enforced. The position of labour tenants in many parts of the country had weakened since the 1936 Native Land and Trust Act, which could require them to give six months' service per year; more was sometimes demanded and rights to land or grazing diminished. In 1964 pressure from farming organizations and officials resulted in legislation that would permit labour tenancy to be abolished in a whole district.

As key arguments, officials cited agricultural efficiency and the technical and environmental benefits to be derived from owners controlling the whole farm. In the absence of a policy of protection for white farmworkers or small farmers, reduction in the number of African tenants was seen as an alternative way of countering *beswarting* of the platteland. 'If farmers were to introduce a system of *cash wages*', so a government commission argued, 'and hire strong young labourers at a higher monthly wage, the number of Bantu in the rural White areas would greatly diminish' (Greenberg 1981:95). It estimated that 1.8 to 2.4 million Africans could be encouraged or compelled to leave the farms.

By the early 1980s, this dire prediction had almost been fulfilled. In 1967 the government announced its intention to end black tenancy within three years and by 1969 these regulations had been applied in most of the grain-farming districts of the Free State and Transvaal where tenancy had persisted. Natal proved to be a more difficult area. Outside the sugar, banana, and wattle belts, undercapitalized farmers feared that they would lose their labour supply and rents. A compromise was reached, lasting till 1980, whereby existing tenancy contracts would be respected but no new agreements allowed. Although various forms of tenancy survived in a disguised way, the axe had finally fallen on the descendants of those who had initially been at the forefront of South Africa's highveld agrarian revolution.

Faced with unpalatable options, or more secure prospects elsewhere, some black tenant families moved voluntarily; many more were pushed. Workers were often dispensed with when farms were amalgamated or sold. The Surplus People Project (SPP), which pooled the research skills of young academics and activists in the early 1980s, calculated that about 1.1 million people were removed from the farms by 1982. A further estimated 600,000 were forced off 'black spots'. These were farms that were owned by African people, some of them since the nineteenth century, which fell outside the designated homelands and therefore became susceptible to appropriation. The amount of land involved was not large, but most of these farms were densely occupied by African tenants, few of whom had the resources or expertise to engage in commercial agriculture. Whites who owned land around the 'black spots' were anxious to have these moved.

Simkins's detailed computations (1983), on which many other sources are based, suggest that the percentage of the total African population on farms declined from 34.9 in 1951 to 31.3 in 1960 and 20.6 in 1980. However, because the rural population was growing so quickly, there was a small increase in absolute terms from 3.4 million to 4.2 million between 1960 and 1980 (about 1 per cent per annum). If the black farm population had been maintained at 31 per cent of the total number of Africans, as it was in 1960, then there would have been at least 6.5 million Africans on the farmlands by 1980. SPP figures suggesting farmland removals of close on 2 million therefore look reasonable, although some families, and especially youths, clearly left the farms before they were forced.

Community protests against removals, notably from 'black spots', were making more impact in the 1980s. Saul Mkize's death, resisting removal from Driefontein in the Transvaal in 1983, marked a turning point. A number of African settlements scheduled for removal from eastern Cape Border farmlands, between the Transkei and Ciskei, were reprieved. These included Mgwali, the old Presbyterian mission, site of the church led in the late nineteenth century by Tiyo Soga, the first African Christian minister. But the movement off farms did not abate. Evidence from the Free State suggests that the number of Africans living on farms in that province peaked in the late 1970s and then declined absolutely, from about 800,000 in 1980 to 600,000 in 1991 (Beinart and Murray 1996).

## Displaced Urbanization

Population movements were taking place in this period at a pace and on a scale that were unprecedented for Africans since Union.

The 'surplus people' and internal refugees of South Africa were not able to choose freely where they went. Megalopolises did not immediately sprout, as in Brazil or Mexico, where the major cities grew so fast. Indeed from 1960 to 1980, the proportion of the total African population in what were classified as the 'white' urban areas actually declined from 29.6 to 26.7 per cent. (This still represented an absolute increase of over 2 million people.)

Settlement, planned and unplanned, was diverted to areas within the boundaries of the homelands, where the population grew from 4.2 million in 1960 (39 per cent of all Africans) to over 11 million in 1980 (52.7 per cent). Perhaps four million of this seven-million increase would have taken place 'naturally'. This was in keeping with the government's intention to ethnicize as many Africans as possible. But few of those absorbed into the homelands obtained agricultural land. The great majority were drawn into closer settlements and new towns of various kinds.

Some found their way into existing rural villages and homesteads. Widespread Betterment had resulted in more concentrated settlement patterns in the old reserves. By 1980 about half of the families in many rural homeland villages were without land. Secondly, some of the surplus people moved into 'growth points' or expanded urban settlements within the homelands, such as Butterworth in the Transkei or Mafikeng in Bophuthatswana, where decentralized industries were being located and urban location-style housing built (**Map 2**). Thirdly, homeland boundaries were redrawn to take in existing urban locations near major cities, which then became large new townships. For example, Umlazi, formerly under the Durban municipality, became part of Kwazulu, and Mdantsane, near East London, became part of the Ciskei. Lastly, government expenditure on African housing was frozen in areas classified as white and diverted through homeland budgets or the South Africa Development Trust (formerly the Native Trust). By the late 1980s the latter had established 74 new towns with a total population of over two million.

Millions of people found themselves in barely planned rural slums, which were urban in respect of their population density and lack of agricultural opportunity, but rural in relation to

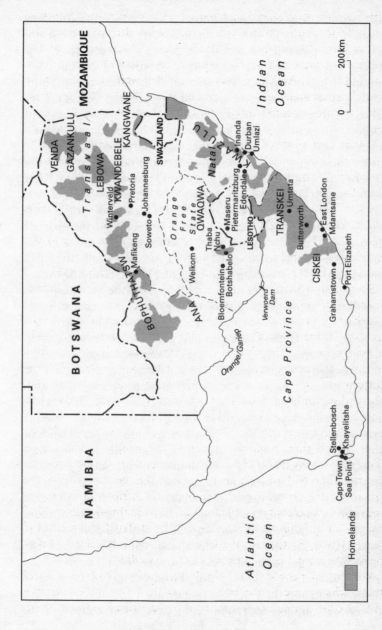

MAP 2. *Homelands and urbanization, 1980s.*

facilities, services, and employment. These were the dumping grounds of apartheid, first documented extensively by the Catholic priest Cosmas Desmond in his book, *The Discarded People* (1971), after a journey through the 'labyrinth of broken communities, broken families and broken lives which is the South African Government's removals policy' (Desmond 1971: 1). They subsequently received extensive media attention, so that images of soulless self-built shanties became indelibly associated, to outsiders as well as their inhabitants, with apartheid. Especially in their earlier years, these were 'wretched and desolate' places like Limehill in Natal—the first to come to Desmond's notice. 'There is not enough water and not enough land for even a meagre subsistence farming. There is no industry and no work within daily reach. The inhabitants struggle against disease on the edge of starvation. It is impossible to say whether the physical degradation or the mental torture of living in such a place is the more terrible' (1971: 1). It was rivalled by places like Sada and Dimbaza in the eastern Cape, Stinkwater and Klipgat in the Transvaal.

Although infrastructure and industry were extended to some resettlement towns, early rural slums were replaced by others on a far larger scale. In the 1970s that part of Bophuthatswana nearest to Pretoria became the biggest single 'close settlement' site, with an estimated 750,000 people. This Winterveld area grew so quickly, not only because it absorbed so many people coming off the farms and homelands, but because it was just about close enough to employment centres for daily commuting. Another striking example, Thaba Nchu, was located in an island of Bophuthatswana in the middle of the Free State. Along with QwaQwa, the tiny homeland for South Africa's Sotho people, it was the only African reserve area in the province. From 1968 the government tried to stabilize the size of Bloemfontein's main location; in some smaller Free State towns the African locations were razed to the ground. Sotho-speakers were supposed to go to QwaQwa and Tswana-speakers to Thaba Nchu. But Thaba Nchu had for a long time housed a diverse population and many Sotho- and Xhosa-speakers found it more attractive, as it was closer to Bloemfontein and the Free State goldfields.

Services and sites in Thaba Nchu were under control of the

Bophuthatswana homeland government. Hard pressed to provide even minimal facilities, officials tended to favour Tswana-speakers. Politicians from QwaQwa, looking for a broader constituency, took up the cause of the dispossessed Sotho-speakers. The central government, anxious to reward Bophuthatswana Chief Minister Lucas Mangope, who had taken Pretoria's offer of independence, agreed to purchase some farms adjacent to Thaba Nchu in order to house those not considered as Tswana. Initially this 10,000-hectare enclave, called Onverwacht (after the farm on which it was located) or Botshabelo (place of refuge), was to become part of QwaQwa, but it never did.

By 1980, a year after its establishment, over 100,000 people had crowded into Botshabelo. Residential plots were supposedly available on production of a reference book and QwaQwa citizenship card; this was largely ignored and people of all backgrounds made their homes there. 'The stands were 30 metres by 15 metres, each consisting of a patch of bare ground with a tin prefabricated toilet whose number—painted on the toilet door—was the new address' (C. Murray 1992: 226). Within six years, by 1985, Botshabelo housed perhaps 200,000–300,000 and rivalled Bloemfontein (265,000), established for over 130 years, and Welkom, the province's largest mining centre. QwaQwa itself grew from a largely rural enclave of under 30,000 in the 1960s, tucked in near the northern corner of Lesotho, to another huge settlement of similar size. Those of Botshabelo's people who could get work commuted 50 kilometres each way by bus to Bloemfontein daily or went for longer periods to the more distant goldfields. New industrial sites were being constructed between Bloemfontein and Thaba Nchu, but the major local employer in 1985, the Country Bird battery chicken farm, had only 500 workers. Lavish subsidies did expand employment by the late 1980s.

Displaced urbanization in places like Winterveld, Botshabelo, and QwaQwa seemed to solve a central problem for white South Africa. African people could not be kept rural and there was no longer any major economic advantage in perpetuating long-distance migrancy. But many African closer settlements, at least till the early 1980s, remained out of the major established cities and out of sight. African workers in these areas could reach employment centres daily and it became government policy to encourage 'commuting' rather than labour migration. This did not mean half-hour car journeys from the northern suburbs of Johannesburg to the city centre—or even hour-long train rides from closer townships like Soweto. 'Commuting' workers generally had to travel further, and in less convenient transport, as was illustrated by the case of KwaNdebele in the Transvaal.

Ndzundza Ndebele people had resurrected their identity and managed to regain land in a segregationist state (**Chapter 4**). A separate homeland did not, however, seem feasible for this small territorial authority, until the government recognized that it might serve also as a zone for displaced urbanization. Additional white-owned farms were bought around the settlement in the 1970s and it too grew wildly from about 32,000 in 1972 to perhaps 200,000–300,000 by 1985. It became a haven not only for former farm-workers but also for about 50,000 refugees from the Winterveld, Bophuthatswana, who felt victimized as non-Tswana.

Those of its inhabitants who could find work had to travel about 100 kilometres daily to Pretoria or East Rand towns. They were dependent on the Putco (Public Utility Transport Corporation) bus service. Begun as a small family business by immigrant Italians who ran buses from Alexandra to Johannesburg at a time when whites were being favoured with licences (**Chapter 5**), it expanded to become the largest bus company in the country. In 1984 its 3,500 vehicles serviced these far-flung African towns, helped by a heavy subsidy from the South African government, which was determined to make commuting work. In 1975 Putco ran two buses a day from Kwandebele; in 1984, 263 (Lelyveld 1985). Commuters would spend over six hours on noisy vehicles with hard seats designed for short hauls, leaving home at 4 a.m. and returning at 9 p.m. In his vivid indictment of government policy, American journalist Joseph Lelyveld remarked that the people of KwaNdebele were 'a nation of sleepwalkers'.

Nationally, transport difficulties were partially relieved in the 1980s by the rapid proliferation of minibus taxis, largely owned and driven by blacks. Between 1970 and 1989, minibus numbers increased from 24,000 to 174,000 (**Table 4**). Journey times were dramatically reduced. Taxis carried 30 per cent of commuters in

1989 and over 40 by 1992. Bustling taxi ranks became a new feature of most urban centres and provided opportunities for informal sector traders. The taxi trade was a key focus for black entrepreneurs in the late apartheid years and also a major cause of conflict resulting from competition over custom and routes.

Given the high rate of population increase and rapid mechanization of farms, South Africa could not have escaped some degree of rural devastation and urban poverty in these decades. Yet the stark division of wealth in the country, the lack of social welfare, and the imperatives of apartheid exacerbated the trials of displaced people. Communities were dislodged and scattered. The benefits of city living, taken for granted by many whites, were absent from most new settlements. Recreational and health facilities, as well as employment, were minimal. There were economic costs, in high fares and transport subsidies, as well as serious social, environmental, and aesthetic costs in this form of urban development.

## Social Division and Politics in the Homelands

Debates about the homelands have been central to critiques of apartheid. The very word 'homeland' has stimulated unease, because it seemed to lend legitimacy to the state's policy of balkanization and exclusion. Opposition groups preferred to retain the word 'reserves' or use Bantustan—the term with central Asian overtones for supposedly inconsequential and backward polities coined in the 1950s, which stuck in critical literature. (It is an irony that a number of these central Asian states became independent in the 1990s after the break-up of the Soviet Union.)

Defending the language of separate development—and trying to make it a reality—was a feature of the Nationalists' task. The arguments for independence used by both the South African government and homeland leaders drew on a more widespread anti-colonial rhetoric. Britain could be seen as conquering the Transkei, and Afrikaners as decolonizing it. Ideas of 'tribe' and chieftaincy had some attraction for African politicians uncertain about the possibility of any real gains in the wide South Africa under apartheid. As illustrated above, there were significant legacies in popular consciousness, which gave homeland politicians some purchase.

Glossy brochures and books illustrated the undoubted beauty of some old reserve areas, as well as investments made into them, but underplayed their poverty. Tables showed that the bigger homelands would not be the smallest states in the world, nor the poorest: the Transkei and KwaZulu, it was argued, were not essentially different from Lesotho, Botswana, and Swaziland. The South African government quickly forgot that it, like its predecessors, had worked hard to incorporate these territories up to the 1950s. This strategy had been reversed when homeland policy was elaborated at that time; the Tomlinson Commission actually envisaged an amalgamation of these territories with South Africa's homelands. Initially, Verwoerd was concerned about the political threat from their independence in the 1960s; now, constrained as they were by Pretoria's power, they were seen as a model. Nationalists' intervention in Lesotho to help secure a more favourably disposed ruler was amongst the first of many regional adventures.

Critics emphasized that Bantustans were not the whole of the historic African homelands and, more especially, that economically and politically they were inextricably part of South Africa. On the one hand, their people had made a central contribution to the development of South Africa and, on the other, they were incapable of producing enough food or achieving 'viability' given the historical skewing of the nation's economy. Homeland policy was particularly disliked because it was used to justify diminishing further the rights of millions of Africans living in the cities and on farmlands. They were threatened with the loss of their already very limited citizenship. Even after consolidation, a number of homelands remained disconnected islands surrounded by a sea of 'white' South Africa.

There is little doubt that the apartheid system, as developed up to the mid-1980s, had the effect of increasing the social chasm and income differentials between the rural homelands and urban areas. Poverty was externalized more systematically to the homelands; it was estimated that on average urban African income was twice that of rural. One indicator, among many, of these inequalities was the rate of mortality of children under 5. A number of countries that had a lower *average* per capita income than South Africa also had lower mortality rates in 1990: these included Iraq (before the Gulf War), Zimbabwe, Botswana, and Vietnam. South Africa's rates were so high, despite its wealth, because the distribution of wealth was so uneven. Although overall national estimates of under-5 mortality declined from about 192 to 90 per 1,000 between 1960 and 1990, figures of up to 300 were cited for some rural homelands in the 1960s and 1970s.

Another indicator was the high rates of child malnutrition, gastro-enteritis, tuberculosis, and other quintessential diseases of poverty. Tuberculosis rates in the early 1980s were probably twice as high in some homeland populations as amongst urban Africans—a figure that closely mirrors estimates of the gap in income—and perhaps twenty times as high as amongst whites. Whereas this disease was carried from the mining centres to the reserves in the early twentieth century, so that the homelands had become crucibles of endemic infection, Packard (1989) argued that by the 1980s it was bouncing back to the cities and peri-urban informal settlements.

Reserve economies had primarily been based upon remnant smallholder agriculture and, increasingly, money from migrant workers. Many sources note the decline of homeland agriculture in the apartheid period and in certain respects they are correct. Surveys from the 1980s suggest that only about 10 per cent of households in the Transkei were significantly involved in agriculture and less than 5 per cent gained a major portion of their living from the land. Yet evidence from the larger homelands such as Bophuthatswana, Transkei, and KwaZulu suggests that total agricultural output did not decline greatly, although it clearly did in much of Lebowa and the Ciskei. There were not fewer agricultural producers in the homelands: 10 per cent of Transkeian households implied 60,000 families—almost as many as the total number of white farming units in South Africa. The problem was that the homeland populations went up so rapidly, and that family size was declining.

There were some successes. In KwaZulu, sugar outgrower schemes for smallholders provided scope for renewal and commercialization of agriculture. Dagga could be a profitable sideline for those prepared to take the risk; it was perhaps becoming the major cash crop in some homeland districts. Families with significant wage income were often most likely to invest in agriculture and livestock as well. But overall production was not increased and large numbers of homeland dwellers, even if they had little other income, were unable to accumulate rural resources.

Whereas Betterment schemes were initially designed in part to control soil erosion and improve the prospects of agriculture, they increasingly became a means of rehousing displaced populations. Even where Betterment plans were relatively successful, they seldom prevented environmental degradation. A major problem reported by anthropologists was that the new villages themselves became the site for ecological damage. Cattle, sheep, and goats still had to be brought back nightly to kraals because of theft and inadequate maintenance of fencing. Livestock were now being returned to more concentrated settlements than before.

Villagization may not have been the only cause of environmental problems. Forms of customary land tenure remained entrenched in many parts of the homelands. Most households in rural settlements retained the right to graze animals on the common pastures that still made up the bulk of land in these areas. Debate now rages as to whether communal forms of tenure have been particularly conducive to environmental degradation, because all livestock owners seek maximum advantage from a resource for which they have no responsibility. Certainly it has been shown that customary tenure by no means always results in environmental tragedy where local political authorities can regulate the use of commons. But in some of South Africa's homelands, where political authority was unstable, controls over land use were uncertain and difficult; recent national surveys suggest that environmental damage has persisted. Communal forms of tenure could also inhibit investment into the land.

Few new villages had piped water, with the result that the streams, springs, and bore-holes near these concentrated settlements could be overstretched. In pre-colonial times, African settlement on the east coast had been dispersed not least in order to minimize this problem. The supply of water was a critical issue not only for health reasons but also because women had to spend so much time and effort in collecting it—an average of three hours daily in some homeland areas. Distance from water sources was of major significance to a household's well-being. Per capita consumption of water, over 200 litres per day for white city-dwellers, could be as little as ten for rural blacks. The drought years of the early 1980s revealed the maldistribution of water with frightening clarity.

Few of the buildings in new rehabilitation villages or displaced towns were initially linked to the national electricity grid, fuelled by South Africa's plentiful supply of cheap coal. Only in the 1970s was progress made with the electrification of major black townships such as Soweto. Many rural people, and those living in a semi-urban situation, had to find their fuel from coal, paraffin, and especially timber. Firewood was collected by women in strenuous and time-consuming journeys. 'One of the clearest images of . . . poverty in the country', Wilson and Ramphele noted, 'is the sight of a group of elderly black women, each carrying home on her head a load of firewood weighing up to 50 kg., passing underneath the high tension cables that carry the electric energy between the towns (and farmsteads) of the Republic' (1989: 44). In one part of KwaZulu, the average distance walked in collecting one head load was over 8 kilometres and the average time for collecting a load 4.5 hours. Women, who made up the majority of adults in the homelands, suffered particularly from the squeeze on rural resources.

Dependence on firewood could have a devastating effect on the environment around large new settlements. In 1976–7, 30,000–40,000 people moved from Herschel, which was about to be incorporated into the Transkei, and other districts to Thornhill, a resettlement camp near Queenstown, where some farms had been bought from white owners. 'From the air', a geographer noted, 'this area stands out as a reddish patch of bare soil, virtually devoid of vegetation. In 1976 . . . [it] had a good cover of thorn trees and bush. By 1981 hardly a tree was to be seen on the slopes of the hill' (Ramphele and McDowell 1991: 44). While systematic farm planning and subsidy probably improved the condition of farmlands, environmental ills were concentrated in the homelands.

Resettlement, environmental problems, poverty, and unrewarding labour characterized many homelands at the height of the apartheid era. In retrospect, the rural revolts and protests of the 1950s proved to be a last attempt to defend the autonomy of the reserves. Many elements of African culture did survive or were reinvented in some form both in town and countryside—for example, bridewealth, Sotho and Xhosa male initiation, Zulu 'traditional weapons' and women's headgear, and African medicine. Pockets of strong rural traditionalism and community life survived, not least because of the lack of modern services. Local languages survived and were taught at homeland schools. But the period from the 1960s to the 1980s marked a new phase of incorporation of the old African chiefdoms, so that their people lost much of their distinctiveness and increasingly reflected the predominant urban and wage-based culture. One indicator was that neo-traditional dress of blankets, beads, and headdresses was fading away. The social bonds that some state ideologues argued they were attempting to preserve tended to erode.

It is inadequate, however, to leave an analysis of the homelands at that: a picture so often presented of social and environmental devastation. They should not be viewed purely in terms of their functionality to the capitalist system or as exhibiting the scars of underdevelopment. In 1980 over 50 per cent of the African population lived within new homelands and their particular pattern of politics and development had important implications for the country as a whole. For the homelands policy to work, even to the extent that it did, local cooperation was required and there were beneficiaries of the system.

The Transkei, flagship of homeland development, was granted self-government in 1963 and elections were held for a legislative assembly. Chief Poto, who led a Democratic Party opposed to many elements of apartheid, won 38 out of 45 seats. Verwoerd had made provision for such an outcome by ensuring that the new authority included ex-officio chiefs. Poto's pro-government opponent, Chief Kaiser Matanzima, persuaded the chiefs in the new assembly to support him. He could play on their insecurities;

many had been threatened in the rebellions of the 1950s and early 1960s. The state of emergency imposed in these years remained in force. Matanzima's Transkei National Independence Party (TNIP) subsequently improved its showing amongst an electorate that recognized that it had no alternative and he effectively introduced one-party rule. Matanzima had a good deal of patronage to dispense.

His path was followed by the other homeland leaders who, with Pretoria's support, veered away from representative forms of government. In this respect, they were more rather than less like independent African states to the north. Where elections continued to be held, the polls were very low. Between 1976 and 1981, four homelands—Transkei, Bophuthatswana, Venda, and Ciskei—accepted independence. Although the South African state took the trappings of independence seriously, they received little recognition beyond Pretoria. In this respect, the international campaign against apartheid was successful.

Not all homeland governments toed Pretoria's line. In Sekhukhuneland, eastern Transvaaal, which became Lebowa, the first elections in 1973 were won by an alliance led by Dr C. Phatudi, a senior education official, which opposed outright independence; he persuaded sufficient of the chiefs to join them. Here electoral politics remained more competitive than in the Transkei: Phatudi's Lebowa Peoples Party was in turn nearly ousted in 1977 by Godfrey Sekhukhune, staunch opponent of apartheid and sympathetic to the ANC in exile. Although in Lebowa, as elsewhere, 'the politics of patronage and sustained opposition proved incompatible', this popular challenge gave warning of the depth of resistance to any formal constitutional separation from South Africa (Delius 1996: 175). It was clear to the government that a status short of independence had to be retained. Lebowa and the small homelands of KwaNdebele, Kangwane, Gazankulu, and Qwaqwa—unlikely candidates for autonomous sovereignty—became 'national states' within South Africa.

Most significantly, Chief Mangosuthu Buthelezi in KwaZulu used the homeland system to its full potential in establishing a powerful hold on his region, but also stopped short of accepting independence. This gave him considerable bargaining power with the state, which was anxious to push him in this direction. Buthelezi, deeply conscious of the historic might of the Zulu, harboured ambitions for more than a localized authority. Far more than other homeland leaders, he was able to canvass popular support as a vocal critic of some elements of apartheid up to the late 1970s. His Inkatha movement, which emphasized cultural renewal and invoked popular Zulu symbols, was far more effective than Matanzima's TNIP, both locally and nationally. Whereas ethnicity in the earlier part of the century often involved defence of rural resources and an old way of life, it was now also mobilized in competition for new economic and political resources.

Pretoria funnelled large quantities of money into the homelands: in 1976, on the eve of Transkeian independence, Bophuthatswana received R37 million, KwaZulu R70 million, and Transkei over R110 million; the latter sum had doubled by the early 1980s. This was over 80 per cent of their total budgets and did represent a substantial boost in expenditure on areas long starved of central government funding. A further irony of apartheid was that the Afrikaner quest to exclude Africans politically entailed far greater commitment to their development and welfare. The costs of the homelands began to outweigh their capacity to subsidize the wages of workers.

One major area of expenditure proved to be land purchase and settlement planning, as the central government finally made good a half-century of promises to extend African-occupied territories. Thousands of white-owned farms were purchased and laid out for African occupation: some for townships, some allocated by homeland leaders to their supporters, but a significant portion for Trust villages in which poor people were beneficiaries. Despite their desperate experience of initial resettlement, those who moved from Herschel to Thornhill in the northern Ciskei, for example, were eventual recipients of some 55,000 hectares of land. The area under exclusive African occupation expanded in the apartheid era. Investment in dams and irrigation projects was no longer confined to white-owned farming districts, as it seemed to hold the promise of denser homeland agricultural settlements.

Much of this money, however, reinforced emerging social

differentiation. Expanding bureaucracies and educational institutions boosted the number of homeland citizens earning reasonable salaries. In the Transkei alone, there were 20,000 in state employ in 1980 and 14,000 teachers taught nearly 700,000 pupils (Southall 1982: 182). All but a few hundred top posts and advisory positions were Africanized. Nationally, the homelands benefited disproportionately from funding for African secondary school expansion, so that by the 1970s perhaps two-thirds of high schools were within their boundaries. A central tenet of apartheid was to divert the ambitions of the African educated classes from major cities to the homelands, where they were expected to help guide the journey towards separate development.

Business as well as bureaucracy provided opportunities. Africans had been permitted to apply for trading licences in the reserves since the 1930s. By 1952 the Tomlinson Commission found about 1,200 African-operated stores in the homelands, nearly as many as white (Union of South Africa 1956: 90). Though these were mostly small outlets—African traders generated only 10 per cent of the estimated £17 million total turnover— this was a considerable platform and their numbers doubled by 1960. Separate development implied that the remaining dispersed network of white-owned stores would be bought out and a protected sphere created for African business. State corporations were established in the homelands, which financed this process— largely completed by the 1980s—and leased or sold sites to blacks. Trade and transport proved the most secure routes, along with public employment, for accumulation.

Up to the 1960s urban and industrial development within the reserves had been minimal and the old magisterial towns remained relatively small administrative, transport, and trading centres. Three processes began to change this. One was the growth of new towns through displaced urbanization. Another was the extension of homeland boundaries to include existing and growing urban townships. Thirdly, while Verwoerd initially disallowed white investment in the homelands, he encouraged industrial decentralization to border industries. These were sited in 'white' territory, but serviced by a black labour force resident in the homelands. The Nationalists pumped subsidies into border industries over many years and also passed a Physical Planning Act, which was in part designed to restrict new employment of Africans in the established industrial centres.

In the late 1960s direct investment by outsiders was allowed in the homelands in order to enhance their economic viability. Some industrialists, especially foreign investors, chose to exploit available subsidies and low wage rates. In the 1970s decentralized industries grew more quickly than those in the older metropolitan centres. Most, but not all, of the homeland factories made products, from matches to clothing, that required limited skills and were cheap to transport to the main urban markets. Casinos, constructed notably by the Southern Suns hotel group, burgeoned within homeland boundaries, where they could circumvent strict South African gambling laws. Sun City, in a segment of Bophuthatswana, was a glitzy and highly successful hotel, entertainment, and gambling venture within easy reach by car from the Rand. White South Africans were its main customers.

Large funds and subsidies pouring into increasingly unregulated governments, Development Corporations, and bureaucracies reinforced neo-patrimonial tendencies. Homeland rulers simultaneously expanded their own security forces, trained by South Africa. Newspaper reports of dubious dealings in the Bantustans—kickbacks, property speculation, and corruption—were legion, a fertile source for investigative journalism. As Streek and Wicksteed argued of Matanzima's Transkei: 'his involvement in corrupt and suspect practices set an example to civil servants and other government employees, and it is not surprising they have done well out of independence' (1981: 234). The Bantustan system created networks of economic and political patronage, with little outside control, reaching down from key figures in Pretoria into homeland administrations, so that many South Africans, white and black, found some self-interest in it. Nevertheless, by the early 1980s *verligtes* were expressing severe doubts about the expense and unworkability of the system. Homeland politicians were under increasing pressure as the youth rebellion of the 1970s became a general insurrection in the 1980s. Their politics became more involuted and violent, capped by a few military *coups.* While some leaders turned more explicitly to ethnic mobilization, many of the homeland elite began to look to national movements.

The legacy of displaced urbanization, poverty, and homeland politics has deeply influenced social developments in South Africa. Although the country was spared from the terrifying famines of Africa in the 1970s and 1980s and from the vortex of civil war, it had many of its own internal refugees. The uprooting of so many people undoubtedly compounded poverty and contributed to the volatility of black politics. Similarly the entrenchment of homelands with their systems of reward through ethnic identification initially helped fuel division between and within African communities. Ironically, in the longer term, the strength of opposition to the homelands has bolstered a national African identity. But there has not been a similar reaction to the corruption that they fostered.

Some of the processes analysed here were partially reversed from the 1980s when the government finally lost control over urbanization. The major established cities again experienced explosive growth (**Chapter 10**); population in the homelands and rural dense settlements stabilized. Nevertheless, the new urban concentrations of the apartheid era will remain part of South Africa's urban landscape. QwaQwa, Winterveld, Kwandebele, and Botshabelo will probably remain almost entirely black settlements, and in this sense the legacy of apartheid will be a long one. But given the problems of large metropolitan areas, there may be long-term benefits to a more dispersed pattern of urbanization—even if these are now hard to discern amidst the poverty and unemployment. In a post-apartheid era, interlinked conurbations could become corridors of growth where the environmental impact of settlement may be more containable than in the older metropolitan areas. They could provide an important stimulus to the surrounding rural districts. One example may be the Bloemfontein–Botshabelo–Thaba Nchu axis, stretching to Maseru in Lesotho, across the centre of the country, already home to over one million people.

# 9

# Black Political Struggles and the Reform Era of P. W. Botha, 1973–1984

### The ANC and the Politics of Exile

From the late 1970s, after three decades of power, the Nationalists were showing signs of vulnerability. The major reason was the growth of political opposition on a number of fronts. In this respect, the Natal strikes of 1973 and the Soweto protests of 1976 were major turning points. By the early 1980s domestic opposition was beginning to link more effectively to the banned political movements, whose survival, largely in exile, proved to be of great importance.

The ANC, PAC, and others initially tried to work underground within the country. The ANC's armed wing, Umkhonto we Sizwe, initially concentrated on the formation of cells and sabotage. These were years of fallen pylons and bombs in public buildings. By minimizing civilian casualties, which it felt morally unjustified, Congress hoped that it might jolt the government into recognizing the need for negotiation. But armed struggle only increased Afrikaner Nationalist resolve, already strengthened by its victory in the Republic referendum. The PAC military wing, Poqo, was less inhibited and did kill some white civilians—actions that attracted more publicity and undermined the ANC's already uncertain strategy of using constrained violence to persuade. In 1964 a group of largely white student activists not based in the Congress movement launched their own sabotage campaign. After a few heady blasts, including the Johannesburg station explosion, they were arrested and station bomber Harris hanged.

Underground movements of all kinds were greatly hampered by the success of the security police in infiltrating them. Mandela was caught in 1962; in 1963 other key Congress underground leaders were found at a farm owned by white Communist Party members in Rivonia, north of Johannesburg. Perhaps 10,000 people were arrested in the early 1960s. Opposition movements still had relatively open recruitment policies and security police were able to find spies, black and white, or extract information from those arrested. Increasingly ruthless methods were used, including torture, which had not been so significant a part of the police repertoire before. The long and sorry saga began of deaths in detention, of prisoners alleged to have thrown themselves out of windows or hanged themselves in their cells. Legislatively sanctioned imprisonment without trial and house arrests were accompanied by an increasingly uncontrolled cop-culture—smashed windscreens and windows, dead cats on gate posts, threatening phone calls, and eventually political killings. Critical film-makers later created an image of blue-eyed police sergeants with searing stares, hard voices, and harder hands; they did exist.

Trust and betrayal became a central nexus in radical opposition politics and the stakes could be very high. It was difficult to be heroic in an atmosphere of suspicion. Nor were activists safe outside the country. Cross-border raids began in 1961 and the web of informers spread abroad with the exile movements. The state succeeded not only in discovering and imprisoning many key political leaders but also in defusing any rapid remobilization. Under Vorster and General van den Bergh the security police, now extended into the ominous Bureau of State Security (BOSS), became a highly effective instrument.

It has been argued that the ANC, Communists, and PAC underestimated the intransigence of the government, and overestimated both the readiness of the people to revolt and the likelihood of international assistance. In abandoning non-violent mass action or worker organization they thus fatally weakened themselves. Yet the security forces were so intent on obliterating radical opposition that there seemed few options left other than a return to cautious reformism or working through the Bantustan system. By the mid-1960s, it was clear that stuttering sabotage would have to be replaced by a more systematic, better-funded military effort based outside the country. Reflecting the methods of liberation movements in the region, the ANC shifted its strategy to guerrilla struggle. Three small expeditions were sent through Zimbabwe with local liberation movement units in 1967–8. They engaged fiercely but unsuccessfully with Rhodesian forces and South African police. With no bases in neighbouring countries, there was little scope for an externally based war, as in Zimbabwe. South Africa's remnant peasantry, difficult to reach and tightly policed, could not provide a platform for sustained guerrilla struggle.

By contrast, the international diplomatic campaign, led by Tambo, who had been sent overseas to open an office in 1960, made more effective progress. The ANC gained access to the United Nations, helped found national anti-apartheid movements, and mobilized funds and resources from the Eastern bloc, African allies, and Scandinavian countries. In the cold-war era, the US and West European governments tended to judge the ANC as revolutionary and to avoid it. A rapidly growing South Africa was seen, although increasingly uneasily, as a good investment and a bastion against communism. But anti-apartheid forces in these countries were able to claim some of the moral high ground. Boycott campaigns involving such varied targets as Outspan oranges, Cape fruit, cultural exchanges, and the arms trade met with some success. As in the case of anti-slavery campaigns over 150 years earlier, it became increasingly difficult to justify apartheid in Western countries.

One of the most significant boycotts was in sport. In a post-colonial age, segregated sport became a major international issue. Demonstrations began in 1960 in New Zealand. Verwoerd and Vorster invited reprisals when they refused permission for Maori members to tour with an All Blacks rugby team in 1965 and for ex-Capetonian coloured cricketer Basil D'Oliveira to join the English touring party in 1968. In the latter year, pressure from African and Asian countries resulted in South Africa's exclusion from the Olympics. When a South African rugby team visited Britain in 1970, the sports boycott came of age in the Stop the Seventy Tour campaign. The Nationalists' response was to tough it out and play with those who would play with them. International control boards in rugby, where the former white dominions were more dominant than in cricket, athletics, and football, took more than a decade to isolate white South Africa; even in cricket 'rebel' tours persisted. But the boycott brought the issue of apartheid into arenas in which people were not usually forced to confront such questions. Opponents of boycotts argued that sport should be kept free from politics; it was an increasingly unconvincing position when the NP's approach was so obviously political. For many white South Africans, whose identity was bound up with sport, creeping international isolation began to have its effects.

Exile movements, dispersed far from their constituencies, searching for diverse international support and fearful of infiltration, are prone to factionalism. Specific organizational and ideological issues did threaten the unity of the ANC: not least the role of the Communist Party and whites, and also the relative weight that should be placed on class or national struggle. Socialist ideas permeated the ANC in exile, but the CP continued to work within the limits of a nationalist rather than explicitly communist struggle. An attempt was made to specify what was implied by a national democratic revolution, based on the Freedom Charter, at a major ANC conference in Morogoro, Tanzania, in 1969. The conference also agreed to allow non-racial membership and to reactivate internal opposition.

If the language of the exile movements sometimes seemed rigid, this was hardly exceptional in the context of left politics in the 1960s and 1970s. There were splits to the Africanist right and socialist left and it was perhaps necessary to police a tight political line when ideological and personal differences could rapidly have produced fragmentation. The Communist Party helped not only to maintain continuity but also to provide a conduit for funding and training in the Eastern bloc. When Mozambique and Angola were liberated and Marxist governments came to power in 1975, the ANC readily found new bases for operation closer to South Africa. By contrast, the PAC fractured and all but collapsed in exile.

ANC prisoners on Robben Island near Cape Town also managed to sustain political solidarity: they formed their own High Organ of Mandela, Sisulu, Mbeki, and Raymond Mhlaba. Especially in the earlier years, discipline and fortitude were essential in coming to terms with an enormously testing prison regime designed 'to break one's spirit and destroy one's resolve' (Mandela 1995: 463–4). 'I was now on the sidelines', Mandela recalled, 'but I also knew that I would not give up the fight . . . We regarded the struggle in prison as a microcosm of the struggle as a whole. We would fight inside as we had fought outside.'

In later years, when greater latitude had been won from the prison authorities and access to books and (censored) newspapers permitted, prisoners developed more systematic educational and political training. Sisulu and Mbeki taught on the history of the ANC, Ahmed Kathrada on the Indian struggle, Mandela on political economy. Established ANC prisoners were able to incorporate youth activists incarcerated after 1976 and many of those leaving the island on conclusion of their sentences threw themselves back into politics. Critically, the prison provided the context for Mandela himself to renew his authority and standing.

'The ANC's survival through the bleak 1960s and early 1970s (albeit in a much-weakened form), had a cumulative—and pivotal—result for the movement. Its long-established traditions and symbols of resistance survived with it, and it would be repopularised—to considerably effect—during the resurgence of militant internal resistance' (Barrell 1988). At home, Congress, like its imprisoned leaders, could remain a powerful memory, standing for a non-racial democracy and 'one man one vote' (in the language of the time), unsullied by the compromises of politics.

### Internal Remobilization: Black Consciousness

While the hiatus in internal black political organization after 1961 was sharp, that in opposition political thinking was less so. By the late 1960s a set of ideas that came to be called 'black consciousness', originating in the churches and educational institutions, were being reformulated. Black consciousness was more an intellectual orientation than a political grouping, difficult to capture analytically because it was represented by a scattering of proponents and small organizations rather than a single party. Protagonists asserted a confidence in being black in the face of bannings, everyday racism, and dehumanization. They confronted the government in the ideological sphere precisely at the moment when its economic success was cresting and the relentless propaganda in favour of apartheid and retribalization seemed to be gaining ground. Their concentration on ideological issues also reflected their caution about open and therefore vulnerable party organization. Moreover, they took issue with the deference and uncertain cultural direction of the African elite.

Use of the word 'black' was in itself a challenge to apartheid's ethnic and racial labelling and an alternative to the negative 'non-white' (*nie-blanke*) or 'non-European', which was in common currency. Terminology has been important in South Africa's political debate and the government's adoption of 'Bantu' rather than native or African was an essential part of its policy. As in the USA, where African-Americans shifted from 'negro' and 'coloured' to black, the use of this word in South Africa set down claims to rights and evoked a new and unified identity. (Black was borrowed from the USA but had been in use in African languages: *abantu abamnyama* meant ordinary or black people in Xhosa.) Steve Biko, the medical student who was one of the key advocates of black consciousness, used the term non-white as late as 1969, switching to black around 1970. Black specifically included coloured and Indian people as well as African. Coloured intellectuals disdainfully prefaced that racial categorization with 'so-called' if they used it at all. This insistence on black was so successful that Botha's government itself renounced Bantu and adopted the term, for African people at least, a decade later.

The amalgam of ideas that made up black consciousness drew on the heritage of Africanism in the ANC and the PAC as well as the strong sense of being African that persisted in the rural areas, in African Christianity, and in everyday associational forms. But the eclectic new black consciousness was not only a local populist ideology; it found much of its additional weaponry in the resounding language of the US civil rights and Black Power movements of the 1960s. Literature of liberation struggles, such as the writings of Frantz Fanon, and images of Che Guevara filtered back, despite banning of individual works. Biko (1978) drew directly on Fanon in his critical article on psychological liberation: 'Black Souls in White Skins'.

In the 'orthodox' churches, which still had very considerable international connections and networks, specifically South African anger was given further focus by international liberation theology. In the 1960s major Christian denominations were coming to terms with decolonization and debates about Third World poverty. The language of Christianity and its political messages were changing. Anglicans, Catholics, and Methodists all threw up individual leaders, both black and white, who maintained a specifically Christian critique of apartheid policy and practice. The Christian Institute, formed in 1963, headed by the renegade Dutch Reformed Minister Beyers Naude, together with the South African Council of Churches, provided a focus for Christian opposition. Hammanskraal, the Catholic seminary north of Pretoria, became a centre for black consciousness meetings, and one of the first specific groupings was the University Christian Movement founded in 1967.

While a significant initial focus of the movement lay in the churches, its central impetus came from educational institutions and student politics. In 1959 African entry into 'white' universities was further restricted and 'tribal' recruiting policies imposed on Fort Hare, *Alma Mater* of many nationalists. New ethnic universities, derogatorily called 'bush colleges', were established within homeland boundaries, in the western Cape for coloured students and at Durban Westville for Indians. They were peopled with conservative Afrikaner academics, while the administration fell under the Department of Bantu Education and the other ethnic subdepartments. Although black university expenditure expanded rapidly, education opportunities were in increasingly segregated spheres.

The National Union of South African Students (NUSAS) had survived as a single non-racial organization and a platform for politicized students both from the English-speaking and black campuses. (Afrikaner students had their own national union.) The English-speaking universities remained important nodes of opposition political culture. Carried by the surge of student protest in Europe and the mood of the anti-Vietnam movement in the USA, students developed a new sense of urgency about political and social change from the late 1960s. The University of Cape

Town sit-in of 1968, triggered by a particularly South African issue—the blocking of Archie Mafeje's appointment as lecturer in Anthropology, apparently under pressure from the government—was one key turning point.

Despite this radicalism, interracial political activity was limited and NUSAS conferences were dominated by the large and articulate white delegations. If the presence of blacks was appreciated, they were more marginalized than they wished. Black students broke with NUSAS in 1968 and launched the South African Students Organization (SASO) in 1969. Biko (1978: 21) argued that white liberals were 'claiming a monopoly on intelligence and moral judgement and setting the pattern and pace for the realisation of the black man's aspirations'. Black people, it was patent, should liberate themselves. Black students also felt that they confronted particular problems in their new institutions, where both intellectual control and discipline were heavy handed. Their debate was not just with white students, but also an attempt to reach back into black communities and counter the ethnicization of black politics through the rapidly evolving Bantustan system.

In 1972 the Black People's Convention was launched as an umbrella body for the black consciousness groups coalescing in many different spheres. Awareness of the emerging trade-union movement led in 1973 to the formation of the Black Allied Workers Union, though some were opposed to the idea of a specifically class-based workers' forum. Black Community Programmes, and especially a flagship community health project in the eastern Cape launched under Mamphela Ramphele, probably expressed the movement's aspirations more closely. Ramphele had been a medical student in Durban, and SASO local chair, who was personally close to Biko and helped him write articles. After he was banned to Kingwilliamstown, she moved to the area in 1974 and Zanempilo (bringer of health) centre became a major new focus for activism.

Black consciousness literature and journalism flourished. Newspapers such as Soweto's *The World*, while not directly espousing these ideas, were increasingly adventurous in coverage of black politics. In 1974 a major rally celebrated the collapse of the Portuguese empire. Leaders began to receive the same treatment of banning, imprisonment, and murder experienced by Congress. Exiled former Turfloop student leader Ongopotse Tiro was killed by a parcel bomb in 1974; Mapetla Mohapi was killed in detention in 1976; Ramphele was banned to the northern Transvaal. The movement needed a high profile and access to the media in order to win support, but this exposed its leaders to retaliation.

If university students and writers were at the ideological heart of black consciousness, school students proved to be its most effective political vanguard. Between 1950 and 1975, the number of African children at school rose from around 1 million to over 3.5 million and the proportion at secondary school from 3 per cent to over 8 per cent. Secondary expansion was especially dramatic between 1965 and 1975, when it increased nearly fivefold to about 280,000. Class sizes averaged over 60 in Soweto and reached 100. Under-trained teaching staff in acutely under-resourced schools found it difficult to cope and corporal punishment was commonplace. Schools became sites of expansion, of expectation, of deprivation, and of explosive political potential.

The school-based South African Students Movement (SASM) was strongest in Orlando, the old heart of Soweto and a politicized area since the 1950s. It drew on flourishing debating societies and the Student Christian Movement, which were encouraged by school authorities, but became penetrated by black consciousness. It included leaders with some experience: the average age for students completing the final school-leaving exam, matric, was 20. SASO was instrumental in 'conscientizing' high schools, and black university student leaders made a direct impact by taking up teaching posts in Soweto: Tiro, expelled from Turfloop university, moved to Morris Isaacson school in Orlando to teach history before he was hounded into exile. SASM challenged the authoritarianism of the Department of Bantu Education, which had cowed teachers and dismissed political activists; it aimed to find a channel for 'needs and grievances' by the formation of Student Representative Councils, which were widespread in the universities.

One of SASM's campaigns was against interschool music competitions, a major extramural interest and commitment of African teachers, which students felt were disrupting education because they took so much time and energy. Choral music was heavily featured on black radio programmes and, while it had strong roots in African churches, it was an activity that was not perceived to threaten the apartheid order. A clear generational challenge was involved, as also in the scholars' campaign against liquor, which reflected awareness of the disruption it caused to education and social life. SASM incorporated the idea of 'the system' into its vocabulary to express the whole oppressive regime that seemed to impinge on people's lives. By the mid-1970s some SASM leaders made contact with ANC members such as Joe Gqabi, later killed by a letter bomb, who were coming off Robben Island.

SASM activists were catalysts in the Soweto marches that rocked the country in 1976, a time of regional crisis and economic recession (**Chapter 7**). Government was reluctant to maintain high subsidies on vital consumer items such as maize and bread for the urban poor. This, coupled with rising unemployment, poor services, rent increases, and urban crowding, exacerbated the effects of the downturn in Soweto. But the protest was specifically against the inequalities of Bantu Education and the introduction of Afrikaans, 'the language of the oppressor', as a teaching medium for some subjects, including maths.

After initiating a schools boycott and successfully resisting the arrest of one of its officials, SASM established an Action Committee and organized a demonstration for 16 June 1976, in which protestors from different schools were to converge and march to Orlando stadium. It was the police overreaction that gave the student struggle its kick-start and helped launch over a year of action. Stayaways, and attacks on government buildings, on police informers, and on beer halls were not new tactics in themselves but achieved a fresh intensity and provoked unprecedented retaliation, leading to hundreds of deaths.

Political mobilization in Soweto schools was all the more remarkable because schoolgoers were in a minority of no more than a third of teenage youths. It was decidedly 'an uprising of school students', Glaser (1998b: 301), argues, 'rather than "the youth", a contemporary catch-all category which often obscures deep cultural divisions'. As their numbers and sense of identity grew in the early 1970s, scholars came under threat of harassment from the ubiquitous Soweto gangs intent on commanding their territories. Student solidarity was not least aimed at defending themselves physically from the gangs. Some attempts were made to 'infiltrate the "*tsotsi* element" and turn their criminal energy towards whites' (Glaser 1998*b* 312). Gangs did participate in arson and looting during 1976; liquor suddenly became freely available. But the student leaders soon found themselves struggling to contain excesses and had to dissociate themselves from crime, which was a major community grievance.

Two striking features of 1976 were the spread of protest to coloured schools in the western Cape and attacks not only on Municipal beer halls but also on shebeens and liquor stores. Students were not fighting for the right to brew and sell liquor but arguing that 'we can no longer tolerate seeing our fathers' pay-packet emptied in shebeens'. Mbulelo Mzamane captured the urgency of the rebellion and the simultaneous informality and portentousness of its language in his novel *The Children of Soweto* (1982: 126):

> Listen our parents
> It is us, your children
> Who are crying;
> It is us, your children,
> Who are dying.
> *Amandla*!

We, the children of Soweto, hereby call upon you all to join us in mourning our martyrs massacred in Soweto by Vorster's fascist stormtroopers.

Elsewhere in the book a student spokesman confronted a cynical shebeen customer: 'You yourselves have been eye-witnesses to all the atrocities perpetrated against us by the System' (1982: 143).

Vorster hit out against 'agitators' in the year following the school protest, so that black consciousness organizations, the South African Council of Churches, and many individuals, black and white, were imprisoned or banned. Soweto's paper *The World,* which had supported the students, was temporarily closed. In 1977 Steve Biko was arrested and died after torture at the hands of the police. Perhaps 12,000 youths fled the country. It was difficult for new black associations to mature and develop nationally or to elaborate specific programmes. But the political 'bounds of possibility' had been extended (Ramphele 1996: 187). Anger and symbols of resistance survived: the clenched fist; the slogan *amandla ngawethu* (power to us, the people); the picture of Hector Peterson, one of the first to be shot, being carried away by anguished scholars. There was a strong belief amongst politicized black youths that 'the system' was so unjust that it could not last.

## Trade Unions

African employment in big-city manufacturing industries (**Chapter 7**) opened new potential for organization. A greater proportion of industrial workers were settled permanently in urban townships—not herded as migrants in compounds; they were also, as a rule, better educated, and a minority were able to find more skilled positions than were generally open in the mining industry. The scope for trade-union activity had been illustrated by the growth of SACTU in the 1950s. It failed to realize its potential, not least because, along with other Congress-linked groups, that federation was weakened by repression in the early 1960s and survived actively only in exile. A number of SACTU organizers went underground as Umkhonto we Sizwe cadres.

While white unions prospered in the 1960s, and some tradition of multiracial activity was maintained in the moderate TUCSA federation, this was a period of deunionization for African workers and of tightening legal restriction on their activities. They were not able to stake their claim equally in competition for the benefits that often accrue in periods of rapid economic growth and relatively high employment. The changing political mood of the early 1970s, however, emboldened black workers. Strikes had never been dependent on unions. In 1971 a partially successful strike by Ovambo migrant workers in Namibia gained considerable publicity. In 1972 Durban stevedores stopped work. And in 1973 the industrial areas around that city were hit by a sustained wave of action.

Interviews with Natal factory workers in 1973 revealed a clear memory of union activity from the 1950s and former members of

SACTU remained in the workforce. Triggered by compounded migrant workers at Coronation Brick and Tile, the strike soon spread to affect 150 factories, including women at the Frame textile works. Wages were at the heart of workers' demands; many also suffered from crowded, dingy hostel accommodation or were forced to live in backyard shacks. Cultural as well as workplace networks provided momentum. A speech to workers by Zulu King Goodwill Zwelithini at the end of 1972 had lifted expectations for a wage rise. Zulu-speaking workers sang the black national anthem 'Nkosi Sikelel' iAfrika' (God Bless Africa), expressed their solidarity in shouts of *Usuthu* for the Zulu royal family, and brandished 'traditional' sticks. Interviewers found that informal leadership networks of *stokvels* and migrant homegroups were also important in mobilization.

The strikes followed a well-established pattern of non-unionized black worker protest but focused attention on the scope for unionization. They also coincided with new intellectual developments. The political traditions and social composition of white South African society were sufficiently diverse to produce, throughout the apartheid era, succeeding generations of dissidents. Most came from middle-class English-speaking families, including a disproportionate number from Jewish backgrounds. Intellectuals both at home and abroad played a significant role in decolonizing minds.

Post-1968 activist fever, together with the challenges of black consciousness and a rediscovery of socialism, helped to refocus radical student opinion. New Left analyses, which swept through British and American universities, and were applied to South African society by expatriate academics, were one influence; African studies as a whole were being transformed. Debates within the Congress movement and the Communist Party in exile filtered back. The legacy of the Natal Indian Congress, which had long battled with the tensions between passive and armed resistance, between elite and workers, and with ethnic divisions, proved important both in London and Durban. Within the country, the Study Project on Christianity in Apartheid Society prompted influential academics such as Richard Turner in Durban to advocate worker organization.

Such analyses provided a means of conceiving South Africa as a peculiar capitalist society in which class as much as race was a primary social division. This gave both succour and meaning to non-racial political beliefs. The late 1960s and early 1970s were a particularly fertile period for white as well as black radical politics, and many new initiatives were generated, from literacy groups to the South African Voluntary Service. White students, linking with black workers and older unionists, especially in Natal, made their most significant impact in espousing the cause of workers where black consciousness seemed to be hesitant.

In 1972 the Workers' Benefit Fund and Institute for Industrial Education in Durban, the Urban Training Project (Johannesburg), and the Wages Advisory Committee (Cape Town) were launched. Durban activists had some involvement in the 1973 strikes. By the mid-1970s fully-fledged African unions such as the General Workers in Cape Town and the National Textile Workers in Durban were established. Some Indian textile workers, inheritors of a strong union tradition, recognized the advantages of cooperation with African workers, and joined the new movement. The African Metal and Allied Workers' Union (MAWU) made rapid strides in a few Natal factories, including British vehicle producers Leyland, and by 1975 had extended to the Rand. Strong links remained between academics, the unions, and service organizations that retained a non-racial leadership.

From the start, great emphasis was laid on democratic structures, shop-floor organization, and elected shop stewards. These were seen as a means of averting some of the weaknesses of black trade unions in the past, where either the leadership had been insufficiently controlled or mass membership had mushroomed then collapsed in the face of repression and failure. The ICU in the 1920s was held up as an example not to follow. The issue of representativeness was all the more important because government and industry attempted to meet the challenge by developing appointed Works and Liaison committees that could provide an alternative channel of communication between employers and black workers.

With the exception of a few in the Cape, the independent

unions tended to be industrial rather than general, concentrating their energies on work-related issues and avoiding open political alignment. While their political potential was patent, they were anxious to walk before they could run. A survey of union members in 1976 found that workers 'contrasted SACTU's concentration on politics on a national level, with the present unions' concern with the day-to-day issues in the factory, and their stress on the need to resolve complaints through shop stewards, and not at the trade union offices' (E. Webster 1987: 20). Although there was widespread sympathy with the Soweto protests of 1976, and stayaways were organized in response to calls from the scholars, the unions avoided direct involvement. The government adopted a relatively cautious approach of containment and, although the unions' legal status was uncertain, did not attempt to dismember them completely.

The new independent unions also suffered in the spate of bannings and detentions after 1976, but they had sunk sufficiently strong roots to survive. They minimized strike action and concentrated on international companies, which were vulnerable to adverse publicity. By the late 1970s a small number of unions were being recognized for negotiation purposes because of the extent of their shop-floor support. In 1979 and 1980 the independent unions formed two federations, the Federation of South African Trade Unions (FOSATU) and the Council of Unions of South Africa (CUSA). The former was explicitly non-racial, while CUSA restricted itself largely to black workers and black leadership. BAWU, associated with the Black Consciousness Movement, which had not developed much in the 1970s, split in 1979. One of its offshoots, the South African Allied Workers' Union (SAAWU), proved especially successful in the eastern Cape, a historically politicized region where black communities were both relatively well educated and relatively poor. It campaigned on community issues and challenged the Ciskei homeland administration, which had recently taken independent status.

## *Crisis, Reform, and the UDF*

Up to the early 1970s Afrikaner *verligtes* emphasized the positive elements of separate development, which many still felt might be attained. It was only a minority, such as a few church figures at Potchefstroom University for Christian Higher Education, who questioned the morality of apartheid. With white confidence shaken by Soweto in 1976, more began to ask harder questions about the feasibility of grand apartheid, the viability of the homelands, and the consequences of mass removals. Elsa Joubert's book, *The Long Journey of Poppie Nongena*, first published in Afrikaans (1978), caught this mood. It was the 'true' story of an Afrikaans-speaking black woman, marginalized by apartheid. Although Joubert denied a political intent, and many reviewers saw the story as a personal tragedy with a Christian ending, it was difficult to escape the devastating indictment of the effects of pass laws, influx control, and resettlement that separated husband and wife, children and parents. It was widely read, serialized in the press, and made into a play.

In 1978 a political scandal broke that played strangely on Afrikaners' self-image. Vorster's security chief and information supremo misused public money in a campaign to persuade the world of the government's credentials. The 'information scandal' was not the first example of corruption, but it came at a difficult time and undermined some of those many who still believed in the morally superior character of the Afrikaner establishment. This spelt the end of Vorster, already a sick man, and P. W. Botha came to power. A long-established party official from the Cape and Minister of Defence, he was a proponent of Armscor and the military.

Botha faced a regional context that had changed radically. White rule was no longer cushioned by the circle of settler and colonial states around it. In the Portuguese colonies of Angola and Mozambique, the metropolitan government itself, rather than settlers, had underwritten the large military effort entailed in controlling an increasingly hostile African population in the 1960s and 1970s. In 1974, when a *coup* in Portugal—prompted not least by the costs of the colonial wars—displaced the fascist government, decolonization followed rapidly. Rhodesian settlers had made their Unilateral Declaration of Independence from Britain after the break-up of Federation in 1965 and fought their own campaign against the black Zimbabwean liberation movements. From the mid-1970s the war intensified and, despite South African assistance and an attempt at an internal settlement, settler rule succumbed in 1979. In 1980 a black Zimbabwe African National Union (ZANU) government under Robert Mugabe was elected.

Pretoria increasingly perceived itself to be subject to a 'total onslaught' from the north. South Africa's hinterland was seen not so much as a source of labour, or avenue for possible expansion, or even as a trading zone, but as a potential threat. The South West African People's Organization (SWAPO) was able to mount an increasingly effective challenge from bases in Angola. South African strategists were deeply concerned that the ANC was finding nearby military bases from which to prosecute its own armed struggle. Because of its proximity and its socialist government, Mozambique was seen as the major potential threat. South Africa fostered the rebel Renamo movement, initially launched by the Rhodesian security forces, to challenge the fledgling Frelimo state.

Vorster had tried hard to develop diplomatic and economic contacts with some African states in order to counteract regional isolation. He had some success with Malawi under the conservative and capitalist President Banda. Botha made renewed attempts to develop a 'constellation' of Southern African states, using both sticks and carrots. But an alternative organization linking the black governments of the region, the Southern African Development Coordination Conference, though beset by problems, confirmed the front-line states' commitment to find a political and economic future outside South Africa's orbit. While Pretoria had long demanded that foreign powers should keep out of its internal affairs, it now felt that the 'total onslaught' justified almost any tactic, short of outright war, on its neighbours. Political and economic destabilization became one of the least salubrious features of Botha's rule. Whereas armed struggle was the weapon of liberation movements until the late 1970s, it increasingly became the instrument of counter-revolution. South

African intervention exacerbated and internationalized regional civil conflicts, with tragic consequences for the people involved.

Regional pressures contributed, along with internal challenges, towards government 'reform' in the period from 1978 to 1984. In 1978 P. W. Botha warned whites to 'adapt or die'. Piet Koornhof, a Broederbonder on the *verligte* wing of the Party, declared in Washington in 1979 that 'apartheid is dead'. Nationalist politicians were far more cautious at home. Nevertheless, as the army rather than the police became central to the security and power structures of the country, so it was recognized that 'hearts and minds' had to be courted more assiduously (**Chapter 10**).

The Soweto school revolt of 1976 forced reconsideration of urban black living conditions. Electrification of Soweto and other townships became a more urgent priority that had many social implications. In 1979 tentative schemes for black private property in the urban areas were reintroduced, twenty years after the government had tried finally to abolish this. Koornhof's much quoted aphorism also indicated that the party was beginning to think of ways to deracialize its ideology and project a more incorporative image—a state that was national in the broader sense rather than simply an Afrikaner state.

Afrikaner businesses, along with industry in general, openly criticized restrictions in the labour market and state monopolies. As the free-market ideology of the Thatcher and Reagan era permeated South African politics, reformers found its combination of more liberal economic policy and conservative social philosophy matched well with their developing perception of the country's problems. Conservative dominance in the West provided something of a respite for white South Africa to work out a reformist strategy, while its rulers could participate in a shared rhetoric against Communism. To a greater extent than before, the government clasped the business community to its bosom. Highly publicized conferences were held in Anglo-American's giant Carlton Centre, Johannesburg, and in Cape Town. Business interests were incorporated more fully into commissions and advisory bodies. The Urban Foundation, a privately funded welfare and research body set up by both English and Afrikaner magnates, became a testing ground for new urban initiatives. 'The ghost of

Hoggenheimer, the capitalist caricature against which the NP used to rail, [had] been laid' (Charney 1984: 273).

A proliferation of government inquiries on key economic issues helped to expand the intellectual and ideological environment for reform. The Riekert Commission (1979) addressed the issue of skill shortages and manpower requirements. While adhering closely to apartheid ideas, it argued that those Africans who did qualify to stay in the cities should have stronger rights as well as greater mobility between urban centres and more control over township government. The Wiehahn Report (1979) advocated some limited recognition for African trade unions as long as they registered and subjected themselves to regulation. The government responded rapidly by passing a new Industrial Conciliation Amendment Act. The De Lange Commission (1981) was the most radical—arguing for a single national Department of Education and gradual equalization of education expenditure. This recommendation had little immediate impact, but, together with the surge in school boycotts, his report helped push the government into massive new expenditure on African education. The scene was set for a further doubling in total African enrolment, and trebling in secondary enrolment, over the next decade. The large gap between average expenditure on white children and that on black began to narrow.

The government had always recognized that it could not rule the country without cultivating some black allies. Whereas in the years up to the mid-1970s, it had concentrated solely on the homeland leaders, attention was now switched also to the urban black middle class. Africans were being offered gradual dismantling of job protection, incorporation in township local government, and the prospect of greater upward mobility. The language of the market seemed to provide increasing scope for blacks to identify with a national capitalist society. Movements like Inkatha, begun essentially as a vehicle for homeland politics in KwaZulu, now found some broader constituency amongst those sharing a free-market approach, and aiming for an internal settlement, who felt that the exile movements were too closely associated with sanctions and socialism.

The logic of apartheid had always been tested by the position of people who were defined coloured and Indian; anomalies and inconsistencies in state policy towards them also prompted reformist thinking. In its quest to create a new race and nation, the government established a partly elected Coloured Persons' Representative Council in 1968. It was to have control over local administration and services within coloured group areas. The Council was not completely boycotted. A new coloured Labour Party chose to mount opposition from within the system. After winning a resounding victory in a 1975 poll, it immobilized the Council and demanded full citizenship for coloured people.

In 1976 a government commission, cognisant of the unworkability of the segregated Coloured Council and the deep anger over Group Areas and District Six, advocated a restructuring of the parliamentary system. *Verligte* thinking was moving towards some kind of group representation in a central parliament. This proved to be an attractive route forward for Botha, who also wished to concentrate more power in his own hands. Reform materialized in significant constitutional change. The upper house of parliament, the Senate, was abolished and a President's Council established in 1980. In 1983 a 'tri-cameral parliament' was approved in a whites' only referendum. Two new national parliaments would be created for coloured and Indian people. While the three bodies would sit separately, their executives would participate on the President's Council, potentially a kind of supra-cabinet from all three parliaments. At the same time, the Presidency was changed from a largely ceremonial to an executive post.

Constitutional reform was clearly an attempt to defuse mounting political opposition, and broke with some key apartheid principles treasured by the NP for over thirty years. But it seemed to offer little more than a new language of white command. The white parliament and NP dominated the President's Council and P. W. Botha became the new President. Spatial segregation and homeland independence remained entrenched. Many of the reform initiatives could be contained within the policy of separate nations, and the apex of the system, the tri-cameral parliament, stopped short of extending political rights to Africans outside the homelands. Although reform policies undoubtedly provided opportunities for the black urban elite, perhaps their most powerful impact was upon Afrikaners themselves: they tore at the heart of Afrikanerdom, for so long educated in the righteousness of its cause. Disagreement within the state and party became endemic—no longer simply a debate between *verligte* and *verkrampte*.

Large sections of the bureaucracy had a particular commitment to protecting the concept of a white state and were uneasy about shifts in ideology. Amongst them were those who had actually implemented and learnt to justify policies such as influx control, labour bureaux, and Bantu Education. Many felt 'it would be chaotic' if Africans had full freedom of movement and employment throughout the country. The older, shrinking constituencies of the NP such as white workers were left behind, together with Nationalist solicitude for the '"little man" in the fields and factories' (Charney 1984: 273). When white miners, by then largely Afrikaans-speaking, struck to defend job reservation in 1978, the government backed management. In the 1981 election, support for far-right groups increased significantly.

In 1982 Transvaal party leader Dr A. Treurnicht left with fifteen MPs to establish the Conservative Party and NP support gradually declined. Some white rural communities in the Transvaal and the Free State, under pressure from drought, high interest rates, and talk of diminishing subsidies, felt threatened by an increasingly insistent language of free markets. The Broederbond, perhaps less influential than at its height, was also deeply divided. After leaning initially towards the Conservatives, its leadership then put its weight behind the NP. The Conservatives and their allies were unashamed in returning to the well-tried political language of racial preservation and the integrity of the *volk*. They hoped that the events of 1982 might herald a repeat of 1914 and 1934, when an exclusivist Afrikaner party broke from those advocating a more inclusive idea of nationalism and started on the long road to power. The changing class character of white society, as well as the new balance of power in the country as a whole, made this an unlikely outcome.

Reform not only split Afrikaners; it provided new opportunities and new dilemmas for popular opposition. Legislation in 1979 extended the definition of 'employee' in the Industrial

Conciliation Act to all black workers, except those from 'internationally recognized' foreign countries. If they registered with the state, the new unions would be able to operate on a more secure legal basis and their members would have the right to strike. But registration also subjected them to constitutional and financial regulation—for example, they would have to provide full details of membership and office bearers. The legislation triggered an impassioned debate within the democratic unions. FOSATU, the Rand- and Durban-based Federation that had largest number of negotiating agreements, decided to approve registration, once it had assurances that migrant workers would be included. It argued that unions needed more stability and muscle; they had to take advantage of political space offered. Western Province unions felt that they had grown successfully without registration, which might hamper democratic structures and freedom of action; they were dependent ultimately upon 'the organized strength of the workers in each factory' (Maree 1987: 182). SAAWU rejected the whole structure of labour legislation.

In 1979 and 1980 a new wave of protest swept the country, reaching its height in the educational institutions. The boycotts and burnings, while similar to those of 1976, were probably more widespread and students developed a wider range of demands including a single education system. Consumer boycotts, which impacted on white businesses, proved particularly difficult for the state to counter. In the late 1970s a rash of new township community associations and issue-oriented 'civics', together with a lively grassroots press, arose in response to government arrests and repression. Strikes in 1979–80 raised the question of the relationship between shop-floor militancy and the community issues in which workers were also involved. Already under pressure to follow SAAWU's lead, other unions were pushed somewhat reluctantly into broader political action. The links established by Oscar Mpetha, a leader of the Cape-based Food and Canning Workers' Union and the ANC in the 1950s, were typical. Released from Robben Island in 1978, he threw himself back into union activities and helped organize the Nyanga (Cape Town) Residents' Association in a bus boycott.

During a dispute at Fatti's and Moni's, the major pasta factory in Cape Town, the African Food and Canning Workers' Union had called for community boycott of the firm's products in order to strengthen their bargaining position. Activists went into the supermarkets, filled trolleys with pasta, and then left them at the checkout counter. A dispute at the Ford factory near Port Elizabeth centred on the political role of a worker, Thozamile Botha, in the militant local Port Elizabeth Black Civic Association, which helped organize a strike. In 1981 strikes on the East Rand also provided the context for stronger linkages between worker and community organizations. Demands for union recognition at Colgate Palmolive resulted in a boycott of that firm's products.

Strikers, especially on the East Rand, took up a wide range of issues—from health conditions to unfair dismissal and demeaning language—on which they had seemed powerless before. White supervisors still used derogatory terms. Indeed unionists felt that racial feeling may have intensified at this time, partly because the emergence of black shop stewards helped to undermine the old lines of authority through whites. Job reservation, already diluted by employers, was further eroded by union demands. As in the late 1940s, these factors contributed to the emergence of the white hard right.

Concerted action both at the workplace and in communities helped the more regulated FOSATU and CUSA unions to grow from about 70,000 signed-up members in 1979 to 320,000 in 1983. MAWU, the main FOSATU union in the key metals sector, had 10,000 members in 1980 and 30,000 by 1982. SAAWU, which kept less systematic records, probably exaggerated its claim of 300,000 members. Whereas initially membership tended to be strongest amongst those with secure urban rights, more vulnerable migrant workers became an important source of growth. In 1982 CUSA relaunched a National Union of Mineworkers (NUM), which soon became the biggest in the country with over 100,000 members. Many sectors remained unorganized; agriculture and domestic service, which together employed nearly half of the five-million African workforce, were hardly touched. Overall membership was probably not more than 10 per cent of African workers. But unions emerged by the early 1980s as a disciplined and highly effective vanguard of resistance.

Reform from above, a response to intense political pressure from below, is a notoriously difficult exercise, which often raises the expectations of the oppressed and unleashes further powerful forces for change. Oppositional culture in the townships, which had found focus in a bewildering range of student, union, and community groups, gradually coalesced in the early 1980s. Some black consciousness leaders, who formed the Azanian Peoples' Organization, explicitly took the PAC name for the country. Most activists saw black consciousness as a phase and moved towards a 'Charterist' or Congress-oriented position. Perhaps three-quarters of those who escaped the country in 1976–7 were shepherded into ANC sanctuaries. Many received training and some managed to return, relaunch the sabotage campaign, and form internal MK cells. Although a string of these were exposed in the Transvaal in 1978, MK guerrillas managed to blow up petrol tanks at Sasolburg.

The Congress of South African Students (COSAS) had become the major vehicle for black student protests at the heart of the 1980 schools rebellion. It subsequently launched Youth Congresses in many centres, incorporating both school-leavers and the young unemployed. As students abandoned black consciousness, they re-established connections with the well-resourced and radical NUSAS groups on English-speaking campuses. Banned activists, together with those coming off Robben Island, cemented links between the new civics and the Congress tradition. The Natal Indian Congress, which refused to participate in elections for the Indian branch of the tri-cameral parliament, provided a further ally in the emerging mass movement.

By 1983 the need for national coordination was patent. In August the United Democratic Front (UDF) was formed at a mass rally in Mitchell's Plain, a new coloured township on the Cape Flats. As the venue indicated, the movement was explicitly non-racial in the tradition of the ANC and also drew on Congress's Christian heritage: radical churchmen such as Alan Boesak, Frank Chikane, and Anglican Bishop Desmond Tutu, who won the Nobel Peace Prize in 1984, joined the platforms and became leading representatives. So did Winnie Mandela, who experienced frequent harassment and banishment during her husband's imprisonment, and had become an international symbol of the survival of the ANC. Albertina Sisulu, formerly a major figure in the ANC Women's League, and wife of the incarcerated Walter Sisulu, became joint president. The UDF looked strongly like an internal wing of Congress, though it did not associate with the armed struggle.

UDF campaigns were organized against the elections to new ethnic parliaments and black local councils. The cycle of insurrection and repression based around schools, universities, factories, and townships that had began in 1976 rose to a crescendo between late 1984 and early 1986 (**Chapter 10**). This marked the turning point for the apartheid state. Some groups identifying with the UDF took a more militant path. The ANC itself was becoming a focus for opposition forces and demands for Nelson Mandela's release from prison became a central unifying call in the external anti-apartheid movements and at home.

In conclusion, we should return to the debate about economic change, apartheid, and its gradual erosion (**Chapter 7**). South African industrial growth under apartheid was initially impressive. Multinationals, mining houses, the state, and agricultural interests were all of great importance in generating capital for investment. This element of the radical argument seems justified. Apartheid did not initially inhibit manufacturing; both local and foreign investors responded favourably to stability, even if this was produced by repression. It is difficult to be certain that growth would have been quicker under a different political regime.

Yet acute skill shortages, technological dependence, and lack of competitiveness evident from the mid-1970s has strengthened the case that apartheid increasingly came to inhibit growth. Capitalists, Lipton argued, lived with apartheid rather than advocated it. Leading capitalists such as Harry Oppenheimer were openly critical of many of its features. They began to attack it more generally and vociferously, not necessarily 'because they were liberals—though some of them were', but because 'apartheid labour policies ... conflicted with their interests and this had dynamic implications for the whole system'. In general, radicals have accepted that apartheid-induced weaknesses were an important reason for economic crisis and reform from the late 1970s.

Both radicals and liberals have recently taken ideology more seriously in explaining segregation and apartheid, and most scholars have also recognized the complexity of interaction between economic interests and political systems. However, in identifying and addressing the crisis of the late 1970s, radicals laid more stress on political struggle and trade unionism, rather than on the interests of business and workings of the market, in highlighting the contradictions, costs, and ultimate demise of apartheid.

# 10

# Insurrection, Fragmentation, and Negotiations, 1984–1994

## Urban Government and the 1984–1986 Insurrection

If the renaissance of black opposition in the 1970s paved the way for political change, the insurrection of 1984–6 made the process very difficult to reverse. Although white authority partially collapsed during the 1980s and early 1990s, Afrikaners were reluctant to sacrifice power and whites in general protective of their wealth. The Nationalists actively pursued a settlement that might secure the position of whites and satisfy their conception of black aspirations but that would fall short of democratic government in a unitary state. While Botha intensified repression, the state also pursued reformist initiatives that laid the ground for some post-apartheid developments.

At the same time, imminent political change intensified divisions in black politics. The ANC and its allies, espousing African nationalist, democratic, and sometimes socialist ideas, appeared to carry majority support. But homeland-based groups, others with an ethnic or conservative outlook, as well as state-supported vigilantes tried to stake their claim. The erosion of state authority was attended by increasing civil disorder and crime. This uncomfortable interregnum bequeathed a difficult legacy to its successor.

The intensity of the mid-1980s insurrection was fuelled both by the NP's intransigence and by economic recession; its form was shaped not least by conflicts over the management of the black urban population. The question of how to govern the new urban millions was starkly posed in the early 1980s. Up to the mid-1970s apartheid logic dictated that homeland development should be prioritized and the black Urban Advisory Councils were relatively neglected. In 1971 authority over city townships was largely removed from municipalities and placed under Bantu Affairs Administration Boards (BAABs), which would both govern them and implement state policy on removals and urbanization.

As part of its attempt to meet the challenge of 1976, the government passed a Community Council Act (1977), establishing a new tier of elected African municipal councils under the authority of the BAABs. This initiative was in keeping with the belated belief that a stable urban black middle class with a greater stake in the system could be essential to the success of reform; some form of local government for African people outside the homelands was clearly essential. The state hoped that 'black councillors would be able to absorb and defuse discontent' (Seekings 1988). In 1982, African local authorities received augmented powers to run their 'own' affairs. Unpopular white BAAB officials, whose image was so deeply bound up with bureaucratic terrorism, were gradually withdrawn from the fractured coalface of urban government.

Although attempts at reform and devolution extended African rights outside the homelands, they further politicized local government. Potentially, urban African people could now exercise some control over matters such as housing, rent, and services, previously the province of authoritarian officials. The central question for urban communities was whether they should participate in state structures that fell far short of granting full civil rights. In the first round of urban council elections in the late 1970s, the government claimed a 39 per cent turn-out of registered voters. This initially lukewarm response soon cooled further. In 1983, when the UDF coordinated a campaign against the elections, perhaps 12 per cent voted. The number of Sowetans who voted in the second election rose from 6 to 10 per cent, but was still under the national average. When elections were held for the Indian and coloured houses of the tri-cameral parliament in 1984, about 13 and 18 per cent respectively voted. The overwhelming decision of black people seemed clear: 'reform' was inadequate and inoperable.

Community Councils did take office and were immediately placed in a difficult financial position. The government aimed to decentralize responsibility not only for spending revenue, but also for the far more fraught task of raising it. This would enable the central state to abrogate some of its fiscal commitments for urban black welfare. The major inheritance of the Community Councils was vast sprawls of low-quality township housing; rents were a major source of income. As the urban population exploded in size, councillors faced a housing crisis. In 1979 the Greater Soweto Council raised rents in a vain attempt to break even. When recession, inflation, and a new Sales Tax bit from 1983, rent increases became more widespread.

Some councillors compounded their difficulties by using their position to their own best advantage. They had access to business sites, licences, information, and excellent opportunities in such fields as supermarkets, liquor outlets, and taxis. Like Afrikaners, they benefited from their relationship with state institutions, and they were widely seen to be corrupt. Popular politics in the urban townships aimed not least at preventing the government from finding allies to work 'the system'. Intense and sometimes violent pressure was put on those Africans viewed as sell-outs. As in earlier contexts, conflict turned inwards against those perceived to betray the community. Especially on the Rand, rent boycotts became a key form of political action, both because these could mobilize large numbers of people and because they struck at the heart of the reforms imposed on Africans.

Up to the early 1980s apartheid planning ensured that much urban growth took place in displaced towns, such as KwaNdebele and Botshabelo, sited within homeland boundaries or away from the main cities (**Map 2**). After that time, patterns of population movement changed radically again, so that millions moved towards the main cities. Pass laws proved incapable of arresting the process and were less vigorously enforced; by 1986 some of the major influx control regulations were rescinded. Durban, said to be one of the fastest growing cities in the world, doubled in size to about 3 million in less than two decades. Cape Town soon rivalled it. Khayelitsha (new home) and neighbouring informal settlements on the Cape flats, which had hardly existed in 1980, were estimated to house three-quarters of a million people by the end of the decade. Cape Town's demographic composition began to resemble that of the other major centres. Many new townspeople lived in backyards and informal shack settlements.

The Rand and southern Transvaal remained by far the largest urban zone and, for the first time since tight controls had been enacted in the 1950s, squatter settlements spread rapidly. In Katlehong south of Germiston, one of the major areas of insurrection, the estimated number of shacks rose from 3,000 in 1979 to 44,000 in 1983, far outnumbering the houses. Under pressure from central government, a prevaricating Community Council attempted to remove squatters in 1984. Here and elsewhere there was defiance and confusion in shack settlements.

In August and September 1984 protests against the inauguration of the tri-cameral parliament and rent rises ended in pitched battles between youths and police. Councillors were killed in Sebokeng; the mayor of Sharpeville was killed on his doorstep after shooting two demonstrators. Insurrections in these townships, including Boipatong and Bophelong, around the southern Transvaal industrial complexes of Vereeniging and Vanderbijlpark, branded the new social geography of the country into national and international consciousness. It was here, as well as the more central Johannesburg settlements of Alexandra and Soweto, that the key political events were played out.

The crisis in South Africa had agrarian and demographic as well as political and economic roots. Proponents of segregation and apartheid always argued that their policies depended on controlling urbanization and they were probably right. By the 1980s unemployment and poverty could no longer be externalized to the homelands, and remnant smallholding could no longer give a majority of African people either significant income or social support. Former farmworkers were being pushed off the land, or leaving it, in droves. An increasing number disregarded attempts to keep them in displaced towns and rural dense settlements. Many now perceived their best opportunity no longer in defending a rural base, but in finding a site, a job, or informal sector income in the cities. Young people asserted themselves politically, strengthened by their numbers as well as ideologies. African people presented themselves in their millions and demanded to be

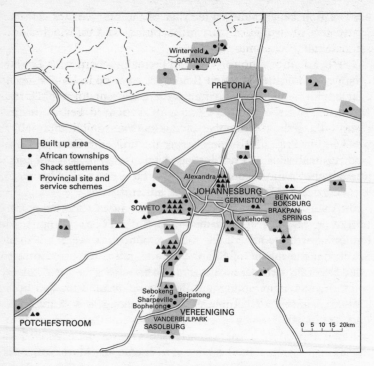

**MAP 3.** *Townships in the Pretoria–Witwatersrand–Vereeniging region*
*Source*: Urban Foundation, 1990.

incorporated in the social order—to be made not only subjects of the state but citizens.

Problems of urban government were compounded by the longevity of the economic downturn. High gold prices, which had helped the country through the oil crisis and recession in the 1970s, declined in 1983. Expensive imports and debt repayments became a financial drain. When Europe began to climb out of its early 1980s recession, South Africa, especially its manufacturing industries, stagnated. The country was no longer so attractive to foreign investors. Despite enormous advances in manufacturing, there were insufficient areas of specialist advantage or independence to cope with international competition. Growing unemployment, estimated at close on 30 per cent for Africans, helped to fuel political turmoil in the mid-1980s, which in turn exacerbated economic difficulties.

After signing a non-agression Nkomati Accord with Mozambique in March 1984, Botha had been received in European capitals and seemed to be winning the argument for his reformist policies. But the 'fruits of Nkomati' shrivelled before the year was out, as insurrection triggered a flight of capital, especially of US firms (Price 1991: 221). Simultaneously, the Rand collapsed to less than half its previous value against the dollar and pound sterling; chronic inflation set in and the foreign debt grew. The government responded by hiking interest rates to over 20 per cent, which had the effect of slowing recovery. Burdened with heavy expenditure on border wars, Botha was hard-pressed to maintain public spending; this helped cement the commitment to privatization. High interest rates also impacted on the indebted agricultural sector and contributed to rural Afrikaner disaffection. One indicator of farming woes was the falling number of tractors (**Table 4**). Inflation had a severe impact on the poor.

Popular struggle reached a nationwide crescendo in 1985 and did begin to achieve its aim of rendering the country ungovernable. Militant youths were on the move, toyi-toying, or jogtrotting in large crowds through the streets, lending urgency to their cause. BAAB offices, police stations, and shops were burnt in the townships. COSAS, a key UDF affiliate, renewed school boycotts. Popular committees and people's courts sprang up, which did, in some zones, briefly take on the governance of their own communities. Activists developed their own 'street sociology and pavement politics'—working hard to define what the national democratic struggle and people's power meant for those on the ground (Bundy 1987). Youthful rebels saw themselves as a 'comrades' movement, aligned with the ANC, and fighting—when necessary as part of the armed struggle—for its aims.

Green, black, and gold ANC banners appeared at rallies where *Nkosi Sikel' iAfrika* and the slogan *Amandla ngawethu* resounded. The term 'Viva', drawn from Mozambique, prefaced long lists of names and organizations, as heroes were pronounced and a history of struggle recalled. Frequent funerals became the site for emotive speeches, expressions of solidarity, and political coordination. Deaths at the hands of police and vigilantes legitimized struggle and provided martyrs. At the funeral of Matthew Goniwe, an eastern Cape activist, and three others widely believed to have been killed by the security forces, the red flag of the Communist Party was also unfurled. People's power gradually rolled back the boundaries of what the government had to consider acceptable. In response, Botha moved large numbers of troops into the townships. Conflict escalated as the state's heavier armoury was countered by street barricades and Molotov cocktails. In a terrifying incident, captured on film in Cape Town, police hid themselves on a lorry, waited till they had been stoned, and then shot their assailants.

In July 1985 Botha declared a state of emergency, which gave the security forces even more formidable powers. Yet the NP still envisaged that repression should be tempered with reform; Western financial institutions and key local corporations expected that its pace would hasten. In August Botha delivered a much-touted speech in which he was expected to lead whites across the Rubicon towards negotiation, and to hold out the prospect of Mandela's release. Troubled by a rising white right wing and angered by youth insurrection, Botha failed to deliver the prepared version; instead he adopted a tone of truculent self-justification, insisting that he would not take whites and other minorities 'on a road to abdication and suicide'. Disinvestment escalated and international banks drew back from rolling over South Africa's short-term loans; the sanctions campaigns were beginning to tell.

A business delegation, led by Gavin Relly, Chairman of Anglo-American, met the ANC in Lusaka—one of the first of a long list of opposition politicians, trade unionists, and intellectuals to make the trip. For powerful sections of the white elite, as well as for the UDF and Comrades, the locus of future political legitimacy was beginning to crystallize. The NP was rapidly losing the support of business, which it had recently courted so assiduously. Interest groups that had coalesced in bodies such as the Urban Foundation increasingly wished to find routes towards some form of national negotiating forum, and recognized the urgency of renewal in urban governance and services. The Progressive Federal Party, which had won 26 white seats in 1981 after the break-up of the old UP, also sought to form a national constitutional convention and met the ANC. Its initiative lacked legitimacy amongst Africans and its links with Inkatha undermined its approaches to the liberation movements.

While the externally based ANC called for ungovernability, it was not able to establish formal internal organization, and a number of Congress and UDF members were uneasy with the excesses of the Comrades. Those aiming to develop 'governability within ungovernability' found it difficult to set up liberated zones in city townships, where the security forces remained active. Some UDF militants justified violence, yet the movement had to be careful not to make itself even more vulnerable to state retaliation by openly espousing armed struggle. Zwelakhe Sisulu, son of the imprisoned Walter and later editor of the UDF-oriented *New Nation* weekly, publicly criticized the meting-out of punishments by youths in the name of people's power.

The most spectacular manifestation of popular vengeance involved 'necklacing' those identified as informers by placing a tyre doused with petrol around the victim's neck and lighting it. The cast-offs of industrial affluence were being recycled to purify society—in the minds of the perpetrators—by fire and death. People's courts, often composed of youths, extended their range to major crimes and political trials. In Alexandra, Johannesburg, activists recognized by 1986 that some rebels were not only 'ungovernable to the enemy', but 'ungovernable to their own organisations' (C. Carter 1992: 126). These tensions were to leave a difficulty legacy for the liberation movements when they came to government (**Chapter 11**).

In Lebowa, youths identifying with the comrades movement killed 32 people accused of witchcraft. 'We realised that those witches kill innocent people,' one recalled, 'the poor people, they just play with them . . . So as the youth we realised that even the poor people, we must help them . . . We must save the community' (Delius 1996: 194). They were helped to identify witches by a local *ngaka* (diviner), who hung a sheet on the wall—an 'African television'—and invited youths to call forth those deemed guilty of acts against the community. Most of the victims were older women. In these impoverished dense settlements, where both schooling and policing had almost ceased, older rural strategies and conflicts were given a macabre new twist, including the use of necklacing.

Responses to the collapse of schooling culminated in the formation of a National Education Crisis Committee in March 1986. It envisioned alternative education and syllabuses and tried to set in place some means to achieve this—emphasizing education for liberation, rather than liberation before education. It could thus encourage the youth to return to school without appearing to support the existing educational system. A host of initiatives dealing with matters from labour, human rights, and industrial health to land, ecology, and economic policy found sharper focus in this insurrectionary period. The basis was laid for opposition intellectual energies, both black and white, to concentrate increasingly on future reconstruction rather than just protest.

Strikes, including major action organized by the revived NUM, reached a crescendo in 1986 and 1987, as workers both expressed their political outrage and struggled to meet the rising cost of living. Successful stayaways cemented links between the independent unions and the UDF civics. In 1985 most of the independent unions came together as the Congress of South African Trade Unions (COSATU). Its leaders were less cautious about congregating 'around the honeypot of popular activity' than FOSATU had been (M. Murray 1987: 192). COSATU supported disinvestment and sanctions as well as nationalization of key industries. Cyril Ramaphosa, general secretary of the NUM, argued that working-class interests and redistribution of wealth should be pushed to the centre of popular struggles. But political unionism had its costs. In Natal, a number of unions had been able to straddle the divide between Inkatha and UDF. COSATU refused to hold back in its criticism of Inkatha, to which some of its members belonged. As Buthelezi retaliated against youths and workers, conflict spilled over into violence.

Despite some dramatic city-centre demonstrations and occasional attacks on white people or their property, the insurrection remained largely confined to black townships and rural districts. Penetrating into white areas in large numbers was difficult; township conflicts and battles for local space were the immediate priorities. Nevertheless, the insurrection made an unprecedented impact on white lives. Even restricted media coverage brought home black anger. Stayaways, strikes, and extended consumer boycotts sucked in large numbers of police and troops. The sheer tenacity of the popular movement demanded attention to its widening demands: the release of political prisoners, abolition of apartheid, and a unitary non-racial democratic political system.

## The State: Militarization, Vigilantes, and Retreat

The state's capacity to ride out the challenge drew on and fed into an increasingly militarized pattern of authority. During the first phase of Botha's rule from 1978 to 1983, the military role in government expanded. This was a new development, justified by the perceived external threat. Although former generals had ruled South Africa till 1948 and Smuts had not been averse to using the armed forces to impose order, civil and military functions had largely been separated following Union. Malan and Verwoerd, hostile to the English-dominated Second World War defence establishment, initially continued the tradition.

By the 1970s the military, especially the army, was Afrikanerized and broadly sympathetic to the Nationalist project. The security apparatus began to impinge on the civil state, blurring divisions and shaping the nature of government. Botha introduced General Magnus Malan, Chief of the Defence Force, into the Cabinet as Minister of Defence. During the 1980s the State Security Council became the linchpin of an elaborate hierarchy of committees forming a parallel state structure. There was not a military *coup*, but a more surreptitious extension of military influence. Estimates suggest an increase in defence expenditure from about 6 per cent of the total budget in 1960 to 15 per cent in 1980 and subsequently to between 17 and 20 per cent. By the late 1980s, Armscor, at the apex of a pervasive 'military-industrial' complex, could claim to be the largest single exporter of manufactured goods.

The ideas of the South African officer class were influenced by counter-insurgency techniques developed to contain the guerrilla struggles of the late-colonial period in Vietnam, Malaysia, and Algeria. The term 'total strategy' was borrowed from the French general Beaufre, who emphasized that in modern warfare the whole society should be involved in a 'dialectic of two opposing wills'. The state should engage at every level with a perceived revolutionary onslaught and attempt to win the 'hearts and minds' of the common people. It was a strategy that reflected Botha's difficulty in recognizing the scale of the political problem and justified simultaneous reform and repression. The government believed it could restore a new legitimacy as apartheid began to crumble.

Total strategy also fitted well with the reinvented traditions of the Afrikaner commando—a people's army defending a nation at war. In 1977 the period of national service demanded from young white men was extended from nine months to two years; they could be recalled for camps or commando service. The number of servicemen who could be mobilized increased to over 400,000. National service sometimes entailed long terms of duty on the Namibian border, even raids into Angola. Hostility to communism, terrorism, the ANC, and opposition movements was inculcated into servicemen. Many learnt a language of male bravado and violence—of themselves as heroes fighting dehumanized targets. State-controlled radio and television became a conduit for total strategy objectives. Private gun ownership rocketed amongst whites in the 1980s. Existing school cadet programmes were expanded. War comics, while hardly unique to South Africa, became a staple of the corner shop. The local version portrayed the *Grensvegter* (border warrior) fighting against the predictable forces of darkness and disorder.

Thus when the insurrection reached its peak, the government was prepared. As reformist strategies promoted by the Department of Constitutional Development and Planning faltered in the face of mass opposition, so more aggressive, hardline 'securocrats' emerged as the dominant force. Protest was the work of agitators, they argued, and it could be halted by removing the leadership. The repressive apparatus of the state was unleashed on an unprecedented scale, but also with 'stamina and steady concentration' (D. Webster 1987: 141). Initiatives such as the Commonwealth Eminent Persons' Group, which promised to facilitate multilateral negotiations, were apparently deliberately sabotaged when the security forces bombed the capitals of three front-line states in May 1986.

In the first eight months of the 1985 emergency, 8,000 people were detained and 22,000 charged with offences arising from protests. In the year from June 1986—when a new emergency was imposed after the first had been briefly lifted because of international pressure—a further 26,000 people were detained. Reporting and especially filming of incidents was far more tightly controlled. Undoubtedly the power of the insurrection had been augmented by its televisual representation locally and internationally. The government also hoped to suppress graphic illustrations of police brutality, which had so undermined the international acceptance of reform.

Faced with an everyday level of dissidence that it was barely able to control, the state persisted in its hard war. Internal professional constraints in the security forces slackened. In addition to the firepower, mass arrests, beating, and torture, sinister evidence of political assassination accumulated. Black policemen, attacked or forced to move out of their homes in the townships, pursued their own vendettas against comrades. Hit squads, some involving white and black members of the security forces, now operated in the country, as they had previously beyond its borders. They drew on members of notorious crack front-line army squads such as Koevoet, which had been particularly brutal in their behaviour. In 1988 these activities were consolidated in the Civil Cooperation Bureau, ultimately under command of members of the Defence Force, whose disruption of the 'enemy' could involve anything from breaking a window to killing.

Faltering attempts to devolve civil authority to black clients were now accompanied by devolution of armed authority to homeland armies, municipal police, and *kitskonstabels* (instant constables) in the townships. Local black powerbrokers and their supporters felt able to take the law into their own hands. These vigilantes had diverse social origins; what they had in common was hostility to the youthful comrades and a readiness to use violence for political ends. By identifying with the state and police, they earned the disdain of rebellious youth.

The clearest early manifestations of this new axis of urban conflict were attacks by migrant workers—urban outsiders living in hostels—on youth rebels in 1976. One issue was access to liquor; another control over crime. Over the next decade, political and generational cleavages deepened, facilitiated by the security services. The death rate escalated. In 1985 and 1986, informal local vigilante groups mushroomed, giving themselves names such as Mabangalala, Witdoeke, and A-Team. To a greater extent than before they had access to firearms. Some were connected with homeland leaders, urban councillors, taxi-owners, and police; some were groups of older men ('fathers') or hostel-based migrant workers. They disrupted zones where UDF authority was being established, removed squatters, and attacked individuals.

'Warlords' could build more organized private armies or posses. In 1985 Simon Skosana, bent on achieving homeland status for KwaNdebele, attacked communities resisting incorporation into his sphere. Vigilantes controlled by a former squatter leader destroyed much of the shack settlement at Crossroads near Cape Town in 1986 after clashing with comrades for control of the area. Over 60,000 people were made homeless. For the security forces, such client groups were a cheap form of reasserting control. The state could dissociate itself from their methods, point to the dynamic of 'tribal' or 'black on black' violence, and project itself as the sole guarantor of stability. Even at the time, there was clear evidence that the security forces were deeply involved. The full extent of dirty tricks by the 'third force', as the ANC named it—drawing on the terminology of the Algerian war of independence—became apparent in court cases and in the Truth and Reconciliation Commission after 1994.

Natal was a major site of violent conflict within and between black communities, as Inkatha attempted to cement its authority over Zulu-speaking areas. Buthelezi, stoned and insulted by black consciousness youths as early as 1978 during the funeral of PAC leader Robert Sobukwe, appealed to tradition and the patriarchal order of Zulu society. Inkatha's Youth League was instructed not to boycott schools, which, leaders argued, were under Kwa-Zulu and not Bantu Education control. Buthelezi increasingly distanced himself from the ANC and UDF as he attempted to forge an image as a moderate leader with a national constituency. His stance against armed struggle, sanctions, and socialism won considerable support from the government, from liberal business leaders, and internationally. For conservative Western leaders like Margaret Thatcher in Britain he offered the first credible alternative to the ANC.

Inkatha's political practice, however, involved extending one-party government in KwaZulu. The movement used its control over housing, pensions, and water in major townships such as Umlazi and KwaMashu (part of Durban but under KwaZulu control) to demand membership and loyalty. Civil servants and teachers found it difficult not to join. Inkatha leaders like Thomas Shabalala of Lindelani, a shack settlement north of Durban, increasingly resorted to violence to enforce political authority. The single incident during the insurrection that resulted in the greatest number of deaths was a battle south of Durban between Inkatha-organized *impis* and squatter communities from the Transkei. Inkatha also attacked a National Education Conference in Durban in 1986.

Between 1987 and 1990, the fiercest clashes took place in the peri-urban townships and settlements around Pietermaritzburg. When people in Edendale township tried to resist incorporation into KwaZulu, it became a battlefield between *amaqabase* (comrades) and Inkatha *impis* brandishing 'traditional' weapons. While Inkatha seemed to forfeit some of the popular support that it had won in its earlier anti-apartheid days, it probably achieved a tighter hold on local politics. Inkatha fighters were better armed and less likely to attract police hostility; most of the 4,000 dead in three years of township carnage in Natal were youths. Although hostility to migrant workers from the Transkei was manifested, this phase of violence was not primarily ethnic in character in that most protagonists were Zulu-speaking. Cleavages were between rural and urban, between generations, between people with different political beliefs and different ideas about Zulu identity and tradition.

To some extent, Botha regained control of the country after 1986. Despite divisions in Afrikanerdom and splits in the government over strategy, the security forces, including the black police, had remained loyal. Though white South African daily life was affected, it was not yet significantly threatened. But his was a tenuous hold, based on increased militarization and unpopular black allies who were not fully under state control. The civil institutions on which the state had relied to control blacks were crumbling. Decentralization of armed authority resulted in a degree of state fragmentation not only in the homelands but, after decades of centralization, in 'white' South Africa itself.

Although the hard war predominated in the second half of the 1980s, Botha could not and did not entirely ignore alternative strategies advocated by *verligte* opinion. To some degree these reinforced the views of counter-insurgency advocates who had convinced themselves that a soft economic and ideological war could win hearts and minds. 'There is presently only a limited section which is really interested in political participation', Magnus Malan argued, 'I think for the masses in South Africa democracy is not a relevant factor' (Centre for Policy Studies 1989). A network of Joint Management Centres was activated to coordinate military, police, and civil functions at a local level, sometimes displacing black Community Councils; they tried to upgrade facilities and living conditions in black townships, offering the promise of a taste of 'the good life'.

Pass laws were formally eased in 1986, after successful legal challenges, and replaced with a policy of 'orderly urbanization'. Abolition of the Mixed Marriages and racial sections of the Immorality Act in 1986 hinted at more far-reaching change. Freehold property rights for Africans in town were extended, as was the state pension system, which became an increasingly significant source of income for the poorest families.

Key Afrikaners close to government were taking initiatives that reflected recognition of the inevitability of change. The Broederbond's reformist agenda had been confirmed by the election of de Lange, *verligte* author of the 1981 education report, as chairman in 1983. He met ANC representatives, notably Thabo Mbeki, at a conference in New York in 1986. Son of ANC and CP eastern

Cape stalwart Govan, Thabo Mbeki had gone into exile in 1962 and had recently been appointed head of international affairs for the ANC. Mbeki had orchestrated and fronted the series of meetings in Zambia. His intellectual breadth, diplomatic skills, and reasonableness impressed and appealed to many of his white interlocutors, including de Lange. From 1987 to 1990, regular informal channels of communication were established in Britain between ANC leaders and Afrikaners such as Willie Esterhuyse, who reported directly to Botha's National Intelligence service. They met at an estate owned by Consolidated Goldfields, near Bath. On the one hand, both sides were seeking to move beyond demonization of the enemy; on the other, they were feeling for disagreements within the opposition's leadership that might open the way for compromise.

In 1985 Botha offered Mandela and other prisoners release on condition that they renounce the armed struggle and violence. Mandela dramatically refused in a speech read by his daughter at a UDF rally in Soweto, the first time for over twenty years his words received such public exposure. Nevertheless Mandela approached Botha to seek a political solution and he had a number of contacts with Kobie Coetsee, Minister of Justice, and members of the Intelligence Service. Now in isolation at Polls-moor prison on the mainland, Mandela was also allowed to meet visiting dignitaries. The prison officer who procured him a new suit for a meeting with the Commonwealth Eminent Persons' Group noted: 'Mandela, you look like a prime minister now, not a prisoner' (Mandela 1995: 629). With the government's knowledge, lawyer George Bizos acted as an intermediary between Mandela and the ANC in exile. Such meetings were kept out of the news and, although Mandela was taken on trips outside prison, he was not publicly recognized. These preparatory contacts inside and outside the country proved to be of great significance in establishing some shared understanding of the political impasse, and the costs of intransigence, amongst the political elite.

Although South Africans were experienced in circumventing trade sanctions, tighter exclusion from international capital markets, disinvestment, and arms embargoes were less easy to counter. Armscor production was sufficient to suppress internal insurrection, but Cuban soldiers and Soviet weaponry in Angola eroded the state's capacity to neutralize opposition on the Namibian border. A major South African offensive launched in 1987 was designed to support Angola's UNITA rebels and undermine SWAPO, as negotiations over Namibian independence broke down yet again. South African air supremacy was challenged and the foray resulted in a severe military setback at Cuito Cuanavale in southern Angola. The government and armed forces were beginning to appreciate the economic costs of prolonged fighting beyond its borders. The death rates of white soldiers caused concern; momentum against military adventures built up in the press, in the white End Conscription Campaign, and amongst Afrikaner intellectuals.

International realignments undermined South Africa's claim that it was the last bulwark against communism. In 1988 the Soviet Union and the USA began to defuse regional superpower conflicts. Gorbachev offered to withdraw Soviet involvement in southern Africa and to put similar pressure on the Cubans, in return for American insistence on free elections in Namibia. The South African government's acquiescence was another critical moment in the shifting balance of power in the region. SWAPO won 57 per cent of the Namibian vote in the 1989 elections and took office in what had been Africa's 'last colony'. As ANC guerrilla activities and the township revolt again escalated in South Africa, and opposition forces amalgamated in the Mass Democratic Movement, the securocrats' blend of reform and repression faltered. A stalemate had been reached in which the opposition could not unseat the government by force and the government could not reassert full control.

## Negotiations and Violence, 1990–1994

It has been rare for a country with such deep divisions of race, wealth, and culture to manage a democratic political transition of the kind achieved in South Africa, or for an undemocratic ruling group to give up power without even more intense conflict or outside intervention. Throughout the period of negotiations between 1990 and 1994, the possibility remained that the country would be sucked into a vortex of violence, or fragment politically. That the outcome would be, in Mandela's words (1995), a 'small miracle' was by no means predictable.

A key element in the transition was the recognition by the leadership of the two main parties involved that they had a sufficient common interest in compromise. They also had sufficient support and authority to bring a majority of South Africans with them and the power, just, to enforce their compromise on recalcitrant parties. They were pushed into discussions by fear of the alternatives and by increasingly adverse socio-economic conditions. South Africa's political elite would not have been unique if they had dragged their country into civil conflict and economic oblivion for the sake of power or ideology. But to some extent they shared a view of the virtues of modernity and progress, which served to underpin discussions. In this context personal relationships, and a stake in a process that attracted international attention, did also matter. So did the global context, especially the passing of cold-war politics.

By the late 1980s a single political party had been in power for forty years. Botha had, however, moved away from the Westminster-type parliamentary system that had served the Nationalists so well. Constitutional reforms such as the executive presidency, the tri-cameral parliament, and the State Security Council had diminished the authority of the NP itself. Agencies of the state had become less accountable, even to the Party, a process emphasized by devolution of power to homelands and urban black councils. The scope for corruption and violence had been greatly extended. Botha had become autocratic and ill-tempered in his relationships, even with his own supporters.

The NP shed much of its right wing to the Conservatives, who in 1987 won over half a million votes and became the official opposition—their support increased further in the 1989 white elections, when they won nearly a quarter of parliamentary seats. Afrikanerdom's political fragmentation and white insecurity fuelled paramilitarism. Its potential was uncertain, because the security forces were one seat of reaction that might turn against the government. For much of the 1980s, the NP had felt deeply constrained by the rumblings in its ranks and losses to the right;

by the end of the decade, they recognized that this gave them more freedom of action.

When Botha suffered a stroke in January 1989, he decided to separate the offices of President and NP leader, both of which he held. In the elections for party leadership F. W. de Klerk, the Minister for National Education, succeeded against Botha's preferred candidates. In August de Klerk also displaced Botha as President. He represented sections of the party that wanted greater control on the executive and further progress in controlled reform rather than the erratic swings between rebellion and repression that had characterized Botha's last few years. This might restore economic growth and international acceptability. The liberal Democratic Party (formerly the Progressive Reform Party) also expanded its vote in 1989 and de Klerk could count on over two-thirds of the white electorate in favour of reform—the number remained stable in a white referendum over continued negotiations in 1992.

De Klerk's background as a politically astute conservative did not prepare his supporters for the pace at which he would act. He was determined to seize the initiative from opposition forces and keep his party and constituency in the political vanguard. He sought to develop a power base and constitutional system that, while it might end the overall political dominance of whites, would protect their position in the country. Agents for the government were engaging in more frequent informal contacts with the ANC, which suggested that negotiations would be possible. While the ANC was not at one yet on this strategy, its Harare Declaration was conciliatory. Mandela had been moved again to a Paarl prison, where he was able to meet a wide range of political contacts. Anti-apartheid movements had projected him globally as the key figure; he was the recognized icon of a new South Africa at home and abroad. After meeting de Klerk in December 1989, Mandela published a forceful statement on the desirability of a negotiated settlement. A number of key political prisoners had already been freed and de Klerk was now prepared to respond.

Mandela's unconditional release in February 1990, together with the unbanning of the ANC and other black political movements, set in train a new phase of politics. It was also an admission that a political settlement required negotiations. Mandela's slow walk to freedom, followed by a cavalcade of cars, was an emotional moment, a televised event of religious intensity—the raising of a man from another world who seemed to carry the promise of salvation.

A wave of optimism was unleashed, the signal for symbolic reclaiming of the country. Blacks were able to move into spaces and institutions that had been barred to them. Pent-up forces of protest were released and, by the middle of 1990, more black councils were inoperative than at the height of the mid-1980s insurrection. Rent, school, and consumer boycotts were renewed and a 'rebel' tour of British cricketers forced to go home. Nevertheless, the ANC initially found it difficult to use the political space that opened up. Congress leaders had to act cautiously in that they still had no formal access to power and their movement, publicly exposed, could still be dismembered. There was no easy walk to democratic elections and they faced acute problems of transforming a liberation movement into a potential governing party.

The ANC hierarchy, many returning from exile, had to find organizational unity with groups forged in the domestic struggle such as the UDF, unions, civics, and highly committed but volatile comrades. ANC branches had to be formed. The role of the SACP, to which a number of ANC and MK leaders belonged, had to be resolved in the face of strident state rhetoric; against international trends, it was successfully relaunched internally at a mass rally in 1990 and, led by almost mythical former exiles like Joe Slovo, seemed to be growing. While all these groupings shared a desire for some form of democratic South Africa, they had different degrees of trust in negotiations. The first full ANC conference took place only in July 1991. Nevertheless an effective understanding was cemented with COSATU and the SACP, which became called the Tripartite Alliance.

Buffeted by the stormy politics of the early 1990s, it was difficult for Mandela to live up to the heroic image that had been constructed around him. But he and the older, non-Communist leaders Tambo (whom he replaced as ANC President in 1991) and Sisulu held control of the movement and worked hard to maintain its moral authority and popularity. The prison years had added to his personal stature and capacity to deal with the media. He could appear as 'communal patriarch, working-class hero, and liberal democrat', appealing simultaneously to a radical mass movement and, as the voice of reason and constraint, to an anxious white population and broader international community. His loyalties were tested by Winnie Mandela's involvement in a criminal trial arising from the murder of youth activist Stompie Seipei. Initially he supported her, but their marriage had faltered; when her activities threatened to undermine both him and the movement, they were separated and she was sidelined.

In the negotiations that continued haltingly from 1990, the ANC aimed for a representative national convention and unitary democratic state. It nevertheless compromised on key issues. Against some internal opposition, Congress suspended the armed struggle in 1990. Its leaders recognized that guerrilla warfare was not their strongest suit; victory in the short term seemed a chimera, while the costs of political violence were potentially great and the lessons of prolonged civil conflict in other parts of Africa stark. Although confident of majority support, the ANC had not yet demonstrated this electorally; rhetoric retained from the liberation struggle was tempered with strategic caution. Chris Hani, leader of MK, was able to represent and contain more impatient elements in Congress until his assassination in 1993.

During the early 1990s the ANC also dropped many of the socialist ideas that had influenced it in exile and were pervasive internally within UDF affiliates and unions. The language of democracy, black advancement, and human rights was more strongly emphasized. The power and persuasiveness of government, financial institutions, corporations, and black business, as well as the realities of a weakened South African economy, influenced ANC economic thinking. This reorientation—the movement had not developed clear economic policies—was hastened by the collapse of communist governments, many of which had helped the ANC in earlier years. The spectre of Mozambique, where the departure of Portuguese settlers and subsequent war left much of the country's infrastructure sabotaged, was before them. Collectivization and nationalization had proved unhappy experiments in Africa and a powerful source of conflict. African countries in general had found it difficult to attract foreign investment; Africa had been falling off the world economic map. Unless South Africa created favourable conditions for investment, the country, already isolated by years of sanctions, might tumble with the rest of the continent. Unlike East Asian states, South Africa was not flanked by economically buoyant neighbours.

When he was released from prison, Mandela affirmed that 'the nationalization of the mines, banks, and monopoly industry is the policy of the ANC and a change or modification of our views in this regard is inconceivable' (Marais 1998: 146). Thinking amongst key leaders such as Thabo Mbeki was already changing and such radical economic ideas were quickly modified. State control of the gold mines, one obvious potential target, raised major problems. Gold exports still brought in a large income, boosted by the weaker rand, but, after the heady peaks of 1980, prices were unstable and profitability uncertain. The skills required to run so complex an industry were unavailable outside the sophisticated multinationals that controlled it. State owner-ship of a contracting industry could lead to direct confrontation with the large and militant NUM, a major political ally. The costs of stabilizing the migrant labour force could also fall on the state.

COSATU itself appreciated the value of some continuity in economic institutions. Ramaphosa of the NUM became ANC Secretary-General and chief negotiator; his own views were chan-ging and he was subject to the constraints of the movement as a whole. Academics linked to COSATU had evolved a relatively moderate social democratic programme of 'growth through redistribution' that prioritized higher government spending on training, welfare, and infrastructure, especially housing. This was temporarily adopted as a slogan for the opposition alliance in the early 1990s. The SACP accepted this commitment to a mixed economy and it was Slovo who suggested a 'sunset' clause with guarantees for existing state employees under a future government.

De Klerk, on his side, revoked racial legislation: the Separate Reservation of Amenities Act in June 1990; the Land Act, Group Areas, and Population Registration a year later. Breaches of racial legislation had been less actively policed in the 1980s, so that a few white residential areas like Hillbrow, Johannesburg's city-centre flatland, went 'grey' and then largely black. Now black people could, in law, live anywhere. The NP opened its membership to blacks and recruited a number of coloured MPs in the tri-cameral parliament, which continued to sit. De Klerk was exploring a new conservative, but deracialized, political alliance.

The NP was reluctant to countenance the kind of unitary state that had proved so valuable for Afrikaner self-advancement and argued that some form of power-sharing would be most conducive to stability. They as well as homeland representatives supported the protection of minority group rights and a federal system, or at least a strong regional tier of government. Decentralization might mean that the NP and its allies could retain more influence at a local level in some areas. While de Klerk soon compromised on ideas about racially based minority protections, his party was more adamant about entrenching private property and a fundamentally capitalist economic system prior to any transfer of power. Here they found themselves increasingly pushing at an opening door in ANC thinking.

Botha's intransigence on political change in the 1980s did not imply abandonment of the NP's shift in rhetoric and policy towards freer markets. Parastatal corporations such as ISCOR (iron and steel), SATS (railways), and SASOL (oil) were partly privatized. It became increasingly apparent that, by placing resources in private hands, radical redistribution might be pre-empted. Education policy mirrored this approach. By 1992 the state foresaw gradual withdrawal of central control; state schools would have more power to run themselves, charge supplementary fees, and shape admission policies.

Although de Klerk frequently met with Mandela, NP strategy suggests that it initially saw protracted negotiations as more likely to favour its interests and increase divisions within the opposition. De Klerk promised to diminish the influence of the security forces and dismantle Joint Management Councils; arms expenditure declined in real terms. A National Peace Accord signed in September 1991 tried to establish codes of conduct for all political groups and security forces as well as community involvement in peace-making; the government was pressurized into appointing the Goldstone Commission 'Regarding the Prevention of Public Violence and Intimidation'. But disorganizing violence, often against ANC supporters, persisted. Between 1990 and 1994, about 14,000 died in political violence within South Africa. As the press and Goldstone increasingly revealed, state security services used violence, or facilitated its use, at critical moments in the negotiations. While the government worked towards a new political dispensation, important elements within the state felt that social disorder, and especially conflict within black areas, might assist them in winning a favourable settlement.

The violence that scarred South Africa was not limited to this nexus of conflict. Surreptitious direct funding for Inkatha by the security services was revealed in 1991, but Buthelezi had his own strategies and goals to pursue. His movement was relaunched as the Inkatha Freedom Party (IFP) to attract a national multiracial following, but this had little impact on its tactics within KwaZulu and Natal. Inkatha supporters responded to renewed ANC mobilization in Natal after Mandela's release by confronting the Comrades in their Pietermaritzburg strongholds, resulting in a brutal 'Seven Day War'. In 1991 Inkatha launched a campaign for support in southern Natal and triggered violence that left many homeless.

From 1990 the Rand as much as Natal was a crucible of conflict. Masked gunmen killed at random on black commuter trains, previously used as vehicles for political mobilization by youths during the emergency. Taxi wars over transport routes escalated. Inkatha started a recruitment drive in hostels and hostel-dwellers armed themselves against township residents. As in Natal, ANC supporters who felt that the state and vigilantes knew only the language of violence resisted and took pre-emptive action against perceived enemies. Meetings between Mandela and Buthelezi in 1991 failed to douse the flaring grass fires of people's anger.

By the early 1990s seven million people were estimated to live in informal settlements that had absorbed large new inflows of people both from township backyards and from the countryside. African people asserted their right to freedom of movement, and occupied municipal and state-owned land on the urban peripheries. Politicized rivalries over scarce resources in volatile and impoverished shack cities resulted in a sequence of clashes. In a number of cases, hostilities broke out between squatters and hostel-dwellers or migrants. Participants and the media sometimes saw allegiances in ethnic terms—for example, between Zulu and Xhosa on the Rand—though such identities were fluid amongst the mobile urban poor. Firearms poured into the urban townships. They were traded across the border from Mozambique, released by security forces to vigilantes, or brought in by MK networks. AK 47 (Kalashnikov) rifles were now in the hands, rather than just the dreams, of Comrades; new weaponry exacerbated conflict and resulted in higher death rates.

Formal negotiations took shape in the Convention for a Democratic South Africa (CODESA) at the end of 1991. Representatives of a wide range of political groups, including homeland governments and ethnic parties, met in the anodyne surroundings of the World Trade Centre, Kempton Park, near Johannesburg airport—a neutral venue unencumbered by history. In many respects, the agreements reached established the key principles upon which a new South Africa would be based: an undivided country; a multi-party democracy; peaceful transition; separation of powers; and a bill of rights that implied protection for private property. Yet CODESA broke down in May 1992 amidst persistent violence and because of the reluctance by the NP and others to accept the logic of a unitary state. The NP wished to ensure a minority veto over constitutional proposals by insisting on a 70 per cent majority in any new parliament for all constitutional decisions; Inkatha tried to entrench the Zulu king. The final plenary 'deteriorated into a verbal brawl' (Ebrahim 1998: 129).

A massacre of residents at the ANC stronghold of Boipatong, near Vereeniging, in July 1992, led the ANC to withdraw temporarily from talks, except for a confidential 'channel' between Ramaphosa and NP chief negotiator, the Minister of Constitutional Development Roelf Meyer. Suspension of CODESA had already spurred opposition forces to intensify mass action in an attempt to force the government to concede the political initiative. In their determination to break the homeland governments, they staged a march in September 1992 against the unpopular military supremo of the Ciskei, Brigadier Gqozo. This was led by key activists such as Hani, Ramaphosa, MK Intelligence Chief Ronnie Kasrils, and Getrude Shope of the ANC Women's League. Gqozo's forces opened fire, killed twenty-nine people and injured over 200; Ramaphosa was nearly hit. The South African Defence Force, which had been present, made little attempt to intervene.

The Azanian People's Liberation Army, armed wing of the PAC, tried to outflank Congress by staging dramatic attacks on white civilian targets along the old colonial faultlines of the eastern Cape border region and the Free State. They hoped to attract radicalized youth frustrated by delays in a political settlement and the ANC's suspension of the armed struggle. Violence, vengeance, and the politics of fear sapped the optimism generated by Mandela's release and CODESA. As policing loosened, a crime wave swept white as well as black communities. Attacks against whites, on farms and in suburbs, became less unusual. Politicized security forces and a Kalashnikov culture threatened to engulf the country; a Lebanese or Yugoslavian future was invoked. Violence was becoming an unpredictable and fragmenting force for all parties, raising the spectre of civil disintegration.

Publicly, the government and the ANC together tried to assume the responsible middle ground in a new Record of Understanding at the end of September 1992. Despite their mutual public recriminations, Mandela and de Klerk continued to meet. Strong personal links were forged between chief negotiators Ramaphosa and Meyer, as well as others sharing what was clearly a historic process that attracted intense international interest. After a *bosberaad* (bush council) in a Transvaal nature reserve where many ANC and NP negotiators met socially for the first time, multiparty talks were restored at the beginning of 1993. These survived the popular anger sparked by the assassination of Chris Hani in April. Right-wing renegades—an English-speaker and a Pole, rather than Afrikaners—were responsible.

Difficulties emanated increasingly from the IFP and the far right. Buthelezi had been an uneasy ally of the Nationalists; they still shared an interest in devolution or federalism and the security forces still colluded with Inkatha *impis*. But, as the NP established a better working relationship with the ANC, Buthelezi effectively threatened secession, and Inkatha's rhetoric brought it closer to

Afrikaner Conservatives, who were floating the idea of a separate Volkstaat. Mangope in Bophuthatswana also explored regional autarky with the white right. The Congress-oriented Transkeian Military Council ruler, Holomisa, by contrast, gave sustained commitment to reincorporation. The very fluidity of politics was reflected by ubiquitous use of the word 'players' to describe participants in political and economic negotiations.

In order to guarantee that any election might be free and fair, the ANC insisted that the government reliquish its monopoly of all instruments of state. The NP initially wished to co-opt additional members to the Cabinet but acceded to the idea of a more evenly balanced Transitional Executive Council at the beginning of 1993. Forward movement resumed in April 1993 with the formation of a Multi-Party Negotiating Forum. This took up the advances made in CODESA and quickly formed a tightly focused Negotiating Council and six technical committees. As early as June 1993 the Negotiating Council fixed the date for non-racial democratic elections in April 1994.

The technical committee on Constitutional Matters set about formulating an interim constitution. After tortuous discussions, a formula was agreed for the Transitional Executive Committee, which was enacted by the old tri-cameral parliament in September 1993. This was perhaps the first 'transitional' Act passed and a remarkable advance into the formalities of power-sharing. The Committee was more than an election monitor and could influence decisions affecting a range of state functions such as policing, defence, and finance. The parties were edging towards a 'marriage of legitimacy and legality,' which could underpin a democratic transition and restore order (Davenport 1998: 52).

At the heart of negotiations were underlying assumptions about the changing locus of power and legitimate authority. The NP increasingly gave way on key issues towards the end of the process, recognizing that there were limits to its likely role; whites were beginning to absolve themselves of prime political responsibility. But a striking feature of the negotiations was the detail in which the new constitutional dispensation was debated and the achievement of agreement by 'sufficient consensus'. Constitutionalism and compromise played a major and sometimes cathartic role. Although some of the most sensitive decisions were reached behind closed doors, or in 'bilaterals', a public discourse of legality helped to counterbalance the often more urgent media coverage of violence and fragmentation. A culture of meetings and a sense that intractable issues could be resolved by discussion pervaded many levels of the society.

ANC constraint was demonstrated in agreements about a Government of National Unity and a potentially unwieldy three-person presidency, all fixed to clear percentages of the vote. Although they preferred a single house of parliament, ANC negotiators conceded the NP's and DP's argument for two—even if they insisted that the upper chamber should be weak. The proposed Constitutional Court underlined the protection envisaged for individuals in a far-reaching Bill of Rights. Though the party's support was small, the DP delegation was effective on these issues and claimed that many of its liberal principles were being enshrined. Such legislation would have been enormously valuable against the arbitrary powers of the state in the apartheid era; it could now in theory protect whites under a black government.

Institutional change ran in tandem with a political settlement. More churches deracialized; large companies speeded up recruitment of blacks. Hospitals were 'opened', initially by mass action. Universities incorporated more black students; by 1993 they were a majority of the intake. The University of the Western Cape, formerly segregated for coloured people, offered greatly expanded access to higher education for Africans and became one centre of reconstruction thinking. Legal Resources Centres, which had challenged apartheid legislation through the 1980s, gave increasing legal purchase to unions, rural land claims, and opposition groups. Elements of the press remained a significant critical force.

South Africans began to discover that they had some things in common. Many people were familiar with more than one language—thus providing scope for cultural fluidity. As black people were drawn into the core political processes, English increasingly became the shared language of national politics. The media, especially some television, began to reflect black aspirations and also to promote a more inclusive South African identity. While television is drawn to images of violence and unobtainable luxury, it also has enormous power to project shared symbols and new roles. Christianity still provided a potent language, so that conciliators such as Archbishop Tutu could draw on a widely understood code of prayer, biblical reference, and forgiveness. For an increasing number of people the aisles of the new cathedrals, the supermarkets, as well as the old, gave access to a common society of consumption.

Non-party associations and interest groups could also stake their claim in the negotiating process. Two such groupings that made an impact—but whose interests were potentially diametrically opposed—represented women and African chiefs respectively (see **Chapter 11** for the latter). The Women's National Coalition was formed in 1991 as a non-racial, cross-party alliance that sought to ensure that South Africa's patriarchal heritage did not remain unchallenged in the transition. Coalition leaders aimed to mobilize women not least by a nationwide consultation to produce a Women's Charter that, echoing the Freedom Charter, would distil demands and policy priorities. As important, they were determined that women should participate fully in the negotiations and that women's rights would be specifically protected in the new constitution.

The ANC provided a major impetus for the Coalition; former exile Frene Ginwala, who became the first speaker of the post-1994 parliament, was its most forceful spokeswoman. Yet it was not simply the ANC Women's League in another guise. NP, DP, even Inkatha members, as well as former UDF activists, became deeply absorbed. In a rapidly changing political world, most parties were sensitive not only to the new language of rights, but also to the unpredictability of electoral politics; the Coalition threatened that women would withdraw support from unreconstructed patriarchal parties. The Women's National Coalition did succeed in placing women on negotiating committees and ensuring that the interim Constitution explicitly outlawed gender as well as racial discrimination. Together with other groups, it helped to ensure that an unusually large percentage of women became members of parliament. It was less successful in its other aim of binding together disparate participants, from Rape Crisis and the black Rural Women's Movement to the South African

Council of Churches and Executive Women's Club, into a sustained movement.

An interim constitution was agreed in November 1993; both Mandela and de Klerk spoke passionately for national unity. They were proclaimed joint winners of the Nobel Peace prize at the end of the year, although they still engaged in public verbal spats. Amidst the heady celebration of political compromise, the settlement came close to being undermined. Youths identifying with APLA and the slogan 'one settler, one bullet' bombed a white suburban church during a service; children were killed by the security forces in a raid on a supposed guerrilla safe house in Transkei. To the echoes of another chant—'kill the Boer; kill the farmer'—murders of isolated white farmers escalated; bombs were planted by right-wing activists, including at the offices of the Independent Electoral Commission. The Afrikaner Weerstandsbeweging (resistance movement or AWB) made paramilitary displays and a fascinated, overindulgent media, sniffing stereotypes and white violence, gave its bombastic leader more than his fair share of coverage.

Right-wing military generals in a new *Volksfront* were potentially more threatening. The possibility of military intervention, with or without de Klerk's authority, on the pretext of curbing the violence for which the security forces were themselves partly responsible haunted the negotiations. Constand Viljoen, *Volksfront* leader, had tried to play a calming role when Afrikaners physically invaded the World Trade Centre negotiations in 1993. He and others met the ANC secretly and initially seemed convinced by Mandela's argument that 'if you want to go to war . . . I must be honest and admit that we cannot stand up to you on the battlefield. We don't have the resources . . . But you must remember two things. You cannot win because of our numbers: you cannot kill us all. And you cannot win because of the international community' (Sparks 1994: 204). Yet the temptation to test their strength was too great. When Mangope announced his final rejection of national elections and Bophuthatswana's reincorporation in March 1994, the homeland's civil servants and police went on strike; his authority as well as civil order collapsed. He called in the *Volksfront*, but in doing so gave an excuse for the

AWB to mobilize their private army; they shot wildly at people in the streets of the homeland's capital. Bophuthatswana troops deserted Mangope and attacked the AWB. The bravado of the white right died with two injured Afrikaners, shot by a uniformed black officer in front of journalists and rolling television cameras. *Volksfront* generals withdrew from their paramilitary operation, which they had barely controlled. In one of its most telling acts, the Transitional Executive Council successfully deposed Mangope and installed direct South African administration.

The IFP played a more sustained destructive hand with maximum effect, combining strategic violence with refusals to sign accords and threats of non-participation. It objected to what it saw as a ANC–NP stitch-up, and was reluctant to accept any outcome that would not give it control of both the old KwaZulu homeland and Natal province. The reckless shooting of IFP protestors marching on ANC headquarters, Shell House, in Johannesburg at the end of March provided them with further self-justificatory ammunition. A ban on traditional weapons could not be enforced; Inkatha spokesmen pointed to the AK-47s in the hands of comrades. Buthelezi's threat was that ultimately he could try to mobilize a guerrilla force in the manner of Jonas Savimbi in Angola.

The IFP finally agreed to participation barely a week before the election, under pressure from an international team of mediators, after a crucial 'bush meeting' in the Kruger National Park. Buthelezi saw this not as a commitment to the national democratic process, but as coming to terms with harsh political realities: 'a power struggle which is pursued with all means possible' (*Guardian*, 23 Apr. 1994). Former allies in the business community and the West, who had supported him in the 1980s, made it clear that he was out of line. The IFP recognized that KwaZulu revenues were deeply dependent on national coffers and that its members could be excluded from the spoils of transition such as positions in the police, army, and civil service. Those implicated in destabilization by the Goldstone Commission may also have been vulnerable. Buthelezi clutched at a major concession: recognition for the Zulu king and traditional authorities; and possible post-election international mediation. Frantic amendments were necessary to all the ballot papers in the shape of a sticker with Inkatha's symbol and name. While the negotiators' wooing of Buthelezi increased his personal stature, it diminished the unpredictable political costs of Inkatha's non-participation. The new government did not have to inaugurate its tenure with a campaign of pacification against sustained violence by a dissident minority that might have undermined a democratic settlement. Perhaps South Africa has experienced its political terrors before its revolution.

In a reaffirmation of public democratic processes, Mandela and de Klerk staged a seventy-minute television debate, in US presidential mode, viewed by an estimated 100 million people worldwide. Deaths dogged the transition to the last. Some were mishaps. Mandela's final rally took place in Athlone, Cape Town, the region with weakest ANC support. As he danced to the ANC song 'Sekunjalo Ke Nako' (Now is the Time) and called for the calming of mass action, three people were crushed to death in a tunnel beneath the packed stadium. It was less easy to call other deaths mishaps: distributors of government pamphlets encouraging people to vote were hacked to death in Ndwedwe, KwaZulu, a fortnight before the election. To the end IFP supporters made it very difficult for other parties to electioneer in their strongholds; some ANC-supporting informal settlements could be equally impenetrable. The Electoral Commission could barely supply and police the ballot in the most difficult areas and there were irregularities. But the election took place, starting on 26 April 1994, amidst national euphoria. The vast majority of eligible South Africans of all backgrounds stood together in the polling queues.

## PART III

# The New South Africa, 1994–2000

# 11

# A New Politics: From Rainbow Nation to African Authority

*The Political Settlement*

A new politics began in South Africa in 1994. Negotiations, elections, and reconstruction released exciting energies as old institutions and practices were reconsidered and fresh models invented. The roots of new approaches lay partly in the opposition political, trade-union, civic, and NGO movements that had flourished in the insurrectionary years. They lay partly in the internal workings of the ANC in exile and at home. But South Africa experienced a negotiated settlement, a transition, not a revolution, in 1994. Important legacies resided in the fragmented institutions left by the Afrikaner National Party's later apartheid strategies, in urban township authorities, in the balkanized homelands, which had done their best to emulate neo-patrimonial African states, in the self-protective impulses of segregated communities. They also lay in a relatively strong private-sector and social institutions, from churches to universities, and in ways of thinking about property and rights that survived the transition. All of these heritages were refracted through the prism of the constitutional settlements of 1994–6, and the new political and social system that they attempted to entrench.

The great majority of commentators on South Africa, whatever their ideological inclinations, celebrated the achievement of a negotiated settlement, the decline in political violence, and the foundations of a democratic political system. Most agreed that key political and moral leaders such as Mandela and Tutu worked hard to articulate a philosophy of reconciliation and of cultural pluralism in the 'rainbow nation'. It is generally recognized that the inheritance taken up by the Government of National Unity

MAP 4. *Post-1994 provincial boundaries*

(to 1996) and the ANC, after years of suppression, division, violence, balkanization, and economic stagnation, was troubled and
difficult. Despite this, they made great strides in advancing deracialization, restoring political stability and developing effective
economic management. The ANC has ruled with the consent and
support of the majority of South Africans.

For some, however, especially African people in the country,
'transformation' has not been sufficiently quick and the legacy of
apartheid remains too vivid. For the left, the ANC has become
trapped in a web of overcautious economic influences and
has sacrificed core aims of addressing widespread poverty and
disadvantage. Others, and not only conservative whites, express
concern about the rapid centralization of political authority and
control; they ask whether South Africa is drifting in the direction

of some African states where, despite recent trends towards democratization, authoritarianism and corruption remain widespread. Many express concern that social dislocation, crime, personal violence—not least against women—and HIV/AIDS might fatally undermine the indisputably important advances that have been made. There is evidence for all of these processes in the new South Africa; it is less easy to identify how significant they may be.

The historic compromise of 1994 found its form in the interim constitution that provided for a parliament based on a non-racial universal suffrage; it would also act as a Constituent Assembly in order to finalize the constitution within two years. Protection of minority groups, for which the NP and IFP had bargained, was achieved only in indirect ways. First, the the Bill of Rights guaranteed key individual freedoms of expression and of association, recognition of property rights, and a constitutional court to defend them. Protection of property was particularly important for whites, because this greatly restricted the scope of action of the government, should it have wished to pursue more radical policies. Existing state employees were assured of their posts and promised relatively favourable terms for retirement.

Secondly, the recognition of traditional authorities remained a crucial concession for Inkatha, as also for chiefs supporting the ANC, although the precise powers involved remained unclear. Thirdly, while the NP and IFP did not secure a federal system in which they believed they might retain regional power, the nine new provinces, incorporating the four old provinces and ten homelands, went some way to realizing a measure of political devolution. Fourthly, the government of national unity would incorporate representatives of political parties in the Cabinet in proportion to the votes they achieved in the 1994 election. The first executive would not initially be chosen, as in many parliamentary systems, only from the majority party.

It was not possible to calculate exactly the voter turn-out in April 1994, because there was no pre-election electoral register: estimates suggested around 90 per cent. The ANC, campaigning in its tripartite alliance with COSATU and the SACP, won 62.6 per cent of the national vote, the NP 20 per cent, and the IFP 10.5

per cent. Neither of the more extreme parties, the PAC or the Afrikaner Freedom Front, registered significant support, nor did the centrist, white-led Democratic Party. Despite irregularities, especially in KwaZulu and Natal, where the result was hotly disputed by the provincial ANC, the process was broadly seen as free and fair. For the ANC and NP, both of which had done as well as they could expect, it was vital to maintain the political momentum and to keep the peace; the results were taken as a reasonable reflection of political opinion in the country. The ANC had demonstrated its popular support and received a strong mandate; Mandela expressed guarded relief that they had not won an even more resounding victory.

Analyses of the election have emphasized how closely voting patterns followed race and region. It is patent that the great majority of African people outside KwaZulu/Natal (KZN), as the new province was called, voted for the ANC, and of whites for the NP, Freedom Front, or DP. But regionalism was not a major feature of the election. It was only in KZN that Africans voted for a provincially based party and there probably only by a relatively small majority. Although the IFP was able to take control of the provincial government, the ANC won wide support in the Durban metropolitan area amongst Zulu-speakers. Apartheid's attempt to retribalize in the homelands helped to cement a national identity, and ethnicity was not expressed elsewhere in African voting patterns.

There were also some less predicted variations. The votes of coloured and Indian people were divided, but tilted towards the NP. This led to a victory for the NP in the Western Cape and a less than comfortable vote of 50 per cent for the ANC in winning the Northern Cape. The NP was successful in associating the ANC specifically with the demands and interests of the vast African informal settlements on the Cape Flats, and with the violence and disruption of the early 1990s. It presented itself as the party of security, safety, property, and homeownerhsip, and the ANC as the party of toyi-toying squatters and youth. African migration to the Western Cape was perceived by some to threaten access to jobs; the vote for the NP was significantly higher amongst less-educated, working-class, and unemployed coloured people. Some coloured voters identified more strongly with F. W. de Klerk, who presented himself as an avuncular elder statesman, and the recently absorbed coloured members of the NP, than with the regional ANC leader, Revd Allan Boesak, who had resigned from the church after denying an extramarital affair with a white woman. Although the NP played on fears about Africans, its Western Cape success depended upon deracialization of the party, formerly an exclusive white preserve.

The ANC faced significant constraints in the constitutional settlement, in the provinces of KZN and the Western Cape, which included the second and third largest metropolitan areas, in the Government of National Unity (GNU), and within its own tri-partite alliance. Mandela in particular was wedded to a rhetoric and strategy of reconciliation. Nevertheless, the period from 1994 to 2000 saw significant centralization of control under the ANC within the country as a whole, and also within the ruling alliance. At the same time, a relatively democratic and open political culture continued to flourish.

Political parties were given greater powers in the electoral system and in the 400-seat parliament than in some other democracies. Proportional representation at a national and provincial level replaced the constituency-based voting system that had historically governed white elections. No names appeared on the ballot papers. The system suited the political brokers of all three of the major parties; key members who may have been vulnerable in local election contests could be placed high on party lists. It undoubtedly helped the ANC to transform the gender composition of parliament: of the first tranche of ANC MPs, over 25 per cent were women. It also probably facilitated retention of non-Africans in ANC lists. After the 1999 election, an estimated 95 per cent of the ANC's support was from African voters, but nearly a third of its MPs were non-African. MPs had to sacrifice their seats if they switched parties, and there was no provision for by-elections; parties could replace members who resigned.

Nelson Mandela, as President, emerged as a conciliator and statesman who commanded respect from a wide range of people in the country. He became a global icon for his skills in negotiation and moral leadership: 'famous above all as the man who forgave the enemies who jailed him' (Sampson 1999: 520). He also ensured that the ANC held to its side of the bargain and accepted the formation of the GNU with de Klerk as one of the two Deputy Presidents. Five additional ministries went to the NP, including key posts of Finance, Agriculture, and Provincial Affairs and Constitutional Development; three went to the IFP, with Buthelezi at Home Affairs.

But Mandela had to make political decisions that favoured some individuals and policies against others. The position of the other Deputy President, which fell to the ANC, was all the more important because Mandela's age precluded a lengthy presidential tenure; he made it clear that he would serve only one term until 1999. Mandela chose Thabo Mbeki, groomed for high leadership by the recently deceased Oliver Tambo, rather than Cyril Ramaphosa. Despite Mandela's concern to balance regional representation in leadership (Ramaphosa originated from the Northern Transvaal), the exile networks, guerrilla movement, and Robben Island links proved important. Mbeki did, as predicted, follow Mandela as President in 1999.

Some key economic posts were assigned to young members of the internal movement. Trevor Manuel, Western Cape UDF activist, appointed initially to Trade and Industry, became Minister of Finance in 1996; Alec Erwin, COSATU leader also in the SACP, was then promoted from Deputy Minister of Finance to Manuel's old post. Unionist Tito Mboweni became Minister of Labour and in 1999 first black head of the Reserve Bank. Ramaphosa stayed on as ANC secretary-general till 1996. Yet commentators at the time perceived seniority and old loyalties to be significant factors for the ANC and Mandela. The costs of disloyalty were demonstrated in the widely reported conflicts with Winnie Madikizela-Mandela and Bantu Holomisa, who had increasingly identified themselves as populists in the ANC. The former had sufficient support within the ANC to secure a Deputy Ministerial post; in 1995, after further financial scandals, and her open attacks on the government for appeasing whites and neglecting the poor, Mandela requested her resignation and divorce followed. Holomisa, the former Transkeian military ruler, also a Deputy Minister, was forced to resign after accusing a Cabinet colleague of corruption. These were exemplary lessons in party discipline and helped to curtail populist and militant rhetoric.

The ANC leadership also extended its dominance in policy processes, in shaping the style of government and particularly the direction of constitutional discussions between 1994 and 1996. Critically, it insisted that power-sharing should not be constitutionally specified over the longer term. Provincial powers, and especially the capacity to raise revenue, were strongly constrained by the centre, from where more than 90 per cent of budgets came. Eleven national languages were equally recognized, and English was clearly to be the language of government. There was no special status for Zulu and Afrikaans, the first and third most widely spoken home languages, used by roughly 23 and 14 per cent of the population respectively (1996 census; Xhosa was second and English fifth).

The possibility of an upper house that might entrench minority rights was jettisoned in favour of a National Council of Provinces. Drawing from the German model, its composition was not majoritarian, in that each province, whatever its population, had ten members. Six were nominated by parties on the basis of the provincial vote, from members of the provincial legislatures, and four were brought in temporarily because of their specialist knowledge. This structure was an attempt to represent provincial interests, but the Council was not directly elected, proved to have weak legislative authority, and has in effect given the ANC further patronage and a larger majority than in the national assembly (Calland 1999).

In restricting provincial freedom of action, the government was not only preoccupied with the provinces it failed to win in the Western Cape and KZN. As important was the lack of administrative capacity revealed in ANC-led provincial governments and their tendency to overspend their budgets. The provinces that included more than one former homeland, such as Mpumalanga, the Eastern Cape, and the Northern Province, which were amongst the poorest, also proved to have acute difficulties in amalgamating their disparate departments and controlling corruption; all had to be bailed out financially by the centre. This was costly, it undermined public spending controls, became politically embarrassing, and hamstrung development programmes.

The ANC central leadership increasingly intervened to appoint its nominees to provinces: the ageing Raymond Mhlaba, a former Robben Island prisoner, but out of his depth as Premier of the Eastern Cape, was replaced by national ANC treasurer and chief whip Arnold Stofile in 1996; Mbhazima Sam Shilowa, former secretary-general of COSATU, was parachuted in to resolve the leadership crisis in the key province of Gauteng in 1999. Central control was seen as essential to cope with the divisive and corrupt political legacy of the homelands. Patrick 'Terror' Lekota, first Premier of the Free State, however, was an effective leader who was ousted for other reasons: Lekota's local opponents, against whom he had taken disciplinary action for corruption, appealed successfully to the ANC centre. Provincial authority is likely to be squeezed from below as well as above. Recent legislation suggests that local government, in rural as well as urban areas, will be strengthened, and given a greater developmental role.

## The ANC Ascendant

The final constitutional settlement helped to trigger the dissolution of the Government of National Unity in 1996. Although Inkatha had been the most reluctant partner, and Buthelezi dissociated himself from the constitutional discussions, he was schooled in the homeland system, and deeply conscious of the benefits of office. Rather it was the NP, which had been more directly involved in forging the details of the new political system, that withdrew. The NP was being bypassed in important decisions and was uneasy about identification with some ANC policies; de Klerk clearly felt that his personal and official status as Deputy President was insufficiently acknowledged. Roelf Meyer, chief constitutional negotiator, was criticized for giving away too much to the ANC. With no guarantee of a role in government after 1999, it seemed preferable to consolidate in opposition.

The decision proved to be rash. The NP did not recognize its dependence on state patronage in maintaining its coherence, especially in the latter part of its rule, when Afrikaner unity was fragmenting. Although it had partly succeeded both in reuniting the white vote, and in deracializing its support base in 1994, Meyer was unable to persuade the party of the urgency of forming a broader non-racial opposition. He resigned and de Klerk stood down as leader in 1997. The weakened New NP could find no effective replacement and was the greatest loser in the 1999 elections, winning only 7 per cent of the vote. It retained its position in the Western Cape government in a coalition with the DP. Had the NP stayed in government, it might have won the time and space to reconstitute itself as the major conservative opposition, defending property rights and Christianity or exploiting issues such as crime and the reintroduction of the death penalty, widely advocated in the late 1990s. Meyer founded a United Democratic Movement with Holomisa as his unlikely partner. Both had a high personal profile, but, with no coherent programme, they secured only 3.4 per cent of the national vote—mainly in Holomisa's old Transkeian base—in 1999.

The government's increasing hold on power tended to fragment the opposition. While the ANC increased its share of the vote to 66 per cent in 1999 (on a lower turn-out), no other party won more than 10 per cent. It is intriguing that white South Africans, formerly so insistent on their collective privilege, were initially unable or unwilling to coordinate a political response to their loss of power. The greatest beneficiary of the realignment was the DP, which won 9.5 per cent to become the official national opposition. With strong roots in the liberal white middle class, close links to big companies, good organization, and experience of municipal government in Cape Town and Johannesburg, the DP also had some credentials in opposing apartheid. Under the aggressive leadership of Tony Leon, its strong free enterprise ideology and consistent criticism of ANC captured some of the NP's constituencies—especially in wealthier Afrikaner, coloured, and Indian suburbs. In 2000 the New NP, weakened by defections, amalgamated with the DP into a Democratic Alliance, which has confirmed that minority middle classes are regrouping behind ideas of good government and the free market. Without signficant African support and leaders—even Holomisa declared his unwillingness to join—it is difficult to see how they could become more than a party of minorities. Yet the formation of the Democratic Alliance did suggest a fascinating white realignment behind an anglophone leader for the first time for a century.

Although Inkatha's share of the national vote was reduced to 8.6 per cent in 1999, largely because of urban losses, it retained the support of its core KZN rural constituency. Mbeki in particular cooperated more closely with Inkatha colleagues and they remained in government after the 1999 election. Holding the IFP in a national coalition has been a masterful means of defusing violent conflict between their followers. The ANC and IFP replicated the strategy in KZN, where neither emerged as dominant, by agreeing on a power-sharing arrangement. Yet there are dangers in this strategy. The IFP has not been committed to democratic processes and has brought homeland practices into central government. The ANC accommodation with the IFP suggests that an essentially African ruling coalition is falling into place; their combined vote, at about 75 per cent, reflects the proportion of Africans in the population. The opposition, by contrast, represents very largely minority groups.

Within the tripartite alliance also, the ANC took a stronger lead. COSATU continued to grow from 460,000 members at its formation in 1985 to 1.3 million in 1994 and 1.8 million by 1999 (Maree 1998: 35–7). Although membership in mining and manufacturing stagnated, reflecting their lack of growth, unions made major gains in the public sector amongst bureaucrats, teachers, and less-skilled workers. Individuals with a background in COSATU certainly remained close to the heart of power, and it also had strong representation on the National Economic Development and Labour Council, set up to advise on policy. Under Shilowa, COSATU made significant gains in parliamentary lobbying and labour legislation (see below). But the unions' influence on more general economic and social policy was already waning before 1994, a trend that was not subsequently reversed.

COSATU's commitment to expand its own democratic practices within the ruling alliance was decreasingly effective as individual ministries rather than the parliamentary caucus became the site of policy formation. Tensions between the government and COSATU were manifest in strikes and mass action intended to influence government policy: in 1995 to secure concessions in the new Labour Relations Act; in 1996 to protect the right to strike and picket in the final Constitution; and in 1997 to win concessions on the Basic Conditions of Employment Act. In August 1999 a major strike by public-sector unions, including teachers, radicalized under COSATU's umbrella, was mobilized around a below-inflation pay offer, which created further strains in the alliance.

Five or six communists were reported in the Cabinet in 1998–9. They included SACP vice-chair Geraldine Fraser-Moleketi, and other central committee members; most whites who achieved office came from a CP background. On assuming the presidency, Mbeki appointed the chair of the SACP Charles Nqakula as his parliamentary adviser. But personal influence was not easily translated into policy. Mandela's arrival at the 1998 SACP Congress was greeted by delegates singing 'asifune [we don't want] iGEAR', acronym for the government's new economic policy (*Star*, 2 July 1998; see Chapter 12). He made an uncharacteristically angry speech, threatening their position in the alliance if they were too critical; Mbeki attacked both the CP and COSATU in this regard. Both Presidents have been careful to incorporate individuals from these movements, so that they have the responsibility and rewards of power, as well as commitment to government. Although they have to some degree been able to keep labour and redistributional issues in the forefront of the government's attention, the cost of staying in the alliance has been acceptance of cautious macroeconomic policies.

A further locus of devolved power in South Africa has been chieftaincy—in this case usually a conservative constituency. Many of the chiefs recognized in South Africa had been, whatever their claims to legitimacy by birth, closely associated with the homeland governments; they came under strong attack in the apartheid era, especially from civics and youth organizations in the 1980s. Recognition of chieftaincy in the interim constitution was not, however, simply a concession to the IFP. Mandela himself, despite his youthful rebellion, was attuned to the patterns of rural traditional authority. In some areas where homeland authority had collapsed, and where civic associations and new local government institutions remained embryonic, established Tribal Authorities were the only functioning system of local government and justice. Most of the major non-Zulu chiefs aligned themselves with the Congress of Traditional Leaders of South Africa (CONTRALESA), established in 1987 and strongly linked to the ANC. Before the 1994 election, the ANC was uncertain about the depth of its homeland support and felt it could not ignore the potential political influence of chiefs.

After making concessions to chiefs in the 1994 settlement, the ANC subsequently seemed to seek ways of retracting. The government fought off a direct challenge from the IFP to retain control over the payment of chiefs. Certainly less than 40 per cent of South Africans, probably fewer, now live in areas where chiefs have significant authority. The government has tried to restrict the reassertion of ethnicity around chieftaincy, or of chiefly control in local government. Tribal claims for land, for example, were not entertained in the 1994 Restitution of Land Rights Act (see below). The wording of the 1996 Constitution implies recognition of chiefs largely in the judicial sphere, as dispensers of customary law, rather than in local administration and land distribution. Customary courts are certainly important in providing a form of justice that is relatively cheap (both for the central government and litigants) and legitimate in the eyes of those who have recourse to it. Such courts also provide an important focus for gatherings in former homeland areas and reinforce old networks of local power. However, it was control over land and administration that had been at the heart of Tribal Authority rule.

Chiefs have not given up their position easily. New local government structures have been difficult to implement. Patekile Holomisa, leader of CONTRALESA, Transkeian chief, and an ANC MP, came to blows with his party in respect of an ex-officio role for chiefs. In an argument that ran counter to democratic ANC principles, he claimed 'we are the guarantors of the rights of our people'. When threatened with expulsion, he argued that 'the potential might of Contralesa is of gigantic proportions ... You ... bear the onerous responsibility of averting the creation of a Renamo or Unita in this land' (Ntsebeza 2000). CONTRALESA formed closer links with Inkatha.

The 1996 Constitution made provision for Houses of Traditional Leaders with an official advisory capacity; six provinces instituted them. While the principle of election seems to be entrenched in local government legislation (1998), research in some former homelands suggests that a form of the Tribal Authorities still operate, and even allocate communal tenure land, as no adequate alternative mechanism has been put in place. CONTRALESA contested new boundaries for local government districts, which it saw as 'a political trick', because they cut across old areas of authority (Ntsebeza 2000). ANC Eastern Cape Premier Stofile argued that royalty is a universal phase in human experience, which should be displaced by democracy and development; Mbeki was more cautious. This remains one of the most uncertain and troubled areas of government policy. The implications of a resurgent chieftaincy could be significant: undermining democratic, representative institutions in the rural areas; and opening the way to neo-patrimonial patterns of authority within government.

In a number of other African countries, regional or ethnic competition for power and resources after independence undermined nationalist movements and precipitated conflict. South Africa is no less a product of colonial boundary-making. African pre-colonial identities and languages remained significant after 1994 and were reasserted at a cultural level; amongst the disparate people labelled coloured there was also some post-apartheid reclamation of cultural identities, as Muslim, or Nama, or San, or Griqua. But, 'political tribalism' or ethnicity and regionalism as a major political force ebbed rather than swelled. Although urbanization by no means rules out ethnic identification, South Africa may be distinctive in the degree to which African people have lost rural ethnic roots. Enforcement of ethnicized homelands in the apartheid era prompted an intellectual backlash, not least within the ANC. Mandela's generalized message of reconciliation, the relatively equal division of provincial resources, and accommodation with the IFP have helped to defuse potential tension. Space was found in the Cabinet for those who might be identified as Zulu-, Xhosa-, and Sotho-speakers as well as white (no longer Afrikaner from 1999), Indian, and coloured. Despite its uncertainty about chiefs, the ANC's success in limiting the purchase and purpose of ethnic mobilization may be an important achievement of its early years in power.

Politically, both central government control and ANC control have been extended, and this has been mirrored in the ever-important military and bureaucratic spheres. In view of the perceived capacity of the white right for disruption, Mandela was particularly concerned about their possible power base within the armed forces and cautious about alienating them. The process of integration between the South African Defence Force, MK, Apla, and homeland armies began under the control of the established forces. While defence and police ministries were taken over by the ANC, many Afrikaner generals initially remained in post. In 1998, however, the chief of the SADF, General Meiring, precipitated his own downfall when he secretly reported to Mandela that Siphiwe Nyanda, former MK commander, was planning a *coup*. Mandela publicized the report, sent it to a judicial commission, and, when they found it to be unreliable, used the opportunity to move Meiring on, and replace him with Nyanda. Racial tensions have by no means dissolved and the costs of rapprochement remain in a swollen defence force. Although defence spending declined as a proportion of the budget, there has not been as significant a peace dividend as expected.

The public services in South Africa have seen previous sweeping changes, following military and political victories; a significant phase of Africanization accompanied homeland self-government. There have been strong grounds for favouring people who were formerly denied access to central government posts on a racial basis, and the upper echelons of the bureaucracy have largely been filled by people who, if not ANC members, were clearly sympathetic to transformation. Initially these included non-African English-speakers who had also largely been excluded under the NP. Tensions leading to the resignation or dismissal of new senior white officials in, for example, Land Affairs and the Land Bank suggested that more thoroughgoing bureaucratic transformation was likely.

Despite the old regime's authoritarian bureaucratic style in its Pretoria heartland, fragmentation, loss of central discipline, and incompetence multiplied within the disparate homeland and racial civil services. This has been a particularly dysfunctional inheritance and reversing these trends a major preoccupation for the new government. Resurrecting a national basis for information and statistics has been equally challenging. The census of 1996 was the first since 1970 that enumerated all people in South Africa. Government agencies have commissioned a wide range of research and statistical collection on issues and areas that have been neglected. Deracialization in elections and in other spheres produced far more systematic polling across the whole of the population than ever before, which will provide a new baseline for understanding social change, political choices, and consumption.

New state-linked institutions, from constitutionally specified bodies such as the Human Rights and Gender Equality Commissions to the statutory Land Restitution and Truth and Reconciliation Commissions, have provided further scope for recruitment into the new governing class. On the one hand, this has greatly strengthened government command of black national talent and, on the other, sapped the strength of NGOs and civics, a source of particular intellectual and activist vitality in the late apartheid years, which was already being weakened by the transfer of foreign donor funds from them to government projects.

Political power has changed dramatically and irrevocably in South Africa. There has been a rapid, tangible formation of a new political class, largely but not only African, straddling parliament, bureaucracy, provincial government, parastatals, commissions, defence force, and many related research and advisory institutions. Identification with a successful political struggle, and with rectifying past injustices, has provided a shared purpose; so has awareness of power and its possibilities. There are signs of an increasingly dominant party embedding itself in the state with wide African support, even if this is less enthusiastic than in 1994. Patronage has made it possible to lure potential opponents into power or ease their path into business.

The change of leadership in 1999 has been seen as part of this process. As Mbeki increasingly shaped policy under the Mandela presidency, distinctions should not be drawn too sharply.

Some differences were inevitable: Mbeki could not attempt to emulate Mandela's avuncular authority and confident self-deprecation. His speeches tend to be less charismatic, but lucid and clear. Mbeki has also followed Mandela in trying to balance interests and representation within the ruling alliance and the ANC itself remains avowedly non-racial, as is evidenced in the disproportionate number of non-African MPs.

Mbeki is, however, seen as less inclusive than Mandela, especially of non-Africans, and less relaxed about opposition, including criticism from within his own party. He seemed to overreact to what was a relatively favourable portrayal of the ANC in the Truth and Reconciliation report and become over-defensive of his view of HIV/AIDs (see below). While Mandela stressed conciliation, Mbeki proclaimed a specifically African Renaissance. When he first canvassed the idea in 1996, in a major speech at the formal adoption of the Constitution, he cited Boer and Khoisan experiences of suffering in defining his own Africanness. The refrain, 'I am an African' was intended as inclusive: 'the constitution whose adoption we celebrate constitutes an unequivocal statement that we refuse to accept that our Africanness shall be defined by our race' (Hadland and Rantao 1999: 107). The idea of a renaissance was a genuine call for continental renewal and an indication of his desire for South Africa to reintegrate itself in Africa. Nevertheless, it was increasingly invoked in the context of affirmative action, African historical achievement, and African cultural ambition.

With a comparative model of African politics before them, some have detected danger signals in such developments for South Africa's fledgling democracy; Africanist rhetoric has certainly accompanied a drift to authoritarianism elsewhere in the continent. However, countervailing interpretations are also possible. The ANC argued for a more unitary system from the outset, not simply because it wished to command the state but in order to counteract powerful centrifugal forces in South African society at a particularly difficult historical conjuncture. To some degree, also, central government has had to assume tighter control as a reaction to incapacity at the provincial level, as well as crime, social disorder, and growing concern about the failure to deliver economic and social benefits.

Although the negotiating parties in South Africa had not all subscribed in the past to the values of liberal democracy, they found this to be an acceptable political and constitutional compromise. The political constraints on the ANC were diminishing by the end of the century, but the movement has been a major force for democratization and the consolidation of its authority does not preclude further maturing of democratic political processes. It may be an irony that South Africa's transition was delayed by white power until the cold war had ended and the West was established as arbiter of world power. An alternative political path implied courting international isolation. International pressures and expectations are conducive to the protection of negotiation, consensus-seeking, and democracy. South African politicians have themselves publicly and regularly reaffirmed their own commitment by acting as mediators or advisers in other conflicts, from the Congo to Northern Ireland, or as advocates of democratization in Africa and the Commonwealth.

South African foreign policy as a whole also suggests that the ANC wishes to sustain its newly achieved moral and democratic authority. Mandela greatly emphasized human rights and non-violent strategies in foreign policy and used his personal presence to pursue these. The collapse of communist regimes that preceded the ANC's entry into government facilitated a shift towards Western governments rather than older allies where the movement had strong diplomatic and funding links. But if the possibility of financial support, and favourable trading relationships with Europe, provided a strong incentive to develop a stronger Western orientation, it was by no means unqualified. Mandela hosted Fidel Castro and maintained links with Gaddafi in Libya; Mbeki sought to act more in concert with African leaders. In both cases, though, South Africa's multiple links could be used to pursue negotiation and stability in keeping with UN and even Western priorities. Many welcomed the advent of a strong regional power that could assist in African peace-making.

Domestically, it is important not to underestimate the significance of the Constitution, which hinges around liberal-democratic values and institutions, and is probably entrenched for at least a further five years from 1999. Institutions such as the constitutional court and parliament's committee system are beginning to bed down. Some committees have conducted well-publicized hearings and made a significant impact on legislation, especially in such fields as labour, justice, and human rights, including the Truth and Reconciliation Act. For example, powerful lobbying by COSATU, welfare groups, and NGOs, together with public hearings by the Portfolio Committee on Welfare, won major concessions on the government's bill for child maintenance grants (1996), and persuaded ministers to increase the amount awarded. Much has depended, however, on activist ANC chairs with particular expertise in their fields, who were prepared to challenge ministers.

Some of the new power brokers have served their apprenticeship in unions, civics, and NGOs, where participatory commitments were strong. Even though a number of ANC MPs moved on to other careers, including backbenchers who felt that they were politically marginalized, an intense political culture of meetings and discussion, of consulting 'stakeholders', to some degree persisted through the first years of the new government. Countless commissions, green and white papers, and consultative processes were set in train on diverse topics from land and environment to education and broadcasting. In every sphere, from politics and culture to commerce and sport, transformation spawned innovative policy strategies, often drawing in a wide range of participants, including international advisers. While this porosity and openness in policy making began to pass in the late 1990s, as ministries, bureaucracies, and powerful interests regroup, it was hardly imaginable under the old regime.

The broader civil society in South Africa, in the press, educational institutions, churches, countless voluntary groups, and the private sector, remained a significant base for a critical intellectual and political culture. Civil society is not enough to underpin a democratic culture, and such associations were not necessarily representative in themselves. But a major strand in the literature on African politics points to the lack of broadly based, diverse, institutional culture as a critical absence in the defence against authoritarianism. 'Transformation' was the watchword of the new political class. At one level it was used to mean deracializing, and opening up layers of society, as well as redirecting institutional energies towards serving the mass of poor black people. If it also means that the ANC will emulate its predecessors in attempting to command too wide a range of institutions and associations, it could undermine the fledgling democracy. With no significant electoral threat, the ANC faced, by 1999, that most difficult of challenges for all ruling groups: political constraint. Mbeki's forthright attack on opportunists in the party at its 2000 national general council conference in Port Elizabeth was a cry for discipline, but was accompanied by renewed determination to 'control all levers of state power' (*Sunday Times*, 16 July 2000).

Understanding of popular and democratic political culture in South Africa also demands consideration of 'communities'—to use a ubiquitous term. While the word has myriad meanings, in this context it referred more usually to localized groupings of the less powerful, poorer, usually black, population and carried with it strong connotations of new political legitimacy. In political discourse, communities could be invoked as a subset of that equally powerful collective notion—the people. Community groups coalesced in civics, resident associations, and similar groups in the 1980s with some leadership structure; their sustained oppositional mobilization provided the backdrop to political transformation. While these groupings have had difficulty converting their energies into representative politics, and are subject to division along many fault lines, some have succeeded in focusing on projects and acting as local pressure groups in the competition for social services, land, or economic benefits. Some civics effectively became local branches of the ANC. Community organizations have also exploited new linkages to government, and developed access to political resources. Ministers and senior bureaucrats sought the legitimacy provided by public engagement with community groups, as well as the media opportunities it offered.

The historic compromise of 1994 and the ANC government both seemed secure at the beginning of the new millennium. Commentators in the media have discussed two potential political forces that might affect this still fragile political stability:

an alternative black party; and a change in ANC constitutional commitments. In respect of the first point, ANC leaders clearly remained nervous about 'populism' and disillusionment that might undermine their political hold. While the scope for political participation greatly increased, the capacity of the state to improve the lot of the majority of people has been limited. Yet the ANC retained great moral and historic authority; its leaders were skilled at drawing in a wide range of constituencies. Though a trade-union-based party has been mooted, COSATU has shown no clear signs of pursuing such a route.

Concerning the second issue, it is possible that power may corrupt its holders, as it has done to previous rulers in South Africa. A large electoral majority over a long period of time could prompt a change of approach within the ANC. This is the most likely factor in undermining the 1990s compromise and the fledgling institutions that have evolved. Yet even without a two-thirds majority, the ANC had achieved its basic constitutional objectives, and its internal political culture and alliances sustained a commitment to democratic processes.

# 12

# Economic Uncertainties: Redistribution, Class Formation, and Growth

*Africans Emergent*

South Africa has been one of the most unequal societies in the world. At the heart of ANC policy, historically, was a commitment to address poverty and social inequality experienced overwhelmingly by black people. During the negotiations of the early 1990s, the ANC dropped many of its socialist ideas and accepted entrenchment of existing private property rights. The key capitalist institutions survived the transition. Use of the term 'comrade' to address supporters of political liberation gradually faded in the 1990s.

While economic reconstruction was widely recognized as an urgent priority, the ANC was prepared to compromise in its economic policy to a greater degree than in other spheres. Not only had the international context changed; for Mandela, the need to work within the Government of National Unity and to build consensus remained critical. But it will be argued here first that more attention should be paid to the trajectory of the African middle class in understanding ideological shifts within the new ruling groups. And secondly that significant strategies of social reform and redistribution were pursued by the government, if not always successfully implemented.

One striking feature of post-apartheid change was rapid upward mobility for the African elite. Political transition threw the shackles off African talent and entrepreneurial ambition; simultaneously major corporations scooped up the most promising graduates. Winning the state proved important for black people, as it was for Afrikaners, not only in providing public sector and parastatal employment, but in facilitating commercial opportunities. In this context, black can be construed in its broadest sense, because those formerly classified as coloured and Indian shared in the new opportunities. In turn, the new economic elite, to some degree interlocked with the political class, helped to define both the direction of social change and government economic policy. Empowerment, a word used globally in the 1980s with reference to the poor and disadvantaged, was unselfconsciously used by the late 1990s in South Africa to mean black business advancement.

Cyril Ramaphosa resigned as ANC general-secretary in 1996, when his immediate political ambitions were thwarted, and moved to the private sector; his decision was taken as indicative of the trajectory of change. He was followed by Tokyo Sexwale, first premier of Gauteng, and Zwelakhe Sisulu, Walter's son and chief executive of the South African Broadcasting Corporation. With the President's public approval, Ramaphosa initially joined Mandela's physician, Dr Nthato Motlana, in New Africa Investments Limited. When *Tribute* magazine, a glossy monthly serving the African business elite, covered this story (July 1996), it featured Ramaphosa on its cover dressed for trout fishing. His enthusiasm for this activity, as well as malt whisky, previously perquisites of wealthier whites, was much touted as emblematic of new ideological and social aspirations.

*Tribute*'s editor, S'bu Mngadi, celebrated 'these high profile members of the new businessocracy', with their 'mergers, acquisitions, consortia, bids and other achievements', who were 'determined to redefine economic power in South Africa'. Estimating the middle class at roughly 5 per cent of 12 million economically active Africans, he argued that, while 'admittedly small, and . . . still on the distant fringes of the mainstream of the economy, they are also laying the foundations for economic emancipation' (*Tribute* 1996). He noted the bid by the National Empowerment Consortium for an Anglo-American subsidiary Johnnic, and compared the process to mobiliziation of Afrikaner business interests and savings after their 1948 victory. One source of savings for African empowerment consortia were trade-union pension schemes. Winning secure pensions for so large a number of workers that the pension funds could become significant investors in the private sector was an extraordinary achievement for the unions to which they could hardly have aspired when the new unionism was launched in the 1970s. It was also further evidence of economic reorientation. Key unionists moved into investment and financial management; after a few rocky years, Johnnic, under former NUM official Irene Charnley, was resurrected as a successful media and communications company.

Many observers were disturbed by the rapidity with which the black beneficiaries of transition, whether in business or politics, seemed to adopt an acquisitive culture and ideology. One of first measures of the new parliament in 1994 was to increase the salaries of MPs and ministers, as recommended by an inquiry set up under the previous administration. Whatever its justification, it was greeted by a flood of adverse coverage; the term 'gravy train' became ubiquitous in the media to describe new government jobs and parliamentarians' perks. Soweto-based *City Press* published a cartoon of one new minister saying to another in a train dining car: 'That's enough gravy. Bring on the champagne' (Meredith 1997: 541). Tutu publicly questioned the wisdom and morality of this pay award. Mandela himself, though living in opulent official residences, and consorting with the rich and famous, remained patently ascetic in his consumption, aside from his flamboyant shirts, and donated a good deal of his Nobel prize to charity.

In their critical book *Comrades in Business*, sociologists Adam, van Zyl Slabbert, and Moodley bewailed 'the readiness of a liberation movement to be liberated into the bourgeois lifestyle of its opponents' as 'many ANC leaders raced to catch up with the finer tastes of the former masters' (1998: 165–6). Journalists complained of 'the BMWs, the cellphones, the celebratory parties'; business publications noted 'the Left goes right into business'. Mngadi argued with some approval that 'black professionals are slowly gravitating towards the white establishment, not confronting it'. Justice Malala, in a full-frontal attack, argued that the 'black middle class' was 'fast becoming the single greatest danger to real transformation in SA' (*SA Times UK*).

There is no doubt that some black people celebrated their political ascendancy and achievements in conspicuous consumption, widely reported, both with praise and dismay, in the press and magazines. There were also clearly individuals whose ideologies and policy changed on the assumption of power. Yet there are limits to analyses that emphasize the apparent betrayal of former values, or that the black middle class are becoming like whites because of their material advance. Analyses of this kind underestimate the depth of an educated black stratum, both within South Africa and in exile, who, although they may have identified with deracialization and the broader political struggle, were not necessarily committed to specific ideologies of transformation. They ask insufficient questions about the size, influence, and ideology of aspirant black professional and business classes in the 1980s and before, for whom opportunities, albeit cramped, were opening up.

Such analyses are also incurious about the scale and character of the expansion in higher education in the late apartheid years, including the opening of access to elite schools and formerly white universities. Opportunities for education and training outside South Africa, including programmes run by Western governments and institutions, multiplied for black South Africans. By 1993 there were nearly as many African enrolments (147,000) in universities as white; if coloured and Indian people are included, whites were a minority of university students and a dwindling one. African university enrolment peaked in 1998 at 218,000, while entry into the tertiary Technikons increased from 44,000 to 134,000 over the same period.

Late-twentieth-century protest in South Africa, as in other places, claimed a share not only in citizenship and power but in wealth and opportunities for consumption. For the youth, Western, especially black American, cultural influences were significant; their struggle was also for baseball caps, trainers and windcheaters, brand-label clothes, reggae and rap (or the South African version, kwaito). Consumption was not simply about fashion, identity, and display: cell phones, for example, may be a status symbol, but, in a country where communications have been extremely difficult for the majority of the population and the national telephone company was tardy in extending services to townships and African rural areas, they present major possibilities for extending social and commercial interaction. Nor should those from wealthier countries and backgrounds be unembarrassed in their criticism of other people's consumption.

African upward mobility should not be exaggerated. By 1999 reports suggested that only 12 per cent of the directors of listed companies were black and Africans were not yet a majority of directors even in black empowerment companies. McGregor's *Who Owns Whom* calculated that black groups held less than 10 per cent of the Johannesburg Stock Exchange's market capitalization in 1997 and that this fell by 2000. There have been some significant mishaps. National Sorghum Breweries, one of the first major companies that an African consortium was assisted to take over—and with a product geared specifically to African markets—suffered major losses and management problems. They were displaced in 1996 by United Breweries, a company from India, which returned the business to profit. (The Indian group also took over Mabula, one of the highest-profile, but financially ailing, white-run private game ranches.)

Deracialization of the state and employment market, as well as affirmative action, were major factors in African mobility. There was clearly a strong case for favouring people in employment previously excluded by race and it was essential to open up the cramped corridors of bureaucracy. The new state did not immediately emulate the ethnic exclusivity of the Afrikaner elite, although the Employment Equity Act, mooted in 1997 and passed in 1999, which threatened racial quotas in private firms, was a significant departure. But public employment and political power were not the only route of black advancement. Increasingly, opportunities for accumulation were being taken in the private sector. Any analysis of the trajectory of change in post-apartheid South Africa must come to terms with the ethos and economic aspirations of this new elite.

## State Policy and Redistribution

Whatever its precise direction, economic reconstruction was an urgent priority. Rates of economic growth in South Africa in the late apartheid years, less than 2 per cent per annum in the 1980s and negative in the early 1990s, were too slow to absorb the increasing population in formal employment, and per capita income was declining. Unemployment figures vary considerably: the 1996 census found 34 per cent of the total economically active population (aged 15–65) unemployed; the figure was 40 per cent for Africans, and close on 50 per cent in the poorest provinces. Some figures are higher at about 40 per cent overall or suggest a fall in formal sector employment from 75 per cent of economically active people in 1980 to little over 50 per cent in the late 1990s. These percentages reflect both an increasing population and an absolute fall in the number of formally employed people (**Figure 4**). None of these figures takes homeland agriculture or the informal sector adequately into account. But clearly manufacturing industry, the motor of growth in the post-war apartheid years, had suffered particularly and commercial farms continued to shed workers and their dependants.

In order to maintain white and international confidence, as well as economic and currency stability, the Ministry of Finance initially remained in the hands of the NP, and the incumbent Governor of the Reserve Bank continued to serve. Mandela himself, who was not centrally absorbed in the details of economic policy, and Mbeki, were convinced of the need for a cautious approach. Despite the economic contraction in its final years, the NP government had tried to maintain spending on the military and whites, at the same time as extending social provision, especially pensions, and education for blacks; it ran up a large deficit, reaching 8 per cent of GDP in 1992/3. Economically sapping interest repayments and inflation might spiral if the government borrowed further to finance public expenditure. The GNU had thus to maintain high interest rates to curb inflation and stringent controls on public expenditure to reduce debt. This was not a recipe for rapid, state-led economic growth.

Economic orthodoxy was also evident in extensions to the policy of privatization set in train by the NP in the 1980s. Gradual dismantling of the complex structure of protectionist rates and tariffs, which surrounded industry and agriculture, offended both COSATU and some agricultural interests. This was reinforced by membership of the World Trade Organization and its liberalized global trading regime. Industries such as clothing and textiles suffered particularly from the cold winds of global competition as well as the displacement of production regionally to the cheaper labour zones of Zimbabwe and Malawi. Yet it was difficult to show that protection had benefited an already declining, and sometimes inefficient, manufacturing sector.

The government and a wide range of economic experts sympathetic to its approach argued that in the long term such macroeconomic strategies, rather than heavy public expenditure, were far more likely to bring the growth and efficiency that might alleviate poverty. Nevertheless, the ANC attempted to pursue some social democratic policies. Although COSATU's 'growth through redistribution' slogan was dropped by 1994, elements of its strategy were incorporated at the heart of the post-apartheid Reconstruction and Development Programme (RDP) launched as a major ANC commitment in the final stages of the 1994 election campaign. Proposed projects included the extension of health services into deprived areas, free health care for children under 6 and pregnant women, the building of a million houses, electrification of 2.5 million homes, domestic water provision, the redistribution of 30 per cent of South Africa's agricultural land, a minimum wage, and deracialized free education for the first ten years of schooling. The defence budget would be slashed and money saved by integrating multiple civil services.

The RDP, under Jay Naidoo, Minister without Portfolio and highest-placed COSATU officer on the ANC's national election list, did provide an important focus for debate and research on redistributive strategies. Joe Slovo, first Minister of Housing, tried to engineer major new urban construction by mobilizing linked private and public funding. NGOs that had focused on resisting apartheid, or forced removals, were drawn into redirecting their energies to land reform, rural water provision, and local government. In 1995 the government evolved a policy whereby poor families could claim R15,000 as part of a housing, upgrading, land purchase, or infrastructure scheme. The RDP was envisaged as demand driven; communities, acting with local NGOs, political groupings, and officials, would themselves help prioritize their requirements.

There were few quick gains. Some officials—for example, in

Agriculture, which remained under NP control till 1996—were unsympathetic. It proved difficult to establish the national inter-departmental coordination to spend the RDP funds, which were top-sliced from other ministerial budgets. In some provinces, local bureaucracies, eroded in the homeland era or preoccupied with their own reorganization, were unable to implement schemes. Money was left unspent, siphoned off by individuals, or sucked into departments that faced acute conflicts. A community-based public works programme was planned with labour-intensive methods that would provide low-wage employment; less than 60 per cent of the money was used and most expenditure took place through NGOs.

Ambitions were then modified and, by the time it was wound up in 1996, the RDP was clearly going to miss its targets. Some of the projects were delegated to individual ministries under the overall authority of Deputy President Mbeki. Achievements were largely in spheres where existing programmes were extended and the capacity and organization were available: in particular water provision, the primary school nutrition scheme, extension of primary health care, and electrification.

ESKOM, not directly dependent on a government bureaucracy, had established itself as one of the largest, semi-privatized corporations in South Africa and perhaps the fifth largest electricity generator in the world. After the 1976 uprising it extended electricity supplies to African townships, notably Soweto. By the mid-1990s over 90 per cent of formal housing in Soweto was connected and 86 per cent of African households in Johannesburg used electricity for cooking (Beall and Crankshaw 2000). ESKOM had spare generating capacity and it was clearly in the corporation's interest to find ways of facilitating consumption in less-favoured townships and informal settlements. Up to 1988, services were extended through institutional bodies, such as municipalities or township authorities, which used billing systems. Conflict over charges for electricity had helped to fuel boycotts in the townships. Inability to collect payment inhibited electrification, especially in informal settlements where few households had registered addresses.

In the late 1980s ESKOM devised a system of extension by

providing pre-payment meters (Electricity Dispensers) for a low connection fee. Consumers purchased cards that gave a known amount of electricity. On the one hand, this largely overcame the problem of non-payment (although not of illegal pirating of power by tapping into lines). On the other hand, meters allowed poor families to monitor use carefully for specific functions, such as lighting, cooking, radio, and television. Overhead cables to individual houses and shacks are a feature of the landscape in informal settlements throughout the country. By the beginning of 1999, 2.5 million pre-payment meters had been installed in South Africa.

Electrification has amplifed the demand for consumer durables and electrical goods, many made in South Africa. The demand for television, as elsewhere a priority even for poor families, has widened rapidly and it has become a major element in national culture and leisure. Its changing audience is reflected in the success of the black soaps from *Egoli* (working class) and *Generations* (upwardly mobile advertising set) to the controversial *Yizo Yizo*, which portrayed black urban youth culture in the starkest terms. In peri-urban and some rural contexts, electrification opens the possibility of switching from firewood and coal as fuel. This might make some contribution to environmental stability, both in removing one source of urban air pollution in Witwatersrand townships and elsewhere in saving vegetation chopped for firewood. Electricity and water on tap ease the burden of domestic labour for African women, but they may also help to snap some of the remaining sinews that hold together old rural lifestyles.

Notwithstanding the demise of the RDP, the first government adhered to its commitment to cut defence spending, which declined at roughly 2 per cent a year. Education became the single most important budgetary head by far, absorbing 22 per cent of total spending by 1999, more than double that devoted to Health (11 per cent) and Social Security and Welfare (9 per cent). Partly because of this spending, and partly because of the difficulty in reforming inherited multiple bureaucracies, public-sector employment also continued to increase, despite frequent threats by the government to cut it. The public-sector wage bill grew at an average of 12 per cent annually between 1995 and 1998, faster than inflation and than national expenditure as a whole. By 1999 public-sector employment costs exceeded 50 per cent of the national budget (excluding interest on public debt). Of more than one million public servants, perhaps over 50,000 were supernumerary.

Although COSATU was an increasingly uneasy partner in the ruling coalition, the dismantling of racial barriers reinforced existing trends towards a real increase in wages for those African people in employment. Nattrass and Seekings (1999) argue that black households with professionals, including teachers and nurses, as well as urban white- and blue-collar workers, 'the social bases of the trade union movement', have benefited disproportionately from government expenditure. COSATU's industrial action (**Chapter 11**) met with some success, so that its impact on labour legislation far exceeded its influence on macroeconomic policy: this was true especially in strengthening rights to underpin collective action and bargaining; and improving basic conditions of employment. The Employment Equity Act of 1999, which aimed to impose racially based quotas on the private sector, could be an important further support to black employees.

Relatively high levels of income tax fall most heavily on the salary-earning middle classes; high avoidance rates have also, it is claimed, been reduced. Total state revenue from this source has been limited by slow economic growth and the stagnation of formal sector employment. Nevertheless taxation has had an impact, especially on middle-income whites. In these ways, government policy has benefited one of its key political constituencies: lower-salaried and wage-earning urban black working people, although they may not have benefited as much as they would have liked, or as much as the top echelon of the black elite.

Despite high rates of unemployment, the poorest segments of society have not been entirely neglected. South Africa's state old age pension system, unusually generous for a country with its per capita income, is a further redistributive measure that goes some way to relieve the most acute poverty. The extension of the state pension was a product of Botha's reform era, initially partly to win legitimacy for the tri-cameral parliament, and then gradually equalized for all racial groups in all areas by 1993. It is paid in cash and means tested at a low level, with the result that the great majority of whites are excluded while about 80 per cent of Africans who qualify are recipients (Case and Deighton 1998). At R370 a month in 1993, and R470 in 1998, the pension kept its real value and exceeded the poverty datum line. A 1993 survey showed that, of 1.6 million beneficiaries, 70 per cent were women, 90 per cent African, and nearly 50 per cent African rural women. Pensions constituted on average over 60 per cent of income for those households that received them. If homeland families once subsidized cheap labour and capitalism, they are increasingly the recipients of transfers—a pensionariat as much as a rural proletariat.

As children in many poorer rural families live with grandparents, or in three-generational households, a practice that may have been reinforced by the pension system, pensions constitute an effective transfer of cash for their welfare also. A new child-maintenance payment was introduced in 1998, which also assisted the poorest households. Although the distribution of large amounts of cash on a regular basis throughout the country provides opportunity for theft and corruption, a great deal of the money finds its way to the poorest families: so much so that the most acute poverty, especially rural poverty, can now be linked to households without access to pensions, as much as to those without wage income, or land and livestock.

One central feature of apartheid was the unequal division of agricultural land by race. Opposition groups had long called for a reversal of these injustices—a highly emotive political issue. Land reform evolved around both legally based restitution and economically driven redistribution strategies; policy was pushed forward by a sympathetic ANC Land Affairs minister, Derek Hanekom, working with NGOs such as the National Land Committee and Legal Resources Centre. Mandela's government quickly put in place a Restitution of Land Rights Act (1994), which invited claims for specific properties that had been confiscated since 1913 under racially discriminatory laws. The conquest of South Africa was complete by this date, so that, critically, earlier dispossession was excluded. The Act did not provide for historical or tribal claims on the basis of occupation before that time.

Processing claims has been slow and a high degree of legal proof of former ownership or possession has been required. The most clear-cut cases have been post-1948 rural 'black spot' and urban group areas removals; even here, earlier compensation in land has to be taken into account. In some urban cases, property itself is not restorable, as it has been subsumed in commercial zones and shopping centres or, as in District Six, Cape Town, is partly under the large site of the Cape Technikon. In the successful Makuleke claim for a northerly portion of the Kruger National Park, the community decided to allow its continued use for conservation, in exchange for payments and projects that might allow them to benefit directly. It is unlikely that much more than 1 per cent of agricultural land can be reclaimed under this Act and delays have caused frustration. But it has been an important political statement, analogous to the Truth and Reconciliation Commission, of the government's preparedness to confront, in a systematic and legal procedure, past wrongs.

Although racial restrictions on landownership were removed in 1991, few black people had the capacity to purchase private farms. Under its redistribution policy, the government planned to help poor African communities to purchase land with generous subsidies and loans. Pilot schemes were set up in each of the nine provinces in 1995, funded largely by foreign donors. Progress proved hesitant and the budget for land purchase was not fully spent by the time the pilot phase was wound up in 1997. Forms of ownership used for such land transfers, involving trusts, were cumbersome to establish; extensive negotiations had to be conducted with communities. New settlements had to be planned. White farmers, especially those on the peripheries of the former homelands, where they were vulnerable to attacks, stock theft, and fence-cutting, were often keen to sell their land, but purchases proved time-consuming to arrange.

The government also had to make hard decisions about further expenditure. There were huge expectations for social services and education, especially around the major cities and small towns; in this context, it was difficult to justify purchasing agricultural land for relatively few people. Demographic growth has been such that there is insufficient land in the country as a whole to provide enough even for minimal subsistence on the land for more than a small proportion of African people. It was not clear that land redistribution was the most effective way to alleviate poverty; some officials expressed concern that production might suffer if too much land went to impoverished communities with no capital to maintain intensive agriculture. Poor people themselves seemed to prioritize secure residential sites as close as possible to employment and services rather than agricultural land—though some still wanted access to grazing land to keep animals.

Especially as government subsidies receded in the 1980s, many commercial farmers had become efficient producers with highly capitalized units that supplied the bulk of an increasingly urban nation's food, as well as key export commodities such as wine and fruit. The government had to consider urban food security and food prices. In fact it diminished protection against some agricultural imports that further favoured consumers. Such concerns and pressures have resulted in a cautious land policy. When Hanekom was replaced by Thoko Didiza as minister in 1999, the emphasis shifted away from communities and towards assisting emerging black farmers who might work as small groups or families on privately owned land.

More land was acquired by black people in the 1990s outside government schemes than through them. Land invasions, evident especially on government- and municipally-owned land in the early 1990s, were generally given legal status by the authorities. Land near cities and small towns remains the main magnet for occupations by the rural poor. It is striking that private farms were not greatly affected, although a few farms that communities felt were due to them under the much-delayed restitution programme were occupied after the Zimbabwean land invasions of 2000; the impact of the latter crisis on South Africa is as yet unclear. Agricultural land is being purchased by individual black people or small groups on the free market and the state seems increasingly committed to facilitating transfers of this kind.

It is an irony that the old regime purchased more land for Africans in order to consolidate the homelands than the new government will as yet contemplate in its land reform programme. The apartheid-period acquisitions probably amounted to more than 5 per cent of agricultural land. Much of it was in the better-watered parts of the country adjacent to the homelands and went to poorer rural families in communal tenure under Tribal Authorities. Yet the ANC government was wisely cautious about further effective extensions of the former homelands, which might have given further power to chiefs, and has been trying to establish the legal basis for alternative systems of tenure.

## The Economy: Growth and Uncertainty

In sum, while the RDP as a whole failed, and economic transformation was unevenly pursued, education and social spending increased in the new South Africa. But, especially after 1996, financial strategy tightened. The RDP was displaced by the Growth, Employment and Redistribution (GEAR) programme, which envisaged 3.5 per cent annual growth, rising to over 6 per cent in 2000, fuelled largely by private and foreign investment. Reductions in the budget deficit and inflation, as well as further privatization and wage restraint, were prioritized. Growth had reached 3 per cent in 1996, the highest for some years, not least because foreign capital had begun to flow back into the country. In 1995, this included a surge of R15 billion of direct investment in production and business establishments—an optimistic celebration of the new South Africa's potential. Economic linkages expanded, especially with the Indian Ocean rim, with Asian and Middle Eastern countries, and, as a relative peace was restored in the subcontinent, with Africa. GEAR aimed to capitalize on these developments.

However, economic optimism and the dividends of the negotiated settlement began to fade by 1996, when direct investment abruptly declined. High crime rates, lack of security, a falling currency, and a well-organized workforce increasingly protected by labour legislation were all seen as disincentives to international companies. In that year, as the GNU was dismantled, and Trevor Manuel took over Finance, speculators drove the rand down, despite ANC protestations of continued economic discipline. Although shorter-term foreign investment in shares and bonds continued to be attracted by the strongly performing stock exchange and high interest rates until early 1998, these proved to be impermanent in a volatile world economy.

South Africa was buffeted by the global financial storms of mid-1998. The fleet-footed managers of Western capital, scared off by, and contributing to, the turmoil in East Asia, Brazil, and Russia, fled emerging markets in general. Shares on the Johannesburg stock exchange, like those in many parts of the developing world, plummeted. The rand fell further; between 1994 and 1998, the value of the South African currency roughly halved from R5 to R10 per pound sterling (R3 to R6 per dollar). Within fifteen years, the South African rand had declined nearly fivefold against the major Western currencies.

The crisis of 1998 had an immediate impact on growth and employment. In its determination to control inflation—below 10 per cent by 1997—and win back foreign investment, the government pushed up interest rates again. The high costs of borrowing affected many sectors, especially industry and agriculture. Economic growth, already slowing in 1997, was barely positive in 1998. The formal sector lost tens of thousands of jobs and consumer spending weakened. Major South African corporations, such as Anglo-American, South African Breweries, and Billiton, resited their head offices in Europe, where they could raise money more cheaply and easily, hold their assets in a less vulnerable currency, and develop their global ambitions. Though this might not directly affect employment in South Africa, it indicated a lack of confidence.

Simultaneously, gold came under a different kind of pressure. With gold no longer essential to back currencies, the longer-term fall in its value provided less incentive for central banks to hold it as security against volatility in currency markets. During the late 1990s central banks in Belgium, Netherlands, and Canada, amongst others, sold some of their gold to invest in assets that might bring better returns; this put further downward pressure on prices. When the International Monetary Fund proposed selling off 10 per cent of its gold in 1999, ostensibly to fund debt relief for the poorest countries, and Britain also began the process, South African mine-owners and the NUM joined forces in protest delegations to Washington and London. They argued that other poor African gold-producing countries, such as Zimbabwe, Ghana, and Tanzania, would suffer along with South Africa.

Temporary delays in sales are unlikely to alter these economic patterns. By 1999 gold made up only 15 per cent of the total value of South African exports. Income from other staple commodities, especially agricultural exports such as wool, have also fallen greatly in value over the long term. The close of the twentieth century probably heralded the end of gold's lustrous pre-eminence. Employment in gold mining declined from heights of around half a million in 1990 to less than 300,000 in 1999; perhaps 100,000 jobs were lost between 1994 and 1999.

It is a tragedy that the global market drove gold prices down—although they remain volatile—at the very moment that South Africa was so much in need of revenue and employment. Lay-offs deeply affected former homelands, such as the Transkei, as well as Mozambique and Lesotho, because so many people in poor rural areas were still partly dependent on miners' wages. The costs of unemployment had already fallen disproportionately on these areas. While a decline in migrant labour might have been welcomed in better times, there were few alternatives for most rurally based families.

Mushroooming informal settlements on city peripheries in the 1980s were replicated in the 1990s by a parallel movement to the well-established small towns in farming areas and former home-lands throughout the country. Such settlements were distinctive for the forest of plastic bags on fences and bushes surrounding them—a measure both of dependence on shop purchases and the lack of urban services. But it is important not to succumb to an analytical closure and see such families simply as terminal victims of the demise of homeland agriculture and farm removals. There is no way back into agriculture for the vast majority of them, even if land reform were to be pursued. Although they were often difficult to discern in the midst of widespread poverty, new strategies of survival and accumulation, from multiple sources, were becoming apparent both in small towns and cities. Informal-sector activities such as small 'spaza' or back-room shops, and the sale of fruit or vetkoek (fatty dough balls) and other food could be a supplement. Bovine head cookers became a distinct presence on Durban's busy Warwick Avenue. Sale of alcohol could be particularly profitable. Livestock numbers in African hands were probably increasing and could bring some income. The demand for transport and shelter created work in local taxi and building businesses. Low-paid, casual labour was available on farms.

Nationally, economic gains and windfalls were not absent. In 1998 world oil prices were low, so that the country was temporarily spared the pressure of rapidly escalating fuel costs, which had made so big an impact in the 1970s. The weak rand also increased the potential for exports. Commodity boycotts of South African goods in the West were rapidly reversed. The armaments industry, a legacy of the apartheid era, was a major beneficiary, exporting to new markets. Exports of wine and fruit in particular boomed, making the rural economy of the Western Cape the most buoyant in the country. Niche markets opened for enterprising entrepreneurs, from a black woman producing red roses for export to Europe to an exporter of mushrooms grown in the damp of disused mineshafts in Kimberley. The government claimed, with some justification, that its cautious financial strategy had enabled the country to survive the economic whirlwinds far better than most; in 1999 interest rates fell sharply and strong growth was predicted for the start of the new millennium.

Tourism also benefited greatly from both political transition and a falling currency. Alongside established zones such as Cape Town and the Western Cape wine route, through mountain scenery, there was growing interest in new sights associated with the political struggle and African experiences. Robben Island, no longer a prison, was sensitively developed as a tourist destination; former prisoners acted as guides. The itinerary of popular Soweto bus tours included visits to a Mandela museum, opened in 1997, to a memorial for Hector Petersen—whose picture came to epitomize the savagery of repression in 1976—and to Winnie Mandela's home in Orlando East. Tourists were offered visits to shebeens, to Wandie's place for African food including dumpling, tripe, vetkoek, samp, and beans, and to the house of Godfrey Moloi, the formidable former gangster and Soweto personality whose autobiography (*My Life*) gave sharp insights into Soweto low life. In 1998 Soweto's first cappucino shop opened. The struggle and poverty, as well as African tradition, could also be commoditized.

Wildlife in the National Parks remained central to foreign conceptions of South Africa's attractiveness. Game farming on private land expanded rapidly as landowners responded to falling returns from livestock and the growing potential of tourism and domestic recreational hunting. There are probably more wild animals in South Africa now than at any time since the late nineteenth century—one reason for environmental optimism. Studies of farm pastures in the semi-arid areas suggest improvements in the density of vegetation as livestock levels have declined.

There was a palpable change in South Africa's economic contours, manifested in the city centres, and the industrial zones. Finance, services, tourism, transport, and a vast range of informal-sector activity now supplemented and supplanted the old core industries. Despite its comparative educational deficit, and continued loss of highly trained people, the country generated significant information technology companies, such as Softline, by 1999 the biggest accounting and retail software provider in South Africa, and second in Australia. Many whites, especially Afrikaners formerly absorbed by the state, moved into the professions and the private sector.

South Africa became a magnet for African immigrants from all over the continent. Some came for the education institutions, cheaper than those in the West but still offering internationally recognized standards. Some brought skills. While the rand was weak globally, it was stronger than many other African currencies, and salaries generally remained higher. Universities, hospitals, and similar bodies employed significant numbers of African professionals. Drug markets attracted criminal syndicates, especially, if newspaper reports are correct, those run by Nigerians. Unskilled workers from the region still sought employment on farms; foreign street traders jostled with local women for sites on city-centre pavements. While the number of new immigrants was uncertain, there were certainly hundreds of thousands, probably over a million; over four million temporary visitors from African countries were recorded in the late 1990s.

The influx of *Makwerekwere* (a street word for African foreigners derived from their unfamiliar languages) was sufficient to occasion alarm, even xenophobia, at many levels of South African society, not least amongst Africans who felt that they created competition for jobs and services. New African minority groups were emerging—an indication that South Africa, for all its economic travails, remained comparatively successful in continental terms.

Democratic transitions are often frail in societies with large impoverished populations and high differentials between rich and poor. Civil disorder and polarized politics can rapidly undermine the political constraint required for democratic processes. The new South African government has made some efforts to address poverty, extend social provision, and enhance opportunity, especially through education. Freedom of movement has been entrenched and formal racial barriers in the economic sphere removed; the significance of these measures should not be underestimated.

But the government inherited an economy that had barely grown for some years; government spending and the public debt were increasing rapidly, while per capita incomes and employment were falling. Increasingly its priority was growth. Together with international pressures, and the changing ideological orientation of the black elite, this implied financial orthodoxy, the courting of foreign investment, and constraints on state expenditure. The state's organizational capacity to deliver social services, housing, and education was also limited. Despite the Masakhane campaign encouraging payment for improved services, the government found it difficult to secure such income and hence finance further provision. The major beneficiaries of transformation were a minority of black people with education and political links, and to a lesser extent those in urban employment. The new elite, however, also inherited the troubled responsibility for alleviation of poverty in the future.

# 13

# Crime, Culture, and Reconciliation
in the New South Africa

## Social Ills: Corruption, Crime, and HIV/AIDS

Post-apartheid South Africa had a president who was globally recognized as a moral leader, but who himself found it difficult to understand the slippage in personal morality and the escalation of crime over which he presided. It had one of the most liberal constitutions in the world, but many people could not enjoy basic rights. Legal protection for women, and a high proportion of female members of parliament, seemed to have little impact on the incidence of rape and personal violence. On the one hand, it was a society brimming with the energy and optimism of reconstruction; on the other, the media dwelt on corruption and inefficiency in public life. It was a society that seemed to evince simultaneously an optimistic openness and frankness, but increasingly reflected pessimism in swift changes of public mood.

In some respects, South Africa's ills became more sharply defined as a new governing class struggled to come to terms with the complexity of its society. Within a few years of the transition, reports of corruption in the bureaucracy were commonplace. Rewards for political loyalty, affirmative action, and access to the state contracts nurtured networks of patronage. Corruption was not a new phenomenon. The old government presided over misuse of government money in a frightening array of secret deals and projects, many designed initially for political or security ends, and in sanctions-busting strategies that provided scope for personal gain. The most chilling of these, involving assassination squads and germ warfare, were only fully revealed during the investigations of the Truth and Reconciliation Commission.

Military adventures in foreign countries and servicing of the homelands provided additional opportunities. The lack of accountability within the homeland bureaucracies led to corrupt behaviour at all levels: from bribes taken for contracts to cash payments demanded for speeding or to transfer pensions. In the final year of the homeland governments, some officials attempted to strip what they could from the sinking ship: cases were recorded of rapid promotions and pay hikes, as well as misappropriation of government vehicles and property. Large sums were siphoned off from the homeland parastatals funding irrigation schemes.

Transactions and appointments at the centre since 1994 have been far more 'transparent' and the highest echelons of ANC articulated a strong internal ethic of public service and accountability. The government has been subject to unparalleled scrutiny in the press; resignations, such as that of Abe Williams, first (NP) Minister of Welfare in the GNU, and Winnie Mandela were enforced. But at the lower levels of government, Lodge (1998) argues, where it was possible for officials and politicians to insert themselves into the circulation of cash, or exploit their positions of authority as middlemen, corruption has persisted, even expanded. Important new welfare initiatives such as the primary school feeding scheme were hamstrung in the Eastern Cape by local agents waylaying central government money. It has been patent that in the new South Africa corruption is a non-racial practice, not least so in the police, where a number of cases have been documented, including collusion in car theft, an omnipresent South African crime. Some white South Africans, cynical about the political transition or anxious to exploit their last moments of authority, and black South Africans, determined upon 'entitlement-seeking', found it difficult to resist.

Mandela, surprised by the reported scale of such misdemeanours, belatedly appointed the judicially led Heath Commission in 1997 to investigate corruption in government; by 1999 it had over 1,000 cases on its books. After intense media pressure, the government forced one of the most senior African civil servants, the Director-General of Home Affairs, to resign in 1999 for alleged fraud and for abusing departmental facilities in running a basketball team; another in Correctional Services followed. Notably, both were in Inkatha ministries. Mbeki was clearly sensitive to what he believed were unfair attempts to characterize the government in general, and Africans in particular, as corrupt. He frequently ascribed corruption to the legacy of apartheid; others labelled press reports of corruption as racist. The ANC publicly recognized the problems of 'careerism, rampant self-interest and corruption' within its ranks; it was unclear how determined they were to act before corruption became the systemic scourge evident in some African countries.

Education was a particularly important element in state policy as a means of reintegrating society, providing opportunity, rectifying racial injustice, and underpinning economic development. Educational provision also seemed to offer hope for black youth, and minimize the possibility of another 'lost generation' spawned by the struggle. The gap between state expenditure per capita on whites and on Africans decreased from about twelve times in the early 1980s to four by 1993. As schools subsequently became increasingly integrated, perhaps the most significant element of deracialization in the country, such calculations were no longer possible, but provincial inequalities were reduced, so that by 1999 wealthier provinces, such as the Western Cape, Gauteng, and Northern Cape, spent less than twice per pupil more than the poorest. Equalizing resources necessitated a hotly disputed attempt to move teachers from better provisioned areas and schools to those with poor provision. Some of those who did not want to move were given the expensive option of early retirement.

Formerly white private schools were amongst the first to incorporate black pupils, and the sector has expanded as both the white and black elite attempt to escape state education. State schools in former white suburbs also charged a fee, although exemption was possible for poor families. These schools included the widest racial mix: children of local residents, of domestic servants, and in some cases black children bussed in from townships. In a study of Cape Town, Anthony Lemon (1999) found that an exclusive English-medium state school with high fees still had 62 per cent white pupils (but its first African head girl), while an Afrikaans-medium school in a less affluent white suburb had equal numbers of white and coloured pupils. Schools in coloured and Indian suburbs, which largely retained their racial character, were taking up to 20 per cent African pupils. Those in African townships and former homelands, now the great majority, remained almost exclusively African.

Redistribution of educational funding was not reflected in the achievement of the bulk of pupils. Matriculation (high school-leaving) exam pass rates amongst African pupils dropped from over 40 per cent in the late apartheid era to 35 per cent by the mid-1990s. Although there were more African girls than boys sitting for the exam, their pass rate was particularly poor. By contrast, the white student pass rate was 96 per cent and rising, with girls doing better than boys. Explanations offered have included the legacy of Bantu Education and inadequate school facilities, continuing disruption from protests, and poorly trained, unmotivated teachers in an expanding system working with new syllabuses. Home conditions were often unconducive to academic achievement. Many youths were absorbed into street life and gangs, while young women found it difficult to escape heavy domestic work and teenage pregnancy. Surveys by the Department of Education also indicated weak levels of achievement—lower than in some other African countries—for junior school pupils. Alongside figures on crime, rape, and AIDS, these were surely amongst the most depressing statistics from the new South Africa.

Despite the new government's commitment, youth culture could not quickly be changed. Some former comrades helped to perpetuate the dominance of the street. Those with education or training had the possibility of making the transition into employment, local politics, or the armed forces. But Thokozani Xaba (1997) suggests that some in Durban who had pursued more vigorously the slogan of 'liberation now, education later' found it difficult to adapt their practices and role when the ANC ended the armed struggle. They had been socialized into a violent masculinity legitimized by the struggle: 'manliness for the young men of the townships meant standing up both to "flush" the security forces and their informers out of the townships as well as to defend their communities.' This brought them social respect as 'comrades', 'young lions', and 'liberators' and also access to young women.

Feeling themselves abandoned and economically disadvantaged in the new order of the 1990s, some in Durban engaged in 'violent criminal activity in order to procure the accoutrements of success' (Xaba 1997). Similarly, even before 1994 key activists in informal settlements such as Phola Park, south of Johannesburg, one of the most militant areas in the country, had had close links with gangs (Reed 1994). A few such groups in Durban and on the Rand kept firearms from the struggle, obtained cheaply from Mozambique, from corrupt army sources, or looted in robberies. They organized heists on security vans, shops, and white properties; they also focused their vengeance on the townships and on young women. Their activities could take the form of gang violence against competitors, for example as the 'cleaners' against the 'dirties' in Kwamashu. Gangs in turn were vulnerable to violence from police and vigilantes; *Ilanga* reported former comrades, 'the abandoned and forsaken precocious heroes', stoned to death for raping a Christian girl.

School failure was one factor feeding into a disaffected youth culture that perpetuated the problem itself and fuelled criminality. Criminal activity as a whole, of course, had far more diverse agents and explanations. The obsession in the media with crime was not simply a moral panic by wealthier people responding to their uncertainty and protecting their self-interest. Crime almost certainly increased. One starting point in understanding this problem was analysis of rapid urbanization, vast informal settlements, and persistent poverty, which underpinned economic desperation. Intense poverty produced a large number of people with little to lose. Poverty does not always produce crime. But it is often noted that many Africans were forced to live in a state of illegality in the apartheid era. To this legacy was added the rejection of government authority during the struggle, the sense amongst some of being beyond the state, and the justification of illegality by the history of oppression. If the government will not redistribute wealth, such an explanation suggests, people will take it for themselves: why rebel when you can rob?

The casual use of violence during crime speaks of alienation and deep social dislocation. Gang culture did not lose its hold in the townships; if anything, it expanded during the political transition boosted by the spread of drugs and the influx of some immigrant groups who run drug rackets. Inadequate policing, the sheer danger of police work, and police collusion must also be part of the picture. In the countryside, there were economic as well as political motivations in widespread killing of white farmers. They were often isolated, they had cash on hand from informal transactions, or vehicles to take. Stock theft from black owners was probably as widespread as from white. Crime clearly paid for some in South Africa. While it may have redistributed resources, this route of survival or accumulation was dysfunctional and a high cost of political liberation.

The idea of social alienation has also been drawn on to explain personal violence and crime against women, in particular by brutalized men who brutalize their women. Campbell (1992) argued that violence by members of Inkatha, both in the public arena against Comrades and in the private sphere against women, was in part a reaction by older men against the undermining of their role as heads of households or as breadwinners: the family became the 'cradle of violence' and 'one area where the power of working-class men has not been threatened by a racial capitalist society'. But rape became so widespread that an analysis must go beyond responses to deprivation and address the carelessness of male behaviour that has evolved in South Africa as a whole, in the townships, and amongst the 'lost generation'. If the figures are correct, and represent a change in behaviour rather than just new reporting, the social alienation and insurrection of the late apartheid period has partly turned inward in what constitutes a war against women.

South Africa was reported to have one of the highest rates of rape in the world—52,000 notified to police in 1998, of which only 3,500 were brought to court, and a similar figure in 1999. Surveys put the actual incidence at many times that number. Many incidents were thought to be gang rapes as an expression of power or bravado, or for enjoyment: 'jackrolling', or 'dipping', in the slang. A Kwamashu (Durban) gang called itself *Bhepa span*, from a Zulu word for crude sex (Leclerc-Madlala 1997). Male gang members on the Cape Flats ingenuously told a television interviewer that young women could join their gang: the initiation rite was gang rape. If male aggression was most pronounced in impoverished communities, more privileged people could also be involved. Pupils interviewed pointed to the involvement of teachers, who threatened girls with failure at school, as well as classmates. Intensive organization and publicity by women's groups brought belated measures to tighten the laws and increase sentences in 1999. The police themselves were reported to be unmotivated on rape, and even involved; male judges were criticized for leniency.

A related issue stalking South Africa's future, along with other countries in the region, was the rapidly increasing incidence of HIV/AIDS. Diagnosed first in 1982, the spread of infection was relatively slow in the 1980s and, despite relatively high rates of sexually transmitted diseases in earlier decades, HIV infection was not expected to make so great an impact in South Africa as further north. But, with few preventative measures, incidence of the disease escalated in the 1990s. New sources of infection were introduced through truckers, migrant workers, immigrants, and exiled guerrillas returning from camps in African countries with a high prevalence. Sexual mores in South Africa, coupled with rapid geographic mobility, limited use of condoms, and deprivation, provided fertile conditions for its spread. Migrant workers, especially on the mines, proved to be particularly susceptible, as also the sex-workers with whom they consorted.

Surveys conducted among pregnant women tested at clinics suggested over 30 per cent were infected with HIV by 1999: rates were higher in rural KZN as well as Gauteng, suggesting that the disease had penetrated well beyond initial nodes of concentration. Most chilling were two widely reported statistics that the incidence of HIV infection was highest amongst young women aged 15–25 and that South Africa was experiencing the highest rate of growth of infection in the world. Although the spread of AIDS was no doubt sometimes a result of unprotected, consenting intercourse, reports from Gauteng suggested that virgins were particularly targeted for sex, both in quest of HIV avoidance and cure. Campbell and Williams (1999) noted that mineworkers interviewed saw AIDS as just one of many dangers at work; their desire for sex *nama nameng* (flesh to flesh), and their lack of clear knowledge of the disease, outweighed the risks in their minds. Leclerc-Madlala found that youths in Durban were reluctant to be diagnosed, and resigned to infection and communal suffering of the kind they experienced in the struggle: 'that way we won't die alone.'

These issues were particularly difficult to confront in the public arena because they raised such sensitive questions about race and masculinity; campaigns implied direct criticism of African men. Although innovative programmes were introduced, and Mbeki himself has appeared on posters advocating safe sex and prevention, the state's response was slow and limited. Opportunities were lost before 1994 and neither Mandela nor Mbeki took a strong lead. Mbeki became embroiled during 2000 in an acrimonious debate when he questioned the accepted causes of infection and the costs of drugs to treat this and other scourges. His concern was to emphasize the relationship of disease in general and HIV/AIDS in particular to poverty and deprivation. The immediate impact of his intervention was to sidetrack preventative campaigns. Yet the criticism he attracted, and the major international conference in Durban in July 2000, may have turned the tide in publicizing the problem. The HIV/AIDS epidemic became central to national politics: it threatened to hit the most vulnerable African people hardest; cast a shadow over political and social advances; required difficult budgetary decisions in what was initially one of the more successful ministries; and called on African politicians to move away from anti-apartheid rhetoric and confront explosive issues of African culture, gender, and sexuality. Predictions of life expectancy fell dramatically.

## Culture, Race, and Reconciliation

South Africa did not suddenly produce a unified post-apartheid national culture. Whites remained insecure and black intellectuals were sensitive to lingering white racism. Many Africans could not take advantage of their new rights. Many remained rooted in specifically African identities. But critics of the pace of transformation in South Africa sometimes overlooked the extent of deracialization after 1994. Education, income, and class increasingly jostled with race as markers of social division. There was evidence of a degree of reconciliation.

Petty apartheid, which segregated everything from post offices to public spaces and beaches, was eroding in the 1980s and disappeared in law. The social geography of conquest and apartheid in some respects remained at the end of the twentieth century in the contrast between commercial farmlands and former homelands, as well as in the structure of cities. Wealth still allowed whites (and increasingly tourists) to predominate in particular settings such as smarter suburbs, restaurants, nature reserves, and beach resorts. But whites were decreasingly able to command exclusive space, so characteristic of the high apartheid years, and their own freedom of movement was increasingly constrained by their sense of insecurity and the threat of crime. Striking juxtapositions were more evident: on the formerly segregated Durban beachfront, black Zionist ministers doused their followers, while bronzed white surfers plunged into the waves beyond them, and cargo vessels stood in the roadstead.

Some black people with sufficient income moved out of the townships into the formerly white city centres and suburbs. Mandela himself bought a house in Houghton, the old elite northern Johannesburg suburb. Johannesburg, still core of the largest conurbation, has, within a short space of time, undergone perhaps the most dramatic transition. The movement of African people into accommodation around the city centre, which started in the 1980s, became an avalanche. Rising crime rates, street hawking, and the apparent incapacity of the state to police the city centre in turn provoked a spatial reaction. The efflux of many companies, the stock exchange, retailers, and tourist services out of the city and north to Rosebank, Sandton, and similar centres accelerated sharply. Surrounded by salubrious suburbs, with shops in malls rather than street frontages, they were more secure although by no means entirely white. White society has also to some degree regrouped itself within the country, moving to the Western Cape, Pretoria suburbs, and other concentrations.

The numbers of whites recorded in the censuses dropped from over 5 million in 1991 to 4.4 million in 1996, from 20 per cent of the population in 1950 to 11 per cent in 1996. While this figure is almost certainly in part due to an overcorrection upwards in 1991 and a possible undercount for all groups in 1996 (African population figures did not rise much), there is other evidence to support the suggestion that the white population is stable if not falling (**Appendix 1**). Birth rates slowed down markedly from 1980. Formal emigration rates were not high, and South Africa was the recipient of some white immigrants. But some younger white South Africans, especially those from anglophone backgrounds with higher education, went searching for new identities, not least Australian, British, and Canadian. They left the country in droves. Some had British passports; others left on holiday or study visas and contrived to establish themselves elsewhere. One marker may be the fall in white university entry from 152,000 to 126,000 and in technikon entry from 71,000 to 37,000 between 1993 and 1999. And the major exodus appeared to be after rather than before higher education; an estimated half of whites qualifying as doctors were leaving.

Newspapers carried advertisements for emigration advice. Many white families now straddled more than one continent; estimates of South Africans in Britain alone exceeded 250,000 by 1999. Despite the relative ease of integration, they began to form a noticeable social group—more so than earlier waves of political and professional exiles. They generated South African tax and finance advisory firms, dental practices, pubs (screening rugby), a weekly paper (*South African Times UK*), a Dutch Reformed Church, retail suppliers of biltong and Ouma's rusks as well as a touch rugby league with other antipodean networks. White South Africans might become a diasporic, or transnational, community.

Whites frequently talked about crime and personal safety as a reason for leaving. Prospects for employment, formerly so secure, were diminishing. Institutions symbolic of specifically European culture such as opera, ballet, and symphony orchestras, which had formerly received major subsidies, seemed threatened. It is an irony that, as English became established as the national language, so the proportion of people with a British background was probably declining. The white population again became more diverse, as it was around the turn of the century, with large new minorities, such as Portuguese and German, who identifed themselves as such. In the big cities, restaurants reflect this ever more diverse immigrant culture, not only of those formerly classified as white.

One of the comments made about the new African elite was their adoption of a globalized culture—or that they were adopting the practices of the former white rulers. The new South Africa certainly remained particularly porous culturally and stylistically, susceptible to the consumer desires that international markets create. It was not the first resort for foreign investors, but it was very much part of global information networks, thoroughly penetrated by advertising and foreign television programmes, and a favoured site for sporting competitions and international conferences. The black middle classes were growing, ideologically varied, and diffuse, both absorbing international currents, and helping to forge new versions of South African modernity. They had something to prove in a post-apartheid context, were ambitious for themselves and for the country, and were beginning to exude the confidence of a major cluster, globally, of African wealth and power.

This did not mean an abandonment of African heritages and identities. African popular culture sometimes self-consciously attempted to marry ideas of Africanness with modern consumer culture. Magazines such as *Drum* and *Pace*, which sold particularly well to an urban, but less select, market than *Tribute* (see **Chapter 12**), can be a useful indicator of cultural concerns. An issue of *Pace* (April 1996) at the same time as *Tribute*'s celebration of Ramaphosa's trout-fishing transition included illustrated features on: 'Ethiopia: Africa's Cradle of Civilisation'; Modjadji, the Lovedu rain queen, whose rainmaking powers appeared to have deserted her; Samkelo Xayimpi, a 12-year-old Port Elizabeth imbongi (praise singer) who, inspired by the performance at Mandela's inauguration, mastered the art and appeared to an audience of millions on TV; and Swazi royals, adorned in African print cloths, at a palace festival with South African stars. These were interlaced with a feature on Solomon 'Sticks' Morewa and South African football, as well as advertisements for upmarket cigarettes and brandy, cosmetics, running shoes, fashion clothes, and watches. African urban culture, while internationalizing, retained local reference points rather than simply becoming white; whites also adapted their cultural and social practices.

In her essay on contemporary Zulu radio drama, Liz Gunner (2000) notes that African language broadcasting services, which have retained their popularity over some decades, received over five million letters from listeners in one year in the 1980s. A drama serial in Zulu on Ukhozi (Eagle) FM, repeated from the 1970s, could attract an estimated 4.5 million listeners in 1999. Called *Icala Lombango* (the succession dispute), it dealt with traditional themes of chieftaincy, competition between wives, and a greedy *inyanga* (doctor) called *Gwiny'inkomo* (cow-gulper). The audience included many in the urban areas of Gauteng and Mpumulanga, as well as in KZN. Contemporary dramas covered a more varied range of themes, including marital breakdown, crime, violence, warlords, AIDS, and accumulators. But they often explored witchcraft, *muthi*, *inyangas*, and specifically African cultural dilemmas in a complex and literary vernacular, both 'wrestling with the present' and 'beckoning to the past'. Oral culture remained of particular importance in transmitting ideas in African communities.

African political leaders, and bodies such as the constitutionally based Human Rights Commission chaired by former black consciousness activist Barney Pityana, frequently reacted against the intensity of reporting on crime, rape, and corruption in the media and the assumption, usually unspoken, that Africans were more to blame. Their discomfort, together with impatience at the rate of transformation in the economic and social sphere, was one factor contributing to a gradual departure from the conciliatory rhetoric so evident in 1994. Such concerns were reflected in continuing accusations of white racism; and, whatever the compromises whites have made, racial prejudices have certainly not disappeared.

Even where white and black intellectuals formerly shared an opposition to apartheid, simmering debates about the nature of racism and the meaning of transformation contributed to splits in a number of institutions. Some white intellectuals—whatever their particular outlook—were labelled as liberals, implying not so much an economic philosophy but a lack of commitment to

339

Africanization as a primary goal of transformation. White intellectuals were challenged in specific institutions, not least universities, and disciplines, including History. As can be seen from the Bibliography of this book, whites—who for so long had differential access to higher education—have written the bulk of professional history, including the rich new historiography of African people in South Africa. Whatever their specific analysis of the African past, their numerical domination created unease. In the process of these debates, black intellectuals extended arguments for affirmative action and put flesh on ideas about the African renaissance—developments that were to some extent harnessed by Mbeki.

But it is easier to list culturally divergent forces than to analyse what South Africans have in common and when they have acted in concert. One significant symbolic indicator may be name changes, which were not a priority—although they were beginning to gather pace. Most significantly, the country retained its old name. The only alternative with some currency was Azania; its association with black consciousness and the PAC ruled it out. Of the provinces, Mpumalanga (initially Eastern Transvaal) and Gauteng adopted African names; the term Transvaal was jettisoned by all northern provinces. The Free State, under an ANC provincial government and with a large African majority, retained its Boer republican roots. KZN is a hybrid and the Northern Cape, Eastern Cape, and Northwest Province were content with neutral geographical nomenclature.

While the Orange River has reverted to the Khoikhoi word Gariep, which was in use until the early nineteenth century, Afrikaans and English names for landscape features have not been changed quickly; rivers, especially on the eastern seaboard, had in any case largely retained their pre-colonial African names. Although many cities have African vernacular names, these remained unofficial everyday usages; neither did cities adopt the names of their African townships, as did Harare in Zimbabwe. There were some plans for changes, notably in honouring Mandela, probably in Pretoria. Airports have been called after their cities, rather than former white Prime Ministers. African leaders have increasingly requested that their African first names are used in public, in place of their Christian names. Mandela, however, retained Nelson, although his praise name Madiba was also frequently used.

The new national flag is an interesting example of hybridity. A competition failed to produce a satisfactory contender and the State Herald, attached to the National Archives and responsible for insignia of all kinds, constructed a final version in 1994, based on his own idea, after extensive consultation. It incorporated no direct symbolism from the past, as did the old flag with its multiple Boer and British referents, but rather embodied a bold modernist multicoloured design. The green, black, and gold of the ANC are present, more so than the blue, orange, and white of the old flag, but they are not entirely dominant and red was introduced. Coming together in the centre of the flag is a forward-looking horizontal V, extending as a bold line to its edge and intended 'as representing the convergence of diverse elements in South African society which then take the road ahead in unison' (Brownell 1995). The anthem is also still an amalgam, drawing together 'Nkosi Sikelel' iAfrika' with 'Die Stem', and can be sung in multiple languages.

Sport, together with its televisual representation, proved a powerful source of national identity and pride. The Rugby World Cup was held in South Africa in 1995, the first major post-boycott sporting event, and a reward for the political settlement. Although rugby was largely a white sport, the event was specifically used by Mandela as an arena to emphasize reconciliation and shared values. He was very present at the final and wore a green and gold jersey with no. 6—that of the South African flank and captain François Pienaar—for the presentations. Pienaar himself proved as able a diplomat as he was captain, sensitive to the symbolic importance of the occasion and projecting the acceptable face of white South Africa. There was an ambiguity to the proceedings: the crowds and the players were largely white; the old South African flag and anthem still jostled with the new; and South Africa's narrow victory over archrivals New Zealand provided a chance for whites to reaffirm their prowess, now as an embattled minority. But a black player, Chester Williams, established himself as a key member of the national team and there were surprising resonances, if still faltering, for a broader constituency. The old African migrants' song 'Shosholoza', about a steam train (stimela) transporting workers, became the ubiquitous anthem for the tournament.

Football, which had a far larger black participation and following, had been ousted from international competition for a longer period, even though the national league had deracialized earlier than other teams sports. By the 1990s professional teams were largely black, including players from other African countries, as was the national team, accepted back into international competition. Dubbed Bafana Bafana, the young men of men, they established themselves through competition within Africa and qualified for the World Cup in 1998. Football was administered by Africans rather than whites—although a foreign coach was introduced for the World Cup—and to a far greater extent than any other sport reintroduced South Africa into wider African networks. Yet the bid to hold the World Cup in 2006 became a national campaign, serving diverse interests. South Africa failed by one vote to secure the competition when the decision was reached in 2000. German success, supported by a block vote of European countries and a Scots New Zealander, occasioned a shared outpouring of South African national anger.

The central formal vehicle for national reconciliation and 'the pursuit of national unity', the Truth and Reconciliation Commission, was a raw experience for whites and blacks. Established by legislation in 1995, and chaired by Tutu, the purpose of the Commission was to elicit in public hearings evidence and confessions about the myriad acts of political violence and violations of human rights during the apartheid era. Minister of Justice Dullah Omar emphasized a 'need for understanding but not for vengeance, a need for reparation but not retaliation, a need for *ubuntu* [humanity] but not for victimisation' (1995). Tutu explained his mission as a contribution to healing the wounds of the past by laying open the cause and nature of the injuries.

South Africa's Commission was one of the most ambitious, and certainly the most open, of the many set up following transitions from authoritarian rule. The hearings, conducted in a number of centres around the country, were highly publicized including television coverage. Participation in the process by those directly involved, both victims and agents of violence, and their families, together with media and public attendance, created tense moments of public drama and personal emotion. Listening to the victims, Antje Krog wrote in *Country of My Skull*, a riveting chronicle of the Commission: 'it is not so much the deaths, and the names of the dead, but the web of infinite sorrow woven around them. It keeps on coming and coming. A wide, barren, disconsolate landscape where the horizon keeps dropping away' (1999: 48). On occasion, victims confronted their torturers or assailants directly.

There was some incentive for those involved in apartheid repression to come clean, because the Commission had powers to grant amnesty from prosecution. Conversely, the threat of legal process would hang over those who did not. Military leaders in particular appear to have negotiated with the government to reveal some of their responsibility, but hoped that, in return for their loyalty to the new state, they might not be pushed too far nor convicted. While some of the material that came before the commission had already been rehearsed in the press, in the Goldstone Commission, or in court cases, a great deal of new evidence was brought, especially about the extent of atrocities and violence by the South African state.

Individual policemen were associated with particular crimes, such as the murders of Biko, Matthew Goniwe, and other activists, and the bombing of Khotso House, premises of ANC-linked groups, in 1988. New evidence was led about Eugene de Kock's destabilization and assassination squad at Vlakplaas, intriguingly multiracial, and the involvement of senior officials and politicians clarified. Chilling details emerged about the chemical and scientific armoury of Dr Wouter Basson and of the extraordinary brutality of individual officers, such as the Cape Town suffocator Jeffrey Benzien, caught up in this system.

The process came under criticism. Most of those aligned with the anti-apartheid struggle refused to admit any equivalence between acts aimed at furthering a politically justified resistance, and those in defence of white rule and apartheid. Many, such as Biko's family, were deeply unhappy that confessed killers might be given amnesty. Some commentators felt that politically weaker white individuals were exposed, while those higher in the command structure seemed to escape. Others, including critics hostile to the old regime, suggested that the TRC, in focusing very largely on the offences committed by those enforcing apartheid, might simply provide a version of events sympathetic to the ANC—a moral justification of its rule.

Some of those implicated seemed to gain public recognition and even celebrity status. In a much publicized and highly critical documentary film on the new South Africa (1998), radical Australian journalist John Pilger highlighted the moment when TV presenter Dali Tambo, son of deceased ANC leader Oliver, hosted a former Vlakplaas operative involved in political killings on his show. As with other guests, he was greeted by a chorus of gyrating young African women. Having earlier spilled his story to the press, and come clean publicly, he was able to sound a reasonable man by continuing his confessional and repentance. Although the TRC itself was clearly not involved, in the eyes of Pilger and perhaps many of his viewers, this was a distasteful offshoot of the TRC's ethos.

The Commission also experienced resistance, most publicly from Buthelezi and former President Botha. Botha refused to appear before it, despite the clear evidence that he and at least some members of his Cabinet, such as Adriaan Vlok, were directly implicated in individual acts of violence, as well as the 'total strategy' policy as whole. Some of the most acute tensions and most difficult legacies lay not between whites and blacks, but within African communities—for example, between Inkatha and ANC supporters. Inkatha's reluctance to cooperate was not the only factor inhibiting investigation. The TRC did less to address these localized conflicts, difficult to research, and their legacy is likely to prove more testing in the longer term.

To a certain degree, the TRC's remit reflected the fact that settlement in 1994 was a set of compromises. The cost of stability may have been a less vigorous prosecution of perpetrators of political crimes. Yet the TRC's hearings were a significant achievement. It had to operate quickly, under considerable constraints, in a context where evidence was being destroyed and obstructionist tactics deployed. Some white South Africans, who were still in a state of denial, were forced to confront what was done in their name by the sheer accumulation of evidence and public exposure—to recognize that apartheid was not simply a failed political experiment. 'The black people in the audience are seldom upset' Krog noted, 'they have known the truth for years. The whites are often disconcerted: they didn't realize the magnitude of the outrage' (1999: 68). Advances were made in further uncovering South Africa's destabilization strategies in the region, which directly and indirectly were responsible for more deaths than those inside the country. At the same time, the Commission, especially in its investigation of the responsibility of business and professions under apartheid, did allow for the ambiguities and unevenness in culpability.

Ultimately its major purpose was to reveal the excesses of an illegitimate system and to give victims a chance to articulate their harrowing experiences in a formal process that, for all its incompleteness, was inevitably quicker and more wide-ranging than full court procedures. Victims could do so with counselling, and with the possibility of compensation—although the government's reluctance to accept the report has greatly complicated the latter process. Victims were invited to, but were not obliged to, extend forgiveness and in this sense exercise power over individuals who had terrorized them or their families. Efforts were made to establish the fate of those who had been killed. Truth is always elusive and reconciliation cannot be a complete process. It requires a certain amnesia and many individuals felt unsatisfied. But the TRC remains an inventive social experiment, drawing on Christian and African ideas and metaphors of confession, revelation, and forgiveness that were familiar to many people in the society. It was an attempt to restore moral order.

Countries do not change overnight. In many respects South African society, already moving away from the high apartheid years in the 1980s, continued to experience rapid transformation. There was no linear progression from an authoritarian racial state to a non-racial democracy, from a country balkanized on ethnic lines to one with a secure national culture. Many of the old fault lines remained and there was still an uneasiness about race.

New chasms of class and gender appeared within the black population: there was a restless edge to the new accumulators; a hardness to masculinity and attitudes to women that seemed to have intensified since political liberation.

By the end of the twentieth century, white domination and apartheid were no longer the key political issues facing South Africa, although it will take many years of active management to overcome the structural inequalities of the past. More important was the government's capacity to reorganize the state, sustain democracy, contain regional and social conflict, as well as address poverty, crime, corruption, and the attitudes of men. The South African state may have been a repressive burden to the majority of people over the second half of the twentieth century. By 2000, as political integration, economic growth, and redistribution became priorities, its defence and maintenance, in modified form, became critical.

The years of political transition loosened the hold of the state over the people. In some spheres, such as regional government, payment for services, and crime, the new state found it as difficult as the old to impose authority. Liberation clearly meant different things to different people. South African society has always been difficult to control and democratic processes will also depend on the people. In South Africa, they may require a preparedness by African voters to use the electoral system and support parties other than the ANC, should the latter drift from its current commitments. They may require popular insistence upon representative structures in the former homelands, where survival of chieftaincy may perpetuate patrimonial practices. Democratic society and civil order may require political constraint, and some acceptance of legality, of other people's rights, and of state authority, on the part of those without, as well as those with, direct access to power.

South African people achieved an extraordinary political and social transition at the end of the twentieth century. It necessitated violence, and imposed many costs, but, unlike Union, it was accomplished without a major war. A carefully considered constitution was put in place that guaranteed individual rights to all. Political violence, if not crime, diminished and a degree of stability was restored. Freedom of movement was entrenched and black people could exercise some of their rights as citizens, rather than subjects. Foreign relations were normalized. There were strong signals of a confident new national culture that remained open to global influences. The state was reunified and a legitimate democratic government in power.

# APPENDIX I.

# Notes on Tables and Figures

It is important to note *which* population figures are given in the following tables, as there is a great deal of variety in the numbers reported in different published sources on South Africa, including other general histories, especially for the years 1980 and 1991. Some anomalies and possible errors are also discussed.

The first simultaneous census counts that included all the people of South Africa were held in the separate colonies in 1904 (**Table 1**). There were census counts in the Boer Republics and the British colonies in 1890–1, but the former excluded the African population (**Table 2**). The figures from 1904 to 1970 include the whole area of South Africa; boundaries were stable over this period.

Between 1976 and 1981 four black homelands, Transkei, Bophuthatswana, Venda, and Ciskei, accepted independence from Pretoria. Most official statistics subsequently exclude their population from the total given for South Africa—for example, the official census figure for 1980 is about 25 million, and for 1991 about 31 million. As a result, the proportion of whites in the population does not decline so markedly after 1970 in official statistics. Figures in the tables published here *include* all the homelands, so that there is a reasonably consistent geographical base to the population statistics from 1904 to 1996. The numbers reported for the independent homelands in 1980 and 1991 vary significantly; totals for South Africa may not correlate exactly with other sources that also try to include them. The 1980 and 1991 census figures have been adjusted by the statistical services for undercounts —this is accepted practice. The upwardly revised figures, which are published as the official results, are reported here.

A post-apartheid census of the whole country was conducted in 1996. The increase of population over 1991 was smaller than

expected: projections made on the basis of that census had antici-
pated over 42 million people by 1996. Urban Foundation projections rose to 47 million by 2000 (see first edition, **Table 1**). Yet the
official count in 1996 was 40.5 million. Detailed commentary on
this anomaly is available on government web sites, including
www.statssa.gov.za/census, **Chapter 7**, 'Issues and Unexpected
Findings in Census '96, and Possible Explanations for them',
and www.statssa.gov.za/census9, 'Calculating the Undercount in
Census '96'. This attempts to explain the apparent slowing of
total population growth between 1991 and 1996 and also the
significant absolute fall in the white population.

It is likely that three factors contributed to these figures:
inflated figures in 1991 owing to overgenerous upward adjustments; an undercount in 1996, especially of the white population
and probably of the foreign African population; and a sharp
actual slowing of the rate of population increase between 1991 (or
earlier) and 1996.

Between 1970 and 1991 census figures did not represent full
counts in respect of the African population. Not only were some
homelands omitted, but neither homeland areas nor the informal
settlements were counted house by house. Some figures depended
on counting structures in aerial photographs and multiplying
them by an average family size. Upward adjustment was then
based on demographic projections. The likelihood is that these
techniques led to an overcount for the African population in 1980
and 1991.

For this reason also, it has been recognized that some of the
population estimates for displaced urban concentrations, such as
Botshabelo in the Free State, made in the 1980s and early 1990s—
and reported in the first edition of this book—were probably
overestimates. The numbers were also based partly on the counting of structures. I have adjusted the figures given in the text,
especially in **Chapter 8**, downwards, but it is still not possible to be
confident of the exact totals in these centres at the time.

The 1996 figures represent an attempt at an actual count of all
the people in South Africa. The upward adjustments were made
on the basis of a post-census random national survey that
recorded the percentage of people missed. This should have been

an accurate assessment. However, there is a possibility that whites were reluctant to give information to black enumerators or survey interviewers in 1996 and were undercounted. It is also possible that upward adjustments made for the white population were inflated in 1991 so that the figure of over 5 million was an exaggeration. There is evidence of significant white emigration after 1991 but this may not have been of the order of half a million people (**Table 2**).

It is also worth noting that 0.9 per cent of people in the 1996 count were unclassified racially. This figure was largest in the Western and Northern Cape, where there is a higher percentage of both white and coloured people and there may have been more uncertainty about racial status in these provinces.

With respect to the rates of increase in various population groups, detailed in **Table 2**, many commentators have noted that the 1921 census figures might represent an undercount because the rates of increase between 1911 and 1921 are lower than for any other period in the twentieth century. The 1921 census may not, however, have been wildly off the mark. It was taken only a few years after the influenza epidemic of 1918, probably the major single demographic check of the twentieth century. Influenza deaths have been estimated at roughly 5 per cent of the black population and 2.5 per cent of the white, totalling about 300,000 in all. If they are taken into account, then the 1921 census is likely to have been of the same accuracy as others, and population growth would have been relatively and remarkably stable for the whole of the first half of the twentieth century at around 2 per cent per annum.

The rapid rates of increase (**Table 2**) for the coloured and Indian population immediately after 1946 are difficult to explain. These figures are taken from *Union Statistics for Fifty Years*. In some other published series the 1946 figures have been revised upwards in order to produce a more even rate of increase. Figures for rates of growth in the African population are calculated on the basis of the official census figures. These rates differ in some official series, such as those published in the annual *Official Yearbook of the Republic of South Africa* in the 1980s. In the *Yearbooks* the rates of increase are calculated on new backward projections of growth and are given as faster in 1951 but slower in 1960. The series reported in this volume suggests that the rate of increase in the African population fell somewhat after 1936 for about twenty-five years. This may be a little difficult to explain, but it is possible, given the argument in **Chapter 8**, that the rapid urbanization of these years, before influx control policies were tightly enforced, contributed to slower African population growth.

Because of the uncertainties reported in respect of the 1991 and 1996 figures, calculations have not been made for the percentage increase of population in 1996 (**Table 2**). They would have shown very slow rates of increase that probably do not reflect the true position. However, there is strong evidence for a significant slowing of population growth after 1980 in the age structure (**Figure 3**). Age breakdowns are given by gender for 1980; they were not available by gender for 1996 so that the charts for this year include male and female.

The 1996 figures (**Figure 3b**) show clearly that, for all population groups, peak birth cohorts were in the 1980s; the subsequent decline was evident for the African population a little later than for others. Nevertheless, the figures available suggest that, while about 44 per cent of the African population was under 15 years of age in 1980, this had declined to 36 per cent in 1996. The slowing of growth coincides almost exactly with a major phase of urbanization in the country (**Chapter 8**). It is likely that it will continue and the post-apartheid government was prepared publicly to encourage and advocate population control: radio jingles advised people to limit their families 'for the sake of the children'. The figures probably do not yet reflect substantial mortality from HIV/AIDS, which is likely to hit people in their 20s, 30s, and 40s first. It is also difficult to predict the impact of immigration from other African countries that might contribute to a counter-trend.

The figures reported in **Table 3** on the urban population also require some comment, because the term 'urban' is difficult to define and becomes increasingly so as the twentieth century progressed. Figures up to 1970 are taken from official census returns. I have placed the figure for 1970 in brackets because it is doubtful. The census reported about 10.5 million in urban areas, which would imply only a 1 per cent increase of the urban population over the 1960 figure. While many Africans were restricted from access to the cities by influx control in these years, nevertheless the figure probably does not reflect the growth of the number of Africans settled in urban conditions within the homelands. The bulk of people within homelands, even when in large dense settlements, were counted as rural (**Chapter 8**).

I have not found an attempt to recalculate urban and rural figures for 1970. This exercise was, however, undertaken by demographers for the Urban Foundation for the years 1980 and 1990. It is the Urban Foundation (1990) figures that are reported here for 1980 and 1991, and they are probably closer to the position on the ground than the official census statistics. I do not know of a similar calculation for 1996 and have thus reported the official census figure of 54 per cent (**Table 3**), which is lower than that for 1991. The 1996 figure is almost certainly an underestimate and results from the way in which the categories of urban and rural were defined. It does not fully take into account all African people who live in dense and closer settlements within the former homelands, or in peri-urban informal settlements. Few people in these settlements have land; most derive their living from wages, welfare payments, or informal sector activities.

A similar problem applies to **Figure 1**, which tries to show the growth of population in the main metropolitan areas of South Africa. It should be noted that the figures are not based on the same geographic area in different years as the metropolitan areas expanded in size. In **Figure 1**, the 1980 and 1991 figures are also calculated from Urban Foundation material and therefore differ from published census figures. The summary of the 1996 census results available at the time of writing did not include separate figures for the metropolitan areas. Figures for 1996 have mostly been taken from the *Official South African Local Government Yearbook, 1997–1998* (Johannesburg, 1998). They are based on different areas from those used for 1991 and are not strictly compatible. The 1991 figures may be slight overestimates. The 1996 figure for the Witwatersrand is from the census for the whole of Gauteng province which was overwhelmingly urban, minus that of Pretoria metropolitan area.

# APPENDIX 2.

# Tables

TABLE 1. *Total population and percentage by race as designated in census*

| Year | Total population | Percentage by race | | | |
|------|------------------|-------|----------|-------|---------|
|      |                  | White | Coloured | Asian | African |
| 1904 | 5,174,827 | 21.6 | 8.6 | 2.4 | 67.4 |
| 1911 | 5,972,757 | 21.4 | 8.8 | 2.5 | 67.7 |
| 1921 | 6,927,403 | 21.9 | 7.9 | 2.4 | 67.8 |
| 1936 | 9,587,863 | 20.9 | 8.0 | 2.3 | 68.8 |
| 1946 | 11,415,925 | 20.8 | 8.1 | 2.5 | 68.6 |
| 1951 | 12,671,452 | 20.9 | 8.7 | 2.9 | 67.5 |
| 1960 | 16,002,797 | 19.3 | 9.4 | 3.0 | 68.3 |
| 1970 | 21,794,328 | 17.3 | 9.4 | 2.9 | 70.4 |
| 1980 | 28,979,035 | 15.7 | 9.1 | 2.8 | 72.4 |
| 1991 | 38,268,720 | 13.2 | 8.6 | 2.6 | 75.6 |
| 1996 | 40,583,573 | 10.9 | 8.9 | 2.6 | 76.7 |

*Note*: See Appendix 1 – Percentages in 1996 add up to 99.1 per cent as 0.9 per cent unclassified.

TABLE 2. *Average annual population increase over previous census year*

A

| Year | Total % increase | African population | % increase | White population | % increase |
|------|------------------|--------------------|-----------|------------------|-----------|
| 1891 | | | | 620,619 | |
| 1904 | | 3,490,291 | | 1,117,234 | 4.63 |
| 1911 | 2.07 | 4,018,878 | 2.03 | 1,276,319 | 1.93 |
| 1921 | 1.49 | 4,697,285 | 1.57 | 1,521,343 | 1.76 |
| 1936 | 2.19 | 6,595,597 | 2.29 | 2,003,334 | 1.86 |
| 1946 | 1.76 | 7,830,559 | 1.73 | 2,372,044 | 1.70 |
| 1951 | 2.10 | 8,560,083 | 1.79 | 2,641,689 | 2.18 |
| 1960 | 2.63 | 10,927,922 | 2.75 | 3,088,492 | 1.75 |
| 1970 | 3.14 | 15,057,952 | 3.26 | 3,752,528 | 1.97 |
| 1980 | 2.83 | 20,984,758 | 3.37 | 4,551,068 | 1.95 |
| 1991 | 2.62 | 28,889,600 | 2.96 | 5,068,110 | 0.98 |
| 1996 | | 31,127,631 | | 4,434,697 | |

B

| | Coloured population | % increase | Asian population | % increase |
|------|---------------------|-----------|------------------|-----------|
| 1904 | 444,991 | | 122,311 | |
| 1911 | 525,466 | 2.41 | 152,094 | 3.12 |
| 1921 | 545,181 | 0.37 | 163,594 | 0.86 |
| 1936 | 796,241 | 2.32 | 219,691 | 1.90 |
| 1946 | 928,062 | 1.89 | 285,260 | 2.65 |
| 1951 | 1,103,016 | 3.51 | 366,664 | 5.15 |
| 1960 | 1,509,258 | 3.55 | 477,125 | 2.97 |
| 1970 | 2,018,453 | 2.95 | 620,436 | 2.66 |
| 1980 | 2,624,007 | 2.66 | 819,202 | 2.82 |
| 1991 | 3,285,718 | 2.07 | 986,620 | 1.70 |
| 1996 | 3,600,446 | | 1,045,596 | |

*Note*: See Appendix 1.

The annual average figures for the period from 1911 to 1951 are taken from the government publication *Union Statistics for Fifty Years* (1960). I have computed the other figures on the basis of census returns and estimates for the independent homelands.

TABLE 3. *Percentage of population in urban areas*

| Year | All | (Total × 1,000) | White | Coloured | Asian | African |
|------|-----|-----------------|-------|----------|-------|---------|
| 1904 | 23 | 1,199 | 53 | 49 | 36 | 10 |
| 1911 | 25 | 1,477 | 52 | 50 | 53 | 13 |
| 1921 | 28 | 1,933 | 60 | 52 | 61 | 16 |
| 1936 | 32 | 3,106 | 68 | 57 | 71 | 21 |
| 1946 | 38 | 4,384 | 75 | 61 | 71 | 23 |
| 1951 | 43 | 5,398 | 78 | 65 | 78 | 27 |
| 1960 | 47 | 7,473 | 84 | 68 | 83 | 32 |
| 1970 | [48] | | 87 | 74 | 87 | [33] |
| 1980 | 54 | 15,704 | 88 | 75 | 91 | 49 |
| 1991 | 63 | 24,411 | 91 | 83 | 96 | 58 |
| 1996 | [54] | 21,781 | | | | |

*Notes*: See Appendix 1. Figures up to 1970 and for 1996 from the censuses. Figures for 1980 and 1991 from the Urban Foundation series, *Policies for a New Urban Future: Urban Debate 2010* (Johannesburg, n.d., 1990?).

TABLE 4. *Motor vehicles*

| Year | Cars | Commercial vehicles | Tractors | Minibuses |
|------|------|---------------------|----------|-----------|
| 1930 | 135,000 | 16,000 | 4,000 | |
| 1940 | 318,000 | 49,000 | 6,000[a] | |
| 1950 | 471,000 | 124,000 | 48,000 | |
| 1960 | 895,000 | 212,000 | 119,000 | |
| 1970 | 1,553,000 | 435,000 | 223,000 | 24,000 |
| 1980 | 2,333,000 | 871,000 | 302,000 | 73,000 |
| 1989 | 3,275,000 | 1,228,000 | 181,000 | 174,000 |

a Figure for 1937.

# APPENDIX 3.

# Figures

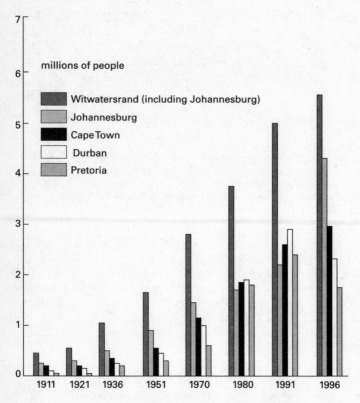

FIGURE 1. *Urban growth, main metropolitan areas, 1911–2000*

*Note*: The figures are not based on the same geographic area in different years, as the metropolitan areas expanded in size. See Appendix 1 for 1996.

*Source*: Census and Urban Foundation (1990).

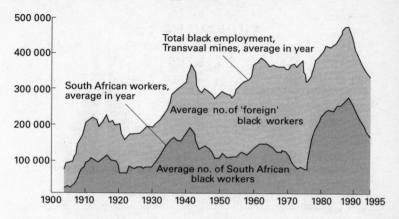

FIGURE 2. *African employment in Transvaal mines, 1900–1995*

*Sources*: Jeeves (1983); Crush *et al.* (1991); South African Institute of Race Relations, *South African Survey*.

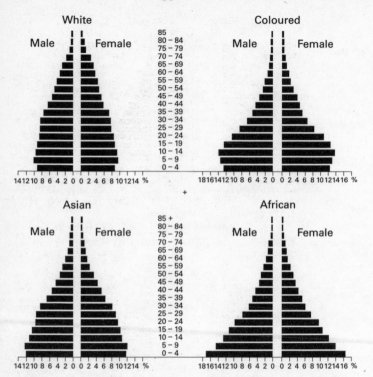

FIGURE 3a. *Age structure of population, 1980*

*Source: South Africa 1986. Official Yearbook of the Republic of South Africa* (Pretoria, 1986), 30, taken from J. L. Sadie, 'Labour Force 2000' in *RSA 2000* Human Sciences Research Council (Pretoria, 1981).

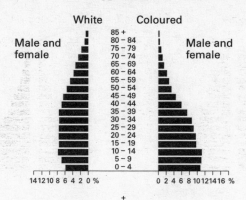

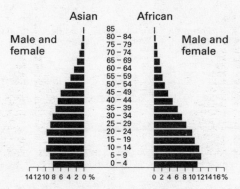

FIGURE 3b. *Age structure of population, 1996*

*Note*: Age breakdowns were not available by gender for 1996 so that the charts for this year include male and female.

*Source*: Census 1996; see Appendix 1, 351.

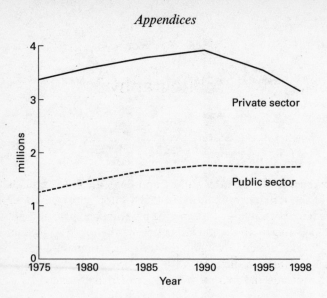

FIGURE 4. *Formal employment in public and private sectors*, 1975–1998
*Source*: South African Institute of Race Relations, *South African Survey*.

# Bibliography

References in the text, by author and date, are listed alphabetically in the References section. In this section short bibliographic notes have been retained to provide preliminary historiographical guidance and to give some indication of the material used in the text. Works are cited roughly in the order that they have been drawn on in each chapter. Only sources in English are listed. *JSAS* indicates the *Journal of Southern African Studies*.

## Introduction

In the large literature published on South Africa, there have been a number of single volume overviews. C. W. de Kiewiet's *History of South Africa, Social and Economic* (Oxford, 1941) is stylish and insightful though now dated. P. Maylam, *A History of the African People of South Africa* (London, 1986), is innovative but strongest on the period prior to 1900. T. R. H. Davenport, *South Africa: A Modern History* (4th edn., London, 1991), is a large comprehensive work, valuable on the details of political history. L. Thompson, *A History of South Africa* (2nd edn., New Haven, 1995), provides a fluent synthesis. N. Worden, *The Making of Modern South Africa: Conquest, Segregation and Apartheid* (Oxford, 1994), and R. Ross, *A Concise History of South Africa* (Cambridge, 1999), both cover the whole of South African history in short volumes: Worden summarizes radical approaches, while Ross ventures more into cultural history. J. Barber, *South Africa in the Twentieth Century* (Oxford, 1999), is a more orthodox political history with some reference to foreign policy. M. Mamdani, *Citizen and Subject: Contemporary Africa and the Legacy of Late Colonialism* (London, 1996), is a fresh examination of South

# Bibliography

Africa in an African context; see J. Iliffe, *Africans: The History of a Continent* (London, 1995), for background. Despite its alarming claim to be the 'Real Story', *The Reader's Digest History Illustrated History of South Africa* (1989) has excellent pictures and a well-informed text; see also S. Spies (ed.), *An Illustrated History of South Africa* (Cape Town, 1986), and N. Parsons, *A New History of Southern Africa* (London, 1982). For single-volume works on political economy that include a strong historical dimension, see B. Magubane, *The Political Economy of Race and Class in South Africa* (New York, 1979), and M. Lipton, *Capitalism and Apartheid, South Africa, 1910–1986* (London, 1985), who approach the issues from a Marxist and liberal position respectively. K. Smith, *The Changing Past* (Johannesburg, 1988), explores historiography. Three edited volumes provide a good introduction to radical historical work: S. Marks and A. Atmore (eds.), *Economy and Society in Pre-Industrial South Africa* (London, 1980); S. Marks and R. Rathbone (eds.), *Industrialisation and Social Change* (London, 1982); S. Marks and S. Trapido (eds.), *The Politics of Race, Class and Nationalism in Twentieth Century South Africa* (London, 1987). B. Bozzoli and P. Delius (eds.), *History from South Africa* (New York, 1990), vols. 46–7 of the *Radical History Review*, includes interesting historiographical surveys.

## Chapter 1

General overviews of African societies include Maylam, *A History of the African People*, and Wilson's chapters in M. Wilson and L. Thompson (eds.), *The Oxford History of South Africa* (2 vols.; Oxford, 1971). M. Hunter, *Reaction to Conquest* (London, 1936, 1964), remains valuable. Sansom's chapter in W. Hammond-Tooke (ed.), *The Bantu Speaking Peoples of South Africa* (London, 1974), is one of the few attempts to write comparatively about coastal and highveld kingdoms. J. Guy, 'Analysing Pre-Capitalist Societies', *JSAS* 14 (1987), on the Zulu, is the fullest analysis of the control of women. C. Bundy, *The Rise and Fall of the South African Peasantry* (London, 1979; Cape Town, 1989), remains a key text. W. Beinart, *The Political Economy of Pondoland 1860–1930* (Cambridge, 1982), explores change in an area less affected by colonization. J. Lewis, 'The Rise and Fall of the South African Peasantry: A Critique' *JSAS* 11 (1984), suggests that the peasantry's opportunities were very restricted. For Natal, see S. Marks, *Reluctant Rebellion* (London, 1970), and N. Etherington, *Preachers, Peasants and Politics in South East Africa, 1835–1880* (London, 1978). Detailed monographs on African societies in the nineteenth century include: J. Guy, *The Destruction of the Zulu Kingdom* (London, 1979); J. B. Peires, *The Dead Will Arise* (Johannesburg, 1989), on the Xhosa cattle-killing; P. Delius, *The Land Belongs to Us* (London, 1983), on the Pedi; P. Bonner, *Kings, Commoners and Concessionaires* (Cambridge, 1983), on the Swazi; K. Shillington, *The Colonisation of the Southern Tswana* (Johannesburg, 1985); K. Atkins, *The Moon is Dead! Give Us Our Money!: The Cultural Origins of an African Work Ethic in Natal, c.1843–1900* (London, 1994). For Plaatje, B. Willan, *Sol Plaatje: South African Nationalist 1876–1932* (London, 1984), and, for Jabavu, L. Ngcongco, 'John Tengo Jabavu 1859–1921', in C. Saunders (ed.), *Black Leaders in South African History* (London 1979). J. and J. Comaroff, *Of Revelation and Revolution* (2 vols.: Chicago, 1992, 1997), develop innovative approaches to cultural and economic interactions during colonization; for religious change, see also P. Landau, *The Realm of the Word: Language, Gender and Christianity in a Southern African Kingdom* (Oxford, 1995), and N. Etherington, 'Recent Trends in the Historiography of Christianity in Southern Africa', *JSAS* 22/2 (1996). Marks and Atmore (eds.), *Economy and Society*, and Marks and Rathbone (eds.), *Industrialisation and Social Change*, contain articles on incorporation, the origins of migrant labour from Mozambique (P. Harries), Cape liberalism (S. Trapido), and early mining (R. Turrell, J. van Helten, and P. Richardson). W. Beinart and C. Bundy, *Hidden Struggles in Rural South Africa* (London, 1987), examines peasant movements.

On early mining, see essays in P. Warwick (ed.), *The South African War* (London, 1981). R. Turrell, *Capital and Labour on the Kimberley Diamond Fields* (Cambridge, 1987), and W. Worger, *South Africa's City of Diamonds* (New Haven, 1987), are important books on diamonds. H. Wolpe, 'Capitalism and Cheap Labour Power in South Africa', *Economy and Society* 1 (1972), republished in W. Beinart and S. Dubow (eds.), *Segregation and Apartheid in Twentieth Century South Africa* (London, 1995), is a major statement of the cheap labour thesis; critiques are included in Delius, *The Land Belongs to Us*, Harries in Marks and Rathbone (eds.), *Industrialisation and Social Change*, Beinart, *Pondoland*, and P. Harries, 'Capital, State and Labour on the 19th Century Witwatersrand: A Reassessment', *South African Historical Journal*, 18 (1986). For the gold mines and migrancy, see A. Jeeves, *Migrant Labour in South Africa's Mining Economy, 1890–1920* (Kingston, Ont., 1985). B. Bozzoli, 'Marxism, Feminism and South African Studies', *JSAS* 9/2 (1983), examines the effects of rural patriarchy on migrancy.

## Chapter 2

For general introductions, see F. Wilson, 'Farming, 1866–1966', in Wilson and Thompson (eds.), *Oxford History*, vol. ii; W. Beinart, P. Delius, and S. Trapido (eds.), *Putting a Plough to the Ground: Accumulation and Dispossession in Rural South Africa 1850–1930* (Johannesburg, 1986), and A. Jeeves and J. Crush (eds.), *White Farms, Black Labour: The State and Agrarian Change in Southern Africa, 1910–1950* (Oxford, 1997). D. Denoon, *Settler Capitalism* (Oxford, 1983), is a useful comparative work. For the western Cape, see R. Elphick and H. Giliomee (eds.), *The Shaping of South Africa, 1652–1820* (Cape Town, 1989); T. R. H. Davenport, *The Afrikaner Bond, 1880–1911* (Cape Town, 1966); H. Giliomee, 'Western Cape Farmers and the Beginnings of Afrikaner Nationalism, 1870–1915', *JSAS* 14/1 (1987); W. James and M. Simons (eds), *The Angry Divide* (Cape Town, 1989); P. Scully, *The Bouquet of Freedom* (Cape Town 1990). On the midland Cape and sheep, Union of South Africa, *Final Report of the Drought Investigation Commission* (U.G. 49–1923), and W. Beinart, 'The Night of the Jackal: Sheep, Pastures and Predators in the Cape', *Past and Present*, 158 (1998). Olive Schreiner's novel, *The Story of an African Farm* (1883), is a very personal evocation of Cape rural society; see D. Opperman, *Groot Verseboek* (Cape Town, 1968), for the poem. M. Legassick, 'The Frontier Tradition in South African Historiography', in Marks and Atmore, *Economy and Society*, is the key critique of the frontier legacy. M. Morris, 'The Development of Capitalism in South African Agriculture', *Economy and Society*, 3 (1976), proposed the model of transition from rent to labour tenancy on the highveld; S. Trapido, 'Landlord and Tenant in a Colonial Economy', *JSAS* 5 (1978), explored tenancy more widely. P. Delius and S. Trapido, 'Inboekselings and Oorlams: The Creation of a Servile Class', *JSAS* 8 (1982), examines the pre-1880 Transvaal. T. Keegan, *Rural Transformations in Industrializing South Africa: The Southern Highveld to 1914* (London, 1987), is detailed on sharecropping and poor whites in the Free State. Solomon Plaatje, *Native Life in South Africa* (London, 1916), remains a key source on the effects of the Land Act but should be read alongside recent writing. W. M. Macmillan, *The Agrarian Problem* (Johannesburg, 1919), and *Complex South Africa* (London, 1930), are still fresh. Bundy, *Rise and Fall*, also includes material on the farmlands. J. Krikler, *Revolution from Above, Rebellion from Below: The Agrarian Transvaal at the Turn of the Century* (Oxford, 1993), examines the state and tenant reassertions in the Transvaal. In *Facing the Storm* (Cape Town, 1987), Keegan presents evocative oral testimony from black tenant families, as do T. Matsetela 'The Life Story of Nkgono Mma-Pooe' in Marks and Rathbone, *Industrialisation and Social Change*, and M. Nkadimeng and G. Relly, 'Kas Maine, the Story of a Black South African Agriculturalist' in B. Bozzoli (ed.), *Town and Countryside in the Transvaal* (Johannesburg, 1983). Maine's life is written in loving detail in C. van Onselen, *The Seed is Mine: The Life of Kas Maine, a South African Sharecropper 1894–1985* (Oxford, 1997); this and his, 'Race and Class in the South African Countryside: Cultural Osmosis and Social Relations in the Sharecropping Economy of the South-Western Transvaal, 1900–1950', *American Historical Review*, 95/1 (1990), are a reminder of the complexity of racial interactions on the farms. H. Bradford, *A Taste of Freedom* (New Haven, 1987), is especially good on the 1920s. C. Murray, *Black Mountain* (Edinburgh, 1992), explores long-term change in the eastern Free State. Railways and transport have been neglected: see general sources and L. Thompson, *The Unification of South Africa* (Oxford, 1960). J. MacKenzie, *The Empire of Nature* (Manchester, 1988), is instructive on hunting; J. Carruthers, *The Kruger National Park: A Social and Political History* (Pietermaritzburg, 1995), and 'Dissecting the Myth: Paul Kruger and the Kruger National Park', *JSAS* 20/2 (1994), on conservation. See also W. Beinart and P. Coates, *Environment and History: The Taming of Nature in the USA and South Africa* (London, 1995).

## Chapter 3

Overviews on the densely covered period of the South African War and reconstruction include C. van Onselen, *Studies in the Social and Economic History of the Witwatersrand, 1886–1914* (2 vols.; London, 1982), and S. Marks and S. Trapido, 'Lord Milner and the South African State', *History Workshop* 8 (1979); both emphasize the centrality of gold and contest D. Denoon, *The Grand Illusion* (Oxford, 1973), which saw less success in reconstruction because of the failure of anglicization. P. Warwick (ed.), *The South African War* (London, 1980), has useful overview articles. On Merriman, see P. Lewsen, *John X. Merriman: Paradoxical South African Statesman* (London, 1982), and *Selections from the Correspondence of J. X. Merriman* (van Riebeeck Society Series, vols. xli and xliv; Cape Town, 1960–9). R. Rotberg, *Cecil Rhodes* (London, 1988), is the largest of many biographies; M. Tamarkin, *Cecil Rhodes and the Cape Afrikaners* (London, 1996), explains his Cape constituency. I. Smith, *The Origins of the South African War 1899–1902* (London, 1996), reasserts a political explanation of the war, building on A. Porter, *The Origins of the South African War* (Manchester, 1980), and Porter, 'The South African War (1899–1902): Context and Motive Reconsidered', *Journal of African History (JAH)* 31 (1990). W. Nasson, *The South African War 1899–1902* (London, 1999), summarizes black involvement, while Greg Cuthbertson and Alan Jeeves (eds.), 'South African War 1899–1902: Centennial Perspectives', Special Issue of *South African Historical Journal*, 41 (1999), reflects new approaches. On mining and labour, see **Chapter 1** and L. Callinicos, *Gold and Workers* (Johannesburg, 1980), and *Working Life, 1886–1940* (Johannesburg, 1987); F. Johnstone, *Class Race and Gold* (London, 1976), and N. Levy, *The Foundations of the*

*South African Cheap Labour System* (London, 1982), provide Marxist interpretations. See Thompson, *Unification*, on constitutional history, S. Dubow, 'Colonial Nationalism, the Milner Kindergarten and the Rise of "South Africanism", 1902–1910', *History Workshop Journal*, 43 (1997), on imperial ideas, and Doreen Greig, *Herbert Baker in South Africa* (Cape Town, 1970), for architecture. Key government documents quoted include Great Britain, *Report of the Transvaal Labour Commission*, Cd. 1897 (London, 1904), and *Report of the South African Native Affairs Commission* (London, 1905). John Buchan, *Prester John* (1910), remains revealing; quotes are from the 1983 Penguin edition. M. Legassick, 'British Hegemony and the Origins of Segregation in South Africa, 1901–14', in Beinart and Dubow (eds.), *Segregation and Apartheid in Twentieth-Century South Africa*, first written in 1972, remains innovative on this key topic, as does M. Swanson, 'The Sanitation Syndrome: Bubonic Plague and Urban Native Policy in the Cape Colony, 1900–1909', in the same volume—originally *JAH*, 18 (1977). For a comparison: J. Cell, *The Highest Stage of White Supremacy* (New York, 1982). F. Reitz, *A Century of Wrong* (1900), partly written by Smuts, for whom see W. K. Hancock, *Smuts*, i. *The Sanguine Years* (Cambridge, 1962). Older books on Afrikaner history are caught up in the ideology of Afrikanerdom. W. de Klerk, *The Puritans in Africa* (Harmondsworth, 1976), should be read alongside A. du Toit, 'No Chosen People', *American Historical Review*, 88/4 (1983), and also L. Thompson, *Political Mythology of Apartheid* (New Haven, 1985). L. Leipoldt, *Bushveld Doctor* (London 1937), is sensitive to popular Afrikaner ideas; see H. Giliomee and H. Adam, *Ethnic Power Mobilized* (New Haven, 1979), and I. Hexham, *The Ironies of Apartheid* (New York, 1981), on their organization. R. Morrell (ed.), *White but Poor* (Pretoria, 1992), and S. Swart, '"A Boer and his Gun and his Wife are Three Things Always Together": Republican Masculinity and the 1914 Rebellion', *JSAS* 24/4 (1998), for new perspectives on poor whites and the rebellion respectively. D. Yudelman, *The Emergence of Modern South Africa* (Cape Town, 1983), remains a key study of white workers, the mines, and the state; see P. Richardson and G. Burke, 'The Profits of Death: A Comparative Study of Miners

## Bibliography

Pthisis', *JSAS* 4 (1978), and J. Krikler, 'The Commandos: The Army of White Labour in South Africa', *Past and Present*, 163 (1999).

### Chapter 4

On Plaatje, see Willan, *Sol Plaatje*, and Plaatje, *Native Life in South Africa*. On the African elite, see A. Odendaal, *Vukani Bantu: The Beginnings of Black Protest Politics in South Africa to 1912* (Cape Town 1981). S. Trapido, 'African Divisional Politics in the Cape Colony, 1884–1910', *JAH* 9/1 (1968), discusses voting politics. D. D. T. Jabavu, *The Black Problem* (Lovedale, 1920), gives a sense of eastern Cape preoccupations and Tuskegee influences. M. Swan, *Gandhi: The South African Experience* (Johannesburg, 1983), is authoritative but critical; for Gandhi's language, see J. H. Stone II, 'M. K. Gandhi: Some Experiments with Truth', *JSAS* 16 (1990). S. Marks, *Reluctant Rebellion* (London, 1970), remains the major analysis of the 1906 revolt in Natal. See also her 'Natal, the Zulu Royal Family and the Ideology of Segregation', *JSAS* 4 (1978); 'Class, Ideology and the Bambatha Rebellion', in D. Crummey (ed.), *Banditry, Rebellion and Social Protest in Africa* (London, 1986), and *The Ambiguities of Dependence in South Africa* (Johannesburg, 1986). N. Cope, *To Bind the Nation: Solomon ka Dinuzulu and Zulu Nationalism* (Pietermaritzburg, 1993), provides more detailed analysis; and, on the symbolism surrounding Zulu royals, see Carolyn Hamilton, *Terrific Majesty* (Cambridge, Mass., 1998). For ethnicity, see L. Vail (ed.), *The Creation of Tribalism* (London, 1990), and P. Delius, 'The Ndzundza Ndebele', in P. Bonner *et al.* (eds.), *Holding their Ground* (Johannesburg, 1990). Beinart, *Pondoland*, looks at chieftaincy. Bradford, *A Taste of Freedom*, concentrates on the rural ICU; see also Beinart and Bundy, *Hidden Struggles*, on East London. J. Wells, 'Why Women Rebel', *JSAS* 10 (1983), and 'The Day the Town Stood Still', in Bozzoli, *Town and Countryside*, explore women's movements, as do articles by Beinart and Bradford in B. Bozzoli (ed.), *Class Community and Conflict* (Johannesburg, 1987). C. Walker, *Women and Resistance in South Africa* (London, 1982), and (ed.), *Women and Gender in Southern Africa* (London, 1991), provide an overview. There are many outlines of nationalist protest, which have helped shape both popular and academic perceptions: H. and R. Simons, *Class and Colour in South Africa, 1850–1950* (Harmondsworth, 1969), is a classic socialist analysis and P. Walshe, *The Rise of African Nationalism in South Africa* (London, 1970), a liberal discussion; M. Benson, *South Africa: The Struggle for a Birthright* (Harmondsworth, 1966), and F. Meli, *South Africa Belongs to Us* (Harare, 1988), are written from within the movement at different periods. B. Sundkler, *Bantu Prophets in South Africa* (London, 1948), is still valuable on African churches; on the Israelites, see R. Edgar, *Because they Chose the Plan of God* (Johannesburg, 1988), and, for a successor movement, see R. Edgar and H. Sapire, *African Apocalypse* (Johannesburg, 1999). On gangs and male associations: van Onselen, *Social and Economic History of the Witwatersrand*, especially 'The Regiment of the Hills' and the 'Witches of Suburbia'; T. D. Moodie, 'Migrancy and Male Sexuality on the South African Gold Mines', *JSAS* 14/2 (1988), 'Collective Violence on the South African Gold Mines', *JSAS* 18/3 (1992), and *Going for Gold: Men, Mines and Migration* (Berkeley and Los Angeles, 1994); K. Breckenridge, 'The Allure of Violence: Men, Race and Masculinity on the South African Goldmines, 1900–1950', *JSAS* 24/4 (1998); W. Beinart, 'Political and Collective Violence in Southern African Historiography', *JSAS* 18/3 (1992); P. la Hausse, 'The Cows of Nongoloza: Youth, Crime and Amalaita gangs in Durban, 1900–1936', *JSAS* 16/1 (1990), and 'The Message of the Warriors', in Bonner *et al.*, *Holding their Ground*.

## Chapter 5

T. D. Moodie, *The Rise of Afrikanerdom* (Berkeley and Los Angeles, 1976), D. O'Meara, *Volkskapitalisme* (Cambridge, 1983), Giliomee and Adam, *Ethnic Power Mobilized*, and P. Furlong, *Between Crown and Swastika* (Middletown, Conn. 1991), are key texts on Afrikaners. I. Hofmeyr, 'Building a Nation from Words: Afrikaans Language, Literature and Ethnic Identity, 1902–1924', in Marks and Trapido (eds.), *The Politics of Race, Class and Nationalism*, moves in new directions on cultural history, as does

# Bibliography

Christoph Marx, 'The *Ossewabrandwag* as a Mass Movement, 1939–1941', *JSAS* 20/2 (1994). Hancock, *Smuts*, ii. *The Fields of Force* (Cambridge, 1968), remains the best biography. M. Lacey, *Working for Boroko* (Johannesburg, 1980), offers a materialist interpretation of segregation; P. Rich, *White Power and the Liberal Conscience: Racial Segregation and South African Liberalism, 1921–1960* (London, 1984), discusses the liberal contribution; and S. Dubow, *Racial Segregation and the Origins of Apartheid in South Africa, 1919–1936* (London, 1989), and *Scientific Racism in Modern South Africa* (Cambridge, 1995), re-examines the variety of ideologies behind segregation. See Walker (ed.), *Women and Gender* for the vote, including the essay by E. Brink on the *volksmoeder*. Yudelman, *Emergence of Modern South Africa*, remains valuable on the state and the mines, as does D. Innes, *Anglo-American and the Rise of Modern South Africa* (Johannesburg, 1984). Union of South Africa, *Report of the Native Economic Commission* (U.G. 22–1932), is a central government document of the inter-war years, and Union of South Africa, *Report of the Native Laws Commission* (U.G. 28–1948), is important for understanding the Smuts government. On industry and unionism: E. Webster, *Cast in a Racial Mould: Labour Process and Trade Unionism in the Foundries* (Johannesburg, 1985); J. Lewis, *Industrialisation and Trade Union Organisation in South Africa, 1924–1955* (Cambridge, 1984); Callinicos, *Working Life*, and I. Berger, *Threads of Solidarity: Women in South African Industry, 1900–1980* (Bloomington, Ind., 1992). B. Hirson, *Yours for the Union: Class and Community Struggles in South Africa, 1930–1947* (London, 1990), discusses a wide range of popular struggles; E. Hellmann, *Rooiyard: A Sociological Survey of an Urban Native Slum Yard* (Cape Town, 1948), remains vivid on the slums; E. Koch, 'Without Visible Means of Subsistence', in Bozzoli (ed.), *Town and Countryside*, provides further background. Novels and autobiographies include M. Dikobe, *The Marabi Dance* (London, 1973); P. Abrahams, *Mine Boy* (London, 1946), and *Tell Freedom* (London, 1954); P. Lanham and A. Mopeli-Paulus, *Blanket Boy's Moon* (London, 1953); and A. Paton, *Cry, The Beloved Country* (London, 1948). On the mineworkers: T. D. Moodie, 'The Moral Economy of the Black Miners' Strike of 1946', *JSAS* 13 (1986), and *Going for Gold*; D. O'Meara, 'The 1946 African Mineworkers' Strike and the Political Economy of South Africa', *Journal of Commonwealth and Comparative Politics*, 13 (1975). Compare D. Hemson, 'Dock Workers, Labour Circulation and Class Struggles in Durban, 1940–59', *JSAS* 4 (1977). On squatters, see A. Stadler, 'Birds in a Cornfield: Squatter Movements in Johannesburg, 1944–1947', *JSAS* 6 (1979), and P. Bonner in Bozzoli and Delius (eds.), *History from South Africa*, and P. Bonner and L. Segal, *Soweto: A History* (Cape Town, 1998). See also Bonner, 'Family, Crime and Political Consciousness on the East Rand', *JSAS* 14 (1988). On Betterment, see W. Beinart, 'Soil Erosion, Conservationism and Ideas about Development', *JSAS* 11 (1984), and for major studies of the rural areas and resistance, see P. Delius, *A Lion amongst the Cattle: Reconstruction and Resistance in the Northern Transvaal* (Johannesburg, 1996), and Anne Mager, *Gender and the Making of a South African Bantustan: A Social History of the Ciskei, 1945–1959* (Oxford, 1999). T. Lodge, *Black Politics in South Africa since 1945* (London, 1983), remains the fullest discussion of the ANC in this period. Voting figures are from K. Heard, *General Elections in South Africa 1943–70* (London, 1974).

## Chapter 6

The early apartheid period has been very thoroughly covered in critical academic and popular writing. See references on Afrikaner history for **Chapter 5**; D. O'Meara, *Forty Lost Years: The Apartheid State and the Politics of the National Party, 1948–1994* (Johannesburg, 1996), is the most comprehensive new study. Older books such as G. Carter, *The Politics of Inequality: South Africa since 1948* (London, 1958), and W. Vatcher, *White Laager* (London, 1965), have considerable interest as responses by concerned foreigners. B. Bunting, *The Rise of the South African Reich* (Harmondsworth, 1963), and A. Hepple, *Verwoerd* (Harmondsworth, 1967), are powerful statements by opposition exiles. Radical critiques by Wolpe, 'Capitalism and Cheap Labour Power', and F. Johnstone, 'White Prosperity and White Supremacy in South Africa Today', *African Affairs* 69 (1970), remain important. H. Adam, *Modernizing Racial Domination* (Berkeley and Los Angeles, 1971), was amongst the first to argue for the flexibility of apartheid. D. Hindson, *Pass Controls and the Urban African Proletariat* (Johannesburg, 1987), challenged the view linking apartheid largely to the extension of migrancy; D. Posel, *The Making of Apartheid 1948–1961* (Oxford, 1991), develops further the arguments about differential impacts of influx control and the Nationalist Party's ideologies. I. Goldin, *Making Race: The Politics and Economics of Coloured Identity in South Africa* (Harlow, 1987), analyses NP attempts to reshape the labour market of the western Cape; see also his essay in Marks and Trapido, *The Politics of Race*. J. Western, *Outcast Cape Town* (London, 1981), is especially interesting on the effects of the Group Areas Act, and Alan Mabin, 'Comprehensive Segregation: The Origins of the Group Areas Act and its Planning Apparatuses', *JSAS* 18/2 (1992), on its origins. G. Pirie, 'Rolling Segregation into Apartheid', paper to the 1990 History Workshop conference, discusses race on the railways. J. Crush, A. Jeeves, and D. Yudelman, *South Africa's Labour Empire: A History of Black Migrancy to the Gold Mines* (David Philip, 1991), is the best overview on this question. P. Bonner, P. Delius, and D. Posel (eds.), *Apartheid's Genesis, 1935–1962* (Johannesburg, 1993), is valuable on a range of state policies: it includes J. Hyslop, '"A Destruction Coming In": Bantu Education as Response to Social Crisis'. See also Hyslop, 'State Education Policy and the Social Reproduction of the Urban African Working Class', *JSAS* 14/3 (1988), and P. Kallaway, *Apartheid and Education: The Education of Black South Africans* (Johannesburg, 1984). Union of South Africa, *Summary Report of the Commission for the Socio-Economic Development of the Bantu Areas within the Union of South Africa* (U.G. 61–1955; Tomlinson Commission; 1956), is the key government document on the homelands. Lodge, *Black Politics*, for the ANC. When I wrote the first edition of this book, there were no adequate biographies of Mandela and it contained minor inaccuracies. This version is guided by N. Mandela, *Long Walk to Freedom* (London, 1995), indispensable on his life, and contextualized by A. Sampson, *Mandela: The Authorised Biography* (London, 1999); Mandela's early speeches were published in *No Easy Walk to*

*Freedom* (London, 1965). Sampson, *Drum: A Venture into the New Africa* (London, 1956), evokes his period editing the magazine, and T. Huddleston, *Naught for your Comfort* (London, 1956), his stay in Sophiatown. Growing academic fascination with this period of urban African culture is evident in P. Gready, 'The Sophiatown Writers of the Fifties: The Unreal Reality of their World', *JSAS* 16/1 (1990), U. Hannerz, 'Sophiatown: The View from Afar', *JSAS* 20/2 (1994), M. Fenwick, ' "Tough Guy, eh?": The Gangster-figure in *Drum*', *JSAS* 22/4 (1996), and R. Nixon, *Homelands, Harlem and Hollywood* (London, 1994). J. Guy and Motlatsi Thabane, 'The Ma-Rashea: A Participant's Perspective', in B. Bozzoli (ed.), *Class, Community and Conflict: South African Perspectives* (Johannesurg, 1987), and 'Technology, Ethnicity and Ideology: Basotho Miners and Shaft Sinking on the South African Gold Mines', *JSAS* 14/2 (1988), provide an insight into the life of migrant workers. P. Bonner and R. Lambert, 'Batons and Bare Heads: The Strike at Amato Textiles, February 1958', in Marks and Trapido (eds.), *The Politics of Race*, is one of the few examinations of SACTU in action; see Beinart in this volume for Pondoland. G. Mbeki, *South Africa: The Peasants' Revolt* (Harmondsworth, 1964), is an early analysis, now dated, of rural rebellions. P. Delius, 'Sebatakgomo: Migrant Organization, the ANC and the Sekhukhuneland Revolt', *JSAS* 15/4 (1989), and Delius, *A Lion Amongst the Cattle*, are valuable on links between the ANC and rural movements.

## Chapter 7

For articles on apartheid and growth, see Johnstone, 'White Prosperity', and others listed for **Chapter 6**. Lipton, *Capitalism and Apartheid*, is a thorough restatement of the liberal position that is in many ways more materialist than 'radical' writing. J. Saul and S. Gelb, *The Crisis in South Africa* (London, 1986), moved the radical argument onwards; see also S. Gelb (ed.), *South Africa's Economic Crisis* (Cape Town, 1991), for survey articles covering manufacturing, the economic crisis, and reform era. Debates are reconsidered in N. Nattrass, 'Controversies about Capitalism and Apartheid in South Africa: An Economic Perspective', *JSAS* 17/4

(1991), and T. Moll, 'Did the Apartheid Economy "Fail"?', *JSAS* 17/2 (1991). Amongst many overview books, J. Nattrass, *The South African Economy* (Cape Town, 1988), is useful on this period; Innes, *Anglo-American*, is a critical analysis of this key corporation. See R. Christie, *Electricity, Industry and Class in South Africa* (London, 1984), for uranium. The annual *Official Yearbooks* published by the South African Government are a valuable source of statistics: figures on cars are from here and H. T. Andrews *et al.* (eds.), *South Africa in the Sixties* (Cape Town, 1962). The social history of white society is covered in popular rather than academic works. A. Drury, *'A Very Strange Society': A Journey to the Heart of South Africa* (London, 1968), is sympathetic but perceptive. P. Joyce (ed.), *Reader's Digest: South Africa's Yesterdays* (Cape Town, 1981), is better on the earlier decades of the twentieth century but well illustrated and suggestive. Jeremy Taylor's song was taken from the record *Wait a Minim*. S. Schama, *The Embarrassment of Riches* (Berkeley and Los Angeles, 1988), discusses Dutch tobacco consumption. J. Cock, *Maids and Madams* (Johannesburg, 1980), was a path-breaking feminist analysis of domestic service. R. Archer and R. Bouillon, *The South African Game* (London, 1979), is interesting on rugby, now supplemented by A. Grundlingh, A. Odendaal, and B. Spies, *Beyond the Tryline* (Johannesburg, 1995), and D. Black and J. Nauright, *Rugby and the South African Nation* (Manchester, 1998). S. Burman and M. Huvers, 'Church versus State: Divorce Legislation and Divided South Africa', *JSAS* 12/1 (1985), analyses changing divorce laws. Adam, *Modernizing Racial Domination*, and Giliomee and Adam, *Ethnic Power Mobilized*, analyse Afrikaner social and economic mobility. H. Suzman, *In No Uncertain Terms* (London, 1994), is a memoir of her political career. S. Marks, *Divided Sisterhood: Race, Class and Gender in the South African Nursing Profession* (London, 1994), explores a major profession for women, and S. Gordon, *A Talent for Tomorrow: Life Stories of South African Servants* (Johannesburg, 1985), records domestics. Studies of African social change in the 1950s and 1960s include: L. Kuper, *An African Bourgeoisie* (New Haven, 1965), on Durban; M. Brandel-Syrier, *Reeftown Elite* (London, 1971); M. Wilson and A. Mafeje, *Langa* (Cape Town, 1963), on

Cape Town; A. Vilakazi, *Zulu Transformations* (Pietermaritzburg, 1965), on a Natal rural community; P. and I. Mayer, *Townsmen or Tribesmen* (1960; 2nd edn. Cape Town, 1971), and B. Pauw, *The Second Generation* (Cape Town, 1973), on East London. Material on Sethuntsa is from P. Becker, *Trails and Tribes in Southern Africa* (London, 1975). On churches: M. West, *Bishops and Prophets in a Black City* (Cape Town, 1979); J. Comaroff, *Body of Power, Spirit of Resistance* (Chicago, 1985). M. Nyagumbo, *Forward with the People* (London, 1980) mentions ballroom dancing. On Soweto gangs, football and styles: C. Glaser, 'Swines, Hazels and the Dirty Dozen: Masculinity, Territoriality and the Youth Gangs of Soweto, 1960–1976', *JSAS* 24/4 (1998); P. Bonner and L. Segal, *Soweto: A History* (Johannesburg, 1998). On liquor: P. la Hausse, *Brewers, Beerhalls and Boycotts: A History of Liquor in South Africa* (Johannesburg, 1988); J. Crush and C. Ambler (eds.), *Liquor and Labour in Southern Africa* (Athens, Oh., 1992); A. Mager, 'The First Decade of "European Beer" in Apartheid South Africa: The State, the Brewers and the Drinking Public, 1962–1972', *JAH* 40 (1999). *Mbaqanga* lyrics are taken from the translation on the record *Mahlathini: The Lion of Soweto*.

## Chapter 8

In addition to sources on apartheid policy, urbanization, and influx control referred to in **Chapters 6 and 7**, C. Simkins, *Four Essays on the Past, Present and Possible Future of the Distribution of the Black Population of South Africa* (Cape Town, 1983), is much quoted on population trends; B. Brown, 'Facing the "Black Peril": The Politics of Population Control in South Africa', *JSAS* 13/2 (1987), deals with some neglected elements of demography. Population figures have also been taken from the censuses and the Urban Foundation series, *Policies for a New Urban Future: Urban Debate 2010* (Johannesburg, 1990). The most striking early account of the population removals was C. Desmond, *The Discarded People: An Account of African Resettlement in South Africa* (Harmondsworth, 1971). A great deal of research was systematized in the five-volume Surplus People Report, *Forced Removals in South Africa* (Cape Town, 1983); this was summarized and given context in L. Platzky and C. Walker, *The Surplus People* (Johannesburg, 1985). For the Free State farms, see Murray, *Black Mountain*, which concludes with a chapter on Botshabelo as a key example of displaced urbanization. See also his 'Displaced Urbanisation: South Africa's Rural Slums', in J. Lonsdale (ed.), *South Africa in Question* (Cambridge, 1988), and with W. Beinart, 'Agrarian Change, Population Movements and Land Reform in the Free State' (Land and Agriculture Policy Centre, working paper 51; Johannesburg, 1996). S. Greenberg, *Race and State in Capitalist Development: South Africa in Comparative Perspective* (New Haven, 1981), makes a comparative analysis of agriculture. For farmworkers, see F. Wilson, A. Kooy, and D. Hendrie (eds.), *Farm Labour in South Africa* (Cape Town, 1977); for Bethal, see Sampson, *Drum*, M. Murray, 'Factories in the Fields: Capitalist Farming in the Bethal District, c.1910–1950', in Jeeves and Crush, *White Farms*, and H. Bradford, 'Getting Away with Murder: "Mealie Kings", the State and Foreigners in the Eastern Transvaal, c. 1918–1950' in Bonner *et al.* (eds.), *Apartheid's Genesis*. M. de Klerk, 'Seasons that Will Never Return: The Impact of Farm Mechanisation on Employment, Incomes and Population Distribution in the Western Transvaal', *JSAS* 11/1 (1984), is important on maize farms. More generally, Lipton, *Capitalism and Apartheid*, includes an strong chapter on agriculture. See M. de Klerk (ed.), *A Harvest of Discontent: The Land Question in South Africa* (Cape Town, 1991), for early debates on land reform, and A. du Toit, 'The Micro-Politics of Paternalism: The Discourses of Management and Resistance on South African Fruit and Wine Farms', *JSAS* 19/2 (1993). J. Lelyveld, *Move your Shadow: South Africa, Black and White* (New York, 1985), is a searing journalistic account of South Africa in the 1980s with reportage from the homelands. A great deal of new socio-economic material was presented to the Carnegie Conference on Poverty in South Africa (Cape Town 1985), summarized in F. Wilson and M. Ramphele, *Uprooting Poverty* (Cape Town, 1989); see R. Packard, *White Plague, Black Labour* (Pietermaritzburg, 1989) for tuberculosis. See P. McAllister, 'Resistance to "Betterment" in the Transkei', *JSAS* 15/2 (1989), and C. de Wet, *Moving Together, Drifting Apart* (Johannesburg, 1995), for the ecological and social effects of rural planning; for Thornhill, F. Kruger, 'The Legacy of "Homeland" Policy', in M. Ramphele and C. McDowell (eds.), *Restoring the Land* (London, 1991). R. Southall, *South Africa's Transkei: The Political Economy of an 'Independent' Bantustan* (London, 1982), and B. Streek and R. Wicksteed, *Render unto Kaiser: A Transkei Dossier* (Johannesburg, 1981), are interesting overviews on the Transkei written at this time; Delius, *A Lion amongst the Cattle*, discusses politics in Lebowa. On industrial decentralization, see William Cobbett *et al.* 'South Africa's Regional Political Economy: A Critical Analysis of Reform Strategy in the 1980s', *South African Review*, 3 (Johannesburg, 1986), and T. Bell, 'The Role of Regional Policy in South Africa', *JSAS* 12/2 (1986).

## Chapter 9

Lodge, *Black Politics*, S. Ellis and T. Sechaba, *Comrades against Apartheid* (London, 1992), Stephen M. Davis, *Apartheid's Rebels: Inside South Africa's Hidden War* (New Haven, 1987), and H. Barrell, 'The Turn to the Masses: The African National Congress' Strategic Review of 1978–79', *JSAS* 18/1 (1992), give a sense of the ANC and Communist Pary in exile. Mandela, *Long Walk to Freedom*, Govan Mbeki, *Learning from Robben Island* (Cape Town, 1991), and M. Dingake, *My Fight against Apartheid* (London, 1987), discuss experiences and political training on Robben Island; for analysis of published personal prison testimony, see P. Gready, 'Autobiography and the "Power of Writing": Political Prison Writing in the Apartheid Era', *JSAS* 19/3 (1993). See S. Biko, *I Write What I Like* (London, 1978), for a key black consciousness text; G. Gerhardt, *Black Power in South Africa* (Berkeley and Los Angeles, 1978), and S. Nolutshungu, *Changing South Africa* (Manchester, 1982), remain important as early analyses. M. Mothlabi, *The Theory and Practice of Black Resistance to Apartheid* (Johanesburg, 1984), reflects the language of the struggle before the insurrection of the mid-1980s. M. Ramphele, *Across Boundaries: The Journey of a South Woman Leader* (New York, 1996), gives an important insight into black consciousness networks and a sometimes critical view of Biko. See Z. K. Matthews, *Freedom for My People* (Cape Town, 1983) on Fort Hare.

# Bibliography

S. Johnson (ed.), *South Africa: No Turning Back* (London, 1988), and R. Cohen, Y. Muthien, and A. Zegeye (eds.), *Repression and Resistance: Insider Accounts of Apartheid* (Oxford, 1990), include useful overview articles on popular struggles. Mbulelo Mzamane's novel, *The Children of Soweto* (Johannesburg, 1982), best captures the mood of 1976; see also Sipho Sepamla, *Ride on the Whirlwind* (Johannesburg, 1981). N. Diseko, 'The Origins and Development of the South African Student's Movement (SASM): 1968–1976', *JSAS* 18/1 (1992,) and her article in Cohen *et al.*, as well as C. Glaser, ' "We Must Infiltrate the *Tsotsis*": School Politics and Youth Gangs in Soweto, 1968–1976', *JSAS* 24/2 (1998), analyse school politics. For trade unions, the *South African Labour Bulletin*, launched in 1974, is an invaluable source; J. Maree (ed.), *The Independent Trade Unions 1974–1984* (Johannesburg, 1987), includes extracts from it; see also S. Friedman, *Building Tomorrow Today: African Workers in the Trade Unions, 1970–1985* (Johannesburg, 1987). Material on Durban strikes is from Institute of Industrial Education, *The Durban Strikes 1973* (Durban, 1974). M. Murray, *South Africa: Time of Agony, Time of Destiny* (New York, 1987), is interesting on the political links of unions; see also A. W. Marx, *Lessons of Struggle: South African Internal Opposition, 1960–1990* (Oxford, 1991). G. Mare and G. Hamilton, *An Appetite for Power: Buthelezi's Inkatha and South Africa* (Johannesburg, 1987), remains the most informative on this topic. R. Davies, D. O'Meara, and S. Dlamini, *The Struggle for South Africa: A Reference Guide to Movements, Organizations and Institutions* (London, 1984), is a valuable reference work. For material on reform, see **Chapters 7 and 8** as well as S. Greenberg, *Legitimating the Illegitimate: State, Markets, and Resistance in South Africa* (Berkeley and Los Angeles, 1987), and C. Charney, 'Class Conflict and the National Party Split', *JSAS* 10/2 (1984). The *South African Review*, compiled by G. Moss, I. Obery, and others (Ravan Press, Johannesburg), of which five volumes were published in the 1980s, is an invaluable source of critical articles on all aspects of economic and political change, while the annual South African Institute of Race Relations, *Race Relations Survey*, is a treasure trove of detailed information.

## Chapter 10

See sources for Chapter 9. I have been partly reliant on the press, especially the *Weekly Mail* and *Guardian* (then separate), on Moss and Obery (eds.), *South Africa Review*, the *Race Relations Survey*, and the journals *Work in Progress* (Johannesburg) and *Transformation* (Durban), which carried debates and analysis of contemporary South Africa. Two *JSAS* special issues: S. Marks and S. Trapido (eds.), *Social History of Resistance in South Africa*, 18/1 (1992); and W. Beinart, R. Turrell, and T. O. Ranger (eds.), *Political and Collective Violence in Southern Africa*, 18/3 (1992), are especially valuable. W. Cobbett and R. Cohen (eds.), *Popular Struggles in South Africa* (London, 1988), contains good coverage of the insurrection, especially J. Seekings, 'The Origins of Political Mobilisation in PWV Townships, 1980–1984'. Volumes in the series *South Africa: Time Running Out* summarize political developments: Robert Schrire, *Adapt or Die: The End of White Politics in South Africa* (London, 1992); T. Lodge and W. Nasson, *All Here and Now: Black Politics in South Africa in the 1980s* (London, 1992). Robert M. Price, *The Apartheid State in Crisis: Political Transformation in South Africa 1975–1990* (Oxford, 1991), is interesting especially on the international dimensions of the mid-1980s crisis, J. Baskin, *Striking Back: A History of COSATU* (Johannesburg, 1991), on unions in the 1980s, and G. Mare, *Brothers Born of Warrior Blood: Politics and Ethnicity in South Africa* (Johannesburg, 1992), on Inkatha and Zulu identity. O'Meara, *Forty Lost Years*, discusses internal Afrikaner fragmentation; H. Giliomee, '*Broedertwis*: Intra-Afrikaner Conflicts in the Transition from Apartheid', *African Affairs* 91 (1992), challenges the link between class and political outlook. Militarization is analysed in P. Frankel, *Pretoria's Praetorians* (Cambridge, 1984); J. Cock and L. Nathan (eds.), *War and Society: The Militarisation of South Africa* (Cape Town, 1989); J. Cock, *Women and War in South Africa* (London, 1992). Centre for Policy Studies, *South Africa at the End of the Eighties: Policy Perspectives 1989* (Johannesburg, 1989), is useful for a perspective of Botha's era; M. Swilling *et al.* (eds.), *Apartheid City in Transition* (Cape Town, 1991), and D. Smith (ed.), *The Apartheid City and Beyond*

(London, 1992), begin to rethink the cities. On violence and political killings: A. du Toit and N. Manganyi (eds.), *Political Violence in South Africa* (Cape Town, 1991), and C. Charney, 'Vigilantes, Clientelism, and the South African State', *Transformation*, 16 (1991). S. Ellis, 'The Historical Significance of South Africa's Third Force', *JSAS* 24/2 (1998), argues for a close relationship between state-sponsored violence and the negotiation process. For personal accounts and interpretations of the negotiations: Mandela, *Long Walk to Freedom*; Sampson, *Mandela*; A. Sparks, *Tomorrow is Another Country* (Johannesburg, 1994); P. Waldmeier, *Anatomy of a Miracle* (London, 1997); A. Hadland and J. Rantao, *The Life and Times of Thabo Mbeki* (Rivonia, 1999). S. Friedman and D. Atkinson, *The Small Miracle: South Africa's Negotiated Settlement* (Johannesburg, 1994) was the last of the *South African Review* series (7); T. Davenport, *The Birth of a New South Africa* (Toronto, 1998), develops constitutional themes; for a more technical discussion and record, see H. Ebrahim, *The Soul of a Nation: Constitution-Making in South Africa* (Oxford, 1998); and for women's roles, S. Abrams, 'Fighting for Women's Liberation during the Liberation of South Africa: the Women's National Coalition', unpublished M.Phil. dissertation, University of Oxford (2000). H. Marais, *South Africa: Limits to Change* (Cape Town, 1998), is a challenging analysis of ANC's economic direction, but less clear about the alternatives. N. Nattrass, 'Economic Restructuring in South Africa: The Debate Continues', *JSAS* 20 (1994), is more supportive of the reorientation; see also responses by Sender and Kaplinsky in this issue.

## Chapters 11–13

Material is inevitably drawn from press reports, observation during visits, and unpublished sources. Of books mentioned for **Chapter 10**, Sampson, *Mandela*, is insightful on his experience of power; Hadland and Rantao, while preliminary, is sympathetic to Mbeki, who has received a far more mixed press than Mandela; Marais, *South Africa*, and Davenport, *Birth of a New South Africa*, contain valuable material and assess the new government's performance up to about 1996. The final constitution has been

printed in a paperback handbook, distributed freely: *The Consti-
tution of the Republic of South Africa, 1996: One Law for One
Nation*, Act 108 of 1996. R.W. Johnson and L. Schlemmer (eds.),
*Launching Democracy in South Africa: The First Open Election,
April 1994* (New Haven, 1994), provides the greatest detail on the
1994 elections, including lengthy regional surveys; for the Western
Cape, see also M. Eldridge and J. Seekings, 'Mandela's Lost
Province: The African National Congress and the Western Cape
Electorate in the 1994 South African Elections', *JSAS* 22/4
(1996). A. Reynolds (ed.), *Election '94 South Africa* (Cape Town,
1994), and *Election '99 South Africa* (Cape Town, 1999), include
useful articles. R. Southall, 'The Centralization and Fragmentation of South Africa's Dominant Party System', *African Affairs*
97 (1998), is an important analysis. On COSATU, the *South African Labour Bulletin* remains informative; see J. Maree, 'The
COSATU Participatory Democratic Tradition and South Africa's
New Parliament: Are they Reconcilable?', *African Affairs* 97
(1998), and E. C. Webster, 'Trade Unions and Democratization in
South Africa', *Journal of Contemporary African Studies* 16
(1998). On the functioning of parliament, R. Calland (ed.), *The
First 5 Years: A Review of South Africa's Democratic Parlia-
ment* (Cape Town, 1999), is concise and clear. Chieftaincy and
CONTRALESA are critically analysed in I. van Kessel and B.
Oomen, '"One Chief, One Vote": The Revival of Traditional
Authorities in a Post-Apartheid South Africa', *African Affairs* 96
(1997), and L. Ntsebeza, 'Attempts to Extend Democracy to
Rural Areas', unpublished paper presented to the African Studies
Seminar, St Antony's College, University of Oxford (2000).
D. Glaser, 'South Africa and the Limits of Civil Society', *JSAS*
23/1 (1997), is largely on the pre-1994 period, but suggestive of
subsequent trends.

H. Adam, F. van Zyl Slabbert, and K. Moodley, *Comrades in
Business: Post-Liberation Politics in South Africa* (Cape Town,
1998) demonstrates a healthy disrespect for the new ruling groups
in South Africa, but is less convincing in its explanations. Figures
on electrification from J. Beall and O. Crankshaw, 'Victims, Villains and Fixers: The Urban Environment and Johannesburg's
Poor', *JSAS* 26/4 (2000), and ESKOM website. N. Nattrass and

# Bibliography

J. Seekings, 'Democracy and Distribution in Highly Unequal Economies: The Case of South Africa', unpublished paper to African Studies seminar, St Antony's College, Oxford (1999), is a sophisticated attempt to analyse the beneficiaries of transition. On pensions, see A. Case and A. Deaton, 'Large Cash Transfers to the Elderly in South Africa', *Economic Journal*, 108 (1998). Land reform and rural livelihoods havè spawned a large literature, though much of it is in semi-published form. Marj Brown *et al.*, *Land Restitution in South Africa: An Independent Evaluation* (Manchester, 1997), is critical of the progress made; M. Lipton *et al.*, *Land, Labour and Livelihoods in Rural South Africa* (2 vols.; Durban, 1996), includes a range of valuable essays and debates. There have been special issues of the *Review of African Political Economy* (1994) and *Journal of Peasant Studies* (1996); B. Cousins (ed.), *At the Crossroads: Land and Agrarian Reform in South Africa into the 21st Century* (Cape Town, 2000) discusses new directions.

Some of the results of the 1996 census are available on the Web, and published in a short volume: F. M. Orkin, *Census in Brief* (Statistics South Africa, Pretoria, 1999). T. Lodge, 'Political Corruption in South Africa', *African Affairs*, 97 (1998), is an effective analysis. A. Lemon and L. Stevens, 'Reshaping Education in the New South Africa', *Geography*, 84/3 (1999), summarizes developments; numbers from the Western Cape are from A. Lemon, 'Shifting Inequalities in South Africa's Schools: Some Evidence from the Western Cape', *South African Geographical Journal*, 81/2 (1999). On crime, masculinity, and gangs: C. Campbell, 'Learning to Kill? Masculinity, the Family and Violence in Natal', *JSAS* 18/3 (1992); D. Reed, *Beloved Country: South Africa's Silent Wars* (London, 1994); T. Xaba, 'Masculinity in a Transitional Society: The Rise and Fall of "the Young Lions"', unpublished paper presented to the Colloquium on Masculinities in Southern Africa, Durban, 1997; and A. Ashforth, 'Weighing Manhood in Soweto', *CODESRIA Bulletin* 3/4 (1999). L. Gunner, 'Wrestling with the Present, Beckoning to the Past: Contemporary Zulu Radio Drama', *JSAS* 26/2 (2000), is a striking analysis of popular culture, as are other articles in this special issue. Information on the flag from interview with F. Brownell, the State

Herald, Pretoria, 1996, and his unpublished paper 'The National Flag of South Africa: Evolution of the Final Design' (1995). The initial, widely distributed leaflet *Truth and Reconciliation Commission* (Justice in Transition, Cape Town, 1995), describes its intentions. A. Krog's reportage in *Country of My Skull* (London, 1999), makes a riveting introduction; A. Norval, 'Truth and Reconciliation: The Birth of the Present and the Reworking of History', *JSAS* 25/3, and M. Lipton's leaflet *Evaluating South Africa's Truth and Reconciliation Commission* (Brighton, 1998), summarize reactions. AIDS statistics are taken from the press; other material from Suzanne Leclerc-Madlala, 'Infect One, Infect All: Zulu Youth Response to the Aids Epidemic in South Africa', *Medical Anthropology*, 17 (1997), C. Campbell and B. Williams, 'Beyond the Biomedical and Behavioural: Towards an Integrated Approach to HIV Prevention in the Southern African Mining Industry', *Social Science and Medicine*, 48 (1999), and R. Shell *et al.*, *HIV/AIDS: A Threat to the African Renaissance* (Johannesburg, 2000).

# References

This list includes only sources to which direct reference is made in the text or from which quotes have been taken. For a fuller list of sources, see the Bibliography.

Abrahams, P. (1946), *Mine Boy* (London).

Adam, H. (1971), *Modernizing Racial Domination* (Berkeley and Los Angeles).

—— van Zyl Slabbert, F., and Moodley, K. (1998), *Comrades in Business: Post-Liberation Politics in South Africa* (Cape Town).

Andrews, H. T. *et al.* (1962) (eds.), *South Africa in the Sixties* (Cape Town).

Barrell, H. (1988), 'The Outlawed South African Liberation Movements', in S. Johnson (ed.), *South Africa: No Turning Back* (London).

Beall, J., and Crankshaw, O. (2000), 'Victims, Villains and Fixers: The Urban Environment and Johannesburg's Poor', *JSAS* 26/4.

Becker, P. (1975), *Trails and Tribes in Southern Africa* (London).

Beinart, W. (1982), *The Political Economy of Pondoland 1860–1930* (Cambridge).

—— and Bundy, C. (1987), *Hidden Struggles in Rural South Africa* (London).

—— and Murray, C. (1996), *Agrarian Change, Population Movements and Land Reform in the Free State* (Land and Agriculture Policy Centre, working paper 51; Johannesburg).

—— Delius, P., and Trapido, S. (1986) (eds.), *Putting a Plough to the Ground: Accumulation and Dispossession in Rural South Africa 1850–1930* (Johannesburg).

Benson, M. (1966), *South Africa: The Struggle for a Birthright* (Harmondsworth).

Biko, S. (1978), *I Write What I Like* (London).

Bonner, P., and Segal, L. (1998), *Soweto: A History* (Johannesburg).

Bozzoli, B. (1983), 'Marxism, Feminism and South African Studies', *JSAS* 9/2.

# References

Bradford, H. (1987), *A Taste of Freedom* (New Haven).

Brandel-Syrier, M. (1971), *Reeftown Elite* (London).

Breckenridge, K. (1998), 'The Allure of Violence: Men, Race and Masculinity on the South African Goldmines, 1900–1950', *JSAS* 24/4.

Brownell, F. (1995), 'The National Flag of South Africa: Evolution of the Final Design', unpublished paper.

Buchan, J. (1983), *Prester John* (Harmondsworth; first published 1910).

Bundy, C. (1979), *The Rise and Fall of the South African Peasantry* (London; Cape Town, 1989).

—— (1987), 'Street Sociology and Pavement Politics: Aspects of Youth and Student Resistance in Cape Town, 1985', *JSAS* 13/3.

Burman, S., and Huvers, M. (1985), 'Church versus State: Divorce Legislation and Divided South Africa', *JSAS* 12/1.

Calland, R. (1999) (ed.), *The First 5 Years: A Review of South Africa's Democratic Parliament* (Cape Town).

Campbell, C. (1992), 'Learning to Kill? Masculinity, the Family and Violence in Natal', *JSAS* 18/3.

—— and Williams, B. (1999), 'Beyond the Biomedical and Behavioural: Towards an Integrated Approach to HIV Prevention in the Southern African Mining Industry', *Social Science and Medicine*, 48.

Carruthers, J. (1994), 'Dissecting the Myth: Paul Kruger and the Kruger National Park', *JSAS* 20/2.

—— (1995), *The Kruger National Park: A Social and Political History* (Pietermaritzburg, 1995).

Carter, C. (1992), 'Community and Conflict: The Alexandra Rebellion of 1986', *JSAS* 18/1.

Case, A., and Deaton, A. (1998), 'Large Cash Transfers to the Elderly in South Africa', *Economic Journal*, 108.

Centre for Policy Studies (1989), *South Africa at the End of the Eighties: Policy Perspectives 1989* (Johannesburg).

Charney, C. (1984), 'Class Conflict and the National Party Split', *JSAS* 10/2.

Christie, R. (1984), *Electricity, Industry and Class in South Africa* (London).

Crush, J., and Ambler, C. (1992) (eds.), *Liquor and Labour in Southern Africa* (Athens, Oh.).

—— Jeeves, A., and Yudelman, D. (1991), *South Africa's Labour Empire: A History of Black Migrancy to the Gold Mines* (David Philip).

Cuthbertson, G., and Jeeves, A. (1999) (eds.), 'South African War 1899–1902: Centennial Perspectives', Special Issue of *South African Historical Journal*, 41.

# References

Davenport, T. (1998), *The Birth of a New South Africa* (Toronto).

Delius, P. (1996), *A Lion amongst the Cattle: Reconstruction and Resistance in the Northern Transvaal* (Johannesburg).

de Kiewiet, C. W. (1941), *History of South Africa, Social and Economic* (Oxford).

Desmond, C. (1971), *The Discarded People: An Account of African Resettlement in South Africa* (Harmondsworth).

Dikobe, M. (1973), *The Marabi Dance* (London).

Drury, A. (1968), *'A Very Strange Society': A Journey to the Heart of South Africa* (London).

Dubow, S. (1989), *Racial Segregation and the Origins of Apartheid in South Africa, 1919–1936* (London).

—— (1995), *Scientific Racism in Modern South Africa* (Cambridge).

du Toit, A. (1993), 'The Micro-Politics of Paternalism: The Discourses of Management and Resistance on South African Fruit and Wine Farms', *JSAS* 19/2 (1993).

Ebrahim, H. (1998), *The Soul of a Nation: Constitution-Making in South Africa* (Oxford).

Edgar, R. (1988), *Because they Chose the Plan of God* (Johannesburg).

Giliomee, H. (1987), 'Western Cape Farmers and the Beginnings of Afrikaner Nationalism, 1870–1915', *JSAS* 14/1.

—— and Adam, H. (1979), *Ethnic Power Mobilized* (New Haven).

Glaser, C. (1998*a*), 'Swines, Hazels and the Dirty Dozen: Masculinity, Territoriality and the Youth Gangs of Soweto, 1960–1976', *JSAS* 24/4.

—— (1998*b*), '"We Must Infiltrate the *Tsotsis*": School Politics and Youth Gangs in Soweto, 1968–1976', *JSAS* 24/2.

Goldin, I. (1987), *Making Race: The Politics and Economics of Coloured Identity in South Africa* (Harlow).

Great Britain (1904), *Report of the Transvaal Labour Commission*, Cd. 1897 (London).

—— (1905), *Report of the South African Native Affairs Commission* (London).

Greenberg, S. (1981), *Race and State in Capitalist Development: South Africa in Comparative Perspective* (New Haven).

Gunner, L. (2000), 'Wrestling with the Present, Beckoning to the Past: Contemporary Zulu Radio Drama', *JSAS* 26/2.

Hadland, A., and Rantao, J. (1999), *The Life and Times of Thabo Mbeki* (Rivonia).

Harries, P. (1982), 'Kinship, Ideology and the Nature of Pre-Colonial Labour Migration', in S. Marks and R. Rathbone (eds.), *Industrialisation and Social Change in South Africa* (London).

—— (1994), *Work, Culture, and Identity: Migrant Laborers in Mozambique and South Africa, c.1860–1910* (Portsmouth, NH).

Heard, K. (1974), *General Elections in South Africa 1943–70* (London).

Hellmann, E. (1948), *Rooiyard: A Sociological Survey of an Urban Native Slum Yard* (Cape Town).

Hirson, B. (1990), *Yours for the Union: Class and Community Struggles in South Africa, 1930–1947* (London).

Hindson, D. (1987), *Pass Controls and the Urban African Proletariat* (Johannesburg).

Hofmeyr, I. (1987), 'Building a Nation from Words: Afrikaans Language, Literature and Ethnic Identity, 1902–1924', in S. Marks and S. Trapido (eds.), *The Politics of Race, Class and Nationalism in Twentieth Century South Africa* (London).

Hyslop, J. (1993), ' "A Destruction Coming In": Bantu Education as Response to Social Crisis', in P. Bonner, P. Delius, and D. Posel (eds.), *Apartheid's Genesis, 1935–1962* (Johannesburg).

Jeeves, A. (1985), *Migrant Labour in South Africa's Mining Economy, 1890–1920* (Kingston, Ont.).

Johnson, S. (1988) (ed.), *South Africa: No Turning Back* (London).

Johnstone, F. (1970), 'White Prosperity and White Supremacy in South Africa Today', *African Affairs* 69.

Joubert, E. (1980), *The Long Journey of Poppie Nongena* (Johannesburg; first published in Afrikaans, 1978).

Keegan, T. (1987), *Rural Transformations in Industrializing South Africa: The Southern Highveld to 1914* (London).

Krikler, J. (1999), 'The Commandos: The Army of White Labour in South Africa', *Past and Present* 163.

Krog, A. (1999), *Country of My Skull* (London).

Kuper, L. (1965), *An African Bourgeoisie* (New Haven).

la Hausse, P. (1990), 'The Cows of Nongoloza: Youth, Crime and Amalaita gangs in Durban, 1900–1936', *JSAS* 16/1.

Leclerc-Madlala, S. 'Infect One, Infect all: Zulu Youth Response to the Aids Epidemic in South Africa', *Medical Anthropology*, 17.

Legassick, M. (1980), 'The Frontier Tradition in South African historiography', in S. Marks and A. Atmore (eds.), *Economy and Society in Pre-Industrial South Africa* (London).

Leipoldt, L. (1937), *Bushveld Doctor* (London).

Lelyveld, J. (1985), *Move your Shadow: South Africa, Black and White* (New York).

Lemon, A. (1999), 'Shifting Inequalities in South Africa's Schools: Some

Evidence from the Western Cape', *South African Geographical Journal*, 81/2.

Lewsen, P. (1960–9), *Selections from the Correspondence of J. X. Merriman* (van Riebeeck Society Series, vols. xli and xliv; Cape Town).

Lodge, T. (1998), 'Political Corruption in South Africa', *African Affairs* 97.

Lugard, F. D. (1929), *The Dual Mandate in British Tropical Africa*, 4th edn. (Edinburgh).

MacKenzie, J. (1988), *The Empire of Nature* (Manchester).

Mager, A. (1999), 'The First Decade of "European Beer" in Apartheid South Africa: The State, the Brewers and the Drinking Public, 1962–1972', *JAH* 40.

Mandela, N. (1965), *No Easy Walk to Freedom* (London).

—— (1995), *Long Walk to Freedom* (London).

Marais, H. (1998), *South Africa: Limits to Change* (Cape Town).

Maree, J. (1987) (ed.), *The Independent Trade Unions 1974–1984* (Johannesburg).

—— (1998), 'The COSATU Participatory Democratic Tradition and South Africa's New Parliament: Are they Reconcilable?', *African Affairs*, 97.

Marks, S. (1970), *Reluctant Rebellion* (London).

—— (1986), *The Ambiguities of Dependence in South Africa* (Johannesburg).

—— (1994), *Divided Sisterhood: Race, Class and Gender in the South African Nursing Profession* (London).

—— and Rathbone, R. 1982) (eds.), *Industrialisation and Social Change in South Africa* (London).

Marx, C. (1994), 'The *Ossewabrandwag* as a Mass Movement, 1939–1941', *JSAS* 20/2.

Matsetela T. (1982), 'The Life Story of Nkgono Mma-Pooe' in S. Marks and R. Rathbone (eds.), *Industrialisation and Social Change in South Africa* (London).

Mayer, P., and Mayer, I. (1960), *Townsmen or Tribesmen* (2nd edn.; Cape Town, 1971).

Mbeki, G. (1964), *South Africa: The Peasants' Revolt* (Harmondsworth).

Meredith, M. (1997), *Nelson Mandela: A Biography* (London).

Moll, T. (1991), 'Did the Apartheid Economy "Fail"?', *JSAS* 17/2.

Moloi, G. (1987), *My Life: Volume One* (Johannesburg).

Moodie, T. D. (1976), *The Rise of Afrikanerdom* (Berkeley and Los Angeles).

# References

—— (1994), *Going for Gold: Men, Mines and Migration* (Berkeley and Los Angeles).

Murray, C. (1988), 'Displaced Urbanisation: South Africa's Rural Slums', in J. Lonsdale (ed.), *South Africa in Question* (Cambridge).

—— (1992), *Black Mountain* (Edinburgh).

Murray, M. (1987), *South Africa: Time of Agony, Time of Destiny* (New York).

Mzamane, Mbulelo (1982), *The Children of Soweto* (Johannesburg).

Nattrass, J. (1988), *The South African Economy* (Cape Town).

Nattrass, N. (1991), 'Controversies about Capitalism and Apartheid in South Africa: An Economic Perspective', *JSAS* 17/4 .

—— and Seekings, J. (1999), 'Democracy and Distribution in Highly Unequal Economies: The Case of South Africa', unpublished paper to African Studies seminar, St Antony's College, Oxford.

Ntsebeza, L. (2000), 'Attempts to Extend Democracy to Rural Areas', unpublished paper presented to the African Studies Seminar, St Antony's College, University of Oxford.

Odendaal, A. (1981), *Vukani Bantu: The Beginnings of Black Protest Politics in South Africa to 1912* (Cape Town).

Omar, D. (1995), *Truth and Reconciliation Commission* (Justice in Transition, Cape Town).

O'Meara, D. (1983), *Volkskapitalisme* (Cambridge).

Packard, R. (1989), *White Plague, Black Labour* (Pietermaritzburg).

Paton, A. (1948), *Cry, The Beloved Country* (London).

Plaatje, S. (1916), *Native Life in South Africa* (London).

Posel, D. (1991), *The Making of Apartheid 1948–1961* (Oxford).

Price, R. (1991), *The Apartheid State in Crisis: Political Transformation in South Africa 1975–1990* (Oxford).

Ramphele, M. (1996), *Across Boundaries: The Journey of a South Woman Leader* (New York).

—— and McDowell, C. (1991) (eds.), *Restoring the Land* (London).

Reitz, F. (1900), *A Century of Wrong* (London).

Richardson, P., and Burke, G. (1978), 'The Profits of Death: A Comparative Study of Miners Pthisis' *JSAS* 4.

Sampson, A. (1956), *Drum: A Venture into the New Africa* (London).

—— (1999), *Mandela: The Authorised Biography* (London).

Schama, S. (1988), *The Embarrassment of Riches* (Berkeley and Los Angeles).

Seekings, J. (1988), 'The Origins of Political Mobilisation in PWV Townships, 1980–1984', in W. Cobbett and R. Cohen (eds.), *Popular Struggles in South Africa* (London).

# References

Simkins, C. (1983), *Four Essays on the Past, Present and Possible Future of the Distribution of the Black Population of South Africa* (Cape Town).

Smith, I. (1996), *The Origins of the South African War 1899–1902* (London).

South African Information Service (1979), *South Africa 1979: Official Yearbook of the Republic of South Africa* (Johannesburg).

Southall, R. (1982), *South Africa's Transkei: The Political Economy of an 'Independent' Bantustan* (London).

Sparks, A. (1994), *Tomorrow is Another Country* (Johannesburg).

Stadler, A. (1979), 'Birds in a Cornfield: Squatter Movements in Johannesburg, 1944–1947', *JSAS* 6.

Stone, J. H., II (1990), 'M. K. Gandhi: Some Experiments with Truth', *JSAS* 16.

Streek, B., and Wicksteed, R. (1981), *Render unto Kaiser: A Transkei Dossier* (Johannesburg).

Suzman, H. (1994), *In No Uncertain Terms* (London).

Swanson, M. (1995), 'The Sanitation Syndrome: Bubonic Plague and Urban Native Policy in the Cape Colony, 1900–1909', in W. Beinart and S. Dubow (eds.), *Segregation and Apartheid in Twentieth Century South Africa* (London).

Swart, S. (1998), ' "A Boer and his Gun and his Wife are Three Things Always Together": Republican Masculinity and the 1914 Rebellion', *JSAS* 24/4.

Thompson, L. (1960), *The Unification of South Africa 1902–10* (Oxford).

Turrell, R. (1987), *Capital and Labour on the Kimberley Diamond Fields* (Cambridge).

Union of South Africa (1923), *Final Report of the Drought Investigation Commission* (U.G. 49–1923).

—— (1956), *Summary Report of the Commission for the Socio-Economic Development of the Bantu Areas within the Union of South Africa*, U.G. 61–1955 (Tomlinson Commission).

van Onselen, C. (1982), *Studies in the Social and Economic History of the Witwatersrand, 1886–1914* (2 vols.; London).

—— (1990), 'Race and Class in the South African Countryside: Cultural Osmosis and Social Relations in the Sharecropping Economy of the South-Western Transvaal, 1900–1950', *American Historical Journal* 95/1.

—— (1997), *The Seed is Mine: The Life of Kas Maine, a South African Sharecropper 1894–1985* (Oxford).

Vilakazi, A. (1965), *Zulu Transformations* (Pietermaritzburg).

# References

Walker, C. (1991) (ed.), *Women and Gender in Southern Africa* (London).

Webster, D (1987), 'Repression and the State of Emergency', in G. Moss and I. Obery (eds.), *South African Review 4* (Johannesburg).

Webster, E. (1987), 'A Profile of Unregistered Union Members in Durban', in J. Maree (ed.), *The Independent Trade Unions 1974–1984* (Johannesburg).

Willan, B. (1984), *Sol Plaatje: South African Nationalist 1876–1932* (London).

Wilson, F., and Ramphele, M. (1989), *Uprooting Poverty* (Cape Town).

Wilson, M., and Thompson, L. (1971) (eds.), *The Oxford History of South Africa* (2 vols.; Oxford).

Wolpe, H. (1972), 'Capitalism and Cheap Labour Power in South Africa', *Economy and Society*, 1, republished in W. Beinart and S. Dubow (1995) (eds.), *Segregation and Apartheid in Twentieth-Century South Africa* (London).

Xaba, T. (1997), 'Masculinity in a Transitional Society: The Rise and Fall of "the Young Lions"', unpublished paper presented to the Colloquium on Masculinities in Southern Africa, Durban.

Yudelman, D. (1983), *The Emergence of Modern South Africa* (Cape Town).

# INDEX

# Index

alcohol 198, 206, 325
  beer brewing 206, 313
  black elite 193
  Cape province 39
  manufacture of 108, 127
  prickly pear liquor 44
  shebeens 196, 238
Alexandra township 132, 257, 261
All Africa Convention (1935) 131
All Blacks rugby team 230
*Amafelandawonye* 106, 133
ANC (African National Congress)
      103–4, 130–1, 152, 252
  armed wing of 168
  ascendancy of 296–308
  business support 260
  careerism 330
  commodity boycott campaigns 209
  Defiance Campaign 151, 167
  economic reconstruction 309–27
  elections (1994) 291–3
  exile 228–32
  farm labour 209
  government negotiations 272–5,
      278–85
  guerrilla activity 229–30, 251, 270
  mass politics 133–4
  Nelson Mandela 166–8
  in 1950s 154–5, 165–6
  provincial government 295–6
  provisional constitution 289–91
  split with PAC 165–6
  trade unions 155–6
  underground movement 167,
      228–9
anglicization 75
Anglo-American Corporation 175–6,
      260, 323
Angola 156, 231, 243, 244, 264, 270
antelopes 44
anti-apartheid campaign, international
      230
apartheid 3, 138, 144–7, 200
  agricultural workers 208
  capitalism and 171–9
  Christianity 240
  de Klerk and 275–6
  domestic service 188
  education 159–61
  government expenditure 224–6

homeland agriculture decline 219
homeland policy 162–5
labour control 155–9
legislation 147–53, 155–6, 158, 159–60
reform 245–52
relaxation of 281
removals policy 210–17, 221–2
social divisions 218–19
sport 186
territorial separation 161–2
unintentional population increase
      203–4
urban spatial division 152–5
APO (African Political Organization) 90
Apostolic churches 198
armoured vehicles 177
arms embargoes 269–70
arms industry 177, 263, 325
Armscor 177, 263, 269
army 245, 263–4, 270, 302
Asiatic Land Tenure Act (1946) 152
assassination squads 343
Athlone rally, Cape Town 285
Australia 145, 182
avocado pears 207
*AWB (Afrikaner Weerstandsbeweging)*
      283–4
Azanian People's Liberation Army 279
Azanian People's Organization 251

BAABs (Bantu Affairs Administration
      Boards) 255
Baker, Herbert 76, 143
balkanization 162–5
ballroom dancing 194
Bambatha, Chief 90, 94, 97–9
bananas 47, 207
Banda, President Hastings 244
banking 52, 175
  Cape Province 42
  central banks 323
  gold prices 323–4
Bantu Authorities Act (1951) 161
Bantu Beer 196
Bantu education, *see* education, black
      South Africans
Bantu Education Act (1953) 159–60
Basic Conditions of Employment Act
      (1997) 299
Basson, Dr Wouter 343

393

# Index

IFP (Inkatha Freedom Party, *formerly* Inkatha) 277, 278, 279–80, 284–5, 291, 300, 333, 344
*Iliso Lomzi* groups 91
illegal brewing 108, 128
immigration, white 73–7, 180, 337
  black 156–7, 204, 326–7
Immorality Act (1950) 147, 268
Impala aircraft 177
Imperial Conference (1926) 114, 117
imports
  arms 177
  economic recession 258
  grain 51
  sophisticated machinery 179
imprisonment, *see* detention
*Imvo Zabantsundu* (Voice of the People) (newspaper) 26, 93
incomes 218–19, 220, *see also* wages and salaries
Independent Electoral Commission 283
Independent Order of True Templars 193
India 179
*Indian Opinion* (newspaper) 94
Indian South Africans 233
  education 330–1
  elite 93–5
  Group Areas 153
  indentured workers 46, 47, 69, 95
  politics 93–5
  representation and rights 137
  restrictions on land purchase 152
  textile workers 241
  trade unions 131
  urban 201
  voting 292
industrial action, *see* strikes
Industrial Conciliation Act (1924) 84
Industrial Conciliation Amendment Act 246, 248–9
Industrial Development Corporation 173
industrialization 86
infant mortality 203, 219
inflation 259, 314, 320
influx controls 158–9, 189, 205, 209, 256
information technology and computers 177, 326
Inkatha (*later* IFP, Inkatha Freedom Party) 224, 246, 261, 262, 266–7, 277

Institute for Industrial Education (Durban) 241
intellectuals 240, 241, 275, 339–40
interest rates 259, 314, 323
International Monetary Fund 323
International Workers of Africa 111
investment
  decline in direct 322
  foreign 173–4, 275
  homelands 226
  pension funds 310–11
  withdrawal of 260
Iran 176
Iraq 219
Iron and Steel Corporation (ISCOR) 115
ironworkers 22
irrigation 43–4, 52, 177–8, 207
ISCOR (iron and steel) 276
Islam 38
Israelites (church) 101–2
ivory 48, 50
*Izwi Labantu* (newspaper) 89

Jabavu, D. D. T. 131
Jabavu, J. T. 26, 89, 92
jackals 45
Jameson, Sir Leander Starr 78
Jameson Raid (1895) 29, 40, 62–3
Japan 174, 182
jazz 153–4
Jewish people 74, 173, 183, 240
job reservation 248, 250
Johannesburg 28, 30, 41, 62, 75–6, 81, 127
  Group Areas 153
  squatter camps 132
  stock exchange 173, 176, 323
  urban segregation 77
  violence 284
Johnnic (Anglo-American subsidiary) 310, 311
Joint Management Centres 268
Joubert, Elsa 243
*Jukskei* (farm and trek game) 185

Kadalie, Clements 104–5, 111
Kahlamba 11
Kalashnikov rifles 278, 284
Kangwane 223
Karoo midlands 41

# Index

Mdantsane 212
mealieboer 55
mechanization 207
media
    insurrectionary period 263
    obsession with crime 332
    promotion of South Africa identity 281–2
    reporting restrictions 265
    total strategy 264, *see also* newspapers; radio; television
Meiring, General 302
Mercedes Benz 182
Merino sheep 22, 40
Merriman, John X. 39, 62, 63, 67, 78, 89
Methodist Church 26, 91, 193
Mexico 145, 178, 212
Meyer, Roelf 278, 279, 296–7
Mfengu people 24–5, 31, 96, 101
Mgijima, Enoch 101
Mgwali mission 211
Mhlaba, Raymond 231, 296
middle class
    black 191–6, 199, 246, 255, 310–12
    white 181–4, 318
migrancy and migrants 24, 198
    African women 92–3
    agriculture 208–9
    *amalaita* groups 109
    apartheid 156–8
    attacks on youth gangs 266
    economic reasons for 32–5
    foreign workers 204, 209
    HIV/AIDS 334
    industrial action 102–3
    *Makwerekwere* influx 326–7
    manufacturing industry 157
    mining industry 27, 28–32, 64, 67–71, 110
    share-croppers 54
    sheep shearing 31
    socially divisive 171
    sugar production 47
    traders 42
    white immigration 73–7
    white women 76–7
millennialism 82
Milner, Lord Alfred 66, 67, 68–9, 73–4, 75
*Mine Boy* (Abrahams) 128

Mines and Works Act (1911) 84
minibus taxis 216–17
mining industry 2
    Afrikaner-controlled 181
    black workers 27–31, 67–71, 84–5, 110, 117, 129, 156–7
    coal 175
    compound organization 111
    copper 175
    diamond 27–8, 29, 30, 41
    English-language press 189
    gold 63–4, 67–71, 86, 110, 116, 117–18, 129, 174–5
    homosexuality 110
    strikes 82–5, 103, 131–2
    taxation 67
    trade unions 131
    tropical recruitment 156–7
    uranium 174, 175
    white workers 74, 82–5, 117
Mirage fighters 177
miscegenation 147
mission schools 160
mission stations 17, 22–3, 25
missionaries 25–6
Mitchell's Plain ( Cape Town township) 251
Mixed Marriages Act (1949) 147, 268
Mkize, Saul 211
Mngadi, S'bu 310, 311
Mobil 176
Modjadji (Lovedu rain queen) 338
Mohapi, Mapetla 236
Moloi, Godfrey 325
Moore, Barrington 171
Morewa, Solomon 'Sticks' 338
Morogoro, Tanzania 231
Moroka Swallows 195
Morris Isaacson School 236
Mosenthals (merchant firm), Port Elizabeth 42
Moshoeshoe, Chief 16, 23
Motlana, Dr Nthato 310
motor industry 173, 241
motorsports 186
Mozambique 49, 64, 66, 168, 180, 204, 231, 243, 244, 259, 274, 324
    southern 32–3, 47, 157
Mpanza, James 132–3, 195
Mpetha, Oscar 249

# Index